COMPUTER SCIENCE RESEARCH TRENDS

COMPUTER SCIENCE RESEARCH TRENDS

CASEY B. YARNALL
Editor

Nova Science Publishers, Inc.
New York

Library of Congress Cataloging-in-Publication Data

Computer science research trends / Casey B. Yarnall (editor).
p. cm.
Includes index.
ISBN-13: 978-1-60021-518-6 (hardcover)
ISBN-10: 1-60021-518-1 (hardcover)
1. Computer science--Research. I. Yarnall, Casey B.
QA76.27.C676 2007
004.072--dc22
2007012174

Published by Nova Science Publishers, Inc. ✢ New York

CONTENTS

PREFACE

Like them or hate them, computers are here to stay. The books in this series present leading-edge research in the field of computer research, technology and applications. Each contribution has been carefully selected for inclusion based on the significance of the research to this fast-moving and diverse field.

Chapter 1 - Within the Internet, there exists a packet-switch network which functions to forward packets from source to destination in order to enable end-to-end connections. The key attribute to enable such a procedure consists of several crucial components, including routing protocol(s), transmission links and routers. While a plethora of literature on routing protocols has been presented in the last decade, the transmission technology is constantly evolving. As a result, provision of tens gigabit fiber links is commonly available now. Yet, the research on high-speed routers is limited insofar and, therefore, increases in its importance. To meet the demands of new multimedia applications, multi-tera routers have been designed. A multi-tera router should have enough internal bandwidth to switch packets between its interfaces at multi-tera rates and enough packet processing power to forward multiple millions of packets per second (MPPS). Switching in the router has been well studied. However, the remaining major bottleneck for a high performance router design is to speed up the multi-memory-access IP packet forwarding engine.

The rate of the packet forwarding engines can be burdened by several factors. The major obstacle lies in the space limitation of IPv4 which leads to the occurrence of classless interdomain routing (CIDR). The address prefix, specifying next-hop for a set of addresses, transforms from fixed length to variable length. Therefore, the packet forwarding engine must be able to derive the best matching prefix (BMP) among the variable-length prefixes. Unlike exact matching, the procedure of BMP requires more pre-computation to enable fast search. The second obstacle would be the incoming IPv6. Although IPv6 can overcome the problem of exhausting IPv4 address space, its huge space also increases the complexity of BMP search. Other factors affecting the speed of packet forwarding engines include the limited storage of high-speed memory, power consumption and the issues of table updates. Since there is no single solution fit under every circumstance, how to select a suitable solution for different applications is thereby important.

To solve these difficulties, numerous algorithms are proposed in the last few years. These algorithms address these performance issues via different approaches. For example, some of them try to compress data structures into high-speed SRAMs, while others utilize the architecture of modern processors. There are some others who resort to hardware implementation. Generally, these algorithms can be categorized into software based and hardware based according to the method of implementation. In this chapter, an introduction of four algorithms will be provided in terms of their major contributions, performance, merits and weaknesses.

Chapter 2 - The creation of the Internet has had several positive and negative results on the world. Additionally, certain aspects of the Internet make it a unique medium of communication with its own set of norms, standards, language, etc. These various factors have influenced children and adolescents. Problematic Internet use, which has become known as Internet addiction, is not limited by demographic elements. However, there may be certain factors about this medium that could make children and adolescents vulnerable to using the Internet in a dysfunctional way. These factors are examined. Additionally, special considerations and treatment options are reviewed for mental health professionals who treat children and adolescents for their problematic Internet use. Future research on particular aspects of problematic Internet use with children and adolescents is suggested.

Chapter 3 - When Feynman introduced his version of quantum computation (QC), it was based on non-relativistic quantum mechanics. But Einstein's special relativity as well as quantum theory, were well established experimentally as the two great physics revolutions of the twentieth century. In fact the theory of light and electrons (quantum electrodynamics (QED)), has led to quantum field theory, which is a logical edifice built on relativity and quantum mechanics.

Because the subject of relativistic quantum field theory (QFT) contains all of non-relativistic quantum mechanics, the authors expect quantum field computation (QFC) to contain (non-relativistic) quantum computation (QC).

By looking at quantum computation with relativity, many new approaches to physics and computation become practically possible. Some of the limitations of Turing computation are also overcome.

In this chapter the authors discuss practically accomplished exact computation over a complex continuum instead of over the integers, symbolic and analog computation, qubits with arbitrary spin, unlimited numbers of qubits and results regarding computational complexity classes which bear on the famous P versus NP problem. The remarkable discovery by Agrawal et al that the problem PRIMES belongs to P, significantly changes notions of what could be called ``strong" or ``hard" computation.

The authors identify a basic problem in QFT, namely Wightman's computation problem for domains of holomorphy, which they call WHOLO. Inspired by the same analytic functions which are central to the famous CPT theorem of QFT, it is possible to obtain a computational complexity structure for QFT and shed new light on certain complexity classes for this problem WHOLO. Possible applications of the work in this chapter to anyons and the fractional quantum Hall effect (FQHE), relate to the physics of knots and braids.

Overall, relativistic quantum computation leads us to much common ground between the disciplines of physics, computer science and mathematics and provides new perspectives on further unsolved problems for the twenty first century.

Chapter 4 - Studying distributed systems is a rich experience that involves many interacting hardware and software components, each component has its distinguishable characteristics and its own way of functioning and interacting. This chapter sheds light on major aspects of distributed systems and their reliability evaluation techniques. First, an insightful coverage, of all issues regarding distributed systems design and functioning, is presented. Then, a comprehensive investigation of different reliability definitions focuses on various complementary views of reliability. Subsequently, a thorough emphasis is accorded to innovative research work dealing with reliability evaluation techniques for distributed systems as a whole as well as for their hardware and software components. Some of the presented work may still need more elaboration but the issues and handling techniques they raise deserve careful follow up.

Chapter 5 - A deployed wireless sensor network is prone to disruptions to communications, degradation and failure of sensor nodes as well as due to limited energy reserves. The network requires a degree of adaptiveness in order to reconfigure itself to sustain operations. Except for extreme environmental conditions, spare sensor nodes pose a significant cost overhead. A wireless sensor network, however, already has some inherent redundancy in terms of the number of nodes as well as the possible communication channels existing between neighbouring nodes. An alternative approach is therefore to exploit software control of this inherent redundancy to detect and reconfigure the network to adapt to node failures and communication disruptions. This research presents two variations of a novel protocol, called SOS, that provide a sensor network with self-reconfigurability as well as selective path redundancy to adapt to network failures and disruptions. Simulations show that SOS compares favourably with existing protocols in terms of performance, reliability and energy efficiency.

Chapter 6 - Iterative algorithms to reconstruct single photon emission computerized tomography (SPECT) data are based on the mathematical simulation of the acquisition process. The reconstruction times of these methods are much longer than that of routinely used reconstruction methods (such as filtered back projection). Java, a platform independent programming language changed the way of software design by using Jini and JavaSpaces, new technologies that have been introduced recently. By applying JavaSpaces, a *space* is used to store objects persistently which can be used also for effective parallel processing. In this paper, the authors report a novel approach for iterative reconstruction of SPECT data by means of JavaSpaces, which uses only a standard personal computer equipment and results in significant improvement of reconstruction time due to the fact that several layers of the object are computed in parallel.

Chapter 7 - Substitutions are typically pervasive in proof procedures for logic programs. This chapter presents a technique relegating the role played by substitutions, thereby simplifying the design of both the inference systems and the search strategies of such proof procedures. The authors method converts logic programs into ``chain" form, whose proof trees have (nontrivial) substitutions only at the leaves. Existing parsers for context-free grammars can then in principle be converted into sound inference systems for chain programs simply by adding unification to the treatment of terminals.

Just as proof trees are simplified in chain programs, so are derivations. Hence, chain programs are also useful for describing search strategies requiring an explicit representation of the derivation tree. The authors apply their technique to the design of deterministic metainterpreters.

Chapter 8 - In this chapter, the authors propose a methodology based on genetic programming genetic programming to automatically generate data-flow based specifications for hardware designs of combinational digital circuits. The authors aim at allowing automatic generation of balanced hardware specifications for a given input/output behaviour. It minimizes space while maintaining reasonable response time. The authors show that the evolved designs are efficient and creative. The authors do so comparing the obtained circuits of some benchmarks against those that were produced by human designers as well as to other evolutionary ones.

To emphasize the applicability of the methodology to real-world problems, the authors use genetic programming as an alternative methodology to automatically generate secure and minimal hardware designs of public-key cryptosystems such as RSA encryption system. The authors evolve optimal hardware circuits for modular exponentiation, which a cornerstone operation in almost every cryptographic system. The evolved circuits minimize both space (i.e. required gate number) and time (i.e. encryption and decryption time). The evolved designs are shielded against side-channel leakage and hence secure. The structure of the cryptographic circuit is random and so the private key cannot be deduced using known attacks. The authors compare their results against existing well-known designs, which were produced by human designers based on the binary method.

Chapter 9 - A common approach of modeling software designs is to represent designs graphically. In the object-oriented design paradigm, the Unified Modeling Language (UML) is a widely used graphical design-modeling method. This paper discusses the big bang graph as an alternative or supplement to UML. The authors compare the big bang graph with the UML and present a translation framework between the two modeling methods. The authors show how to expand the big bang graph to model aspect-oriented and procedural designs. The authors discuss using the big bang graph as a design-analysis platform and the state space embedded in the graph. Finally, the authors discuss the potential applications of the big bang graph in formalizing software measures and calculating design.

Chapter 10 - The authors' symmetric key crypto-system is based on walks on a bipartite graph. The general idea is to treat vertices of a graph as messages and arcs of a certain length as an encryption tool. Starting from the plain text (vertex v_1 of graph), the authors consider a one-step walk as an arc that connect v_i to the next vertex v_{i+1} and which uses one character of the password. The adjacency matrix of this graph consists of a simple system of equations. A plain data is seen as an n-tuple in a Galois finite field $GF(2^8)$. The authors show that using this special family of graphs, for any password of length m, $m<(n+5)/2$, any cipher data (vertex in the graph) will have a unique path (walk) in the graph. Furthermore, our crypto-system has a linear complexity and it resists to different type of adversary attacks.

In: Computer Science Research Trends
Editor: Casey B. Yarnall, pp. 1-57
ISBN 978-1-60021-518-6

Chapter 1

PROGRESS IN IP PACKET FORWARDING RESEARCH

Pi-Chung Wang
Department of Computer Science,
National Chung Hsing University,
Kuo Kuang Road, Taichung

Abstract

Within the Internet, there exists a packet-switch network which functions to forward packets from source to destination in order to enable end-to-end connections. The key attribute to enable such a procedure consists of several crucial components, including routing protocol(s), transmission links and routers. While a plethora of literature on routing protocols has been presented in the last decade, the transmission technology is constantly evolving. As a result, provision of tens gigabit fiber links is commonly available now. Yet, the research on high-speed routers is limited insofar and, therefore, increases in its importance. To meet the demands of new multimedia applications, multi-tera routers have been designed. A multi-tera router should have enough internal bandwidth to switch packets between its interfaces at multi-tera rates and enough packet processing power to forward multiple millions of packets per second (MPPS). Switching in the router has been well studied. However, the remaining major bottleneck for a high performance router design is to speed up the multi-memory-access IP packet forwarding engine.

The rate of the packet forwarding engines can be burdened by several factors. The major obstacle lies in the space limitation of IPv4 which leads to the occurrence of classless interdomain routing (CIDR). The address prefix, specifying next-hop for a set of addresses, transforms from fixed length to variable length. Therefore, the packet forwarding engine must be able to derive the best matching prefix (BMP) among the variable-length prefixes. Unlike exact matching, the procedure of BMP requires more pre-computation to enable fast search. The second obstacle would be the incoming IPv6. Although IPv6 can overcome the problem of exhausting IPv4 address space, its huge space also increases the complexity of BMP search. Other factors affecting the speed of packet forwarding engines include the limited storage of high-speed memory, power consumption and the issues of table updates. Since there is no single solution fit under every circumstance, how to select a suitable solution for different applications is thereby important.

To solve these difficulties, numerous algorithms are proposed in the last few years. These algorithms address these performance issues via different approaches. For example, some of them try to compress data structures into high-speed SRAMs, while others utilize the architecture of modern processors. There are some others who resort to hardware implementation. Generally, these algorithms can be categorized into software based and hardware based according to the method of implementation. In this chapter, an introduction of four algorithms will be provided in terms of their major contributions, performance, merits and weaknesses.

1. Introduction

The Internet is a global computer network that began as the ARPANET, an U.S. Department of Defense project to create a nation-wide computer network that would continue to function even if a large portion of it were destroyed in the war or natural disaster. However, the Internet was changed in 1992, when commercial entities started offering Internet access to the public. In addition, the Internet is used to provide enterprise communications. As personal computers became more affordable, people also began to connect to the Internet through **Internet Service Providers (ISPs)**. Due to the advance of the World Wide Web and the promise of future e-commerce, we have seen that the traffic in the Internet doubles every 3 months [1]. The number of hosts on the Internet has been growing exponentially, as shown in Figure 1. In addition, the introduction of the Gigabit Ethernet for LANs and the audio/video traffic generated by the multimedia applications increase the demand for higher bandwidth on the Internet. For example, the required bandwidth for high definition TV (HDTV) quality video is 20 to 40 Mbps or 2 to 6 with MPEG compression. When the network has to support a large number of such connections, the aggregate bandwidth requirement is high.

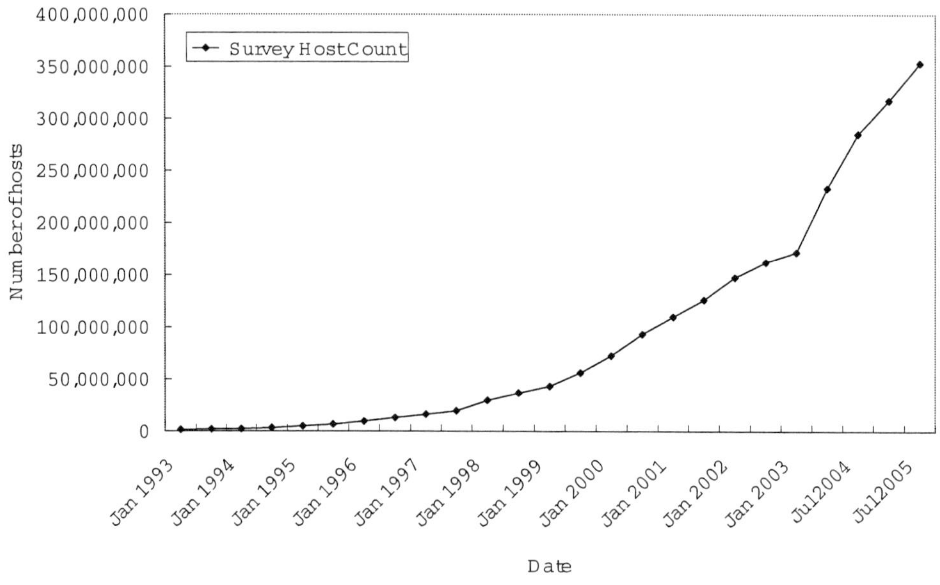

Figure 1. The Number of Hosts on the Internet.

Internet consists of different subnetworks which are interconnected via gateways, routers, switches and various transmission facilities. **Internet Protocol (IP)** provides the functionality for connecting end systems across multiple networks which may use different protocols. This message (called **packet**) transfer process is called **packet forwarding**. The packets traverse from source to destination through links and routers, it is just like the way a postal mail traverses from post office to post office through delivery channels. Each post office uses the destination address on the envelope to decide where to forward this mail. In the same way, routers decide to forward a packet based on a destination address (**DA**) that is placed in the packet header, this process is called IP address lookup (or IP lookup, for short). Thus routers can forward packets through the Internet all the way to their destinations.

In addition to the basic packet forwarding based on destination address, the new requirements are emerging. To support security, quality of server (**QoS**) or specific business policies, user traffic may be further classified according to a maximum of eight fields: source/destination IP address (32 bits), source/destination transport-layer port numbers (16 bits for TCP and UDP), type-of-service (**TOS**) field (8 bits), protocol field (8 bits) and transport-layer flags (8 bits) with a total of 120 bits. This new forwarding type is called Layer 4 Switching because routing decisions can be based on headers available at Layer 4 or higher in the **Open Systems Interconnection (OSI)** architecture. Layer 4 switching offers increased flexibility: it gives a router the capability to block traffic from a dangerous external site, to reserve bandwidth for traffic between two specific sites or to give preferential treatment to one kind of traffic over other kinds. Traditional routers do not provide service differentiation because they treat all traffic in the same way. The process of mapping packets to different service classes is referred to as *policy-based routing*.

Speeding up the packet forwarding in the Internet backbone requires high-speed transmission links and high performance routers. The transmission technology keeps evolving and provision of gigabit fiber links is commonly available. For example, the high speed fiber links up to OC-192 (10 Gbps) are commercial available. Consequently, the key to increase the capacity of the Internet lies in fast routers [2]. A multi-gigabit router must have enough internal bandwidth to switch packets between its interfaces at multi-gigabit rates and enough packet processing power to forward multiple millions of packets per second (**MPPS**) [3]. Switching in the router has been studied extensively and solutions for fast packet processing are very popular. As a result, the remaining major obstacle for the high performance router design is the slow, multi-memory-access *IP/policy lookup* process.

In the past few years, new protocols such as tag switching and IP switching have been proposed to avoid the need for doing address lookups. This is because earlier algorithms for address lookups were too slow. The IETF has also instituted the Multiprotocol Label Switching (MPLS) [4] charter to study the use of label switching. Label switching is a generalization of tag and IP switching. MPLS proposes using labels to avoid address lookups and policy-based routing, it tends to achieve better traffic engineering. However, the MPLS efforts primarily focus on achieving better traffic engineering, as opposed to avoiding address lookups or policy-based routing because the average utilization of Internet backbone networks is estimated at 15% [5]. However, these solutions cannot completely avoid the need for IP lookups, thus it still requires fast address lookup algorithms for both protocols.

1.1. IP Address Lookup

The size of a IPv4 packet header is 20 bytes without extensions. It contains the source and destination addresses. An IP address consists of a network identifier and a host identifier. Routing is solely based on the network identifier. Originally, the network identifier had a predetermined length, indicated by a prefix in certain address bits which specified the address class: 0 indicated class A with 8-bit network identifiers, 10 indicated class B with 16 bits, and 110 indicated class C with 24-bit identifier. The class-based structure are proved too inflexible and wasteful of the address space. As a result, it is outmoded by the introduction of classless interdomain routing (CIDR) [6] in 1993.

With CIDR, IP routes have been identified by a ⟨routing prefix, prefix length⟩ pair, where the prefix length varies from 1 to 32 bits. Arbitrary aggregation of networks are allowed to reduce routing table entries, as well as increase the utilization of address space. Suppose all the subnets in a big network have identical routing information except for a single, small subnet that has different information, rather than having multiple routing entries for each subnet in the large network, just two entries are needed: one for the big network and a more specific one for the small subnet. The entry-length distribution of a sample CIDR routing table from the network access point (**NAP**) Mae-East is shown in Figure 2. Although the class-based address structure has been abolished, it is still visible in routing table entries since the numbers of prefixes with length 16 and 24 bits (formerly class B and C, respectively) are more than other lengths, especially the 24-bit prefixes. Although the CIDR results in better usage of the available IP address space as well as decreases the number of routing table entries, it also increases the processing power requirement for doing IP lookup.

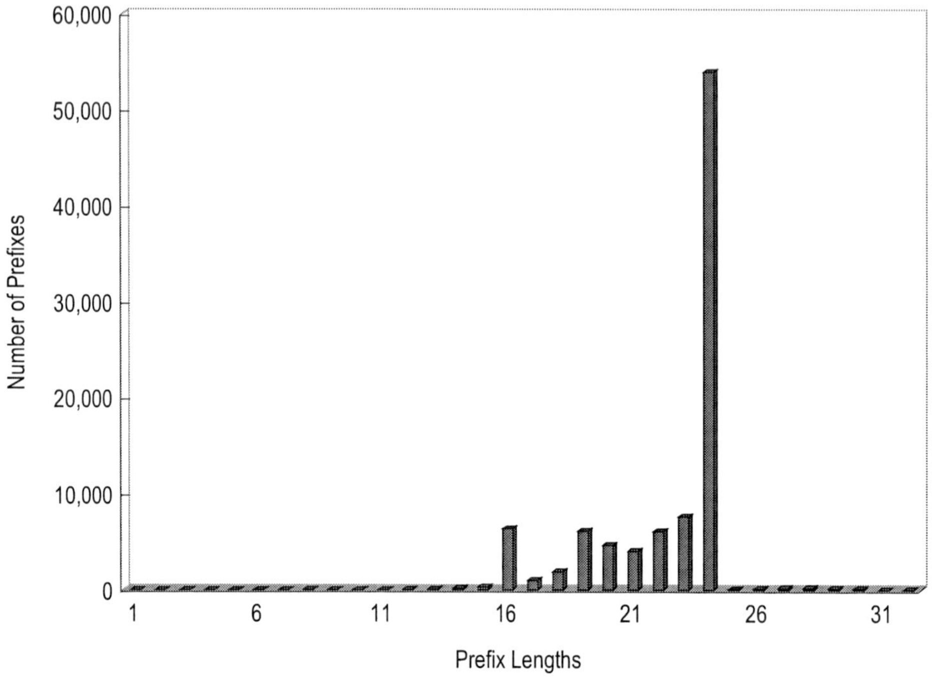

Figure 2. The Prefix Length Distribution.

An IP address can be split into network and host identifiers from any point. The network identifier is the prefix that is stored in the routing table. For instance, the address 140.113.215.213 gives the network identifier 140.113.208 with 20-bit prefix and 140.7 with 12-bit prefix. An address that would match both prefixes in a router should consequently be routed according to the information kept for the longer one, which is 20-bit prefix in this case. We call this **Best Matching Prefix (BMP)** problem.

To solve the BMP problem, traditional exact-matching lookup algorithms, such as hash and CAM, cannot be applied trivially due to two facts: 1) the prefixes length is variable and 2) there are multiple matching prefixes to the same DA. Thus it is time-consuming to search for the BMP, especially in a backbone router with a large number of table entries.

Most routers have a default route that is given by a prefix of length zero and therefore matches all addresses. The default route is used consequently if no other prefix matches. The backbone routers in the Internet are required to recognize all network identifiers and cannot resort to the default route. Thus their routing table is larger than other routers. Although the address structure for IPv6 is not public available, there are suggestions to keep the variable-length network identifiers. As result, the longer address length of IPv6 will only compound the problems of routers.

The result of an IP-address lookup in a router is the port number and next-hop address that should be used for the packet. The next-hop address is used to find the physical-link address for the next downstream router when the interconnection is via a shared-medium network (e.g., Ethernet address). The next-hop is not needed for point-to-point links, and the corresponding routing-table entry would only contain the output port number. Even when next-hop addresses are needed, they are much fewer addresses than the entries in the routing table. One can use an 8-bit pointer pointing to an array that lists the next-hop addresses.

2. IP Address Lookup: A Brief Overview

There has been a remarkable interest in the organization of routing tables during the past few years. The proposals can be separated into hardware and software based solutions.

- Hardware-based Solutions

  For years, designers of fast routers use caching to claim high speed IP lookups. This is problematic for several reasons, potentially diluting the cache with hundreds of addresses that map to the same prefix. Second, a typical backbone router of the future may have hundreds of thousands of prefixes and be expected to forward packets at tera-bit rates. Although studies have shown that caching in the backbone routers can result in hit ratios up to more than 90 percent [7,8], the simulations of cache behavior were done on large, fully associative caches which are commonly implemented using CAMs. CAMs, as already mentioned, are usually expensive. It is not clear how set associative caches will perform and whether caching will be able to keep up with the growth of the Internet. So caching does help, but does not avoid the need for fast BMP lookups, especially in view of current network growth.

  Besides cache schemes, Degermark *et al.* [9] proposed a trie-like data structure. A major concern in their work is the size of the trie to ensure that it fits in on-chip cache memory. The main idea of their work is to quantify the prefix lengths to levels of 16, 24 and 32 bits and expand each prefix in the table to the next higher level. Using this structure, it is able to compact a large routing table with 40,000 entries into a table with 150-160 Kbytes size. If implemented in hardware, the minimum and maximum number of memory accesses for a lookup are two and nine, respectively. Gupta *et al.* presented fast routing-lookup schemes based on a huge DRAM [10]. The scheme accomplishes a maximum of two memory accesses for a lookup in a forwarding table of 33 megabytes. By adding an intermediate-length table, the forwarding table can be reduced to 9 megabytes; however, the maximum number of memory accesses for a lookup is increased to three. When implemented in a hardware pipeline, it can achieve one route lookup every memory access. This furnishes about 20 MPPS. Huang *et al.* [11] further improve it by fitting the forwarding table into SRAM.

- Software-based Solutions

  Regarding software solutions, algorithms based on tree, hash or binary search have been proposed. Srinivasan *et al.* [12] present a data structure based on binary tree with multiway branching. By using a standard trie representation with arrays of children pointers, insertions and deletions of prefixes are supported. However, to minimize the size of the tree, dynamic programming is needed. In [13], Karlsson *et al.* solve the BMP problem by *LC tries* and linear search. Waldvogel *et al.* proposed a lookup scheme based on a binary search mechanism [14]. This scheme scales very well as the size of address and routing tables grows. The scheme requires a worst-case time complexity of log_2(address bits) hash lookups. Thus, five hash lookups are needed for IPv4, and seven for IPv6 (128-bit). This software-based binary search work is further improved by employing a cache structure as well as using multiway and multicolumn search techniques [15]. For a database of N prefixes with address length W, the native binary search scheme needs O($W \times logN$) searches. This improved scheme takes only O($W + logN$) searches.

In the following, we present three algorithms for IP address lookup. One is suitable for hardware implementation, one for software implementation and the other for both.

3. IP Address Lookup with Hardware Pipelining

First, we present a BMP scheme for hardware implementation in [16]. Based on the implementation, the forwarding table would be reduced to enough small to fit into SRAM with very low cost. For example, a large routing table with 53,000 entries can be compressed to a forwarding table of 540 Kbytes. Most of the address lookups can be accomplished in a single memory access. In the worst case, the number of memory accesses for a lookup is two. When implemented in pipelined hardware, the scheme can achieve one address lookup per memory access. With state-of-the-art SRAM technology, this mechanism can achieve more than 100 million lookups per second.

3.1. Related Works

Several works have been proposed with novel data structures to reduce the complexity of longest-prefix matching lookups [9, 12–15]. These data structures and their accompanying algorithms are designed primarily for software implementation, they are usually unable to complete a lookup in one memory-access-time. The most straightforward way to implement a lookup scheme is to have a forwarding table for each IP address, as depicted in Figure 3. However, the size of the forwarding table (next-hop array; NHA) is too large (4 GBytes) to be practical.

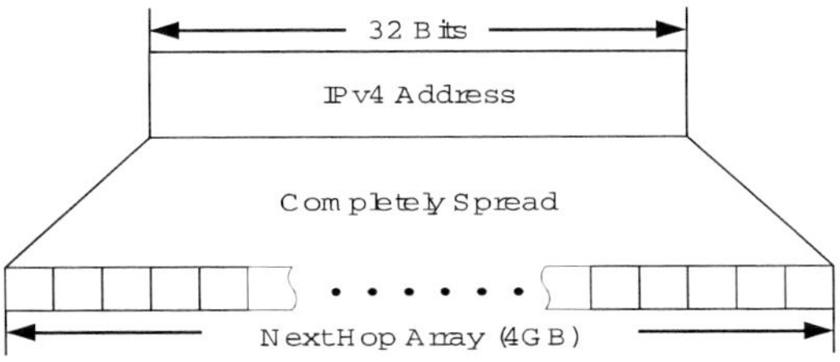

Figure 3. Direct-lookup mechanism.

To reduce the size of the forwarding table, an indirect lookup mechanism, as shown in Figure 4 [10], can be employed. Each IP address is split into two parts: 1) segment (16-bit) and 2) offset (16-bit). The segment table has 64K entries which record either the next hop of the route or pointers pointing to the associated **Next-hop Array** (**NHAs**). Each NHA consists of 64K entries, each entry records the next hop for the destination IP address. This scheme uses a maximum of two memory accesses for a lookup in a 33-Mbyte forwarding table. By adding an intermediate-length table, the forwarding table can be reduced to 9 Mbytes; however, the maximum number of memory accesses for a lookup will be increased to three. When implemented in hardware pipeline, the scheme can accomplish one address lookup every memory access and achieve up to 20 million lookups per second.

In [11], Huang *et al.* further reduced the size of the associated NHA by considering the distribution of the prefixes belonging to the same segment, as demonstrated in Figure 5. With 45,000 routing prefixes, it results in about 750K entries in the NHA. With 1 byte per entry, the total required memory size (including segment table) is more than 1 MBytes, and the required number of memory accesses is two. By employing the concept of compression, the required memory size can be further reduced, but the number of memory access would be increased to three. The time complexity for building the so-called **Code Word Array** (**CWA**) and the **Compressed NHA** (**CNHA**) is $O(n\log n)$ [11], where n denotes the number of prefixes in a segment. However, due to the mechanism of compression, it is needed to rebuild the CNHA for updating the forwarding table. Since the routing updates may occur every few seconds, the performance might degrade severely due to the memory bandwidth contention.

3.2. NHA Construction Algorithm

By observing the sample routing table in Figure 6, one can find that all routing prefixes are belonging to the same segment $\langle 63.192 \rangle$. In Huang's algorithm, the total required entries

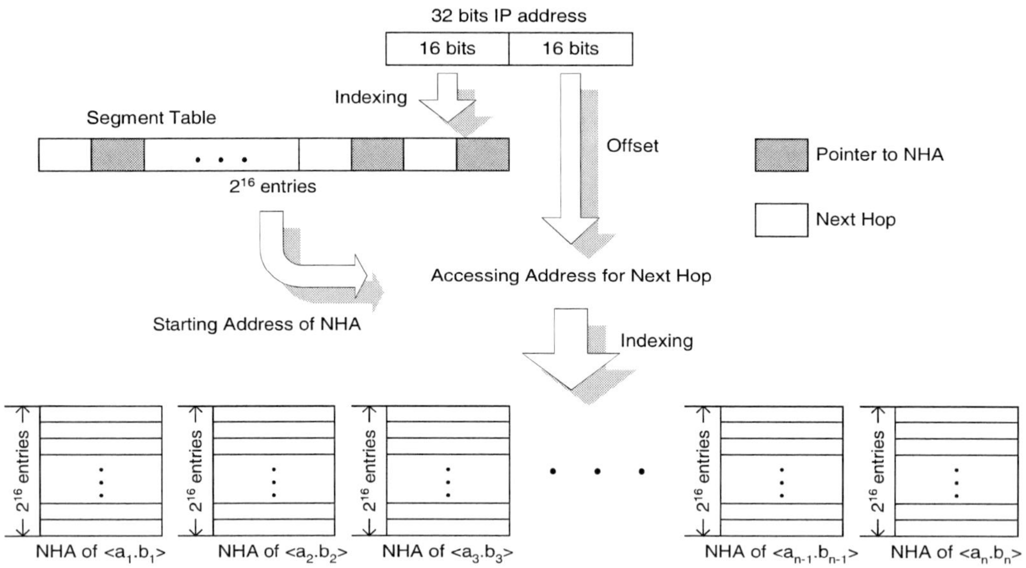

Figure 4. Indirect-lookup mechanism.

in an NHA would be $2^{(20-16)} = 24$. After a further analysis of these prefixes, one can find that the first 17 bits $\langle 00111111110000000 \rangle$ of these prefixes are the same. Since the longest prefix length is 20, this means that only the 3-bits variation is needed to build an NHA with $2^{(20-17)} = 23$-entries for these 6 prefixes, as shown in Figure 6. The longer the common part is, the shorter the NHA entries will be. The only problem is how to represent the extra prefix information. To deal with this issue, few prefix bits and its length are added to the entry of the segment table. This will increase the size of the segment table as a trade off. Those entries with no routing prefix information, such as P_5, should be filled with a default route.

The NHA construction algorithm for a segment is given bellow. Let l_i and h_i be the length and output port identifier of a routing prefix p_i, respectively. The *cprefix* represents the common part of routing prefixes beyond the first 16 bits in a segment, and *clength* is the valid length of *cprefix*. *Mlength* equals to the longest prefix length in the segment minus 16, thus, $clength \leq Mlength$. Let $p_i(x, y)$ represent the bit pattern of p_i from the x_{th} bit to the y_{th} bit. The entries from $V(p_i(clength + 16, l_i)) \times 2^{Mlength-(l_i)-16}$ to $V(p_i(clength + 16, l_i)) \times 2^{Mlength-(l_i)-16} + (2^{Mlength-(l_i-16)} - 1)$, where $V(p_i(a, b))$ represents the value of bit pattern $p_i(a, b)$. Besides, most routers have a default route with zero prefix length which matchel addresses. The default route is used consequently if no other prefix matches. Thus the table is initially assigned the default route for possible reference to these entries.

NHA-Construction Algorithm
Input: The set of routing prefixes of a segment.
Output: The corresponding NHA of this segment.

Step 1. Let l_i and h_i be the length and output port of a routing prefix p_i, respectively.

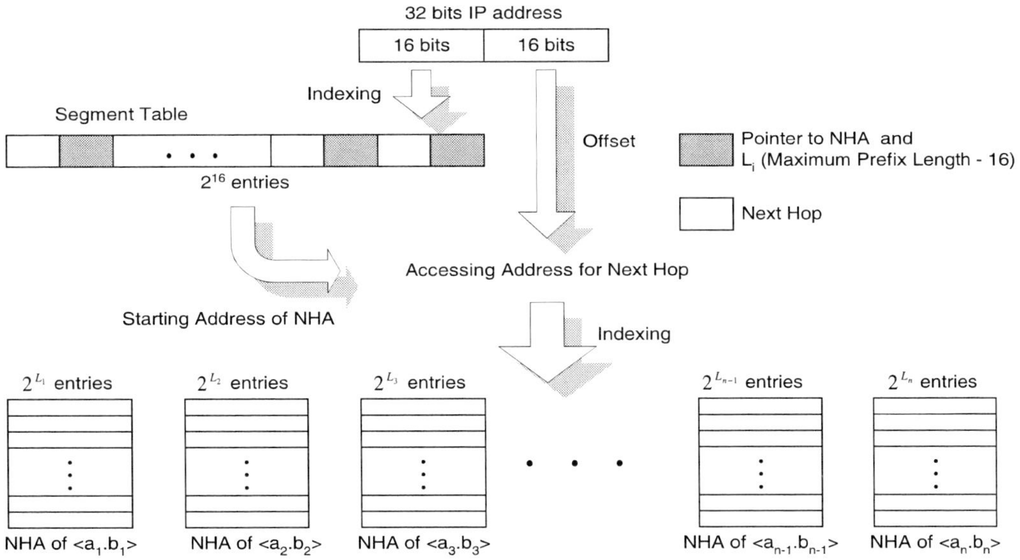

Figure 5. Indirect-lookup mechanism with variable offset length.

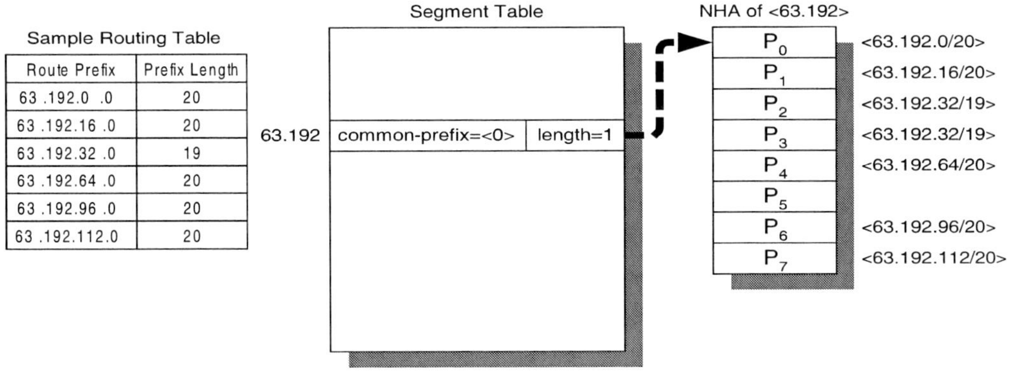

Figure 6. The resulting NHA from the sample routing prefixes.

Step 2. Let $P = \{p_0, p_1, ..., p_{n-1}\}$ be the set of sorted prefixes of an input segment. For any pair of prefixes p_i and p_j in the set, $i < j$ if and only if $l_i < l_j$.

Step 3. Let $cprefix = p_0(17, i_0)$,$clength = l_0 - 16$ and $Mlength = l_{n-1} - 16$.

Step 4. For $i = 0$ to $n - 1$ do
cprefix=common bits between *cprefix* and $p_i(17, l_i)$.
clength=valid length of *cprefix*.

Step 5. Construct the NHA with $2^{Mlength-clength}$ entries and set an initial value to the default route.

Step 6. For $i = 0$ to $n - 1$ do
Calculate the range of updated entries and set h_i.

Step 7. Stop.

Let us use an example to show how this algorithm works. Consider the set of sorted prefixes in Figure 7. In Step 4, all prefixes are examined once for deciding the *cprefix* and *clength* value, and it results in a single bit "0" for *cprefix* and thus *clength* is 1. Since *Mlength* is equal to 8, the constructed NHA is with $2^{8-1} = 128$ entries. After constructing the NHA, the table is assigned with default route as the initial value because the routing prefixes cannot cover every entry in NHA. Then the first prefix $\langle 24.48.8/22/10 \rangle$ will be fetched. The $8_{th}(= 2 \times 2^{8-6})$ to $11_{th}(= 2 \times 2^{8-6} + 2^{8-6} - 1)$ entries are the associated entries for $\langle 24.48.8/22/10 \rangle$ and will be overwritten with the output port value 10. The process is repeated for other prefixes. When processing the prefix $\langle 24.48.9/24/7 \rangle$, one can find that the value of 9_{th} entry is 10, which is defined by prefix $\langle 24.48.8/22/10 \rangle$, but the prefix $\langle 24.48.9/24/7 \rangle$ is a longer one. To satisfy the longest prefix matching, the 9_{th} entry will be overwritten with 7 again. Since the prefixes have been sorted by their lengths, this process can be done trivially.

Sample Prefixes

Prefix	Length	Output Port
24.48.8	22	10
24.48.40	22	1
24.48.56	23	10
24.48.80	23	7
24.48.82	23	7
24.48.9	24	7
24.48.10	24	10
24.48.12	24	7
24.48.13	24	1
24.48.55	24	1
24.48.84	24	7

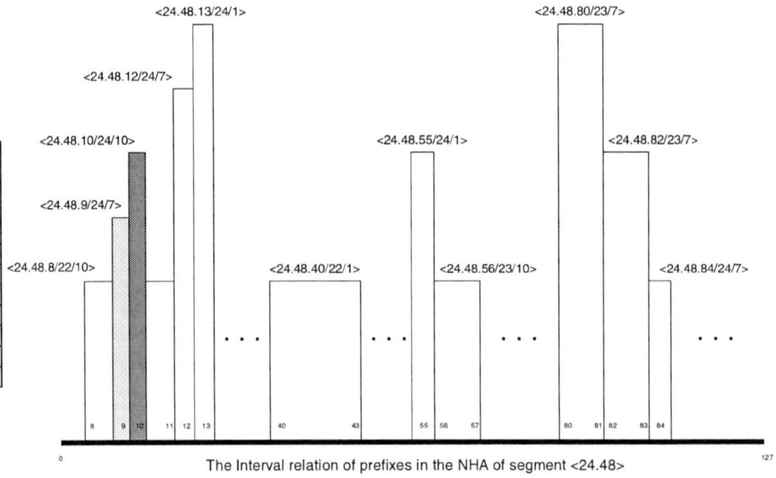

Figure 7. The NHA construction example.

Obviously, the computation cost is low. If a new routing prefix is received, it will recalculate *Mlength*, *cprefix* and *clength*, which is same as Step 4, and rebuilds the NHA if its size is changed. By applying the algorithm, the number of entries of the generated NHA can be 25% less than Huang's algorithm. The detailed organization of the segment table and the hardware architecture will be addressed below as well as the effect of the *cprefix*.

3.3. NHA Compression Algorithm

In the NHA construction algorithm, the size of the generated forwarding table would be around 1.2 Mbytes with one byte per entry which includes 3-bit *cprefix*. Moreover, the NHA can be further compressed based on the distribution of output port count within the NHA. The distribution, which is generated from traces of several main NAPs, is shown in Figure 8. It is observed that approximately 54% segments consist of less than two output ports and 96% segments use less than four output ports. Thus fewer bits are enough to encode the output port identifier in an NHA. Two extra fields, *cbits* and *base*, are appended to the entry of the segment table. At first, a bit-vector is used to record all possible output port identifiers, which are then encoded using the smallest port identifier as the *base*. Each associated NHA entry will be set to the value of its output port identifier minus the *base*. Also, the required bits are set to *cbits* for each entry. Thus the *base* can be read before indexing the associated NHA, and the physical output port index can be calculated by adding the base index to the NHA indexing result. This process can be completed within two memory accesses plus the calculation time which can be ignored. the detailed compressed-NHA construction algorithm is listed below.

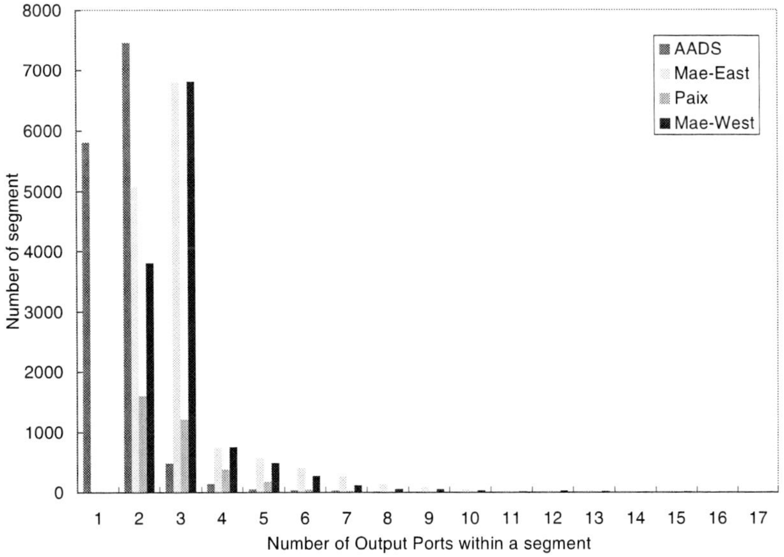

Figure 8. The distribution of output port count within a segment.

Compressed-NHA Construction Algorithm

Input: The set of routing prefixes of a segment.

Output: The corresponding compressed NHA of this segment.

Step 1. For each prefix, calculate *cprefix*, *Mlength* and *clength*. Also, records the output port value in the output port vector.

Step 2. Construct the index table from the output port vector and calculate the *cbits* and *base* value according to the output port count.

Step 3. Construct the NHA with size $2^{Mlength-clength} \times cbits$.

Step 4. For each routing prefix
Calculate the index value of an output port by subtracting the base value.
Calculate the range of updated entries in NHA and fill it with index value.

Step 5. Stop.

Although the table compression ratio in the scheme is not so notable, it is able to accomplish an IP lookup with two memory accesses. Also the scheme is implementation feasible with pipelining hardware. Notice that in Huang's algorithm, the memory locations accessed in the second and the third lookup are the same because it appends the CNHA to the tail of the CWA. Therefore, it may cause the structural hazard for implementation in pipelining hardware. Such potential structural hazard can be avoided in the scheme without requiring any specific hardware such as dual port memory.

3.4. Hardware Implementation

A feasible high-level hardware architecture of the lookup scheme is shown in Figure 9. When a DA is fetched, its first 16 bits are used as an index to the segment table. The value of pointer/next_hop field in the corresponding entry records the next hop if it is smaller than 256. The value will be forwarded to the selector directly. Otherwise, it records the starting address of the associated NHA. Then the bit pattern *DA(clength, Mlength)* is used to compare with the *cprefix* stored in this entry. If two values are identical, then *V(DA(clength, Mlength))* plus the value of the pointer is used to access the NHA. The physical output port can be derived by adding the *base* with the value fetched from NHA. Otherwise, the default output port will be forwarded to the selector.

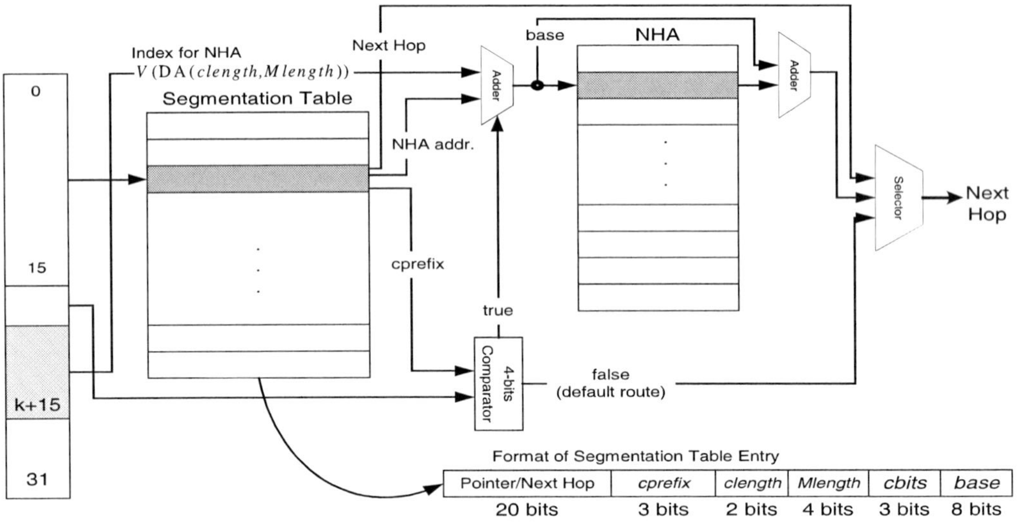

Figure 9. Hardware architecture of the lookup scheme.

The entry of the segment table consists of 6 fields: pointer/next_hop, *cprefix*, *clength*, *Mlength*, *base* and *cbits*. The length of pointer/next_hop is 20 bits which can map to 1 mega memory addresses, this is more than five times the space required for storing the whole NHAs generated from the real world routing tables. Since the maximum prefix length minus the length of segment (16) is smaller than 16, the length of *Mlength* is 4 bits. Trivially, the base is 8 bits and the maximum number of encoded bits is 8. Thus the bit count of *cbits* is 3. If the length of *cprefix* is 3, then the *clength* is 2 bits. As a consequence, the length of each entry is 40 bits, and the size of the segment table is $2^{16} \times 40$ bits, i.e.,

320 Kbytes.

3.5. Performance Analysis

The IP address lookup scheme aims at two targets, one is to reduce the memory space needed for the forwarding tables, and the other is to speed up the IP lookup process. Note that the current backbone routers have a routing table with about 53,000 entries. We use the logs of publicly available routing tables as the basis for comparison. These tables are offered by the IPMA project [17], they provide a daily snap shot of the routing tables used by some major NAPs.

To further realize the effect of the extra *cprefix*, we use the trace available in the router of Mae-East NAP to present the relation between the total number of entries in NHAs and the length of *cprefix*, as shown in Figure 10. By coupling the effect of *cprefix*, the number of entries can be 25% less than that required in Huang's algorithm. Although as the length of *cprefix* increases, the number of NHA entries is reduced, it has to increase the entry length of the segment table, thus results in a larger segment table. From the observation of Figure 10, the suitable *cprefix* length should be no more than 3 by considering both segment table size and the number of NHA entries.

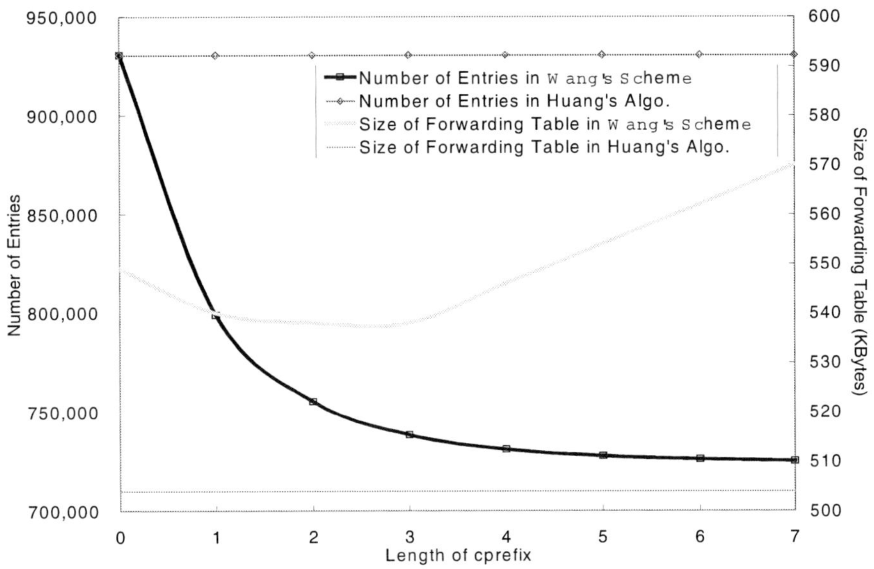

Figure 10. Effect of the Length of *cprefix*.

In Table 1, we log five traces to build the forwarding table for illustrating the effect of the scheme. Although the size of the forwarding table might become larger as a trade-off for throughput improvement, we can find that the required memory size does not increase too much, or even decrease in two traces (PacBell and Paix). This is because that the use of *cprefix* reduces the number of NHA entries effectively. While in the traces of two backbone NAPs (Mae-East and Mae-West), the memory increment is notable, this is due to the diverse routing prefixes in the backbone, in which the effect of *cprefix* is degraded.

Table 1. The comparison of memory requirements.

Site	Routing Prefixes	Wang's Scheme (Kbytes)	Huang's Algo (Kbytes)
AADS	23,426	396	403
Mae-East	53,226	538	504
PacBell	29,942	258	412
Paix	11,498	328	351
Mae-West	33,332	529	454

3.6. Summary

In this section, we introduce a fast IP lookup scheme that requires less memory space, and it can be implemented with high-speed SRAM. By employing an efficient compression scheme, the size of the forwarding table can be reduced significantly. For example, a large routing table with 53,000 routing entries can be compressed to a forwarding table of 540 Kbytes with the cost of less than US$30. Most of the address lookups can be done in one memory access, with the worst case, two. Furthermore, the scheme can avoid the structural hazard for hardware pipelining. When implemented in hardware with pipeline technique, it can accomplish one address lookup in a single memory access and achieve approximately 100 million address lookups per second with current 10ns SRAM.

4. Performance Enhancement of IP Forwarding Using Routing Interval

Nowadays, the commonly used table lookup scheme for IP routing is based on the so-called classless interdomain routing (CIDR). With CIDR, routers must find out the BMP for IP packets forwarding, this complicates the IP lookup. Currently, this process is mainly done in software and several schemes have been proposed for hardware implementation. Since the IP lookup performance is a major design issue for the new generation routers, the properties of the routing table are investigated and a new approach for IP lookups is presented in [18, 19]. This approach is not based on BMP and thus significantly reduces the complexity. By applying the approach, the computation cost of existing schemes can be significantly reduced. Moreover, the performance of the binary search on prefixes is improved to 30 MPPS and 5,000 route updates per second under the same experiment setup with an even larger routing table. With the state-of-the-art 700 MHz CPU, it can achieve more than 70 MPPS in average.

4.1. Routing Interval

According to the concept of CIDR, each IP address might be covered by multiple routing prefixes. However, only the longest one indicates the next-hop. From the geographical characteristic of the destination location, a new routing concept based on the following observations is presented. Before presenting our approach, it is necessary to define the segment for IP address. Here each IP address can be divided into two parts: segment (16 bits) and offset (16 bits).

The density of routing prefixes for segments is related to its hop-count: From the network topology, all networks (including enterprise, campus, ISP) are physically interconnected through trunks. Since there are multiple trunks for neighbor cloud to connect with each other, the number of routing prefixes is large and with disorderly information. On the other hand, the routing prefixes are simple and much fewer for the remote cloud, i.e., farther geographical region.

The number of routing prefixes is sparse in IP network: Although the number of Internet hosts increases exponentially, the distribution of routing prefix is still very sparse. For example, there are $2^3 2$ IP addresses but only about 56,000 routing prefixes in current backbone router (Mae-East 8/12/2000). There is less than one routing prefix per segment on average. We use the routing tables offered by the IPMA project [17], which provides a daily snap shot of the routing table used by some major NAPs, as basis for our experiment. The number of prefixes whose length is longer than 16 bits in each segment is shown in Figure 11. From the experimental results, we observed that most of routing prefixes identify the next-hop only for few segments, this phenomenon is called as routing locality. It also reflects the property that most prefixes are related to neighbor clouds.

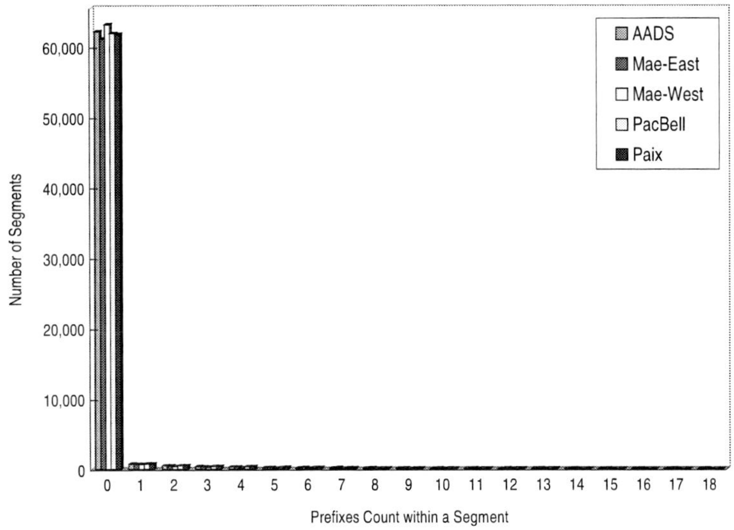

Figure 11. Prefix Count Distribution.

In a router, the number of possible next-hops for a segment is always much less than the total number of ports: The number of distinct next-hops in a routing table is limited by the number of other routers or hosts that can be reached in one hop, it is clear that these numbers would be small even for large backbone routers. For the enterprise or campus routers, the extensive use of default routes for outside destinations further reduce the routing table and the number of next-hops. It results in that few routing prefixes are used to define the routes for most segments. Hence the number of next-hops for most segments is small and hence less than the number of related routing prefixes, as shown in Figure 12.

From the above discussion, a new routing concept "Routing Interval", which

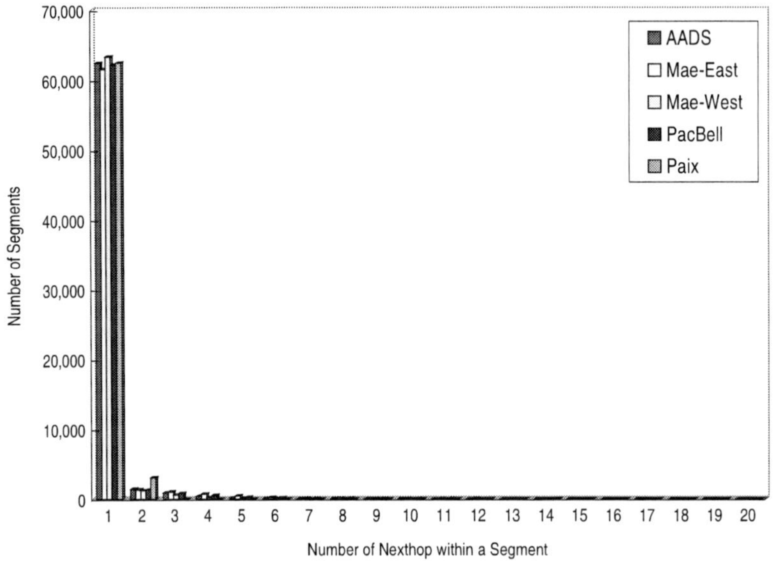

Figure 12. The Distribution of Next-hop Count within a Segment.

fully utilizes the aforementioned properties, is introduced. By sorting the routing prefixes based on their lengths, a next-hop array contains entries, which correspond to all intervals. In addition, each entry also records the related next-hop. For example, there are three routing prefixes $140.113.0.0/255.255.0.0/NH_1$, $140.113.3.0/255.255.255.0/NH_2$ and $140.113.0.0/255.255.255.0/NH_3$ with length 16, 24, 24, respectively. First, the routing prefix $140.113.0.0/255.255.0.0/NH_1$ creates an IP address interval $140.113.0.0 \sim 140.113.255.255/NH_1$. When the next routing prefix $140.113.3.0/255.255.255.0/NH_2$ is processed, the interval is further partitioned into three regions, $140.113.0.0 \sim 140.113.2.255/NH_1$, $140.113.3.0 \sim 140.113.3.255/NH_2$ and $140.113.4.0 \sim 140.113.255.255/NH_1$, respectively. According to this simple rule, three routing prefixes results in five intervals based on the next-hop value and record each with $\langle begin\ address, end\ address, next - hop\rangle$. This tuple is named as "Routing Interval", as shown in Figure 13.

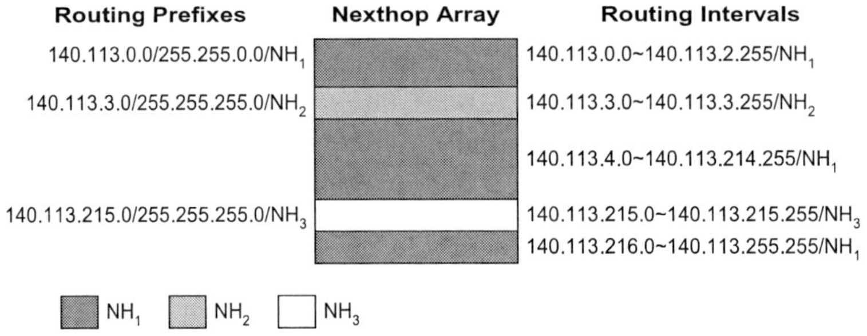

Figure 13. Routing Interval Example.

Most of existing algorithms use different approaches to handle the BMP problem and result in either complex data structure or extra storage, or both. The most significant benefit to transform the routing prefix into routing interval is that the complexity of BMP problem can be removed. For example, each node in Patricia trie consists of three pointers, one for prefix entry and two for child nodes due to possible longer match. Although various implementations of the Patricia trie have been proposed and significantly improve the performance, it can be further enhanced via applying the routing interval. The inefficient data structure can be simplified, with which each node may contain either a prefix pointer or two child pointers, but not both. With low transformation cost, the BMP problem is reduced into a much simpler search problem. The algorithm of transformation is addressed below. Notice that the idea is completely different from the previous work [20], which concerns how to reduce the number of routing prefixes, while the concept of routing interval focuses on how to remove the BMP problem.

Theoretically, the maximum number of generated routing intervals is $2N - 1$, where N is the number of routing prefixes (including default route). However, the experiments show different results. The result generated from the large routing table (Mae-East) is shown in Figure 14. The number of routing intervals is less than that of routing prefixes in this case. There may be three reasons: (I) A region which indicates identical next-hop value has to be represented by several routing prefixes due to the limitation that the occupied region of routing prefixes must be with the order of 2. (II) Some routing prefixes belong to the same routing interval, thus they can be merged into a single interval. For example, there are two routing prefixes, $140.113.0.0/16/NH_1$, $140.113.3.0/24/NH_1$, with difference prefix length and identical next-hop value. The routing prefix $140.113.3.0/24/NH_1$ is redundant and can be removed. (III) There are zero-range intervals which can be eliminated. This phenomenon can be understood after the discussion in Section 4.2.1.. The results of other NAPs are shown in Table 2, where the value below is the number of routing prefixes. In most of the numerical results, the generated numbers of intervals are fewer than that of the routing prefixes.

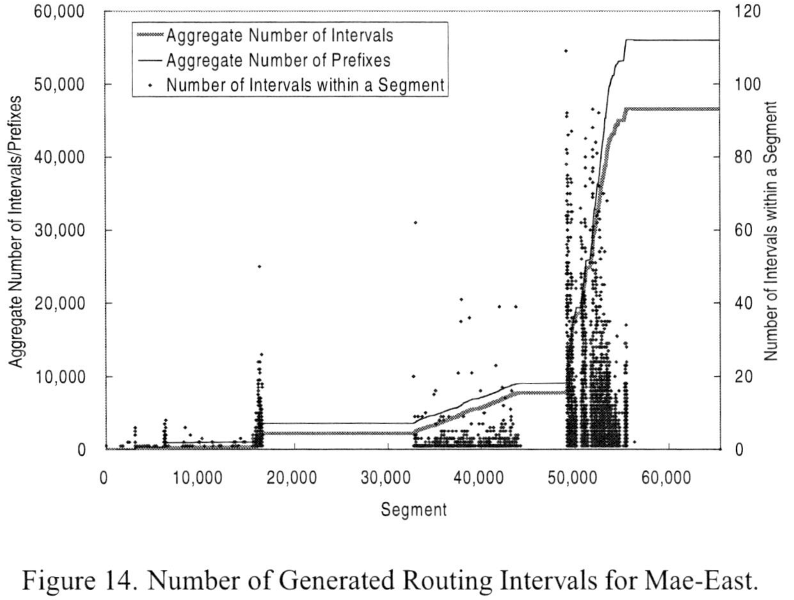

Figure 14. Number of Generated Routing Intervals for Mae-East.

Table 2. Comparison of Routing Prefixes/Routing Intervals in Different Dates.

Date	AADS	Mae-East	Mae-West	PacBell	Paix
9/9/1999	9,287 35,769	44,233 47,784	28,853 28,998	22,263 26,278	9,341 9,270
12/22/1999	12,075 17,460	44,904 52,372	30,387 30,688	21,141 25,406	8,711 9,237
5/15/2000	24,451 23,515	42,800 53,226	30,492 33,514	23,619 29,959	8,944 11,587
8/12/2000	23,411 26,109	46,557 56,039	30,501 31,060	25,807 33,680	14,201 13,878

For most of the segments, the routing information, including the next-hops and routing prefixes, is very simple. Further, the distribution is related to the network topology. The routing information is more complex for the nearby region (in topology). Therefore, it is possible to improve the IP lookup scheme based on these characteristics by converting the hierarchical routing prefixes into flat routing intervals. With the concept of routing interval, complexity of IP lookup can be greatly reduced. Next, how the existing schemes can take advantage of this concept is shown in the following.

4.1.1. Qualitative Analysis and Enhancement with Existing Routing Schemes

The scheme proposed by Waldvogel *et al.* [14] performs the IP lookup based on the lengths of the prefixes. The prefixes with the same length are stored in a hash-table. The binary search is used to find out the longest prefix, and one hash-table lookup is performed at each step of this search. However, to find out the BMP with binary search is not trivial. For each prefix with length L, an extra marker will be added to the hash table with length 1 to $L-1$ to indicate that there exists a longer match, so that it will lookup the longer-prefix hash table. Furthermore, the best match prefix for the marker should also be calculated to avoid misleading. While the routing prefixes is replaced by the routing intervals, it does not need to change the basic mechanism, but the pre-computation of best match for each marker can be removed. Since no misleading will happen with the usage of routing interval, there is no backtracking problem. Thus, the pre-computation cost can be saved while simplifying the data structure of forwarding table.

To migrate the routing prefixes to routing intervals here, the routing intervals must satisfy that the region of each interval can be represented as the power of two. For example, an interval whose region is six will be cut into two intervals with region value four and two respectively. A sample result converted from Figure 14 is shown in Figure 15. The number of the processed intervals would be a trade off between simplified construction and searching algorithm.

Another scheme proposed by Srinivasan *et al.* [12] consists of two parts. In the first part, it reduces the number of distinct prefix lengths. With dynamic programming, the optimal expansion level can be calculated. Consequently, it constructs the trie based on the results. Leaf pushing and cache line alignment are used to improve the performance. While

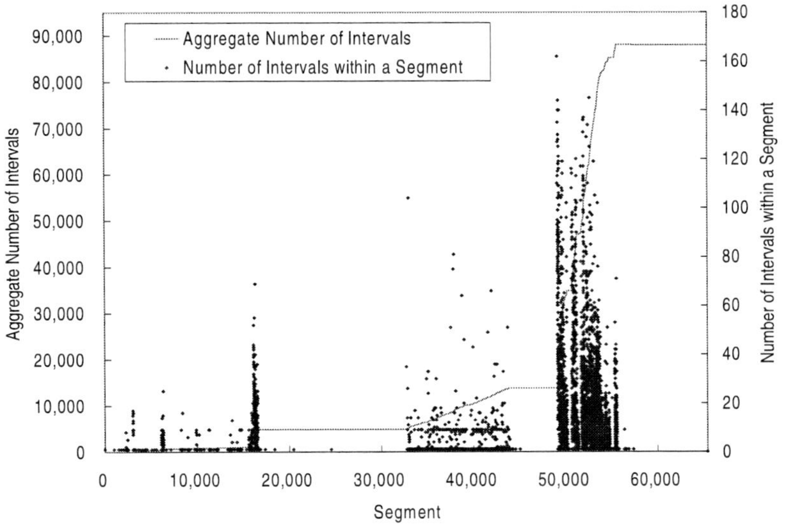

Figure 15. Number of Processed Routing Intervals for Mae-East.

applying routing intervals, the operation of leaf push can be eliminated because the longer match will not occur. Each element in the node indicates a pointer to either the next node or the prefix table. In fact, leaf pushing is conceptually similar to our idea, but ours is more generalized. In [12], the authors address how to improve the performance of binary search on hash table. By applying the routing interval concept, the enhancement discussed above can be applied, too.

In [13], Nilsson *et al.* use the skill called level compression tries (*LC tries*) to reduce the height of trie. The basic idea is: since there is a fixed cost for comparing strings whose lengths are equal or less than the machine word, it is therefore more efficient to compare more bits at a time to reduce the number of comparisons and memory accesses. However, to improve the efficiency of data structure, they didn't handle the BMP problem in the trie. Each internal node keeps the number of nodes and the address of the leftmost one. The search only stops at the leaf node, which contains the pointer to the prefix table. Once the pointed prefix doesn't match, it will jump to the shorter prefix of current one indicated in this entry. Therefore, it deals the BMP problem with linear search, this might result in poor performance in some cases.

Applying routing interval can eliminate the aforementioned problem. If the trie is constructed with routing intervals, each interval will correspond to a leaf node in the trie. Once the search reaches the leaf node, the best matching will be found. Since no linear search is needed, the prefix table can be removed.

4.2. IP Address Lookup by Using Routing Interval

We have introduced three enhancements to previous schemes and show the advantages of using the routing interval. Basically, it can simplify the data structure and reduce the precomputation cost that leads to low table construction time. It might also reduce the required memory storage and the number of accesses in some cases. The transformation from routing prefix to routing interval is essential to design an effective routing scheme. Consequently, an efficient transformation method is presented as well as an IP lookup scheme, which further takes advantage of routing intervals. The algorithm can handle 5,000 route updates per second, which includes the interval transformation and forwarding table construction.

4.2.1. Routing Interval Transformation

According to the routing interval concept, each routing prefix implies a routing interval that can be identified by just appending (32-prefix length) 0's and (32-prefix length) 1's as starting and ending address, respectively. For example, routing prefix $P_i = \langle 140.113.0.0/16/NH_i \rangle$ is with a routing interval $\langle S_i = 140.113.0.0, E_i = 140.113.255.255, NH_i \rangle$. However, it is an imprecise routing interval since it overlaps with other routing interval in the boundary that causes the ambiguous address lookup. Consequently, the major purpose of routing interval transformation is used to partition the routing intervals precisely.

The insertion of a routing prefix will generate at most three routing intervals which are $\langle unknown, S_i - 1, unknown \rangle$, $\langle S_i, unknown, NH_i \rangle$ and $\langle E_i + 1, unknown, unknown \rangle$. The transformation algorithm is used to determine these unknown values. Basically, the transformation from routing prefix to interval is irreversible because the hierarchical information carried in routing prefix is removed. Each route update will cause the re-transformation of the routing interval. To make it easier for implementation, two link-lists, L_1 and L_2, are adopted. The former is used to store the generated routing interval formats, and it is initialized to empty. The latter is used to store the possible routing interval $\langle E_i + 1, unknown, unknown \rangle$ and it is implemented as a stack, which performs "push", "pop" and "modification" operations.

With the sorted routing prefixes, let S_i, E_i and NH_i be the starting address, ending address and the next-hop of the routing interval P_i, respectively, where $S_1 \leq S_2 \leq \ldots \leq S_N$ (N is the number of routing prefixes, $1 \leq i \leq N$). At the beginning, we append the interval $\langle 0, unknown, default\ route \rangle$ to L_1 and push the interval $\langle 255.255.255.255, 255.255.255.255, default\ route \rangle$ into L_2. To simplify the description, we use the subscript *top* and *rear* to represent the starting address, ending address and next-hop of the top and rear routing interval in L_1 and L_2, respectively. For each routing prefix with imprecise routing interval $\langle S_i, E_i, NH_i \rangle$, we first check whether S_{top} (i.e., the starting address of the top interval in L_2) is smaller than S_i, if so, $E_{rear} = S_{top} - 1$. Then, we pop the top element, say, $\langle S_{top}, E_{top}, NH_{top} \rangle$, of L_2 and append it to the rear of L_1. After that, we update NH_{rear} with NH_{top}. We repeat these steps until there is no smaller interval in L_2, i.e.,$S_{top} \leq S_i$, and modify E_{rear} to $S_i - 1$. It means that there exist an interval $\langle S_{rear}, S_i - 1, NH_{rear} \rangle$. Moreover, we must check whether S_{rear} is equal to S_i or not. If yes, then we replace NH_{rear} with NH_i. Otherwise, we append $\langle S_i, unknown, NH_i \rangle$ to L_1. Since it belongs to an interval which is not defined clearly, we must further check whether S_{top} is equal to $E_i + 1$ or not. If $S_{top} = E_i + 1$, then we replace NH_{top} with NH_i. Otherwise, we push an interval, $\langle E_i + 1, unknown, NH_i \rangle$, into L_2. Finally, we pop all intervals stored in L_2 and append them to L_1 sequentially. The detailed algorithm is listed as below.

Routing Interval Transformation Algorithm

Input: N routing prefixes.
Output: The set of ordered routing intervals.
Let S_i and E_i be the starting and ending address, NH_i be the next-hop of i_{th} routing prefix, respectively. (The subscript top and $rear$ represent the starting address, ending address and the next-hop of the top and $rear$ interval in L_1 and L_2, respectively.)
Let $P = P_1, P_2, \ldots, P_{N-1}$ be the set of sorted prefixes of an input segment.
For any pair of prefixes P_i and P_j in the set, $i < j$ if and only if $S_i < S_j$.
Append interval $\langle 0, unknown, default\ route\rangle$ into L_1 and push interval $\langle 1111\ldots1, 1111\ldots1, default\ route\rangle$ into L_2.
For $i = 1$ to N **do**

1. For the imprecise interval $\langle S_i, E_i, NH_i\rangle$ of i_{th} routing prefix. Check if S_i larger than S_{top}.

2. If yes, modify E_{rear} with $S_{top} - 1$. Pop the top interval from L_2 into L_1. Then modify NH_{rear} with NH_{top}.Repeat step 1&2 until the result of comparison is false.

3. Consequently, modify E_{rear} as $(S_i - 1)$.

4. Check if $S_{rear} = S_i$,
   4.a If yes, overwrite NH_{rear} with NH_i.
   4.b Otherwise, append $\langle S_i, unknown, NH_i\rangle$ into L_1.

5. Check if the $S_{top} = E_i + 1$,
   5.a If yes, overwrite NH_{top} with NH_i.
   5.b Otherwise, push $\langle E_i + 1, unknown, NH_i\rangle$ into L_2.

Push all intervals stored in L_2 and append into L_1.
For all generated intervals **do**
    Merge two successive intervals with identical next-hop.
Stop.

In Figure 16, we use an example to illustrate the process of the routing interval transformation. After processing the routing prefix P_3, the top element of L_2 and rear elements of L_1 are $\langle E_3, unknown, NH_3\rangle$ and $\langle S_3, unknown, NH_3\rangle$, respectively. For the routing prefix P_4, it is firstly compared with S_{top}. Since S_{top} is smaller than S_4, E_{rear} is modified to S_i. It pops the top element, $\langle E_3 + 1, unknown, NH_3\rangle$, of L_2 and append the popped element to the rear of L_1. Then we modify NH_3 with NH_2. Since there is no smaller interval in L_2, we replace E_{rear} with $S_4 - 1$. It further checks whether S_{rear} is equal to S_4 or not. Because they are different, it must append the interval $\langle S_4, unknown, NH_4\rangle$ to L_1. In addition, S_{top} is unequal to $E_4 + 1$, thus it pushes the interval $\langle E_4 + 1, unknown, NH_4\rangle$ into L_2.

After processing all prefixes, the ordered intervals are listed in the array. The time complexity of the transformation algorithm without the prefixes sorting is $O(M) = O(2N - 1) = O(N)$ where M is the interval count and N is the prefix count.

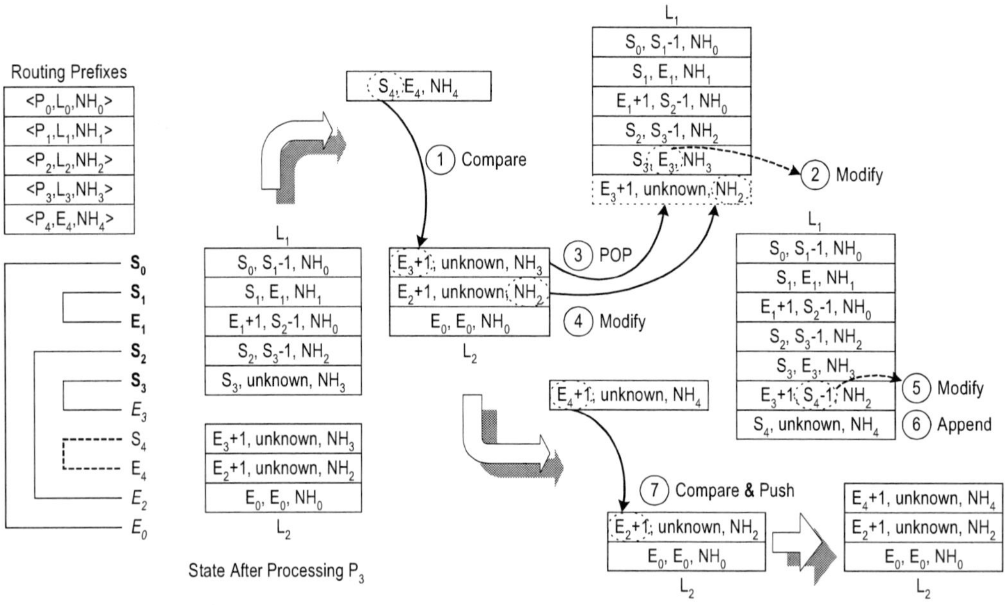

Figure 16. An Example of Routing Interval Transformation.

4.2.2. Modification of Binary Search for Speedup

In [15], Lampson *et al.* use two copies of the routing prefixes, one copy is padded with zeros and the other with ones, for IP lookup. With pre-computation, it can perform the prefix matching with binary search in a sorted array containing these extended prefixes. The required memory of forwarding table is about 1 Mbytes, which cannot fit into the L2 cache of most modern CPUs. Recall that a CPU READ to a byte will prefetch an entire cache line into the L2 cache, multiway search with cache line alignment are used to improve the performance. In spite of its scalability to IPv6, the route update will cause the reconstruction of the forwarding table, which costs about 350 ms in the worst case.

The performance can be greatly improved by adopting the routing interval. The mapping of previous scheme from routing prefix to routing interval is shown in Figure 17. From the right part of Figure 17, one can see that a native binary search can support IP lookup without any further pre-computation. Moreover, the number of entries (M) is always less than that of previous scheme ($2N$). However, the problem of route updates remains, there is no existing update technique that is faster than just building a table from scratch. Another problem resulted from the unbalanced interval distribution, as shown in Figure 11, might degrade the efficiency of binary search.

To alleviate both problems, an IP address is split into two parts: the segment (16-bit) and the offset (16-bit), and add a segment table which extract the prefixes with length less than 16, as used in [15]. Each entry of the segment table consists of two fields: address of the first interval and the number of intervals, as shown in Figure 18. If the interval count is zero, the value in another field indicates the next-hop. Otherwise, it will perform a binary search to the intervals whose first 16 bits are the same. With 2 bytes for each field, the size of segment table will be 256 Kbytes.

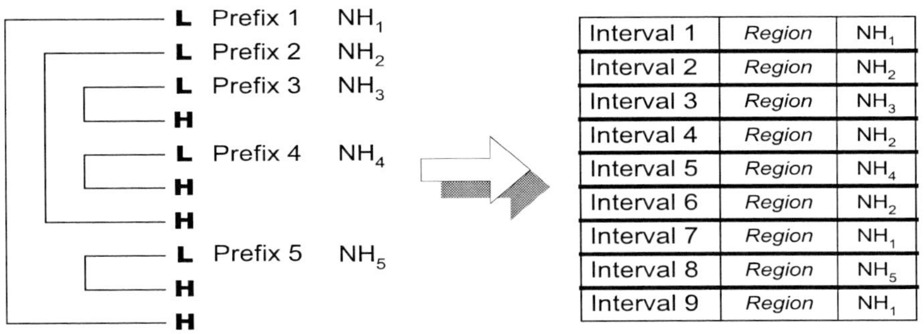

Figure 17. Mapping from Previous Scheme into the Routing Interval Scheme.

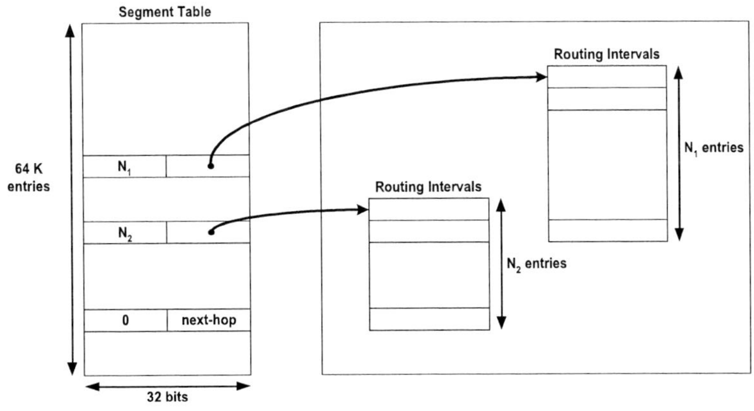

Figure 18. Binary Search With 16-bits Segment Table.

4.2.3. Further Improvement with Memory Bus Alignment

To achieve better lookup performance, two requirements should be met. At first, the size of forwarding table should be small enough to fit into the L2 cache. By constructing the forwarding table, the total size including segment table is less than 480 Kbytes for Mae-East routing table. Consequently, the data structure for binary search should comply with the memory bus. Unlike the cache line alignment described in the previous scheme, our improvement focus on the characteristic of memory bus between L1 and L2 cache. Most modern CPUs have large bus width, such as 64-bits, for access efficiency. Therefore, two intervals (5-bytes for each) is merged into one entry with 8 bytes, as shown in Figure 19. The binary search will test two routing intervals within one L2 cache access. The size of forwarding table can be reduced and the lookup speed can be fastened.

4.2.4. Complexity

In Table 3, we show the complexity required for different software-based schemes. Note that these complexity measures do not indicate anything about the physical speed or actual memory usage. In the worst case, the number of routing intervals is twice of the number of routing prefixes. We will show the realistic performance metrics in the next section.

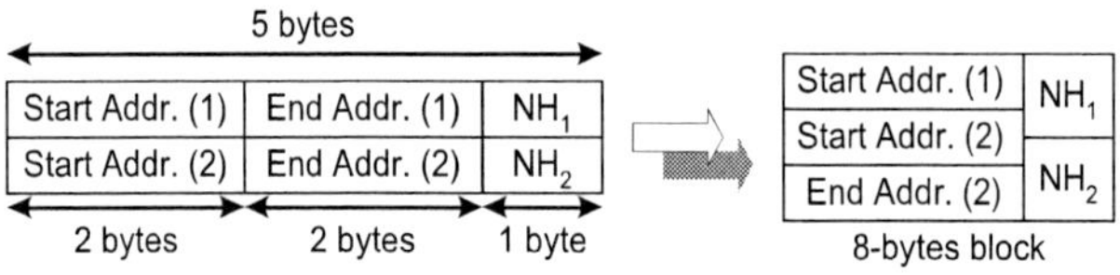

Figure 19. Memory Bus Alignment for Access Efficiency.

Table 3. Comparison with the Existing Works.

Algorithms	Build	Search	Memory
Patricia Trie	$O(NW)$	$O(W)$	$O(NW)$
Binary Search on Hash Tables	$O(N log_2 W)$	$O(log_2 W)$	$O(N log_2 W)$
Multibit Trie	$O(hW^2)$	$O(h)$	$O(hN)$
LC Tries	$O(hN)$	$O(h)$	$O(hN)$
Multiway Search	$O(N)$	$O(log_M(2N))$	$O(2N)$
Routing Interval Scheme	$O(N)$	$O(log_2(2N))$	$O(2N)$

N: the number of the prefixes, W: the length of the address,
h: the height of the trie, M: the number of branches

4.3. Performance Evaluation

To simplify the comparison with multiway search, we use a comparable platform as used in previous work [15]. We choose a 300-MHz Pentium II running Windows NT that has a 512-Kbytes L2 cache. We also use another 700-MHz K7, state-of-the-art high performance CPU, to show what performance level we can achieve. Five routing tables from the IPMA project are used for the experiment. We will show the performance of the scheme with respect to three metrics: worst/average search time, storage and construct/update time.

The detailed performance metrics are shown in Table 4. The routing interval scheme works very well even with a large routing table. The update time represents the cost of table reconstruction for the segment with most intervals. Both construction and update time are accounted as the cost of interval transformation. The scheme can support at least 5,000 route updates per second which is much faster than 100 update/s as required in some BGP implementation [15]. The reason for the shortened build/update time is that our table construction is very simple. With link-list implementation, no large memory copy is needed in the interval transformation. Moreover, the construction of memory-bus-alignment array is much simpler than any existing schemes. The constructed forwarding table is small enough to fit into CPU L2 cache. Besides, the memory bus alignment helps improve the access efficiency as well as decrease the number of entries with a factor of 2. For the routing table of Mae-East, the worst-case forwarding rate is larger than 4 MPPS. If the weight of each IP address is the same, the average forwarding rate is about 30 MPPS. As used in practical environment, the performance would be better due to the locality of traffic flows.

Consequently, the routing interval scheme is compared to multiway search. The result generated from the routing table of Mae-East is shown in Table 5. Note that numbers measured on 200-MHz Pentium Pro have been proportionately scaled to 300 MHz, as used

Table 4. Performance Evaluation with Five Routing Tables.

Performance Metrics	AADS	Mae-East	Mae-West	PacBell	Paix
Prefix Count	26,109	56,039	31,060	33,680	13,878
Interval Count	23,411	46,557	30,501	25,807	14,201
Memory Required (Kbytes)	374	459	393	372	327
Build Time (msec)	93	141	109	110	62
Update Time (μsec)	183.6	183.6	121.1	183.6	121.1
Average Lookup Time (nsec)	34	39	34	32	29
Worst Case Lookup Time (nsec)	244	244	244	244	244

in [15]. The critical build/update problem is significantly improved. This is mainly because the pre-computation cost for solving the BMP problem is removed in the routing interval scheme. Moreover, the transformation from routing prefixes to intervals is performed cost effectively with link-list implementation. As a result, the build/update cost can be reduced significantly. Since no pre-computation information should be carried, the forwarding table is very simple and efficient. It can fit into the CPU L2 cache, thus results in better lookup performance. Therefore, even with slower L2 cache (150 MHz vs. 200 MHz), the worst-case lookup time is much shorter than that in multiway search.

Table 5. Comparison with Multiway Search.

Performance Metrics	Multiway Search	Routing Interval Scheme
Worst Case Lookup Time (nsec)	330	244
Worst Case Update Time (msec)	352	0.2
Build Time (sec)	5.8	0.14
Memory Required (Kbytes)	950	459

In Table 6, we further compare the routing interval scheme to other existing algorithms. Again, we proportionally scaled all results of previous works to 300 MHz CPU to ease the comparison. The worst-case lookup time of *LC tries* [13] is not addressed in the literature so we fill it with the average lookup time. Another important factor not shown in the table is the cost of route update which is not addressed in the papers on *LC tries*, binary search on hash tables, and Lulea compressed tries. However, all these schemes potentially require changing the complete data structure during a route update, they are likely to feature slow insertion/deletion times. Although the worst-case lookup time of multibit trie [12] is better than the scheme, we used a larger routing table for experiment (56,039 vs. 38,816). Also, their worst-case update time (2.5 msec) is much larger than ours.

From the results of performance evaluation, the routing interval scheme not only reduces the memory size significantly, outperforms the existing schemes in lookup speed, but also provides a much faster routing-table update. Furthermore, it just uses simple data structure and address lookup operations. Finally, we employ the state-of-the-art AMD 700 MHz CPU to investigate the possible highest performance of the scheme. As shown in Ta-

Table 6. Comparison with Other Existing Works.

Previous Schemes	Worst Case Lookup Time (ns)	Memory Required (Kbytes)
Patricia Trie	1,650	3,262
Binary Search on Hash Tables	650	1,600
Lulea Scheme	409	160
Multiway Search	330	950
LC tries	(*)500	464
Multibit Trie	236	640
Routing Interval Scheme	244	459

(*)This is the average performance since the worst-case performance is not addressed.

ble 7, the average packet-forwarding rate is above 70 MPPS with 6 MPPS in the worst case. Thus, both build and update time benefit from the upgrade of CPU speed.

Table 7. Performance Evaluation with 700 MHz CPU.

Site	Required Memory (Kbytes)	Build Time (msec)	Update Time μsec	Average Lookup Time (nsec)	Worst Case Lookup Time (nsec)
Mae-East	459	70	117	22	153

4.4. Summary

In this section, we present a new concept named "routing interval" which can be used to resolve the BMP problem and significantly reduces the routing complexity. A routing interval transformation algorithm is introduced to support an efficient IP address lookup. Via experiment, both the table construction time and table size can be reduced significantly. The routing interval scheme not only reduces the memory size requirement significantly, outperforms the existing schemes in lookup speed, but also provide a fast routing-table update. The constructed forwarding table is small enough to fit into the CPU L2 cache. By using the fast table-reconstruction algorithm, it is able to provide more than 5,000 route updates per second. This feature is preferred to the backbone router for handling the frequent route updates. With memory bus alignment, the routing interval scheme can further achieve 70 MPPS with state-of-the-art 700 MHz CPU. These results demonstrate that the scheme is efficient and flexible for IP packets forwarding.

5. High Speed IP Lookup Using Level Smart-Compression

In the following, we introduce a new trie-based data structure: *Level Smart-Compress tries* (*LS tries*). By using the new data structure, the size of the forwarding table can be compressed to less than 900 Kbytes for a large routing table with 100,000 routing entries. It can accomplish one IPv4 route lookup with a maximum of nine memory accesses and support incremental updates. The heuristics named core-leaf decoupling is presented to further improve the lookup performance and IPv6 scalability.

5.1. Trie-Based Algorithms

5.1.1. Patricia Trie

The trie is a general-purpose data structure for storing strings. The idea is very simple: each string is represented by a leaf in a tree structure, and the value of the string corresponds to the path from the root of the tree to the leaf. This simple structure is not very efficient. The number of nodes may be large and the average depth (the average length of a path from the root to a leaf) may be long. The traditional technique to overcome this problem is to use *path compression* when each internal node with only one child is removed. Of course, it has to somehow record those nodes which are missing. A simple technique is to store a number in each node, called the *skip* value, which indicates how many bits have been skipped on the path. A path-compressed binary trie is sometimes referred to as a Patricia trie, which is implemented in the IP lookup of NetBSD [21, 22]. Consider the example shown in Figure 20. There are five bit streams in the left part. Based on the given routing table, the constructed Patricia trie is shown in the right part of Figure 20. Basically, it processes an address one bit at a time.

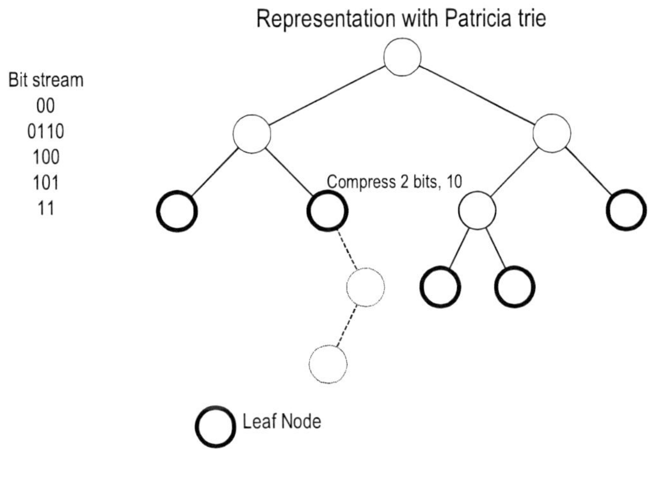

Figure 20. Representation of Patricia Trie.

5.1.2. Level Compression Trie

One might think of path compression as a way to compress the parts of the trie that are sparsely populated. Level compression [23] is a recently introduced technique for compressing parts of the trie that are densely populated. The idea is to replace the i highest complete levels of the binary trie with a single node of degree 2^i; this replacement is performed recursively on each subtrie. The level-compressed version of the trie in Figure 20 is shown in Figure 21. In Figure 21, one might find that there are eight leaves generated but only five route prefixes in the table. Accordingly, three nodes are over-generated in the trie, which is noted in Figure 21.

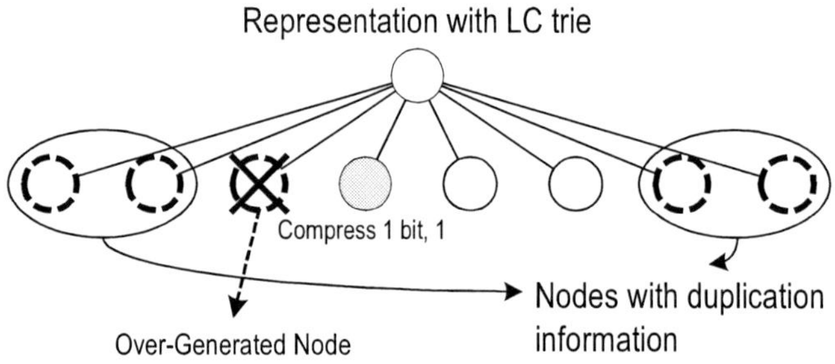

Figure 21. Representation of Level-compressed trie.

The performance of the LC-trie is much better than that of the Patricia trie since comparing strings of lengths equal to or less than the machine word size has basically a fixed cost, thus it is more efficient to compare more bits at a time in order to reduce the number of comparisons and memory accesses.

However, the implementation in [13] uses array representation by laying the LC-trie nodes out in breadth first order (first the root, then all the trie nodes at the second level from left to right, then third level nodes etc.). Each node only carries the first address of its children. While performing address lookup, the procedure stops only when the leaf node is reached. Yet the fetched node may not be the BMP due to path compression. If the prefix in the node doesn't match the address, the shorter prefix of the node will be tracked until matched. Furthermore, the array layout and the requirement for full subtries make updates slow in the worst case. Further, it might cause almost every element in the array representation to be moved. Thus while LC-trie have reasonable average lookup speeds, they feature long insertion time and worst-case lookup performance.

The data structure presented in [12] is similar to LC-trie. It is also a binary trie structure, and it allows multiway branching. By using a standard trie representation with arrays of children pointers, insertions and deletions of prefixes can be supported. However, to minimize the size of the initial trie, complex dynamic programming is used.

5.1.3. Lulea Compressed Trie

The Lulea scheme compresses multibit trie nodes so that the entire data structure can now be placed in SRAM. In contrast with the Patricia/LC tries to compresses the trie structurally, Lulea scheme compresses the information in a node. The nodes are compressed by representing repeated elements in a node array only once and using a bitmap to specify the number of times an element gets repeated, as shown in Figure 22.

To speed up the counting of set bits, the algorithm accompanies each bitmap with a summary array that contains a cumulative count of the number of set bits associated with fixed size chunks of the bitmap.

The Lulea scheme features compact storage but it has two disadvantages. First, counting bits requires at least one extra memory reference per trie node. Second, the implicit use of

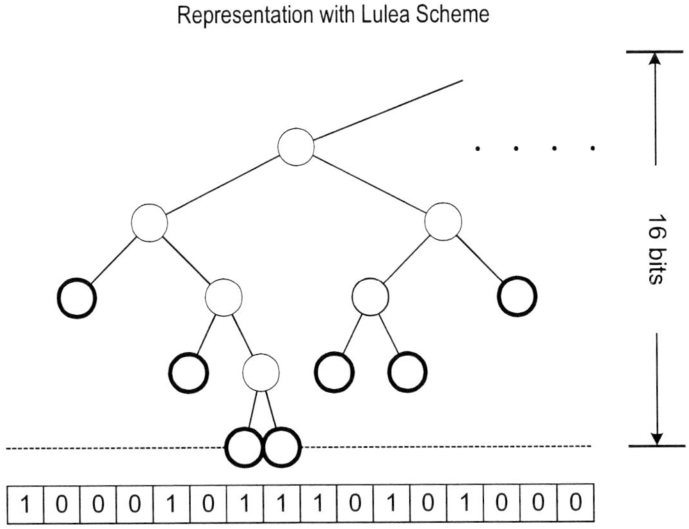

Figure 22. Representation of Lulea Compressed trie.

leaf pushing, makes the worst-case insertion time large. A prefix added to a root node entry can cause information to be pushed to thousands of leaf nodes.

5.2. Level Smart-Compression Tries

Figure 23 conceptually depicts the architecture of the IP router, which mainly consists of a network processor and a forwarding engine. The forwarding engine employs a forwarding table (FT) downloaded from the network processor to make the routing decision. The network processor executes the routing protocols, such as RIP and OSPF, and maintains a routing table (RT) and a dynamic forwarding table for fast updates. Once the route is updated, the forwarding table in the network processor will be renewed. Consequently, the forwarding engine will update its table based on the update information from the network processor without downloading a new forwarding table.

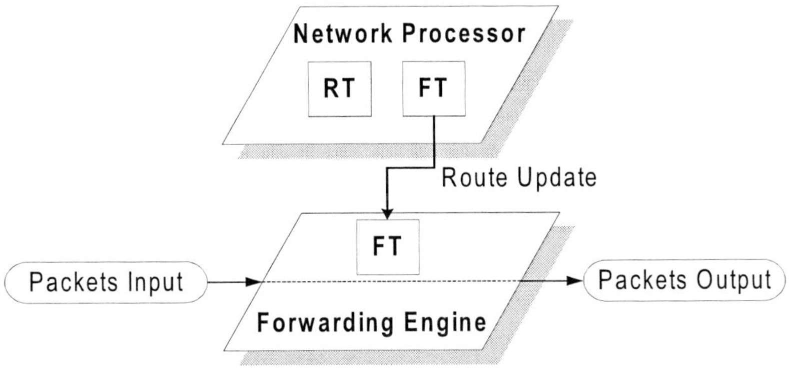

Figure 23. Architecture of the IP Router.

5.2.1. Level Smart-Compression Tries

If routing-table can be fit into the high speed SRAM, the performance can be promoted significantly. The data structure of level smart-compression tries (LS tries) is presented to achieve this goal. We use a simple binary tree as an example to explain the basic idea. As shown in Figure 24, the binary tree is constructed from the sample routing table. The bold circle indicates a node/leaf that identify a prefix. If the leaf node can be reached without traversing the internal node (thin one), the tree size can be further reduced, also the lookup performance can be increased. It is different to the ideas used in the Patricia tries and LC tries. In the former,only the one-child path is reduced, while in the later extra storage might be required to full expansion. With the scheme, only the necessary nodes are generated to greatly reduce the size of the forwarding table.

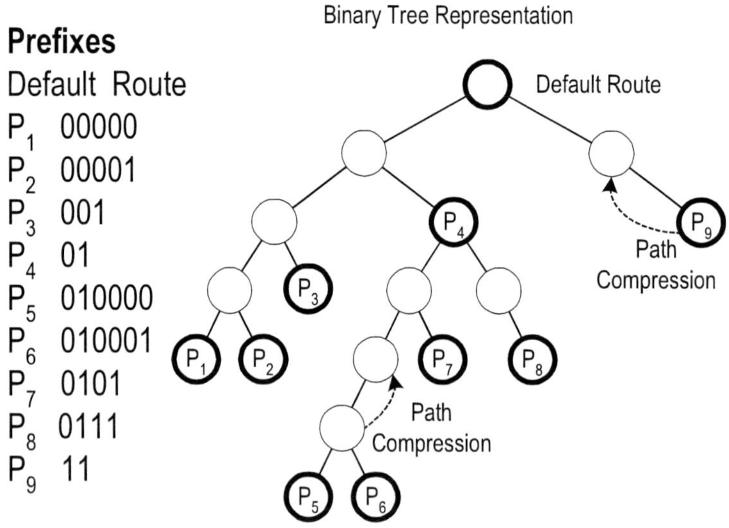

Figure 24. Representation of the Bit Stream With Binary Tree.

The data structure consists of the intermediate node and the leaf, as shown in Figure 25 and Figure 26, respectively. The value 2^N and 2^M indicate the number of branches which the intermediate node and the leaf will "administer", respectively. In the intermediate node, it consists of two parts: a head and a pointer. In the node head, the next-hop and length of the current BMP is recorded. It will be referenced only when the search is stopped as fetching a non-available value (NA) which indicates that there is no more specifically matched prefix. For example, P_4 will be used when search for "01001*" in Figure 24. It is called as a potential prefix since it is referred only when the destination address no longer match specific one. The deployment of this information can avoid the complex route update resulted from leaf-pushing, which will be explained in the subsection 5.2.2.. The node pointer is mainly used to indicate the address of the children. The one-bit flag is used to identify whether a child is an intermediate node or a leaf. Since the position of the leaf is variable, an extra field with x bits is used to record its relative depth in the intermediate node. The node information and pointer are stored in two different arrays with one-to-one mapping and the later will be referred only when the non-available value is read in the node pointer or the leaf.

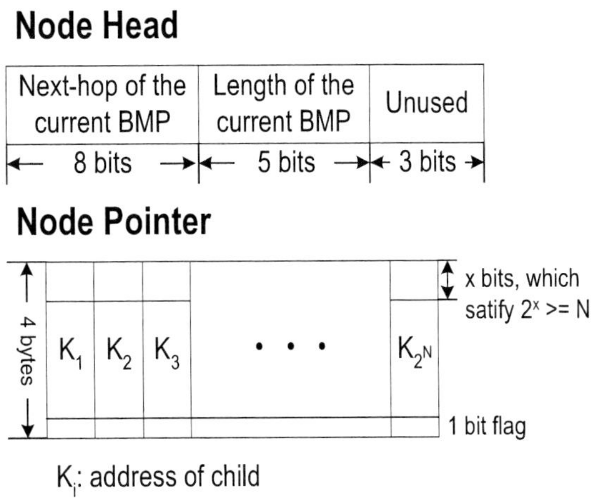

Figure 25. Intermediate Node of LS trie.

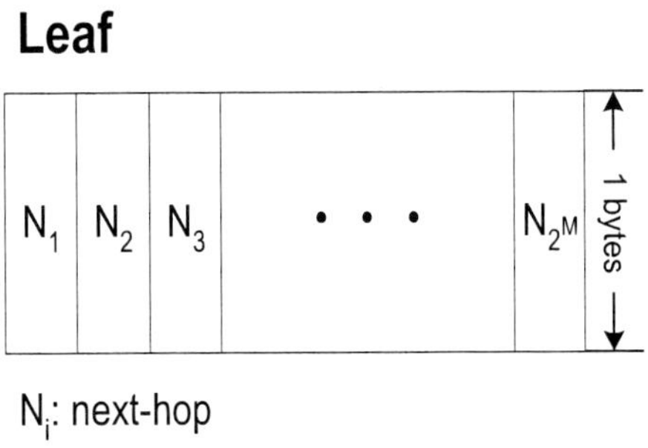

Figure 26. Leaf of LS trie.

The data structure of the leaf is a next-hop array which consists of 2^M elements, as shown in Figure 26. It is generated by expanding M bits of the route prefixes.

Before constructing the forwarding table, a binary tree without path compression is generated from the original routing table. Then the binary tree is traversed with DFS. Firstly, the distance between the current node and the deepest node is checked whether it is less than or equal to M. If yes, a leaf is generated by expanding all routing prefixes included in the subtree. Otherwise, the left and right child nodes will be traversed to construct the forwarding table. In addition, it should decide whether to construct an intermediate node by dividing the current depth to N. If the result is zero, an intermediate node will be generated. The pseudo code of the construction algorithm is shown below. The parameter "Parent" is used to identify the related intermediate node for the leaf.

LS trie Construction Algorithm

Input: The root of the binary trie which is constructed from the routing table.

Output: The forwarding table.

Constructor (Parent, Root, Depth, Prefix) {

```
  IF ((the deepest child depth in the subtree - Depth) is less or equal to M)
    Generate_Leaf (Parent, Root);
  ELSE {
    If (Root−>Prefix not equal to NULL)
      Prefix=Root−>Prefix;
    If ((Depth mod N) is equal to 0)
      Parent=Generate_Intermediate_Node(Root,Prefix);
    Constructor(Parent, Root−>Left_Child, Depth+1);
    Constructor(Parent, Root−>Right_Child, Depth+1);
  }
}
```

By applying the algorithm to the binary trie in Figure 24, the constructed forwarding table is shown in Figure 27 (N=3, M=3). The node head and the depth of the node information are ignored since both values can be derived from Figure 27 easily. Note that the routing information in P_4 will be pushed to its descending leaves or nodes. By using the node head, the information pushing is bounded to one level, thus the update complexity can be reduced. Yet the number of leaves is not optimal. Consequently, two improvements, which can further reduce the number of leaves, are presented.

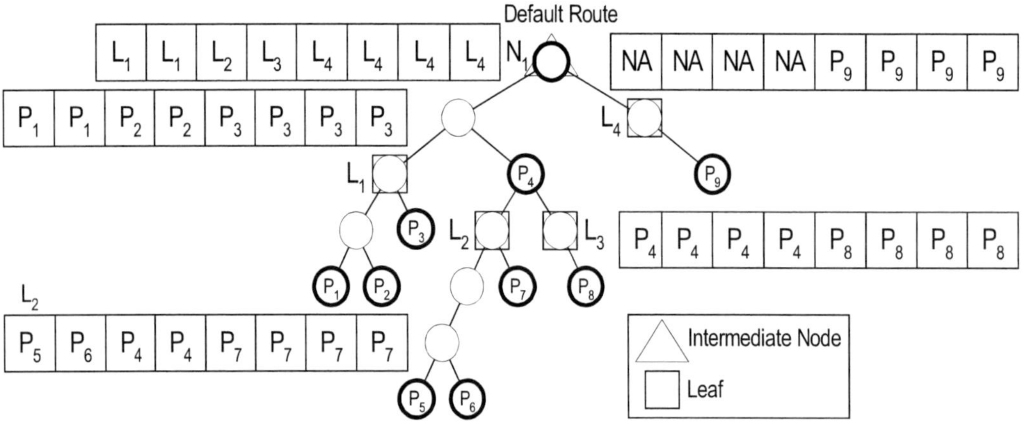

Figure 27. Generated LS trie (N=3, M=3).

Firstly, the algorithm is modified to increase the leaf utilization by raising the leaf position. For example, the L_1, L_2 and L_4 in Figure 27 only indicate at most three routing prefixes which is much fewer than the maximum prefixes available in a leaf (2^M). To revise it, a new rule is added to the algorithm. The leaf will be generated only when the difference between the current node and the longest prefix invoked is equal to M. In case the difference is longer than M, the algorithm will be called recursively. As a result, there might be another leaf under a generated leaf, such as two route prefixes which one is a shorter prefix of another one.

Secondly, some prefix information can be included in the intermediate node directly without adding another leaf. For example, L_4 can be erased by recording the prefix P_9 in N_1. The modified construction algorithm is shown as follows and the enhanced forwarding table is shown in Figure 28. Obviously, the number of leaf nodes is greatly reduced.

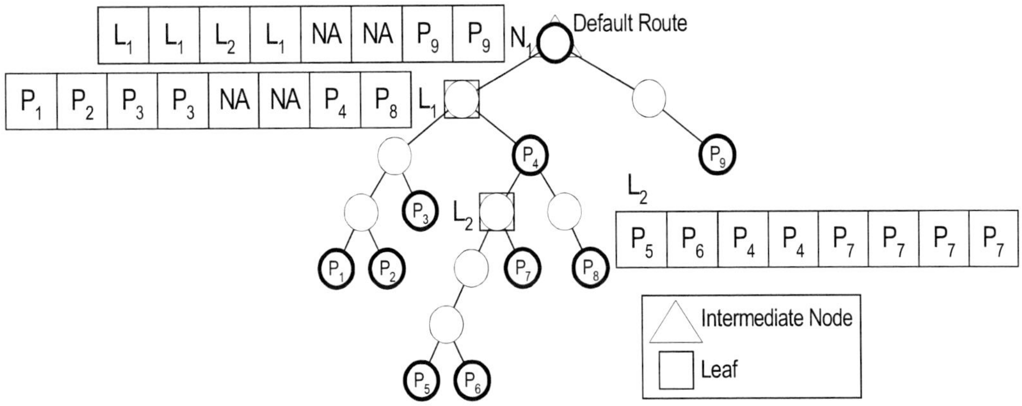

Figure 28. Enhanced LS trie (N=3, M=3).

Modified LS trie Construction Algorithm

Input: The root of the binary tree which is constructed from the routing table.

Output: The forwarding table.

```
Constructor (Parent, Root, Depth, Prefix) {
  IF ((the deepest child depth in the subtree - Depth) is equal to M)
    Generate_Leaf (Parent, Root);
  ELSE {
    If (Root− >Prefix not equal to NULL)
       Prefix=Root− >Prefix;
    If ((Depth mod N) is equal to 0)
       Parent=Generate_Intermediate_Node(Root,Prefix);
    Constructor(Parent, Root− >Left_Child, Depth+1);
    Constructor(Parent, Root− >Right_Child, Depth+1);
    If ((the length of the longest unprocessed prefix - Depth) is equal M)
       Generate_Leaf(Parent,Root);
  }
}
```

By using the algorithm, the detailed child information is recorded in the intermediate node to guide the lookup. Also, it is different for those existing schemes to use level compression [12, 13]. The idea used in the existing schemes might generate unused nodes, but not in the scheme.

To perform an IP lookup, the destination address is split into N-bit chunks, and these chunks are used to follow a path through the tries until a leaf address or next-hop value in the node pointer is fetched. In the latter situation, the search procedure is terminated. Otherwise, relative depth of the fetched leaf is recorded to decide the M-bit chunk of the address which can be used to access the entry in the leaf. If NA is read in the intermediate node or leaf, for example, to search “100000” in Figure 28, the BMP information in the node head would be used.

5.2.2. Route Update

As the topology of the network changes, new routing information is disseminated among the routers, leading to changes in routing tables. As a result of the change, one or more entries must be added, updated or deleted from the table. Because the action of modifying the table can interfere with the process of forwarding packets, various route updates and the relative procedures are considered.

The route updates can be separated into three conditions: **route change**, **route insertion** and **route deletion**. Before considering the route update procedure, the field "prefix length" is necessary to be added to the next-hop field of the leaf in the forwarding table maintained by the network processor in Figure 23.

- **Route Change:** For the prefixes located in the leaf, the update can be done by checking and updating the entries with equal length in the leaf. Otherwise, the BMP information of the intermediate node head or its descending leaves will be modified. Thus only the leaves/nodes in one level will be affected in the worst case. As a result, maximum $2^M \times 2^N$ entries will be modified.

  While the head information of the descending nodes is changed, this update will not be forwarded to its leaves/nodes. However, this requires slight change in address lookup procedure. Originally, only the head information in the last node before fetching the leaf will be used. This might cause error result after route changes because the update information may not be broadcasted to the nearest node. To correct this, the longest prefix information in the head is memorized while traversing the trie for possible referring.

- **Route Insertion:** When a route prefix is inserted, the procedure is akin to the route change. However, it might need to generate a long path due to a long prefix insertion. In this case, maximum $32/N$ nodes will be generated.

- **Route Deletion:** The procedure is equal to change the route of the deleted prefix to the route of its shorter prefix. To accomplish this update, the route information of the last matched prefix before reaching the deleted one will be used to refresh the entries which refer to the deleted prefix.

In the worst case, $maximum(2^M \times 2^N, 32/N \times 2^N)$ entries will be updated for IPv4. Assuming that the 5-ns SRAM is used with setting $N = 4, M = 4$, the worst-case update time is 1.28 μsec

5.3. Core-Leaf Decoupling

By observing the data structure of the trie, one may find that most memory accesses refer to the nodes (we use the term *core* to refer the internal nodes of the trie hereafter.) since only one leaf will be accessed in a address lookup. Thus if the core size can be reduced to fit into a higher-speed memory, the performance can be improved dramatically. For example, the core can be located into the CPU L1 cache and the leaves to the CPU L2 cache. If the speed of the L1 cache is twice of the L2 cache, the total lookup time will be reduced to half approximately. By extending the size of leaf, the number of nodes will decrease as well as the core size.

Note that the total required memory space might increase due to a larger-size leaf is used. To alleviate this, a simple array compression scheme can be used. As described in [11], only the variable part in the next-hop array is recorded in a separate entry-array and the original one will be replaced with a bitmap. Each bit in the bitmap maps to an entry in the leaf where the bit is set to one when the array values change. In spite the compression can reduce the size of leaves, one extra memory access is required to access the entry-array. An example of table compression for the L_2 in Figure 28 is shown in Figure 29.

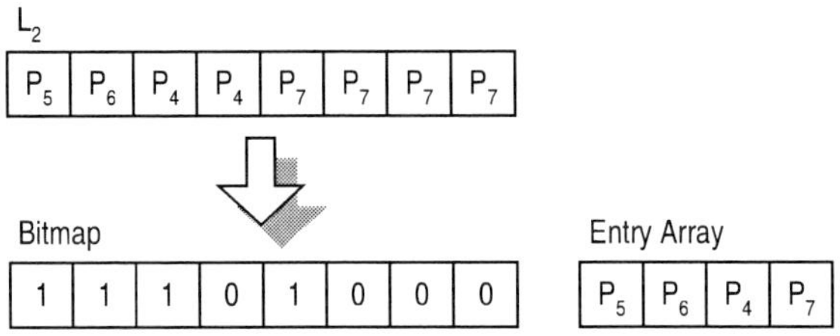

Figure 29. Table Compression Example.

5.4. Performance Analysis

In Table 8, the performance of the scheme ($N = 4, M = 4$) is presented. The value in the parentheses is the number of memory accesses. Even for the large routing table with more than one hundred thousand entries, the table size is small enough to fit into the high speed SRAM. We assume that the memory access time is 5 ns and nine memory accesses are required to accomplish one lookup, the worst-case lookup time is less than 50 ns, i.e., 20 MPPS can be achieved in the worst case.

Table 8. Performance Evaluation with Six Routing Tables.

Site	Routing Prefixes	Memory Required (Kbytes)	Worst-case lookup performance (nsec)
AADS	24,470	373	40
Mae-East	58,101	565	45
Mae-West	36,943	454	45
PacBell	32,338	428	40
Paix	13,395	254	40
NLANR	102,271	866	45

In Table 9, we further compare other existing algorithms with the LS tries. The worst-case lookup time of LC tries [13] is not addressed in the literature so we fill it with average lookup time. Obviously, the scheme outperforms the existing schmes in lookup speed. Although we use a table which is much larger than the tables used in Lulea scheme, LC tries and multibit trie, the average required storage is the lowest besides the Lulea scheme. Also, except Patricia trie and multibit trie, the rest of schemes all potentially require changing the complete data structure during a route update, thus feature slow insertion/deletion speed.

Table 9. Comparison with Other Existing Works.

Previous Schemes	Worst Case Lookup Time (ns)	Memory Required (Kbytes)
Patricia trie	1,650	3,262
Binary search on hash tables	650	1,600
Lulea scheme	409	160
Multiway search	330	950
LC tries	(*)500	464
Multibit trie	236	640
LS tries	45	866

(*)This is the average performance since the worst-case performance is not addressed.

To test the performance of core-leaf decoupling, the setting of N and M is changed to 4 and 8, respectively. The value in the parentheses is the required storage after applying compression. Obviously, the size of the nodes is much less than that of the leaves. Even with compression, the size of the nodes is about third to quarter of the leaf size. Such as the leaf size of NLANR is compressed from 1.2 Mbytes to 320 Kbytes. Thus the total size of the trie is less than the 512 Kbytes L2 cache of the modern CPUs.

Table 10. Performance Evaluation with Core-Leaf Decoupling.

Site	Routing Prefixes	Core Size (Kbytes)	Leaves Size (Kbytes)	Total Size (Kbytes)
AADS	24,470	40	628 (166)	668 (206)
Mae-East	58,101	51	867 (230)	918 (281)
Mae-West	36,943	45	738 (196)	783 (241)
PacBell	32,338	42	699 (185)	741 (227)
Paix	13,395	33	424 (112)	457 (145)
NLANR	102,271	119	1,201 (319)	1,320 (438)

5.5. Summary

In this section, we show how IP-routing tables can be succinctly represented and efficiently searched by structuring them as LS trie. Furthermore, incremental update is supported. Our data structure is simple and not based on any ad hoc assumptions about the distribution of the prefix lengths in routing tables. Even a the routing table with more than 100,000 entries, the size of the forwarding table is still smaller than 900 Kbytes in our approach. The incremental update algorithm is also provided. Each address lookup can be accomplished within nine memory accesses. With the heuristic, core-leaf decoupling, the frequent-access nodes can be put into high speed memory. Through simulation, the scheme outperforms most existing schemes.

6. Fast Packet Classification by Using Tuple Reduction

In addition to the basic packet forwarding based on destination address, the new requirements are emerging. To support security, quality of server (**QoS**) or specific business policies, user traffic may be further classified according to a maximum of eight fields: source/destination IP address (32 bits), source/destination transport-layer port numbers (16 bits for TCP and UDP), type-of-service (**TOS**) field (8 bits), protocol field (8 bits) and transport-layer flags (8 bits) with a total of 120 bits. This new forwarding type is called packet classification. Packet classification offers increased flexibility: it gives a router the capability to block traffic from a dangerous external site, to reserve bandwidth for traffic between two specific sites or to give preferential treatment to one kind of traffic over other kinds. Traditional routers do not provide service differentiation because they treat all traffic in the same way. The process of mapping packets to different service classes is referred to as *policy-based routing*. In this section, we present the background of packet classification and a new algorithm in [24].

6.1. Introduction

IP networks are rapidly evolving toward a QoS-enabled and multimedia-friendly infrastructure. In the **DiffServ** model, resources are allocated differently to various aggregated traffic flows according to the differentiated services codepoint (DSCP field). The edge routers positioned at administrative boundaries, for example, the boundary between two ISPs, as shown in Fig. 30, set the DSCP field. Packet classification is the process of identifying packets based on specific rules. It has been extensively employed in the Internet for secure filtering and service differentiation by administrators to reflect policies of network operations and resource allocation. Using the pre-defined filters, the packets can be assigned to a given DSCP field. Packet classification is a key component that determines to which forwarding class a packet belongs. Clearly, the performance of packet classification is important in the deployment of new services, including VoIP, VoD and video conferencing, which have strict QoS requirements. The potential future popularity of multimedia services is such that the filter database will be large. Also, packet classification with a potentially large number of filters is difficult and exhibits poor worst-case performance [25].

The classifier and the filter must be defined before the problem can be formally described. A classifier includes a set of filters to divide an incoming packet stream into multiple classes. A filter $F = (f[1], f[2], \dots, f[k])$ is called k-dimensional if it has k fields, of which each $f[i]$ is a variable length prefix bit string, a range or an explicit value of a packet header. A filter can be any combination of fields; the most common fields are the IP source address (SA, 32 bits), the destination address (DA, 32 bits), the protocol type (8 bits), port numbers (16 bits) of source/destination applications and protocol flags in the packet header. A packet P is said to match a particular filter F if for all i, the i_{th} field of the header satisfies $f[i]$. Each filter has an associated action. For example, the filter F=(140.113.*, *, UDP, 1090, *) specifies a rule that addresses a flow belongs to the subnet 140.113, and uses

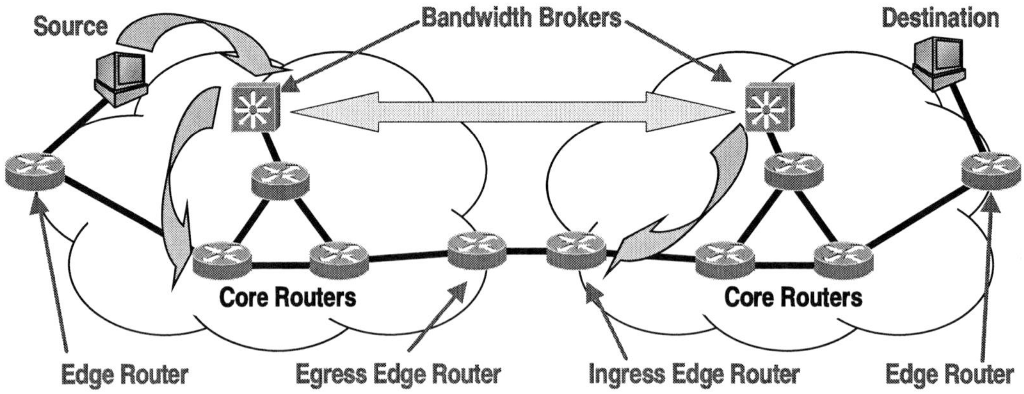

Figure 30. DiffServ Framework.

the progressive networks audio (PNA); the rule may assign the flow's packets with high queueing priority. The filter is usually assigned a cost to define its priority of the matched filters. The least-cost matched filter will act to process the arriving packets, such that the packet classification problem is a least-cost problem.

Hashing is an extensively applied method for performing fast lookup. Many hash-based schemes have been presented for solving the Internet lookup problem [14,26,27]. The tuple space search is a well-known two-dimensional (*source address prefix, destination address prefix*) solution which is based on multiple hash accesses for various filter-length combinations [26, 28]. The rectangle search, one of the tuple-based algorithms, is proposed and shows the lower bound $O(2W - 1)$ of the lookup speed, where W is the length of the IP address. The rectangle search is highly scalable with respect to the number of filters. However, it suffers from the memory-explosion problem. Also, the lookup is not sufficiently fast. For example, through experiments, the required entries are determined to be as large as twelve-fold filters and each packet classification requires approximately 40 hash accesses in a 100K-filter database. Consequently, it cannot support a gigabit throughput.

In the following, an efficient scheme for improving the rectangle search is presented. The scheme consists of two parts. The first presents the **"Tuple Reduction Algorithm"**. Duplicating the filters dramatically reduces the number of tuples. Dynamic programming is used to optimize the tuple reduction and two heuristic optimization methods are introduced to simplify the optimization process. The primary goal of the spatial optimization approach is used to minimize the required storage while the speed optimization approach can further increase the lookup speed. By the tuple reduction, all the performance metrics, including storage, speed and implementation complexity, are enhanced. The second part presents the **"Look-ahead Caching"** scheme, which can further improve the lookup performance. The basic idea is to prevent unnecessary tuple probing by filtering out the **"un-matched"** situation of the incoming packet. Obtained by combining the tuple reduction algorithm and look-ahead caching, the experimental results show that the lookup speed increased by a factor of six while requiring only around one third of the required storage.

6.2. Previous Works

Several algorithms for classifying packets have recently appeared in the literature [25, 26, 29–34]. They can be grouped into the following classes: linear search/caching, hardware-based solutions, grid of tries/cross-producting, recursive-flow classification, and hash-based solutions. The following briefly describes the important properties of these algorithms. Assume that N is the number of the filters, k is the number of classified fields and W is the length of the IP address.

Linear Search/Caching: The simplest method for packet classification involves a linear search of all the filters. The spatial and temporal complexity is $O(N)$. Caching is a technique frequently used at either the hardware or the software level to improve the performance of linear search. However, the performance of the caching depends critically on each flow's having large number of packets. Also, if the number of simultaneous flows exceeds the cache size, then the performance is severely degraded.

Hardware-based Solutions: A high degree of parallelism can be implemented in hardware to provide a speed-up advantage. In particular, ternary content addressable memories (TCAMs) can be used effectively to look up filters. However, TCAMs with a particular word width cannot be used when flexibility of the filter specification is required. Manufacturing TCAMs with sufficiently wide words to contain all bits in a filter is difficult. It also suffers from the problem of power consumption and scalability [28]. Lakshamn *et al.* presented another scheme that depend on a very wide memory bus [30]. The algorithm reads Nk bits from memory, corresponding to the BMPs in each field, and determines their intersection to find a set of matching filters. The memory requirement for this scheme is $O(N^2)$. The hardware-oriented schemes rely on heavy parallelism, and involve considerable hardware cost; the flexibility and scalability of hardware solutions is very limited.

Grid of Tries/Cross-producting: Specifically for the case of two-field filters, Srinivasan *et al.* [30] presented a trie-based algorithm. The algorithm has a memory requirement of $O(NW)$ and requires $2W - 1$ memory accesses per filter lookup. It is a general mechanism, called cross-producting, which involves BMP lookups on individual fields, and the use of a pre-computed table to combine the results of individual prefix lookups. However, this scheme suffers from a $O(N^k)$ memory blowup for k-field filters, including $k = 2$ field filters.

Recursive-flow Classification: Gupta *et al.* presented an algorithm that can be considered to be a generalization of cross-producting [25]. After BMP lookup is performed, a recursive flow classification algorithm hierarchically performs cross-producting. Thus k BMP lookups and $k - 1$ additional memory accesses are required per filter lookup. The algorithm is expected significantly to improve average throughput, but it requires $O(N^k)$ memory in the worst case. Also, in the case of two-field filters, this scheme is identical to cross-producting, and hence has a memory requirement of $O(N^2)$.

Hash-based Solution: This solution is motivated by the observation that, although filter databases include several different prefixes or ranges, the distinct prefix lengths tend to be few [26]. For example, backbone routers have around 60K destination address prefixes, but only 32 distinct prefix lengths exist. Hence, all the prefixes can be divided into 32 groups, one for each length (W). Since all prefixes in a group have the same length, the prefix bit string can be used as a hash key, leading to a simple IP lookup scheme, which requires $O(W)$ hash lookups, independent of the number of prefixes. The algorithm of Waldvogel [14] performs a binary search over the W length groups, and has a worst-case time complexity $O(logW)$.

The tuple space idea generalizes the foregoing approach [14] to multi-dimensional filters [26]. A tuple is a set of filters with specific prefix lengths, and the resulting set of tuples is called a **"tuple space"**. Since each tuple has a specific bit-length of each field, these bit-lengths can be concatenated to create a hash key, which can be used in performing the tuple lookup. The matched filter can be found by probing each tuple alternately, and tracking the least-cost filter. For example, the two-dimensional filters $F = (10*, 110*)$ and $G = (11*, 001*)$ both belong to the tuple $T_{2,3}$ in the second row and third column in the tuple space. When searching for $T_{2,3}$, a hash key is constructed by concatenating two bits of the source field with three bits of the destination field. Even a linear search of the tuple space represent a considerable improvement over a linear search of the filters since the number of tuples is typically much smaller than the number of filters.

The rectangle search, a tuple-based algorithm, was proposed to improve the performance of the tuple lookup [26]. The lower bound has been demonstrated to be $O(2W-1)$ given a $O(W \times W)$ rectangular tuple space, where W is the number of distinct prefix lengths. The primary aim is to eliminate a set of tuples during each probing, as depicted in Fig. 31. Tuples above T are eliminated if the probe of tuple T returns **"Match"**. Otherwise, tuples to the right of tuple T are discarded. Markers and a pre-computation mechanism are required to reach this goal. Assuming that the number of filters is N, a rectangle search requires NW memory space. Notably, reducing the number of distinct lengths would increase lookup performance. Furthermore, the number of generated markers can be eliminated under certain conditions.

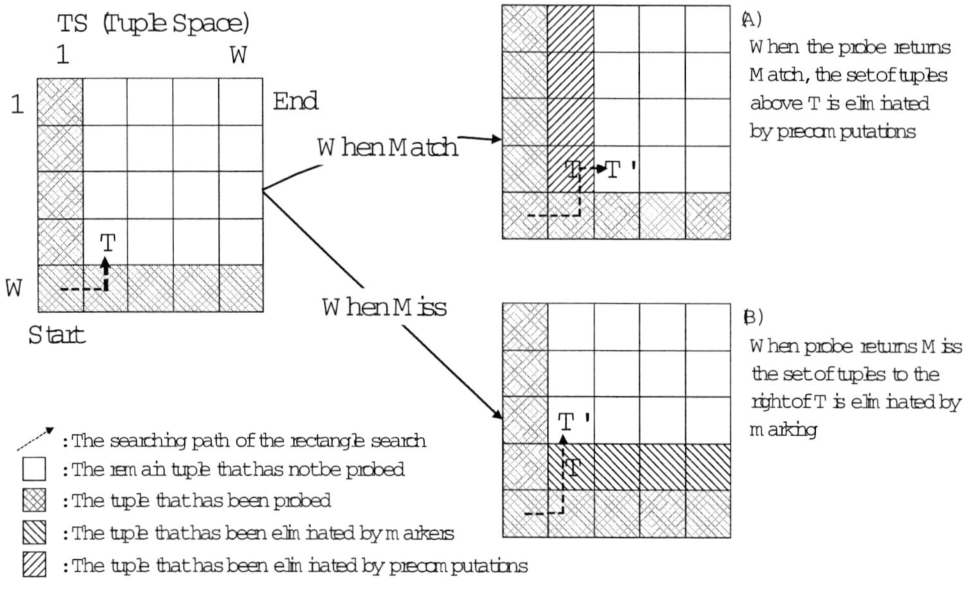

Figure 31. Rectangle Search Algorithm.

6.3. Tuple Reduction Algorithm

For a given **TS**, pre-computation and markers are used to perform a rectangle search. Assume that the filter database contains 203 filters, which occupy five tuples, as shown in Fig. 32. Each filter must generate one marker in each left-side tuple to indicate the existence of a long potential matched filter. Accordingly, 703 markers are generated, resulting in 906 entries. The size explosion is caused by the unbalanced distribution of routing prefix lengths, which is currently common in the Internet [10, 12–14]. Clearly, reducing the number of tuples to promote a native rectangle search is an important issue.

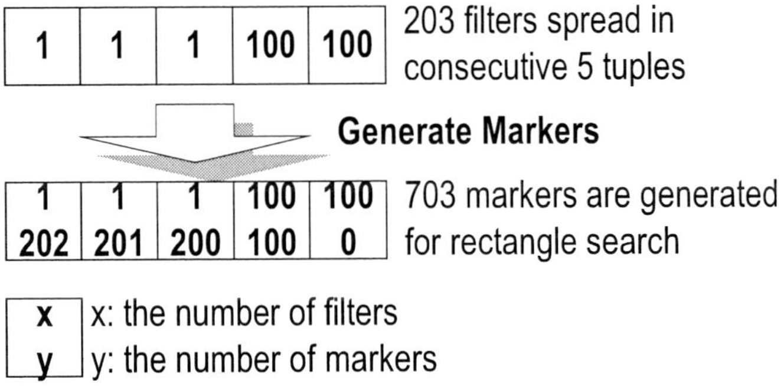

Figure 32. Relationship between the Filters and the Markers.

6.3.1. Filter Expansion

The lookup performance of the rectangle search can be improved by reducing the distinct lengths. A well-known capability, based on duplicating entries, can be used, as described in [12]. Dynamic programming is used to minimize the increasing storage required by the duplication of entries. The other algorithms [9–11, 13] are based on a similar mechanism, but have additional compression schemes. Briefly, the algorithms in this category depend on either large storage or complex compression logic, which must be traded off to increase throughput. However, faster lookup can be obtained with a smaller storage in the rectangle search because the reduction of the tuple also results in fewer generated markers. Figure 32 considers the same example as presented in Fig. 33 to facilitate the explanation. The three filters with short prefixes are expanded to the fourth tuple, corresponding to a longer filter. The number of required markers is reduced drastically by the expansion of filters.

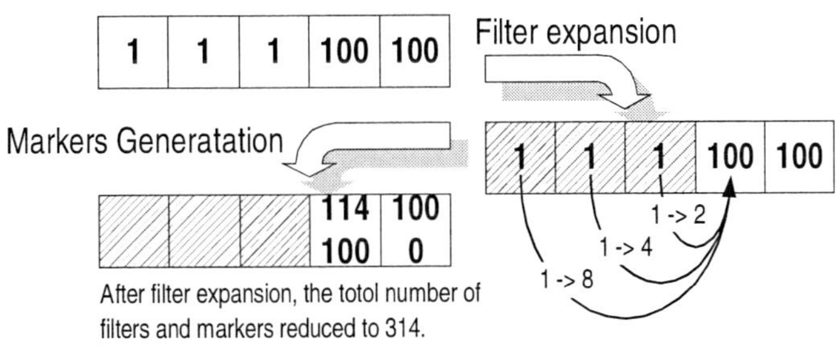

Figure 33. Tuple Space with Filter Expansion.

Figure 34 depicts a two-dimensional filter expansion. The filter $f(11*, 10*)$ at the tuple $T_{2,2}$ is expanded to the destination tuple $T_{3,3}$. Firstly, the source prefix of f is expanded from 11* to the prefixes 110* and 111*. By the same procedure, the destination prefix is expanded from 10* to 100* and 101*. After both the source and destination prefixes are expanded, the cross-product of the two sets of prefixes are obtained, yielding four new filters $f_1(110*, 100*)$, $f_2(111*, 100*)$, $f_3(110*, 101*)$ and $f_4(111*, 101*)$, whose actions equal that of f.

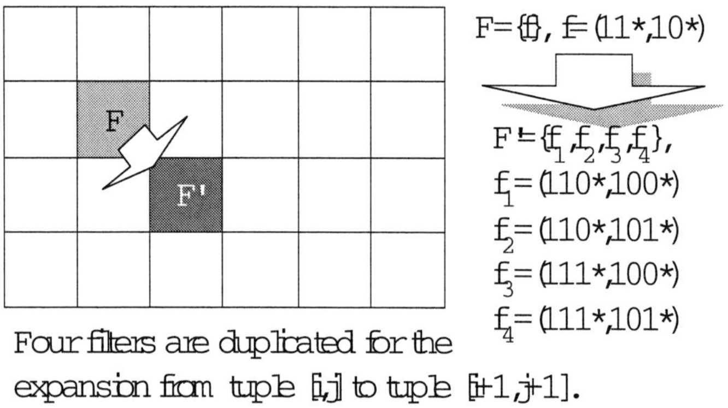

Figure 34. Filter Expansion.

6.3.2. Two-Dimensional Tuple Reduction to Minimize Storage

The tuple reduction algorithm presented herein is a space-optimization scheme in which the decision to expand the filter is made independently for each tuple. The design principle is to minimize the required storage by converging the tuple space. In the following, dynamic programming and two heuristic methods are introduced to minimize storage.

Dynamic programming is used to perform the optimal filter expansion with minimal cost. Figure 35 illustrates the cost of a filter expansion. The cost is determined by several contributing factors, including the number of duplicated filters due to the expansion as described above, the number of original markers in the source tuple and the number of markers generated of the duplicated filters. The original markers are eliminated by the expansion of the filter. The number of markers of the duplicated filters is also important. The original filters, the duplicate filters and the markers must be simultaneously considered to determine the minimal expansion cost. The minimal expansion cost can be formulated as a recursive equation, as shown below. The number of the filters (tuples) in the tuple (tuple space) is defined as $|T|$ ($|TS|$). To simplify the expression, a tuple at the i_{th} row and the j_{th} column is labeled as $T_{M(i,j)}$ using the following one-to-one mapping function $M(i,j) = (i+j-2) \times (i+j-1)/2 + j$. Consequently, the tuple space can be equivalently represented by a set $T_1, T_2, \ldots, T_{|TS|}$.

$$\begin{aligned} DynaP(TS) = \; & \min_{i=1}^{|TS|}\{DynaP(TS - T_i) + \min_{j=1}^{|TS|}\{Expansion(T_i, T_j) \\ & - Sum\_of\_Filters(T_i)\}\}, where \end{aligned} \quad (1)$$

$$Expansion(T_{src}, T_{dest}) = 2^{Dist(T_{src},T_{dest})} \times |T_{src}| \times Left\_Tuples(T_{dest}); \quad (2)$$

$$Sum\_Of\_Filters(T_{M(R,C)}) = \sum_{col=C}^{C \leq W} |T_{M(R,col)}|; \quad (3)$$

$$Left\_Tuples(T) = Number\, of\, tuples\, in\, the\, left\, side\, of\, T. \quad (4)$$

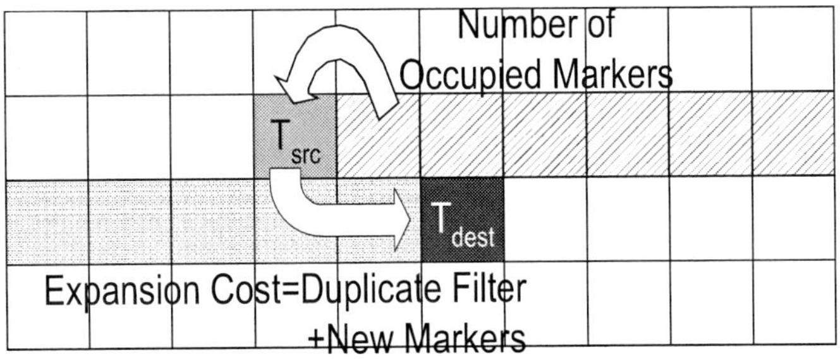

Figure 35. Dynamic Programming for Expanding the Filter.

The cost function is $f(\alpha) = \alpha \times f(\alpha - 1) + \alpha^2$, where α is the number of tuples and α^2 is the complexity of determining to where a tuple is expanded. Thus, the cost-function is exponential ($f(\alpha) \leq 2^{\alpha}$). Although an optimal solution can be derived, dynamic programming is time-consuming.

6.3.3. Semi-Optimization Algorithm

A heuristic semi-optimization algorithm that restricts the expansions is adopted to reduce the time complexity. The new algorithm expands tuples only to those with large number of filters because the cost of expansion to those tuples is usually higher than that to others. Thus, expansion begins from tuples with the fewest filters. The number of expansion combinations can be considerably reduced to $|TS| \times |TS|$. Moreover, expansion is allowed within a predefined region, such as a 3×3 region, from the source tuple, $T_{i,j}$ to $T_{i+2,j+2}$. The semi-optimization algorithm is described below. The tuples are sorted by the number of filters. In the iteration i $(1 \leq i \leq |TS|)$, $Cost\_Old$ refers to the current cost of T_i without expansion. T_{dest} is the best expanded tuple of tuple T_i within the restricted region. $Cost\_New$ shows the new cost of tuple T_i is expanded to T_{dest}. If the $Cost\_New$ is greater, it continues to process the subsequent iteration. Otherwise, the filters in T_i are expanded to T_{dest}.

Semi-Optimization Algorithm
[Functions]
$Markers(T)$: Generated markers for the filters in tuple T.
$Optimal\_Expansion(T)$: Optimal expansion for tuple T within the restricted region.
[Input] Ascending-ordered Tuples $\{T_1, T_2, \ldots, T_M\}$
[Output] Optimized Tuples
For $(i = 1; i \leq M; i++)$ {
    $Cost\_Old = |T_i| + Markers(T_i) + Sum\_of\_Filters(T_i);$

$T_{dest} = Optimal\_Expansion(T_i)$;
$Cost\_New = Expansion(T_i, T_{dest})$;
If $(Cost\_Old \geq Cost\_New)$
Expand Tuple T_i to T_{dest};

}

6.3.4. Tuple Reduction in Area of Sparse Filter

The semi-optimization algorithm achieved a near-optimum rectangle search. Some tuples are eliminated by trading off storage. Most existing IP address lookup schemes have to deal with an unbalanced length-distribution of routing prefixes. Although large filter databases are not yet commonly available, the authors believe that unbalanced distributions will continue to be prevalent. A randomly generated filter database with 100K filters is used to illustrate the phenomenon, as shown in Fig. 36. Each tuple is positioned according to its length combination and colored according to the number of filters. Most filters are in the region from the upper-left tuple $T_{16,16}$ to the bottom-right tuple $T_{24,24}$ because most routing prefixes have a length of 16-24 bits [14]. Relatively few tuples are occupied by filters in regions **A, B, C, D** and **G** when the **TS** is separated into nine regions. Although regions **F, H** and **I** include more occupied tuples, the density of filters is lower than that of tuples in region **E**. Essentially, too many tuples with few filters represent the primary factor reducing the search rate because the cost of access is the same, independently of the number of filters in each tuple.

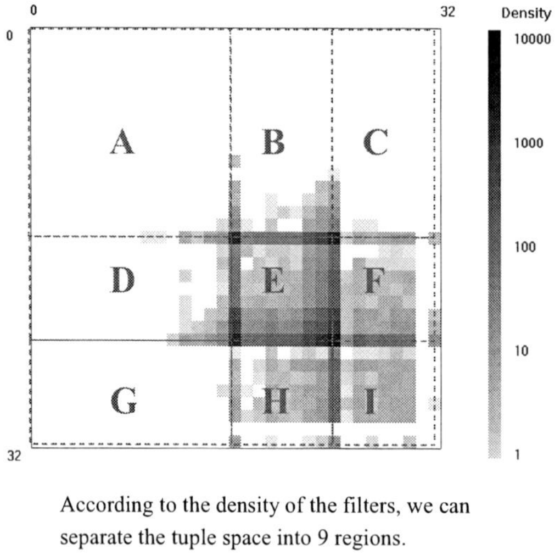

Figure 36. Unbalanced Filter Distribution.

This work proposes an enhancement of tuple reduction by collecting filters within sparse regions into a target tuple in the lower-right hand corner of the region. Thus, the nearest non-empty tuple is expanded into the target tuple. If the number of aggregated filters does not exceed a certain threshold, $MAX\_FILTERS$, the procedure will be repeated. Otherwise, another target tuple in this region is chosen and the procedure is then performed.

6.3.5. Further Optimizing of Lookup Speed

The optimization algorithms presented above efficiently reduce the required storage; however, the lookup speed is not yet maximal, primarily because the self-absorbed expansion of each tuple cannot systematically reduce the number of rows and columns. Hence, the other heuristic approach for eliminating the tuple probes by restricting the filter expansion to specific rows/columns is considered. Restated, the selected rows and columns interlace to generate a set of grid-cells and the filters are expanded to the nearest tuples in the grids. The required storage will be enlarged because of the restriction, and dynamic programming is used to minimize it.

Several items must first be defined. Assume that the resulting tuple space has r rows and c columns. The function $F(P)$ is defined as the minimal cost of a specific (r, c) combination where $r + c = P$ and $2 \leq P \leq 2W$, as shown in Eq. 5. For each (r, c) combination, $\binom{W}{r} \times \binom{W}{c}$ row/column selections exist. The closest tuple to T_i is expressed as $T_{closest}$, which conforms to the (row, column) selection results. The resulting (row, column) selection will satisfy $\min_{P=1}^{2W} F(P)$. However, the complexity of computation is markedly increased ($2W \times W \times \binom{W}{r} \times \binom{W}{c}$) since the results of each combination are calculated from scratch. Although recording the executed results for later reference can reduce costs, a more efficient approach is introduced here. First, the number of filters of each row and column are calculated. Thus, the rows and columns are sorted according to the their summations. The minimal cost of each (r, c) combination can be derived easily by selecting the rows and columns with the highest value. Although the results may not be optimal, the computational cost is reduced greatly.

$$F(P) = \min_{\substack{for\ all\ (row,column)\\ combinations}} \sum_{i=1}^{|TS|} (Expansion(T_i, T_{closest}) - Sum\_of\_Filters(T_i)), ;\ where\ r+c = P. \quad (5)$$

6.4. Look-Ahead Caching Mechanism

The space occupied by each filter can be intuitively assumed to be small since only specific services require the setting up of filters for packet classification. Also, multiple filters are unlikely to be defined over a specific address space. Thus, filter matching might be rare in tuple probing. Look-ahead caching is presented to filter out the **"un-matched"** case of each incoming packet using dual-hash architecture to eliminate unnecessary tuple accesses during the rectangle search.

The look-ahead cache includes as many tables as tuples. Figure 37 depicts the basic mechanism. For each incoming packet, the look-ahead cache is probed firstly. If the probing indicates a miss, no matched filter is present in the corresponding tuples; thus, the tuple access can be bypassed. Otherwise, the tuple will be probed for **"possible"** matched filter.

For each table, the number of entries is identical to the number of corresponding tuples but each entry is much smaller so that they can fit into high-speed SRAM. An entry in the look-ahead cache has three fields, **Tag**, **Empty** and **Collision**, as shown in Fig. 38. The source and destination prefixes are extracted from the original filter and mapped onto the

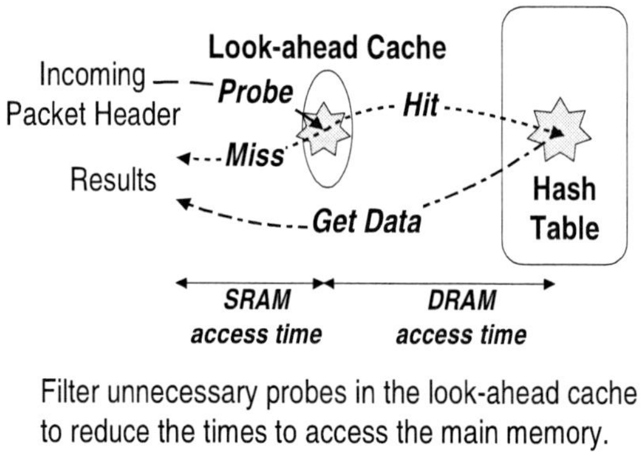

Figure 37. Concept of the Look-ahead Caching.

Tag using the function $TAG\_FCN()$. The Tag is used to specify whether a filter occupies the entry. Its length is defined by the size of SRAM. The **E** (Empty) bit states the status of the corresponding entry in the tuple. If this entry contains no filter (that is, the E bit is set to one), the look-ahead cache probing returns "false" and tuple probing can be skipped. The **C** (Collision) bit states whether multiple filters map onto the entry (such that, the collision occurs in the hash entry).

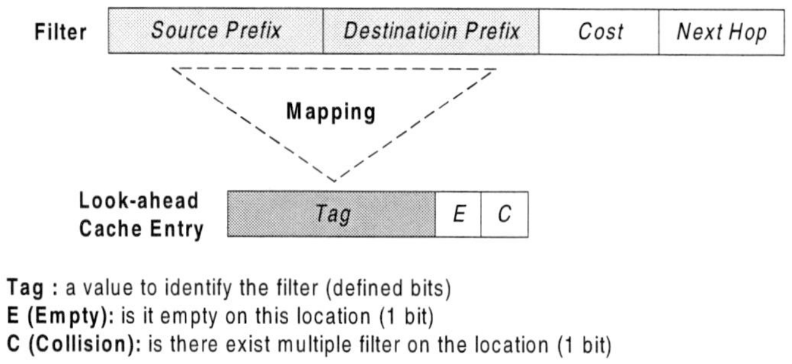

Figure 38. Data Structure of the Look-ahead Cache Entry.

Figure 39 presents the tuple space search with look-ahead caching. When a tuple is initially probed for a packet with header Y, the entry location in the look-ahead cache is calculated using the hash function $INDEX\_FCN(Y)$ and the tag value $TAG\_FCN(Y)$. After the cache entry is retrieved, the **Empty** bit and the **Collision** bit of the entry are tested. If the **Empty** bit of the entry is set to one, then the entry is empty, and a **miss** is returned. Otherwise, the **Collision** bit is checked. If it is set, the collision occurs, and these filters must be accessed and compared one by one. Otherwise, $TAG\_FCN(Y)$ is compared with the Tag of the fetched entry. If they differ, a **miss** is returned, and tuple access can thus be avoided. Otherwise, the corresponding entry in the tuple is probed for possible matching.

6.4.1. Realization of Parallel Hardware

Experiments that will be discussed in Section 6.5. will reveal that look-ahead caching can markedly enhance the lookup performance of a rectangle search. However, the look-ahead

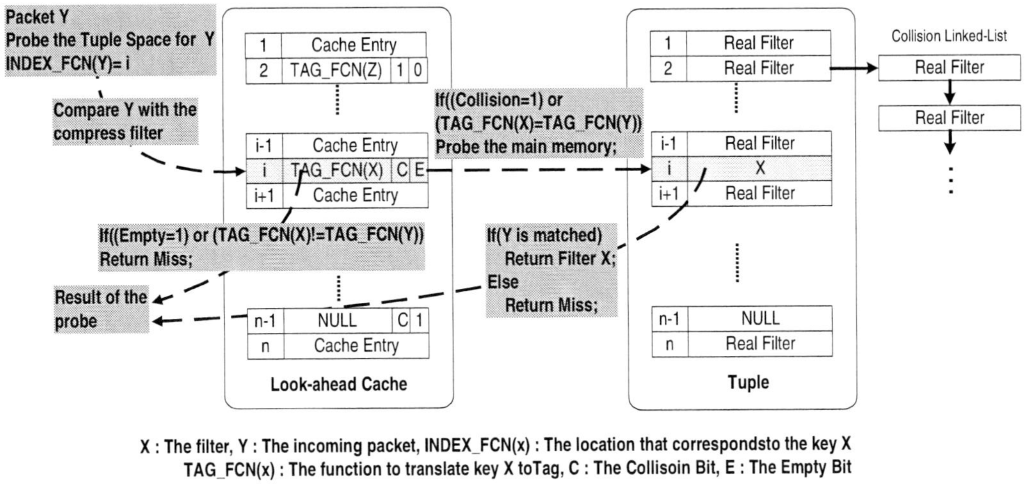

Figure 39. Lookup Procedure with Look-ahead Caching.

cache always waits for the access to a tuple since the access time of DRAM is much greater than that of SRAM. Thus, the design principle that governs hardware implementation is to keep the look-ahead cache as busy as possible.

According to Fig. 40, the implementation involves a network processor, SRAM and DRAM. A network processor includes multiple processing elements (PEs) and request queues. PEs are connected to request queues through the shared buses. The look-ahead cache and tuples are located in the SRAM and DRAM, respectively. The request queues are used to resolve the memory bottleneck by simultaneously accessing the look-ahead cache and the tuples. When the queue of the look-ahead cache is empty, the idle PE issues another packet header for classification. Sets of PEs ($\lceil$DRAM access time/SRAM access time$\rceil$) are required to keep the look-ahead cache busy. Let the access time of the DRAM and SRAM be 25 ns and 5 ns, respectively. $\lceil 25$ ns$/5$ ns$\rceil = 5$ PEs are deployed. The look-ahead cache is always busy so the mean lookup time is reduced to *"Number of Tuples Probing*$\times$*DRAM Access Time"*. However, deploying multiple PEs raises a new issue. That is, in the worst case, the time taken to accomplish single packet classification is the product of the number of PEs and "the worst case lookup time without parallel implementation". The packet might undergo a longer delay in the router than it would under the native scheme. For example, each classification is assumed to require P tuple accesses. Given five PEs, the maximum delay in the classifier is $5 \times (P \times 25$ ns$)=125P$ ns. In the worst-case of 64 tuple probes, the holding time is 8 μs. However, the delay is tolerable for presently available services.

6.5. Performance Evaluation

This section presents the experiment results to demonstrate that the tuple reduction algorithm increases the lookup speed and reduces the memory requirement. Synthetic filter databases are used to evaluate the performance, mainly because filter databases are normally considered to be commercial secrets and most are relatively small, including those considered in [26] and [25].

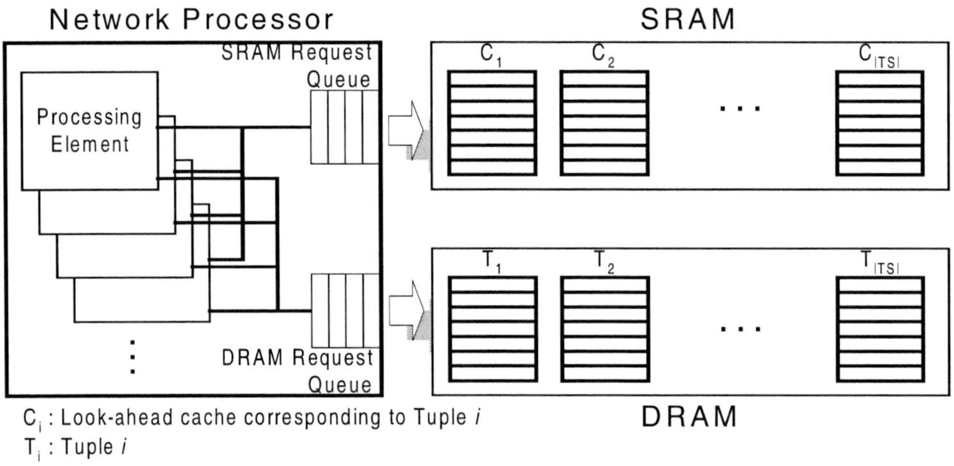

Figure 40. Realization using Parallel Hardware.

The routing table includes 102,309 prefixes, downloaded from the NLANR [8] as a basis for synthesizing filters. Sampling the routing prefixes randomly produces 12 ⟨source prefix, destination prefix⟩ filter databases. The minimal database contains 1K filters; and the sizes of the databases increase to 5k, 10k, 20k, 30K, and so on, and up to 100K filters. Look-ahead caching is not used in the first part of experiments to realize the effect of tuple reduction.

The effect of tuple reduction is firstly specified using the filter distribution, as shown in Fig. 41. Figure 41(a) shows the filter distribution in the original **TS** for the 100K-filter database. It is comprised of 350 tuples, and leads to several tuples with few filters. After the semi-optimization algorithm is applied, the TS is reduced to 85 tuples, as shown in Fig. 41(b). However, several tuples contain few filters ($<$ 100 filters). Applying the tuple reduction to the sparse region (*MAX_FILTERS=1,000*) can reduce the number of the tuples to 55, as shown in Fig. 41(c).

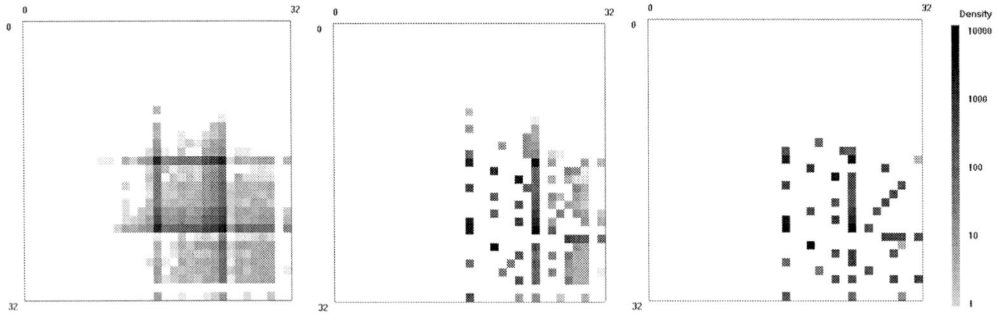

(a) The distribution of the original database (350 tuples). It is easy to see that there are many tuple with few filters and the performance of searching is poor.

(b) After the semi-optimization, the number of tuples is significatly reduced, but there are still some tuples with few filters.

(c) After collecting the filters on the sparse regions, the number of the tuples is usually reduced below 50.

Figure 41. Filter Distribution after Filter Expansion.

Figure 41(c) clearly shows that expanded tuples are disordered and wide-spread, resulting in increased search time since it ties to the sum of the numbers of rows and columns. The speed-optimization algorithm can improve the performance by expanding simultaneously the tuples in identical rows or columns. Although the number of occupied tuples is not markedly changed, the numbers of the rows and columns are reduced, as shown in Fig. 42.

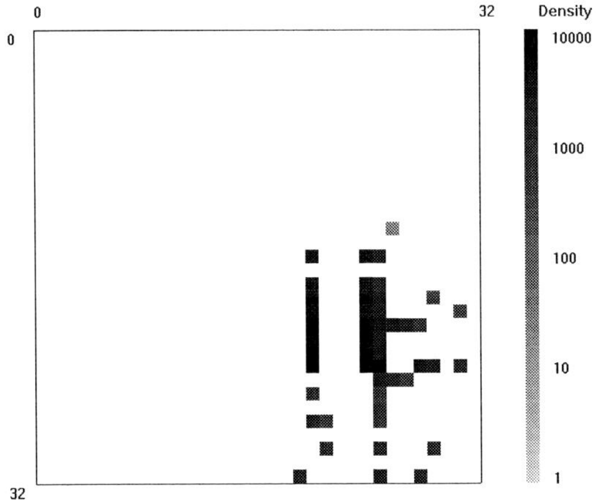

Figure 42. Filter Distribution after Speed is Optimized.

Figure 43 compares the number of the occupied tuples within various databases. The term "space-optimization" is used to refer to the combination of the semi-optimization algorithm and sparse-region reduction. The curve generated by the rectangle search is varies slightly because of the random generation of the filter databases. Both algorithms outperform the rectangle search since occupied tuples are noticeably eliminated when the optimization of speed further eliminates tuples because of the restrictions of expansion. After tuple reduction, the new schemes can achieve a throughput comparable to that of the rectangle search, even using a simple linear search. Furthermore, the number of occupied tuples is very stable with respect to the number of filters. Consequently, the new algorithms can provide much sustainable throughput. Also, memory management can be simplified with many fewer tuples.

Figure 44 presents the number of filters and generated markers. Though the number of entries is proportional to the number of filters, the rate of increase in the number of filters and markers of the new algorithms is much less than that of rectangle search, mainly because tuple reduction also leads to a requirement for fewer entries. Clearly, both algorithms are better than the native rectangle search. The speed-optimization algorithm requires more entries than the space-optimization algorithm as a trade-off for fewer tuples.

Table 11 lists detailed results concerning occupied tuples and generated entries. The speed-optimization algorithm depends on fewest tuples while the space-optimization generates fewest entries. If an 80-bit filter (32-bit source prefix, 32-bit destination prefix, 8-bit cost and 8-bits nexthop) is used, then the required memory can be derived. Using a 100K-filter database, the three schemes require 12,586 Kbytes, 3,280 Kbytes and 4,909 Kbytes. Apparently, the new schemes are very efficient, and are thus suited to large filter database

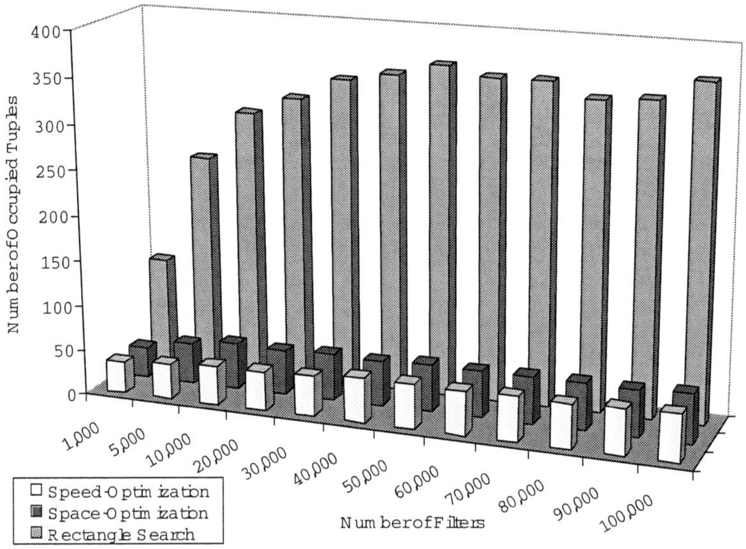

Figure 43. Number of Occupied Tuples.

and implementation using high-speed memory.

One hundred million packets are randomly generated and the number of tuple probes recorded to demonstrate the lookup speed of the new scheme. Figure 45 shows the search performance. The number of tuple probes equals the number of occupied tuples since each tuple is probed in a linear search. The scalability of the rectangle-based algorithms is demonstrated. The lookup time is relatively stable with respect to the number of filters. Although the rectangle search significantly improves the linear search, the tuple reduction algorithms can further reduce the tuple probing to a near-optimal level.

Table 12 presents in detail the results of the investigations into the search speed. The space-optimization algorithm probes 19 tuples for the least-cost filter in a 100K-filter database, while the rectangle search probes 44 tuples on average. The speed-optimization algorithm can further reduce the number of probes to 14 and triple the throughput of the rectangle search. Simultaneously considering the storage and speed enhancements, the space-optimization and speed optimization improve the rectangle search by factors of 8.8 $[(1, 288, 823/335, 882) \times (44/19)]$ and 8.0 $[(1, 288, 823/502, 734) \times (44/14)]$, respectively. The speed-optimization algorithm can perform one lookup per 575 ns in the worst case when commercially available 25-ns DRAM is used. The average lookup time is 350 ns; that is, two OC-48 links can be supported by an average packet size of 256 bytes.

The effect of the look-ahead cache is now examined. The performance obtained using the rectangle search can be examined since the look-ahead cache can also be coupled to any tuple-based algorithm. The experimental results in Fig. 46 indicate that the number of tuple probes in the three schemes is decreased as the size of Tag increases. Even using a zero-length tag, the required tuple probing can be further reduced by the effect of the **E** bit. However, once the size of the tag exceeds 8 bits, the benefit of look-ahead caching is eliminated. Two factors may impact the performance. The first is the number of markers. The markers related to each matched filter are probed in the packet classification. Thus, the minimum number of probes is bounded by the number of columns. Another factor is

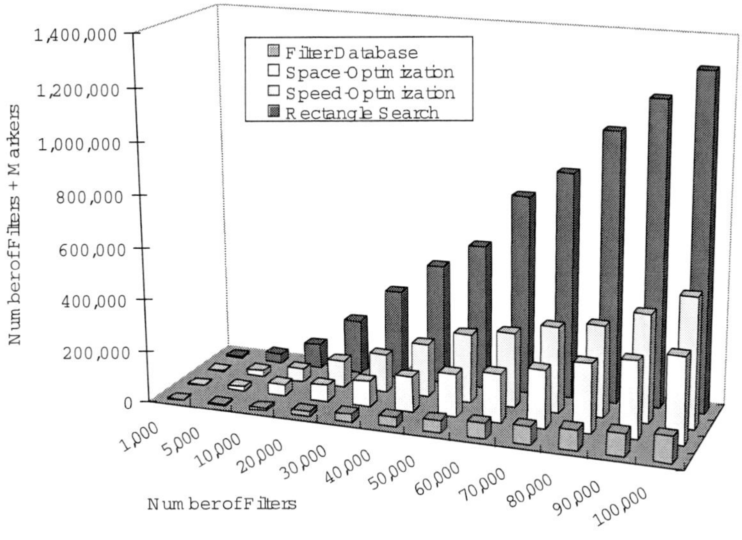

Figure 44. Number of Searchable Entries.

the hashing efficiency. In the experiments, the hash function caused around 26% of the collisions, implying that 26% of cache accesses result in tuple probing, independently of the tag field. Therefore, if the hash efficiency can be improved, the effect of the look-ahead caching may increase.

Table 13 presents the detailed results concerning look-ahead caching. Notably, when the tag size falls to zero, the length of the tag is one since 1 bit remains as an **E** bit. In the rectangle search and space-optimization, an 8-bit tag is required to ensure significant performance enhancement. However, the speed-optimization algorithm only requires 2 bits, mainly because disordered tuples in the rectangle search and space-optimization cause pre-computation information and markers to be spread across more tuples, increasing the hit probability of the look-ahead cache. Unlike the tuple storage, the cache size required by space-optimization and speed-optimization is sufficiently small to fit into a high-speed SRAM at relatively low cost.

The following formula is used to calculate the total search time of the tuple reduction schemes.

$$\begin{aligned}\textit{Total Search Time} = {} & \textit{Number of the Look-ahead Cache Probing} \times \textit{SRAM Access Time} \\ & + \textit{Number of Tuples Probing} \times \textit{DRAM Access Time}\end{aligned}$$

Assume that 5-ns SRAM and an 8-bit tag are used. The mean search time of 270 ns (19×5 ns + 7×25 ns) can be derived for the space-optimization scheme using 409-Kbyte SRAM. Compared to the rectangle search, which requires 620 ns (44×5 ns + 16×25), the tuple reduction scheme provides a twofold improvement while requiring only one quarter of the SRAM. Furthermore, deploying pipeline hardware can further enhance these improvements. The maximum packet delay under parallel implementation is 2.375 μs (125×19 ns) , which is satisfactory. However, the mean lookup time is reduced to 175 ns and an OC-192 throughput is achieved. The mean lookup time of the speed-optimization scheme is the same as that of space-optimization, but using only 245-Kbyte of SRAM.

Table 11. Comparing Storage.

Filter Databases	Rectangle Search		Space-Optimization		Speed-Optimization	
	Tuples	Entries	Tuples	Entries	Tuples	Entries
1K	119	6,472	34	2,775	35	3,572
5K	241	35,440	44	17,110	39	23,566
10K	296	95,206	51	46,616	43	50,971
20K	316	209,574	49	63,805	43	104,224
30K	340	344,592	51	100,260	45	147,224
40K	350	466,714	50	136,367	50	206,482
50K	363	560,438	53	168,339	50	265,299
60K	354	767,865	52	188,627	49	290,059
70K	355	872,355	53	225,106	50	332,293
80K	339	1,043,683	53	270,266	49	355,983
90K	343	1,176,061	52	299,550	51	418,469
100K	366	1,288,823	55	335,882	52	502,734

6.6. Summary

Packet classification is a highly effective primitive for associating a policy-defined context with each incoming packet, so as to permit packet handling using DiffServ actions to activate multimedia services. However, implementing at high-speeds with a large number of rules is difficult. This study proposes various methods for improving both performance and the storage of the rectangle search algorithm. The way in which filter expansion can be applied to the rectangle search to reduce the number of markers and tuples in the first part is addressed; then space and speed optimization techniques are introduced. Space optimization can minimize storage requirements. A semi-optimization algorithm is also presented by restricting the expansions because of the high cost of dynamic programming. The tuple reduction over a sparse area is introduced to reduce the number of tuples. Therefore, the row and column-based expansion is presented as speed optimization. While the algorithm is not storage-optimized, the lookup time is reduced by the regular tuple distribution. Furthermore, "look-ahead caching", which is based on the assumption of a low filter-hit-ratio in the Internet, is introduced. The experimental results obtained by combining the tuple reduction algorithm and look-ahead caching show that the lookup speed was increased by a factor of six while required storage was reduced to only about a third. With an average packet size of 256 bytes, the tuple reduction scheme can provide OC-192 throughput, even in a large database with 100K filers.

7. Conclusion

This chapter presents several efficient and scalable algorithms for IP forwarding engine in Internet routers. These algorithms allow lookups at gigabit speeds even in software. A good lookup algorithm should satisfy: **simplicity, small storage, fast update, IPv6 scalability and parallelism**. However, some of these item might need balance among themselves. For

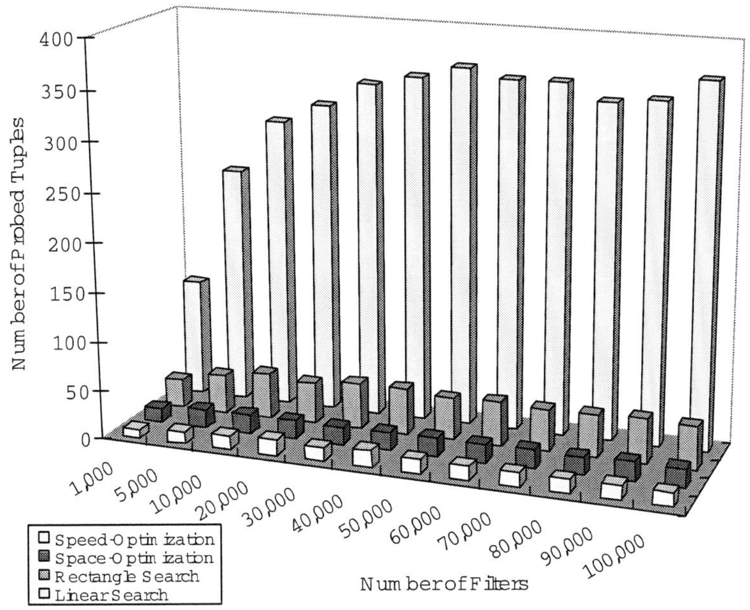

Figure 45. Average Search Performance.

example, a fineness compression may largely reduce the required storage, but might result in increasing complexity and slower lookup speed. On the other hand, with less required storage, if the table can be fitted into the high-speed memory, it might result in higher lookup speed. But the compressed data structure may not support incremental update.

We now review the main ideas of these algorithms and outline the principles underlying each idea.

Pipelined Indirect Indexing: The first algorithm is based on indirect indexing. According to the sparse distribution implied in the current routing table, the number of entries can be reduced by just adding few fields. Furthermore, a new compression scheme is presented to solve the structural hazard, thus can be implemented in hardware pipelining. The experimental results demonstrate that the table size is small enough to fit into SRAM. The scheme cannot support incremental update and future IPv6 lookup, however, its implementation is relatively simple.

Binary Search on Routing Intervals: The major complexity of IP address lookup ties to the BMP problem. It is observed that the route aggregation implied in the Internet causes a special property called "routing locality". By adopting this property, the routing prefix is transformed to "**Routing Interval**". With the routing interval, the complexity of BMP algorithms can be removed. The routing interval can be applied to most existing IP lookup algorithms. With binary search, the address lookup speed can outperform the existing scheme.

LS trie: Trie-based algorithm is the most straight-forward solution for address lookup. By introducing the concept "Level Smart-Compression", the advantages of LC-tries and binary trie are combined. With the LS trie, the size of the forwarding table is significantly reduced and the incremental updates is supported. It also provides the flexibility by separating the internal nodes and leaves to conform the memory hierarchy.

Table 12. Comparing Speed.

Schemes	Rectangle Search			Space-Optimization			Speed-Optimization		
Speed	Min	Avg	Max	Min	Avg	Max	Min	Avg	Max
1K	23	29	36	10	14	21	7	9	17
5K	31	39	48	15	19	24	9	12	20
10K	33	46	57	16	19	28	10	14	22
20K	30	42	53	14	19	27	11	16	22
30K	35	47	58	13	18	26	11	14	22
40K	30	47	59	14	18	26	12	17	24
50K	27	43	56	14	19	27	11	15	22
60K	31	45	60	13	18	26	10	14	21
70K	28	43	56	13	19	27	11	14	22
80K	30	44	57	14	18	27	10	14	22
90K	31	46	59	16	20	29	11	15	22
100K	28	44	59	13	19	26	9	14	23

Table 13. Look-ahead Cache Performance.

Schemes	Performance Metrics	Tag Size (bits)						
		0	2	4	8	16	24	32
Rectangle Search	Cache (Kbytes)	157	628	942	1,570	2,826	4,083	5,339
	Average Probes	35	34	34	16	15	15	15
Space-Optimization	Cache (Kbytes)	41	164	246	409	737	1,064	1,391
	Average Probes	15	15	15	7	6	6	6
Speed-Optimization	Cache (Kbytes)	61	245	367	612	1,102	1,592	2,082
	Average Probes	9	7	7	7	6	6	6

Tuple Reduction: Last, we extend the algorithm from IP address lookup to the policy-based routing. To solve the two-dimensional filters lookup, the tuple reduction algorithm uses the pre-computation to improve the lookup speed and storage over previous scheme simultaneously. Several heuristics are also provided to improve the lookup performance.

Recently, the research focus has been moved from IP address lookup and packet classification to deeper packet inspection by filtering predefined strings in the packet payload. The applications of deep packet inspection include virus detection, intrusion detection and data secrecy. Since these problems, including IP address lookup, packet classification and deep packet inspection, can be transformed into the problem of computational geometry, we believe that the advance in IP address lookup and packet classification could benefit to the solution of deep packet inspection.

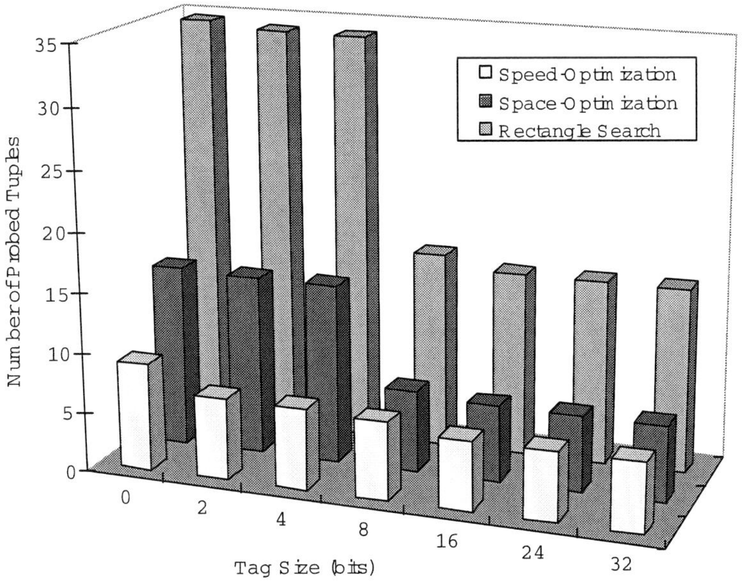

Figure 46. Average Number of Tuple Probes.

References

[1] A Tam. How to Survive as an ISP. In: *Networld Interop*; 1997. .

[2] S Keshav and R Sharma. Issues and Trends in Router Design. *IEEE Communication Magazine* 1998;36(5):144–151.

[3] C Partridge, *et al.* A 50-Gb/s IP Router. *IEEE/ACM Trans On Networking* 1998; 6(3):237–248.

[4] IETF MPLS Charter. Multiprotocol Label Switching See *http://www.ietf.org/html-charters/mpls-charter.html*, 1997;.

[5] AM Odlyzko. Data Networks are mostly empty and for good reason. In: *IT Professional*; 1999. .

[6] Y Rekhter, T Li. *An Architecture for IP Address Allocation with CIDR*. RFC 1993; (1518).

[7] C Partridge. Locality and Route Caches. In: *NSF Workshop on Internet Statistics Measurement and Analysis*; 1996. .

[8] NLANR Project. National Laboratory for Applied Network Research. See *http://www.nlanr.net*;.

[9] M Degermark, A Brodnik, SCarlsson, and S Pink. Small Forwarding Tables for Fast Routing Lookups. In: *ACM SIGCOMM*; 1997. p. 3–14.

[10] P Gupta, S Lin, and N McKeown. Routing Lookups in Hardware at Memory Access Speeds. In: *IEEE INFOCOM*; 1999. p. 1240–1247.

[11] N Huang, S Zhao and J Pan. A Novel IP-Routing Lookup Scheme and Hardware Architecture for Multigigabit Switching Routers. *IEEE JSAC* 1999;17(6):1093–1104.

[12] V Srinivasan and G Varghese. Fast IP lookups using controlled prefix expansion. *ACM Trans On Computers* 1999;17:1–40.

[13] S Nilsson and G Karlsson. IP-Address Lookup Using $LC-Tries$. *IEEE JSAC* 1999; 17(6):1083–1092.

[14] M Waldvogel, G Varghese, J Turner and B Plattner. Scalable High Speed IP Routing Lookups. In: *ACM SIGCOMM*; 1997. p. 25–36.

[15] B Lampson, V Srinivasan and G Varghese. IP Lookups Using Multiway and Multicolumn Search. *IEEE/ACM Trans On Networking* 1999;7(4):323–334.

[16] Pi-Chung Wang, Chia-Tai Chan and Yaw-Chung Chen. A Fast IP Lookup Scheme for High-Speed Networks. *IEEE Communications Letters* 2001;5(3):125–127.

[17] Merit Networks Inc. Internet Performance Measurement and Analysis (IPMA) Statistics and Daily Reports. *IMPA Project* See $http://www.merit.edu/ipma/routing\_table/$;.

[18] Pi-Chung Wang, Chia-Tai Chan and Yaw-Chung Chen. Performance Enhancement of IP forwarding by using Routing Interval. *Journal of Communications and Networks* 2001;3(4):374–382.

[19] Pi-Chung Wang, Chia-Tai Chan and Yaw-Chung Chen. Performance Enhancement of IP Forwarding by Reducing Routing Table Construction Time. *IEEE Communications Letters* 2001;5(5):230–232.

[20] RP Draves, C King, S Venkatachary and BD Zill. Constructing Optimal IP Routing Tables. In: *IEEE INFOCOM*; 1999. p. 88–97.

[21] R Stevens and G Wright. *TCP/IP Illustrated-Vol. 2: THe implementation*.; 1995. .

[22] K Sklower. *A tree-based table for Berkeley unix*.; 1991. .

[23] A Andersson and S Nilsson. Improved behavior of tries by adaptive branching. I*nformation Processing Letters* 1993;46(6):295–300.

[24] Pi-Chung Wang, Chia-Tai Chan, Shuo-Cheng Hu, Chung-Liang Lee and Wei-Chun Tseng. High-Speed Packet Classification for Differentiated Services in NGNs. *IEEE Transactions on Multimedia* 2004;6(6):925–935.

[25] Pankaj Gupta and Nick McKeown. Packet Classification on Multiple Fields. In: *ACM SIGCOMM*; 1999. p. 147–160.

[26] V Srinivasan, G Varghese and S Suri. Packet Classification using Tuple Space Search. In: *ACM SIGCOMM*; 1999. p. 135–146.

[27] Daxiao Yu, Brandon C Smith, and Belle Wei. Forwarding Engine For Fast Routing Lookups and Updates. In: *IEEE Globecom*; 1999. p. 1556–1564.

[28] Pankaj Gupta and Nick McKeown. Algorithms For Packet Classification. *IEEE Network Magazine* 2001;15(2):24–32.

[29] V Srinivasan, G Varghese, S Suri and M Waldvogel. Fast Scalable Level Four Switching. In: *ACM SIGCOMM*; 1998. p. 191–202.

[30] TV Lakshman and D Stidialis. High Speed Policy-based Packet Forwarding Using Efficient Multi-dimensional Range Matching. In: *ACM SIGCOMM*; 1998. p. 203–214.

[31] Anja Feldmann and S Muthukrishnan. Tradeoffs for Packet Classification. In: *IEEE INFOCOM*; 2000. p. 1193–1202.

[32] M Buddhikot, S Suri and M Waldvogel. Space Decomposition Techniques for Fast Layer-4 Switching. In: *IFIP Sixth International Workshop on High Speed Networks* ; 2000. .

[33] Thomas Woo. A Modular Approach to Packet Classification: Algorithms and Results. In: *IEEE INFOCOM*; 2000. p. 1213–1222.

[34] Pankaj Gupta and Nick McKeown. Packet Classification using Hierarchical Intelligent Cuttings. In: *Hot Interconnects VII*; 1999.

In: Computer Science Research Trends
Editor: Casey B. Yarnall, pp. 59-70
ISBN: 978-1-60021-518-6

Chapter 2

INTERNET ADDICTION IN CHILDREN AND ADOLESCENTS

Keith W. Beard
Marshall University, Huntington, West Virginia, USA

Abstract

The creation of the Internet has had several positive and negative results on the world. Additionally, certain aspects of the Internet make it a unique medium of communication with its own set of norms, standards, language, etc. These various factors have influenced children and adolescents. Problematic Internet use, which has become known as Internet addiction, is not limited by demographic elements. However, there may be certain factors about this medium that could make children and adolescents vulnerable to using the Internet in a dysfunctional way. These factors are examined. Additionally, special considerations and treatment options are reviewed for mental health professionals who treat children and adolescents for their problematic Internet use. Future research on particular aspects of problematic Internet use with children and adolescents is suggested.

The Impact of the Internet

The development of the Internet has had a very positive influence for many people. Economically, the Internet has provided business and financial opportunities (Beard, 2002). Socially, users are able to meet others similar to them and foster favorable impressions. The Internet allows people to make friends, maintain relationships, play games, gain emotional support, and learn about other cultures (McNamee, 1996; Parks & Floyd, 1996; Scherer, 1997). With regard the physical and mental health, using the Internet may provide relief from anxiety and depression by acting as an escape or helping the person gain needed support and education about their problem (Armstrong, Phillips, & Saling, 2000; Harmon, 1998; Kraut et al., 1998; Pocius, 1991; Shotton, 1989; Suler, 1996a; Young, 1996b, 1997, 1998b). It has even been suggested that the Internet has increased the self-concept that some people hold about themselves. Shotton (1989) described how the Internet has allowed those who are knowledgeable in the computing market to offer advice to those less knowledgeable. This has resulted in higher self-esteem and self-confidence, and improved self-concept for those helping others. Computer and Internet use have also allowed people to increase their knowledge about various related technologies. It has been suggested that there has been an improvement in writing abilities and intellectual growth for some people as a result of their computer and Internet use.

In contrast, the Internet may have created a new set of difficulties for the general population. Several studies have illustrated that there are a significant number of people who report averse consequences from their Internet use (Coopers, Griffin-Shelley, & Delmonico, 2001; Young, 1997, 1998a, 1998b). Researchers (Stern, 1999; Winn, 1985; Young, 1998b) have compared the introduction of the Internet to the introduction of the television when identifying potential negative impacts. It was initially thought that the television would bring families together. Griffiths (1997) and Winn (1985) claim that the television has separated families. In the same way, the Internet is providing a backdrop for several critical family problems (Oravec, 2000). Griffiths (1997) and Winn (1985) go on by stating that even though families are spending time together watching television, their interaction is minimal and quality time may now be consumed by television viewing. Like television, the Internet may contribute to decreased family interaction. Television has also allowed families to avoid confronting their problems which then grow and become more difficult to resolve. The researchers go so far as to claim that television has played an important role in the disintegration of the family. Also, like television, the Internet can be detrimental to physical development and growth by limiting activity. Pike (1999) goes on to compare these two mediums. She characterizes the Internet as television on steroids. However, the difference is that television shows end where as the Internet provides a sense of "boundarylessness" that can be enticing to a person.

Beard (2002) states that another negative consequence of the Internet has to do with the content that is obtained. For example, there is an abundance of misinformation that can be perpetuated. It can be difficult to obtain desired information because of the numerous web sites that have to be reviewed and sorted through in order to find the desired material. Other issues with the content on the Internet include the fact that people have more access to pornographic material. This has lead to some people being fired from their jobs and conflict in relationships. Dangerous information can be obtained from the Internet such as instructions for how to make a bomb out of common household items.

Negative consequences with interpersonal relationships can occur as a result of Internet use. People can create new identities or misrepresent themselves (McCormick & McCormick, 1992). Adolescents may be particularly susceptible to this behavior since they are often unhappy with their appearance and are involved with the developmental task of integrating various roles into a unified identity. As a result, this misrepresentation can cause disappointment if a pen-pal is never met or there is disappointment after he/she was met (Turkle, 1996). Another dangerous misinterpretation of identity can occur as a result of sexual predators easily soliciting large numbers of children and adolescents in a relatively anonymous environment (Dombrowski, LeMasney, & Ahia, 2004). Armstrong et al. (2000) and Young (1995, 1996b, 1998a, 1998b) report other interpersonal relationship issues such as less time is spent with people in the user's life resulting in impatience, arguments, and a strain in the relationship. A person's school work, extracurricular activities, or after-school employment may suffer if too much time is spent scanning the Internet. The Internet may also contribute to people escaping from social interactions and hinder the development of social skills (Beard & Wolf, 2000).

Young (1995, 1998b) described how schools are rushing to add Internet access for students. There is an underlying belief that children need Internet access in order to stay competitive in the global marketplace. However, one survey (Barber, 1997) revealed that 86 percent of responding teachers, librarians, and computer coordinators did not believe that Internet use improved classroom performance. These respondents claim that the Internet is too disorganized and unrelated to the school curriculum. Not only can inaccurate information be perpetuated quickly but much of the information is unattainable (McCormick & McCormick, 1992; Turkle, 1996). Only 9 percent of the estimated 800 million web pages are covered by the top 11 search engines ("Search Engines," 1999). Schools have cut funding for programs in the creative arts and invest the money in a technology that may not provide benefits to the students (Young, 1995, 1998b).

The Internet Culture

There may be qualities with this medium of communication that have allowed an Internet culture to develop. The Internet culture has its own set of values, standards, language, signs, and artifacts (Beard & Wolf, 2000; Correll, 1995; Friess, 1998; Griffiths, 2001; Parks & Floyd, 1996; Suler, 1996b; Young, 1997, 1998a). Symbols and initials have been given meanings. For example, "LOL" stands for "Laugh Out Loud," "IMHO" stands for "In My Humble Opinion," and ":-P" represents "I'm sticking my tongue out" (Friess, 1998). The exchange of these standards and signs can express deep meaning and psychological bonds may develop quickly (Correll, 1995; Kiesler et al., 1984; Suler, 1996b; Young, 1997, 1998a). The person reading the symbols is able to create in the writer what their ideal person would be but this creation is based only on words.

For many, the main attraction to the Internet is the anonymity (Correll, 1995; Griffiths, 1997; Kiesler, et al., 1984; Young, 1997, 1998a, 1998b). Unlike face-to-face communication, demographics have to be announced in order to be known (Correll, 1995). Many Internet users take on different personas when on-line (Kandell, 1998; Suler, 1996b; Young, 1997, 1998a, 1998b). Users may change their persona and create different profile information about themselves depending on their mood or desires. As mentioned previously, this may be particularly attractive for adolescents as they go through some of the development tasks associated with this period. An identity crisis can occur as adolescents begin to integrate various roles into a solid identity. Questions may develop such as, “Who am I?” or “What am I going to be?” This aspect of the Internet and the factors associated with identity development may join to provide adolescents with an opportunity to “try on” different identities and determine what “fits” for them. Young (1997, 1998a, 1998b) found that some users chose identities that were an ideal self that represented the opposite of what the person is in real life. As a result, the chosen persona is a way to fulfill unmet needs. Others chose a persona that represented an emotion or trait that may be repressed. Some users even take on a different gender, age, or race. The impact of taking on a different persona for adolescents, and those interacting with that person, needs to be studied further.

King (1996) and Young (1997, 1998a, 1998b) believe that Internet users tend to take more emotional risks and may express opinions on-line that they are unable to express to others in the real world. This creates a deep need to continue these bonds and receive the support that they are lacking in the real world. Adolescents may be particularly vulnerable because they often feel isolated. As a result, these bonds made over the Internet may take on even more significance in the adolescent's life. However, the commitment of friends on the Internet can be ended with the simple click of a button. The Internet offers the illusion of companionship without the demands often placed on friendships. Interestingly, even though people were more embarrassed about meeting face-to-face after interacting via the Internet, they actually reported liking each other better (Correll, 1995; Kiesler, et al., 1984). Kiesler and colleagues (1984) specifically address this social psychology aspect of electronic communication in the results of their study which explored the physiological arousal and affective consequences of computer communication. Results suggested that computer-mediated communication is not physiologically arousing. However, there can be affective consequences with computer-mediated versus face-to-face communication when people are getting to know each other. Affective consequences include changes in emotionality, interpersonal attraction, responsiveness to others, and self-disclosure.

Users are not shy to express positive and negative feedback to those they communicate within this forum. It is not unusual in this culture to ask personal questions upon the first on-line meeting between two users (Kandell, 1998; King, 1996; Suler, 1996b; Young, 1997, 1998a). The lack of face-to-face communication may also create a feeling of safety and encourage more flirtation and overtures of friendship (Harmon, 1998; McCormick & McCormick, 1992; Morahan-Martin & Schumacher, 2000; Suler, 1996b).

Young (1997, 1998a, 1998b) explains that the Internet environment allows for any virtual experience. If the person desired to hurt his or her teacher, the person can go into a Multi-User Dungeons and Dragons (MUDS) or on-line gaming site and blow up an enemy. If the person fantasized of ripping off the clothes of an attractive man or woman it can be simulated in a cybersex encounter. If the person wanted to know what it would be like to be bisexual, the person can go on-line and engage in a fantasy. Once these unconscious drives are brought to the conscious mind it becomes difficult to suppress them again. As a result, the Internet user may begin to blur the distinction between their real-world personality and their on-line persona.

Problematic Use of the Internet

Beard and Wolf (2000) believe that problematic Internet use can be found in any age, social, educational, and economic range. Excessive Internet users have been called Internet addicts, pathological Internet users, computer addicts, computer mediated communication addicts, and computer junkies. The term that has been most often used for problematic Internet use is "Internet addiction." This includes a mixture of obsessive-like characteristics and impulse control problems related to a person's Internet usage resulting in a preference for on-line rather than in-person interactions (Beard & Wolf, 2000; Pratarelli, Browne, & Johnson, 1999). Each of the previously listed terms reflects a different understanding of the nature of excessive Internet use. The most popular term utilized is "Internet addiction." While this term will be used throughout this chapter, it is my position that this term does not accurately reflect the phenomenon of excessive Internet use. While there are commonalities between excessive Internet use and an addiction, excessive Internet use does not result in all of the symptoms and behaviors associated with a chemical addiction, such as physical withdrawal. Moreover, comparison of excessive Internet use with pathological gambling suggests that this behavior with the Internet may be better classified as an impulse control disorder rather than an addiction (Beard & Wolf, 2000; Young, 1998b). Given the issues outlined above, terms such as excessive, problematic, or maladaptive Internet use are most optimal for describing this behavior as they involve fewer theoretical overtones than terms such as "Internet addiction."

Media attention has stereotyped those who are Internet addicted as predominantly young/adolescent, introverted, and computer-oriented males (Scherer, 1997; Young, 1996a, 1998a). While this stereotype may have been true in the past (Pocius, 1991), the availability of computers and the easy access for everyone to the Internet is quickly challenging this notion and causing researchers to re-assess their previous conceptualizations of what characteristics a person addicted to the Internet may possess (Armstrong et al., 2000). Now, most Internet users are young students (Treuer, Fabian, & Furedi, 2001). Young's (1998b) findings demonstrated that the number of male and female computer and Internet users may be changing. She reported that 61 percent of her respondents were women. It is suspected that the change in Internet use is related to the availability of this technology.

Subjects, who completed a survey posted on the Internet and met a proposed criteria for problematic Internet use (Young, 1995, 1996b, 1998a, 1998b), described their personality as bold, outgoing, open-minded, and assertive. Many of the Internet users reported being depressed, lonely, having low self-esteem, and anxiety. Pathological Internet users typically score higher on loneliness scales than non-pathological Internet users (Morahan-Martin & Schumacher, 2000). The Internet may provide pathological users with a way to express themselves that is considered more satisfying than previous coping skills. Other common personality characteristics included having pride in their intellect, and the use of the defense mechanism called intellectualization (Correll, 1995; Pocius, 1991; Shotton, 1989).

New users could be more vulnerable to the development of pathological Internet use. Twenty-five percent of those who completed Young's (1996b, 1997, 1998a, 1998b) survey on the Internet reported becoming addicted to the Internet within the first six months on-line. She went on to report that 58 percent of the respondents met her criteria for Internet addiction within one year. Most felt intimidated by the computer initially but began to feel a sense of competency and exhilaration from mastering the technology and learning to navigate the applications quickly (Kandell, 1998; Kraut et al., 1998; Shotton, 1989; Young, 1996b, 1997, 1998a, 1998b).

The survey administered by Young (1996b, 1997, 1998b) also found that her addicted respondents used the Internet an average of 38 hours a week. In general, adolescents have been found to use the Internet more hours than adults (Kraut et al., 1998). Young (1998b) explains that respondents admitted to trying to cut down on their Internet use and failing despite significant problems it was causing. Nearly 80 percent of Internet addicts engage in two-way communication forums such as chat rooms and interactive games. The greater the availability of the Internet, the increased chance that people will engage in various activities offered on the Internet.

Problematic Use by Children and Adolescents

Children and adolescents are becoming active users of the Internet (Young, 1998b). It has been suggested by Young (1998b) that many parents are unaware about what their children do on the Internet. Some parents may not even know how to turn on the computer. There are parents who have banned the use of the Internet or controlled access for fear of exposing their children to pornography and contact with pedophiles that frequent sites for children and adolescents. Neither being unaware of nor prohibiting the use of the Internet will help parents confront the issues that the Internet raises concerning their children and adolescents.

Young (1998b) pointed out that students are primed for Internet access. Most are typically exposed to computer games, digital music players, cell phones, and digital cameras. If they have not already been introduced to the Internet by high school, these other technical gadgets prepared them to learn about and embrace new technology. When examining adolescents, it has been discovered that their perception of how useful the Internet is was a major variable in predicting whether an adolescent would become addicted to the Internet (Xuanhui & Gonggu, 2001).

Warning signs that give evidence that a child or teen is abusing the Internet have been suggested by Young (1998b). The child may be excessively fatigued due to a change in sleep patterns because of excessive on-line use. Academic problems may be noticed. Parents may believe that the child is spending their time on the computer working on class assignments when the child is actually on-line. A child who is dependent on the Internet typically spends more and more time on-line which results in negative ramifications on the child's daily routine, school performance, and parental relationship (Lin & Tsai, 2002). Additionally, the child may show a decline in other hobbies because the Internet becomes the only non-curricular activity. The child may withdraw from friends and make emotional attachments with those on the Internet. Adolescents who are dependent on the Internet may even go as far as believing that their excessive Internet use enhances their peer relationships (Lin & Tsai, 2002). Anger, irritability, edginess, and acting out may result from a decrease in Internet accessibility; this experience has been coined the "cybershakes" (Young, 1998b). A youth's reaction to limits being set on Internet use may provide further evidence of possible Internet addiction behaviors.

Clearly, pathological Internet use may be an indication of other underlying problems. Young (1997, 1998b) discussed how children may use the Internet to alleviate depression, anxiety, and to escape from family discord. Real-life problems return after this temporary alleviation. As a result, these problems may now be seen as even more difficult to endure. Depression, guilt, and loneliness deepen as a byproduct of excessive Internet use (Morahan-Martin, 1999). Young (1997, 1998b) continues, stating that these feelings push the person into going on-line for even longer periods of time. This same cycle is also seen in alcoholics and compulsive gamblers as they engage in their addictive behaviors.

It is normal for adolescents to be plagued with feelings of low self-esteem. Some adolescents become dependent on the social contact they receive from the Internet. Children and adolescents may be seeking out confidants on the Internet to discuss issues that they feel others in the real world, such as their parents, will not understand. Adolescents form such strong connections with others on the Internet that they often consider each other a "cyberbro" or "cybersis" (Young, 1998b).

Young (1997, 1998b) also suggested that the Internet may attract children with Attention Deficit Hyperactivity Disorder (ADHD). Those children diagnosed with ADHD may find the Internet appealing because of the abundance of stimulation and rapidly changing material.

Causes of Internet Addiction

The cause of Internet addiction is more than likely a multifaceted phenomenon (Wang, 2001). From a sociocultural stand point there may be familial, social, and cultural dynamics that prompt excessive Internet use. For example, the person may use the Internet to escape family conflict. From a social aspect, some people may lack certain social skills that would enable them to fulfill these social needs in places other than the computer. Likewise, modeling may play a role. Children and adolescents may see their primary care giver, other adults, or peers engaging the various activities and material offered on the Internet and then model that behavior. Additionally, children and adolescents can witness and experience peer pressure from those around them engaging in Internet use. There may be the expectation from friends for the Internet user to engage in various on-line activities. Likewise, cultural factors such as the push to be a "technologically advanced society" or the necessity to use the Internet for school assignments could encourage Internet use to a point that is detrimental to the person. The environment in which the Internet is being used could also increase the potential for pathological use. Using the Internet in the comfort of one's home can increase the chances that the person will not want to leave this environment.

Treatment Considerations with Children and Adolescents

Marlatt (1985) feels that the focus of treatment should revolve around the assumption that people can learn effective ways to change their addictive behaviors regardless of how the problem developed. Likewise, addictive behaviors are controllable behaviors even though their cause may be determined by multiple factors. Therefore, ideal intervention programs should include behavioral, cognitive, and lifestyle changes.

When intervening with children and adolescents the therapist often works closely and intervenes with the care givers. Stanton and Heath (1997) reported how family disruptions and stress may promote the onset of addictive behavior. These same disruptions and stresses may influence how family members enable, encourage, or overlook addictive behaviors such as Internet use. Families may rationalize the pathological Internet use as a phase that will be resolved in time (Young, 1995, 1996b, 1998a). Learning ways to handle family crises and stabilizing the family are the goals. Family therapy may be a necessary treatment modality. When treating the family system, the family becomes the "client." Young (1995) suggested that the family be educated on how the Internet can be addictive. Exploration into previous family problems is needed since this may be a reason why the child or adolescent sought out the Internet and began using this technology in a maladaptive way. There should also be some effort to reduce the blame placed on the Internet addict for their behaviors. The family is also encouraged to help the Internet addicted child find new hobbies, take time for him/herself, and listen to the child's feelings. Stanton and Heath (1997) continued stating that the family has to learn how to go on with life without the use of the Internet or with specific modifications so that problematic Internet use will not recur. The family may need to be reorganized and members will be expected to take on their expected roles in the family. These roles may have shifted when the addicted person began having a problem. Care givers should be supportive but not enable excessive Internet use by aiding children with excuses for why the child missed school or failed an assignment. It is important to validate the child for any effort that is being made.

Young (1998b) suggested that a therapist assist care givers in establishing agreed upon reasonable rules and goals regarding Internet use. If there is a division regarding how to parent between the care givers, the child may use this to create an even larger divergence. Peele and Brodsky (1991) stressed to the care giver that lecturing the child is typically an ineffective and counter-productive intervention. Acknowledging and exploring reasons why the child may be using the Internet may help the parent understand the issue at hand and how to best deal with it. Young (1998b) continues, stating that the child may feel blamed or criticized for his/her Internet use. The care giver can learn how to effectively reassure the child that this is not the case and focus the concerns over specific changes such as fatigue, declining grades, and social withdrawal. It is vital that the parents are consistent with the rules that are established. The care givers should encourage other activities to fill in the time gained by decreasing Internet use.

Young (1998b) also recommended that care givers get on-line and see what their children could be exposed to on the Internet. This could also result in the care givers modeling appropriate Internet use (Peele & Brodsky, 1991). Children and adolescents can learn to emulate their parent's responses to situations such as what to do if inappropriate web sites are accessed or what to do if someone the child or adolescent does not know attempts to contact them. Care givers can also learn how to take a proactive stance and talk to children about the Internet just as they would talk to them about drugs and alcohol.

Finally, Young (1995, 1998b) suggested that families find support in groups for other addictions such as Al-Anon. Information about dealing with any addiction in the family can be obtained at these meetings. Even if the person only goes and listens to the experiences of family members of alcoholics they will see similarities in their situations, feel validated, and less alone. Parents may be able to seek support regarding their Internet addicted child from a parent's association and as a result, they may find that other parents are experiencing similar difficulties.

Future Research and Conclusions

When examining Internet addiction one factor that needs to be taken into consideration is the limited empirical research on Internet addiction. Likewise, the empirical research that has been conducted contains methodological flaws that could impact the results. Additionally, the term "Internet addiction" has been used to denote all types of abuse with a variety of Internet applications and there is a controversy over whether it should even be called an addiction (Beard, 2002; Beard & Wolf, 2000; Scherer, 1997). Some researchers (Young, Pistner, & O'Mara, 1999) have claimed that there are numerous subtypes of Internet addiction such as Cybersex, Cyber-relationships, online stock trading, information surfing, and computer games. However, even if this is the case, it is not uncommon for a single word to describe a diverse category of behavior (Jaffe, 1990).

Areas that need further exploration include prevalence rates and issues related to specific populations. There could be issues that need to be taken into account when assessing various ethnic groups, income levels, individuals with various mental disorders, and differences between adolescents and children. Walther and Reid (2000) agreed, stating that past research has ignored a broader range of participants.

Research that includes retesting participants and replication of various studies is also needed (Walther & Reid, 2000). Young (1995, 1997, 1998b) suggests that longitudinal studies of the Internet and its users be done. This may reveal certain personality traits, family dynamics, social support, or communication skills that promote Internet addictive behaviors. Additionally, there may be undiscovered differences between new and old users. Since the Internet is readily available and user-friendly, the characteristics of those who may become addicted to the Internet could be shifting.

Future research also needs to focus on what it actually is about the Internet that children and adolescents find addictive (Griffiths, 1998; King, 1996; Walther & Reid, 2000; Young, 1997, 1998b). Is it the computer? Is it the typing? Is it the information gained? Is it the anonymity? Is it the interactions with other users? Is it the types of activities in which the individual is engaged? (Beard, 2002; Beard & Wolf, 2000). Young (1996b, 1998b) makes the important point that the Internet addict may not be addicted to the Internet per se, but addicted to the application, emotional state, or mental response that is received from on-line behaviors. All of these factors could play a role in making the Internet reinforcing. Therefore, the Internet may not be addictive but how it is used may be the addictive aspect of this technology (Harmon, 1998). Additionally, it is unknown how important individual characteristics are in determining if applications are addictive (Pocius, 1991; Walther & Reid, 2000). Likewise, it is assumed that off-line activities are healthier than on-line behavior but this has not been examined (Walther & Reid, 2000).

Goolkasian (1995) and Young (1995, 1996b) recommend that those involved with youth be aware of this growing phenomenon and the role that mental health professionals and other's involved in a child's life can take with addressing Internet use and abuse. These difficulties should be examined in a proactive manner rather then waiting for the crisis to occur and then "picking up the pieces." Mental health professionals pride themselves on their ability to predict behavior. Introducing new technology and simultaneously using what we know about the mental, social, and physical aspects of people to counteract negative effects may lessen the onset of difficulties and the formation of crises.

There are millions of people on the Internet and the number keeps growing. In 2002, Neilson/NetRatings report that over 422 million people in 21 countries had access to the Internet in their homes (Mariano, 2002) with each U.S. citizens averaging 35 on-line visits in one month from their home computers in 2007 (Nelison/NetRatings, 2007). Since the concept of Internet addiction is a new phenomenon, mental health professionals and school counselors need to be alerted to the fact that many individuals may be reluctant to seek treatment believing that the clinician will not take their difficulties seriously. Keeping an open mind that there could be problems with how some children and adolescents use the Internet, trying to understand why this technology is used in a maladaptive way, and recognizing the signs and symptoms of Internet addiction will be beneficial for all of those involved.

The continuing debate over the existence of Internet addiction will probably go on for some time. Regardless of whether or not the term Internet addiction is used, there are children and adolescents who are developing a harmful dependence on the Internet. Anything can become addictive when it becomes obsessive (Walther & Reid, 2000). Regardless of whether this problematic behavior is a result of the Internet itself or some other factor, there is a problem in how some children and adolescents use the Internet and steps need to be taken to help these individuals.

References

Armstrong, L., Phillips, J. G., & Saling, L. L. (2000). *Potential determinants of heavier Internet usage. International Journal of Human-Computer Studies*, **53**, 537-550,

Barber, A. (1997, March 11). Net's educational value questioned. *USA Today.* pp. 4D.

Beard, K. W. (2002). Internet addiction: Current status and implications for employees. *Journal of Employment Counseling,* **39**, 2-11.

Beard, K. W., & Wolf, E. M. (2001). Modification in the proposed diagnostic criteria for Internet addiction. *CyberPsychology & Behavior,* **4**, 377-383.

Correll, S. (1995). The ethnography of an electronic bar. *Journal of Contemporary Ethnography,* **24**, 270-298.

Dombrowski, S. C., LeMasney, J. W., & Ahia, C. E. (2004). Protecting children from online sexual predators: Technological, psychoeducational, and legal considerations, *Professional Psychology: Research and Practice*, **35**, 65-73.

Friess, S. (1998, February 3). A place where no one knows your name. *The Advocate.* 24-31.

Goolkasian, P. (1995). Psychology and its role in information technology. *Behavior Research Methods, Instruments, & Computers,* **27**, 109-115.

Griffiths, M. (1997). Psychology of computer use: XLIII. Some comments on 'Addictive Use of the Internet' by Young. *Psychological Reports,* **80**, 81-82.

Griffiths, M. (1998). Internet addiction: Does it really exist? In J. Gackenbach (Ed.), *Psychology and the Internet* (pp. 61-75). San Diego, CA: Academic Press.

Griffiths, M. (2001). Sex on the Internet: Observations and implications for Internet sex addiction. *Journal of Sex Research*, **38,** 333-342.

Harmon, A. (1998). Researchers find sad, lonely, world in cyberspace. *New York Times.* Retrieved January 10, 2001, from http://www.nytimes.com/library/tech/98/08/biztech/articles/30depression.html

Jaffe, J. H. (1990). Trivializing dependence. *British Journal of Addiction,* **85**, 1425-1427.

Kandell, J. J. (1998). Internet addiction on campus: The vulnerability of college students. *CyberPsychology & Behavior,* **1**, 11-17.

Kiesler, S., Siegel, J., & McGuire, T. W., (1984). Social psychological aspects of computer-mediated communication. *American Psychologist,* **39**, 1123-1134.

King, S. A. (1996). *Is the Internet addictive, or are addicts using the Internet?* Retrieved January 9, 2002 from http://rdz.stjohns.edu/~storm/iad.html

Kraut, R., Patterson, M., Lundmark, V., Kiesler, S., Mukopadhyay, T., & Scherlis, W. (1998). Internet paradox: A social technology that reduces social involvement and psychological well-being? *American Psychologist,* **53,** 1017-1031.

Lin, S. S. J. & Tsai, C. (2002). Sensation seeking and Internet dependence of Tawainese high school adolescents. *Computers in Human Behavior*, **18**, 411-426.

Mariano, G. (2002). Web usage grows across globe. Retireved June 20, 2007 from http://news.com.com/2100-1023-934655.html

Marlatt, G. A. (1985). Relapse prevention: Theoretical rationale and overview of the model. In Marlatt, G. A. & Gordon, J. *Relapse Prevention.* New York, NY: The Guilford Press.
McCormick, N. B. & McCormick, J. W. (1992). Computer friends and foes: Content of undergraduates' electronic mail. *Computers in Human Behavior,* **8**, 379-405.
McNamee, S. (1996). Therapy and identity construction in a post-modern world. In D. Grodin, & T. R. Lindlof (Eds.), *Constructing the self in a mediated world. Inquires in social construction.* Thousand Oaks, CA: Sage Publications, Inc.
Morahan-Martin, J. M. (1999). The relationship between loneliness and Internet use and abuse. *CyberPsychology & Behavior*, **2**, 431-439.
Morahan-Martin, J. M. & Schumacher, P. (2000). Incidence and correlates of pathological Internet use among college students. *Computers in Human Behavior,* **16**, 13-29.
Neilson/NetRatings (2007). U.S. average web usage month of May 2007 home panel. Retrieved June 20, 2007 from http://www.netratings.com/reports.jsp?section=pub_reports &report=usage&period=monthly&panel_type=2
Oravec, J. A. (2000). Internet and computer technology hazards: Perspectives for family counseling. *British Journal of Guidance & Counseling*, **28**, 309-324.
Parks, M. R., & Floyd, K. (1996). Making friends in cyberspace. *Journal of Communication,* **46**, 80-97.
Peele, S., & Brodsky, A. (1991). *The Truth About Addiction and Recovery.* New York, NY: Simon & Schuster.
Pike, R., (1999). *Log on, tune in, drop out.* Retrieved January 10, 2002 from http://abcnews.go.com/sections/living/DailyNews/netaddiciton032699.html
Pocius, K. E. (1991). Personality factors in human-computer interaction: A review of the literature. *Computers in Human Behavior*, **7**, 103-135.
Pratarelli, M. E., Browne, B. L., & Johnson, K. (1999). The bits and bytes of computer/Internet addiction: A factor analysis approach. *Behavior Research Methods, Instruments, & Computers*, **31**, 305-314.
Scherer, K. (1997). College life on-line: Healthy and unhealthy Internet use. *Journal of College Student Development,* **38**, 655-665.
Search Engines. (1999, July 30). *Entertainment Weekly,* **496**, 81.
Shotton, M. (1989). *Computer Addiction?* New York, NY: Taylor & Francis, Inc.
Stanton, M. D., & Heath, A. W. (1997). Family and marital therapy. In J. Lowinson, P., Ruiz, R. Millman, and J. Langrod (Eds.), *Substance Abuse: A comprehensive textbook, third edition.* (pp. 448-454). Baltimore, MD: Williams & Wilkins.
Stern, S. E. (1999). Addiction to technologies: A social psychological perspective of Internet addiction. *CyberPsychology & Behavior*, **2**, 419-424.
Suler, J. (1996a). *Computer and cyberspace addiction.* Retrieved January 9, 2002, from http://www1.rider.edu/~suler/psycyber/cybaddict.html
Suler, J. (1996b). *Why is this thing eating my life? Computer and cyberspace addiction at the "Palace."* Retrieved January 9, 2002 from http://www1.rider.edu/~suler/psycyber/ cybaddict.html
Treuer, T., Fabian, Z., & Furedi, J. (2001). Internet addiction associated with features of impulse control disorder: Is it a real psychiatric disorder. *Journal of Affective Disorders*, **66**, 283.

Turkle, S. (1996). Parallel lives: Working on identity in virtual space. In D. Grodin, & T. R. Lindlof (Eds.), *Constructing the self in a mediated world. Inquires in social construction.* Thousand Oaks, CA: Sage Publications, Inc.

Wang, W. (2001). Internet dependency and psychosocial maturity among college students. *International Journal of Human-Computer Studies*, **55**, 919-938.

Walther, J. B., & Reid, L. D. (2000). Understanding the allure of the Internet. *Chronicle of Higher Education,* B4-B5.

Winn, M. (1985). *The Plug-In Drug. New York*, N.Y.: Viking Penguin Inc.

Xuanhui, L. & Gonggu, Y. (2001). Internet addiction disorder, online behavior, and personality. *Chinese Mental Health Journal*, **15**, 281-283.

Young, K. S. (1995). *Internet addiction: Symptoms, evaluation, and treatment.* Retrieved January 9, 2002, from http://www.netaddiction.com/articles/symptoms.html

Young, K. S. (1996b). *Internet addiction: The emergence of a new clinical disorder.* Retrieved January 9, 2002, from http://www.netaddiction.com/articles/newdisorder.html

Young, K. S. (1997). *What makes the Internet addictive: Potential explanations for pathological Internet use.* Retrieved October 25, 2001, from http://www.netaddiction.com/articles/hatbitforming.html

Young, K. S. (1998a). *The center for on-line addiction - Frequently asked questions.* Retrieved January 9, 2002, from http://www.netaddiction.com/resources/faq.html

Young, K. S. (1998b). *Caught in the Net.* New York, NY: John Wiley & Sons, Inc.

Young, K. S., Pistner, M., & O'Mara, J. (1999*). Cyber disorders: The mental health concern for the new millennium*. CyberPsychology & Behavior, 2, 475-479.

In: Computer Science Research Trends
Editor: Casey B. Yarnall, pp. 71-92
ISBN 978-1-60021-518-6

Chapter 3

WHY EINSTEIN'S RELATIVITY IS RELEVANT TO QUANTUM COMPUTATION

A. C. Manoharan[*]
California State University Stanislaus, Turlock, CA 95382 USA

Abstract

When Feynman introduced his version of quantum computation (QC), it was based on non-relativistic quantum mechanics. But Einstein's special relativity as well as quantum theory, were well established experimentally as the two great physics revolutions of the twentieth century. In fact the theory of light and electrons (quantum electrodynamics (QED)), has led to quantum field theory, which is a logical edifice built on relativity and quantum mechanics.

Because the subject of relativistic quantum field theory (QFT) contains all of non-relativistic quantum mechanics, we expect quantum field computation (QFC) to contain (non-relativistic) quantum computation (QC).

By looking at quantum computation with relativity, many new approaches to physics and computation become practically possible. Some of the limitations of Turing computation are also overcome.

In this chapter we discuss practically accomplished exact computation over a complex continuum instead of over the integers, symbolic and analog computation, qubits with arbitrary spin, unlimited numbers of qubits and results regarding computational complexity classes which bear on the famous P versus NP problem. The remarkable discovery by Agrawal et al that the problem PRIMES belongs to P, significantly changes notions of what could be called "strong" or "hard" computation.

We identify a basic problem in QFT, namely Wightman's computation problem for domains of holomorphy, which we call WHOLO. Inspired by the same analytic functions which are central to the famous CPT theorem of QFT, it is possible to obtain a computational complexity structure for QFT and shed new light on certain complexity classes for this problem WHOLO. Possible applications of the work in this chapter to anyons and the fractional quantum Hall effect (FQHE), relate to the physics of knots and braids.

Overall, relativistic quantum computation leads us to much common ground between the disciplines of physics, computer science and mathematics and provides new perspectives on further unsolved problems for the twenty first century.

[*]E-mail address: Manoharan@att.net

Keywords and phrases: quantum field computation, quantum computation, computing, relativity, holomorphic, analytic, real computation, quantum field theory, analog, symbolic, complexity classes.

1. Introduction

Feynman believed [39] that his greatest research contributions were in the area of quantum electrodynamics (QED). QED is a relativistic theory of photons and electrons and is a discipline contained within a wider subject of quantum field theory. In later life Feynman, with others before him, originated a fertile new subject of quantum computation (QC). It would be nice to relate these two areas of research, i.e. quantum computation and quantum field theory computation (quantum field computation (QFC)), in directions of his main interests. It is possible to attack some of these complicated problems even now, as this chapter addresses. New results are obtained. There is a further motivation, since people are now trying to relate Feynman's space-time path integrals [21, 22] to computational methods in quantum field theory. Our approach to computation of quantum transition amplitudes is motivated through the analytic functions [42] which are the basis for the famous CPT theorem of Pauli, Lüders and Jost.

The two great physical theories of the twentieth century were *quantum theory* and *relativity*, both of which generalize classical Newtonian mechanics. Quantum mechanics and classical mechanics are special limiting cases of quantum field theory. By taking the limit as the velocity of light $c \to \infty$ we expect to get non-relativistic quantum mechanics. The limit as Planck's constant $h \to 0$ gives classical mechanics [21].

1.1. Historical Highlights of Quantum Field Theory

In 1946 the US National Academy of Sciences announced [39] the *Charles L. Meyer Nature of Light Award* for which the best researchers in the world competed. It would be for a *"comprehensive contribution to a logical, consistent theory of the interaction of charged particles with an electromagnetic field including the interaction of particles moving with high relativistic speeds"*. The prize went to C. J. Eliezer [13] who (incidentally from the Dirac school in England) submitted a beautiful essay entitled *"The Interaction of Electrons and an Electromagnetic Field"*. The Lamb shift was discovered shortly thereafter. The free electron or bound electron in an atom also interacts with the (Maxwell) electromagnetic field, which itself was the cornerstone to Einstein's special theory of relativity. Thus quantum mechanics by itself via the Dirac equation did not correctly predict small experimentally observed deviations like the Lamb shift. This necessitated evaluating radiation corrections to quantum mechanics and its calculation by Bethe and Schwinger [4], and these endeavors established remarkable successes in quantum field theory. Neither quantum theory nor relativity can be ignored. Quantum field theory is a logical and natural result of combining quantum theory and relativity.

1.2. Computers and Computation

In the same twentieth century, the mathematical theory of *computation* was developed and the *electronic computer* was invented. Gate implementation for the standard classical computer or *Turing machine* can be based on classical mechanics; in the sense that the gates, ideally in the absence of perturbations (depicted by the electrical engineering term *noise*), could even consist of perfect billiard balls, in an extreme case.

Meanwhile, we have become increasingly dependent on computing machines, and there are more models of computation. By Church's thesis [1], to state it simply, all *reasonable* models of computation are equivalent. At the present time, there appear to be three principal models of computation, which have grown largely independently. The models are, *quantum field computation (QFC)*, *real computation (RC)* and *quantum computation (QC)*. It is proposed and argued here that these three models of computation are indeed significantly related. Hopefully, from a unified point of view, there is much more to be learned about computation.

Unity of these computational models is not surprising because physicists generally believe that quantum field theory contains quantum mechanics, which in turn contains classical mechanics.

Correspondingly, we present the (quantum field computation) thesis:

A. *Quantum field computation contains quantum computation as a proper subset* .

B. *Quantum field computation involves more elaborate computational tools than quantum computation (e.g. infinite dimensional Hilbert spaces, some methods of real computation, and holomorphic functions)*.

On the other hand it might be argued that quantum methods may not be suitable for certain real computing problems. A simple argument is that mathematics is a much wider subject than physics; not all of mathematics is necessarily applicable to physics. But in a practical implementation of quantum computation, it is the physics that applies to the quantum machine. Quantum computation can take care of small errors, using appropriate error correction schemes.

At present, quantum field theory is regarded only as an asymptotically valid theory [48]. Some of the difficulties, although not so bad as in classical mechanics, are inherited from classical mechanics itself, for example, the infinite self-energy of the electron. Because of present unknowns in quantum field theory, we regard this thesis as not completely in the realm of provability. For example, problems of infinities and renormalizability extend to many areas of physics. We expect that well developed future generalizations of physics theories, which include non-abelian gauge theory, general relativity (Einstein gravitation), and perhaps supersymmetry, will replace quantum field theory in the above thesis, with additional and more elaborate computational tools brought into play.

1.3. Quantum Computation (QC)

Based on quantum theory, with others before him, Feynman proposed *quantum computation* [14]. In quantum computation, as opposed to Turing computation, qubits (quantum

[1] Needless to say, Church's thesis in any of the historically proposed forms, was justifiably never supposed to be provable, nor requiring proof.

binary digits) are used in place of classical bits. A bit could be in one of two discrete states, 0 or 1. A qubit, on the other hand, corresponds to a 2 level quantum system, like a spin $1/2$ state of an electron. We can have a complex linear superposition of wave functions (eigenstates) of a 2 level quantum system so that two complex number amplitudes (in $\mathbb{C}^2$) are involved in each qubit. Feynman hoped to exploit the quantum system itself by making it do the computation, but practically, decoherence *noise* is a serious implementation problem even with very much less than 10 qubits. Yet, considerable progress is being continually made on practical applications.

As a result of Feynman's proposal there has been an enormous amount of research, not only on quantum computation, but also on quantum cryptography. The efforts in this regard are to seek improved ways of performing computations, including a refinement of Church's thesis by Deutsch [12] to tackle quantum computation, or building new types of computing machines. It is hoped that not only exponentially faster computation will be achieved [41], but that better understanding of computational complexity will come about [3, 36].

1.4. Real Computation (RC)

In another direction, the classical discrete digital Turing computer [45] has been generalized to include the possibility of computing over the continuum [6, 5]. This generalization is called *real computation.* [2] The need for doing this is because computing over the continuum is more appropriate to the way we do analysis, physics, numerical analysis and engineering problems. Accordingly, the classic logic theory of computation was enhanced with analysis, topology and algebraic geometry.

Until recently, it was considered unthinkable to speak of computing over a continuum, for example, over the infinite number of points in the real interval $[0, 1]$, without approximating at a finite number of points. But Tarski, in a little known paper [43], proved completeness over the reals for elementary algebra and geometry. The complexity was extremely high (exponential), but Smale *et al* [6, 5] have rectified that situation. Tarski's result is in contrast to Gödel's famous theorem [37] of incompleteness of arithmetic over the integers $\mathbb{Z}$, and to Turing's theorem [45] of undecidability of the Halting problem for computation over the integers $\mathbb{Z}$.

A question was raised by Penrose [38] as to whether the Mandelbrot set was an (albeit beautiful, picturesque) example of an undecidable set (i.e. a recursively enumerable set that is not recursive). It was concluded that it was not possible to answer this question because there was no proper definition for computing over the continuum. One problem is: how does one feed a real number, consisting of an infinitely long sequence of bits, into a computing machine in finite time? A proper definition was indeed given in the work of Smale *et al* [6, 5] on real computation, and the question on the Mandelbrot set was answered in the affirmative. (The proof hinges on the fact that the Hausdorff - Besicovitch dimension of the boundary of the (2-dimensional) Mandelbrot set is indeed equal to 2.)

In fact, Tarski hoped to build a machine which would compute over the reals. But it is now possible to do some simple real computation even on a Turing machine. Our thesis on quantum field computation relies heavily, not only on the fact that quantum field theory

[2] The complex continuum as well as the real continuum can be handled.

generalizes quantum theory, but also on our actual practical examples of exactly computing over the continuum.

Real computation is a computing model that is based on classical mechanics and classical dynamical systems. But classical mechanics could also be extended to include relativity, resulting in relativistic mechanics [40].

1.5. Quantum Field Computation (QFC)

In studying atomic phenomena, classical mechanics has been replaced by quantum mechanics. Correspondingly the classical computer could be improved with a quantum computer. But we could also think of more general models of computation based on adding relativity to quantum theory to get relativistic quantum field theory, and consider appropriate quantum field computation models.

In an approach to the central computer science problem of the P (Polynomial time) versus NP (Nondeterministic Polynomial time) [37]) complexity classes, a *quantum field computer* has been proposed [15]. Under consideration were topological quantum field theories, and physical systems which contained non-Abelian gauge terms in the Lagrangian. The initial preparation of states was supposed to be consistent with *knot* types [3].

Of course, in a general situation, as in non-Abelian gauge theories, string theories (including general relativity), superstring theories, or topological field theories [50], quantum field computation would be an immensely difficult undertaking. Although it has not been possible to obtain stronger computation in this manner [16], this work has provided tools for quantum field computation.

Moreover, due to the work of Wightman on relativistic quantum field theory (incorporating Einstein's special relativity and employing analytic functions of several complex variables) many of the components for some quantum field computation are already available [42, 21]. Some additional computation methods are described in [31, 32].

In this chapter the approach is based on mathematical physics but the results also impact computer science.

In section 2 we discuss relationships between the main computation models. Next, in section 3, we consider the particular quantum field theory enhancements to the quantum computational model, that we will need. Analog and symbolic computation are related in section 4. Section 5 deals with uniformity of computation over different values of the function index and in different space-time dimensions. Section 6 discusses complexity classes and section 7 concludes with an outlook for the future. Appendix A states our definition of the complex space $\mathbb{C}^\infty$ which is used in this chapter and Appendix B recalls a theorem on maximal bounds (namely, generalizations of upper bounds) for holomorphy envelopes, in the theory of analytic functions of several complex variables for QFT.

[3]The user-friendly, interactive and animated color graphics "SnapPea" program (due to Weeks) for creating knots and studying hyperbolic 3-manifolds is available : [47, 33]

2. Relationships Between Computation Models

There is a remarkable relationship between quantum field computation and real computation. Computation over the continuum [4] appears in quantum field computation as well as in real computation. In the former, it is already possible to compute over *cells* which are actually certain chunks of the continuum space $\mathbb{C}^n$ of n (i.e. several) complex variables.

We might say this comes about because it is natural to consider a physical or quantum system in the continuum limit. In fact Isaac Newton, when studying gravitation, found it natural to consider a continuous distribution of matter to model the earth's gravitational action at external points. From continuum quantum mechanics, by combining relativity, we have quantum field theory, a system with an infinite number of degrees of freedom. The development in real computation of the Newton endomorphism method in numerical analysis follows naturally from Newton's continuum limit.

Real computation could also be regarded as a stepwise form of *analog computation* working within a continuum.

Conversely, quantum (mechanics) computation would be suspected to be a discrete finite case of quantum field computation where the number of qubits is finite, and the corresponding Hilbert vector space is a finite dimensional vector space.

At the present time, in some approaches, quantum computation proceeds as a time evolution over a finite number of discrete time intervals, whereas time must be regarded as a continuous variable. (Continuous variable quantum computation has also been done [10].) Yet, space and time are interwoven in relativity, depending on the frame of reference: thus the need to handle the problem in a covariant manner. Also, because a quantum field computation model does exist, it is important to say that quantum computation can therefore benefit by including considerations of relativity, methods of computing over the continuum, and an unbounded number of qubits (infinite dimensional [5] Hilbert space).

The important concepts for quantum computation are unitary transformations, finite superposition of states, entanglement, and quantum cryptography. Superposition is standard also in quantum field theory. Entanglement is a rather interesting form of superposition (which is of course available in quantum field theory too), with applications to quantum teleportation considerations and quantum cryptography [7, 2], and relies often on a basis of EPR (named after Einstein, Podolsky and Rosen) or Bell states. The EPR *gedanken* (thought) experiment itself, is now regarded as the first demonstration of a particularly strange form of non-local structure in quantum mechanics. At the present time we can say

[4]When we speak of *computation over the continuum*, it means a generalization, in the complex number field, of the methods of *real computation*, and should not be confused with simply the use of continuous variables instead of discrete variables in quantum mechanics. We deal with exact computations of domains of holomorphy and exact analytic extensions of domains for functions of several complex variables.

[5]Historically Hilbert came up with the space l_2 of absolutely square convergent infinite sequences. Later the space L_2 of Lebesgue square integrable functions also came into play because of the need to handle discrete variables as well as continuous variables in quantum mechanics. The transition to a countably infinite dimensional space was a departure from finite dimensional (Euclidean metric) vector spaces. Von Neumann set up quantum mechanics in Hilbert space, but Dirac's earlier work had wanted a more general space due to improper functions like the Dirac delta function. The QFT formulation of Wightman, on which we rely for our work in this chapter, uses Hilbert space and Schwartz *distributions* to take care of improper functions. There is another technique for quantum mechanics, which is in terms of Gel'fand *generalized functions* and *rigged Hilbert spaces*.

that quantum mechanics (without hidden variables) has been confirmed within experimentally available accuracies.

In the non-relativistic treatment of quantum mechanics of the atom with its orbiting electrons, concepts of angular momentum are important. These appear naturally as irreducible representations of the rotation group.

Just as the rotation group is of importance in non-relativistic quantum mechanics (with Euclidean geometry), the Lorentz group (with Minkowski geometry) is relevant to relativistic quantum mechanics. The Lorentz group contains the rotation group as a subgroup.

Thus a basic symmetry group in quantum mechanics is SU(2), the special (determinant $= 1$) unitary group of 2×2 complex matrices. This is also the universal covering group of the rotation group (real special orthogonal group) SO(3) in 3-dimensional space. (Of course SU(2) is only a basic group out of which other symmetries are built up (using tensor products) in quantum mechanics. For example, in the case of a small number n of entangled qubits, mathematical properties, involving Lie groups and Lie algebras, in $\otimes_1^n SU(2)$ appear to be relevant [28]. A satisfactory mathematical understanding of the entanglement of many states is yet an unsolved problem.

We would also like to point out that combining of symmetry groups occurs also in the example of the *Standard Model of Elementary Particle Physics* [6] , based on the gauge group $SU(3) \otimes SU(2) \otimes U(1)$ [48, 23, 46]. This model of elementary particles might appear to be esthetically ugly, but is a great success based on experimental facts, and is the best we have at present.

SU(2) is a proper subgroup of SL(2,$\mathbb{C}$), the universal covering group of the Lorentz group, which is the symmetry group for relativity in the usual 1-time and 3-space dimensions. Hence SL(2,$\mathbb{C}$) is the (basic) group appropriate for the quantum field computation model we use here, in this chapter, but not necessarily for future models.

Consider, for example, the EPR states. One particular EPR state, based on electron spins , can be written as

$$\{|01\rangle - |10\rangle\}/\sqrt{2},$$

or equivalently as

$$\{|\downarrow\uparrow\rangle - |\uparrow\downarrow\rangle\}/\sqrt{2},$$

where, in the usual description, the first qubit refers to Alice and the second to Bob. They prepared the entangled state, perhaps on Earth when they were together, and now Bob could be in the Alpha Centauri system, at a space-like separation from Alice on Earth. This is simply the singlet state for adding two spins of $1/2$, where we have a simultaneous eigenstate of the total spin angular momentum $S = 0$, and the total z-component of spin $S_z = 0$.

So what is happening here is that we have two qubits, each of which is represented in a 2-dimensional vector space over $\mathbb{C}$, and then a linear superposition of tensor products of the two qubits in the 4-dimensional [7] tensor product space. This superposition cannot

[6]The symmetries for elementary particle fields, namely colored quarks, leptons, vector bosons, gluons and photons (less of course the graviton) are represented here, thus combining *quantum chromodynamics* (QCD) and the Weinberg Salam *electroweak theory*.

[7]Due to normalization of state vectors in quantum mechanics, and choosing an overall phase factor, the complex dimension decreases by 1 each case.

in this simple example, nor in general, always be expressed as a tensor product of any two qubits i.e. the qubits are said to be *entangled*. Hence we can proceed to define entanglement states for n qubits, or n quantum systems, and also frame the definition in terms of density matrices. (It is possible also to have entangled states for photons, which can have horizontal or vertical polarization. Entanglement produces quantum interference between photons.)

Addition of angular momentum of spins $1/2$ appears here as $D^{1/2} \times D^{1/2} = D^1 + D^0$, in terms of decomposition of representations of the rotation group in 3- dimensional space. In quantum field computation, this group is enlarged to the group SL(2, $\mathbb{C}$), which covers the restricted (proper, orthochronous) Lorentz group. In general, one can build up from irreducible representations $D^{(j/2,k/2)}$ of SL(2,$\mathbb{C}$).

The concept of electron spin $1/2$ is added on to (non-relativistic) quantum computation in an *ad hoc* fashion. But Dirac showed that electron spin naturally follows from considerations of relativity, and the requirement of first order differential equations [4] [8]. Entanglement of quantum states is also applicable to the relativistic theory, i.e. to quantum field theory. Indeed, experiments verify that quantum rather than classical field theory gives the correct results [29, 51]. Very recently [17] it has been shown that relativistic quantum entanglement is a most interesting subject. Spin and momentum entanglement are not separately invariant and become mixed when viewed by a moving observer. Much earlier [9], it was shown that new issues would be realized when considering relativistic massive particles in the EPR-Bohm gedanken experiment.

Quantum entanglement can be compared with *topological entanglement* [24]. With the analytic function approach studied in this chapter, there is also another type of entanglement, namely, *analytic combinatorial entanglement* [32]. The diagrams exhibited in this cited reference illustrate this type of entanglement.

3. Field Theory Enhancements to Quantum Computation

Quantum field theory not only includes all of quantum mechanics, and classical mechanics, but much more in the form of well-known results. Examples are, discrete anti-unitary symmetries, namely, CPT invariance; also the well-known spin statistics connection [42]. Our purpose here is to exploit results that enhance quantum computation, through working with a relativistic quantum field theory model.

Non-relativistic quantum mechanics is not complete because radiative corrections have to be made to it, using field theory. In dealing with a system corresponding to an infinite number of degrees of freedom, it is well known historically that formulations of quantum field theory like perturbation theory lead to infinities resulting in the need for renormalization. Nevertheless, quantum electrodynamics has turned out to be "the most accurate theory known to man" [9]. Dirac, Schwinger and Feynman are some of the principal contributors to quantum electrodynamics (the spectacular history of which is related in [39]) and hence to quantum field theory [48]. Relativistic covariance is of paramount importance in correctly performing the renormalization process.

[8]Einstein was so impressed with this achievement that he referred to Dirac as "the greatest genius of the twentieth century".

[9]This statement is attributed to Feynman.

If there is some way we can avoid approximations due to series expansions of perturbation theory, and also avoid renormalization problems, at least up to our point of departure of computational enhancements, we should do so. Fortunately we can achieve this by working within the Wightman formulation [42, 21] of quantum field theory. We are dealing with fields in the Heisenberg picture without using perturbation theory nor any particular time frame related Hamiltonians. We recall, using Dirac's quantum terminology, that in the Heisenberg picture (in contrast to the Schrödinger picture) the quantum state vectors (bras and kets) are stationary (do not vary with time) while the quantum field operators carry the full interaction. Heisenberg discovered quantum mechanics, in a form which was called matrix mechanics, and the Schrödinger equation (which is used often in quantum computation) came later. Dirac related these apparently different versions of quantum mechanics through his *transformation theory*, so that there is either a Heisenberg picture or an alternate Schrödinger picture for viewing quantum mechanics. The Heisenberg picture is preferable in relativistic quantum mechanics because time is not separated from space nor treated in a preferred manner as it is in the Schrödinger picture.

The theory is in terms of analytic functions (Wightman functions) of several complex variables. These functions arise from their boundary values which are vacuum expectation values (in Dirac's *bra - ket* notation) of the form

$$\mathcal{W}_m(x_1, x_2, \ldots x_m) = \langle \Omega | \phi^{(1)}(x_1)\phi^{(2)}(x_2)\ldots\phi^{(m)}(x_m)|\Omega\rangle \tag{1}$$

of products of m quantum field operators ϕ in a separable [10] Hilbert space. $|\Omega\rangle$ denotes the unique vacuum state. These transition amplitudes $\mathcal{W}_m$ are called Wightman distributions. They are boundary values of analytic functions called Wightman functions, denoted by $W_m(z_1, z_2, \ldots z_m)$ where each x is the real part of the corresponding z, i.e. $x_i = \Re z_i, i = 1, 2, \ldots m$. We summarize the physical foundations for this in the next subsection.

Wightman reconstructs quantum fields uniquely from these analytic functions. This is called the *reconstruction theorem*.

3.1. Physical Requirements for Relativistic QFT

We recall some basics of the known and solid mathematical physics foundation [42, 21], due to Wightman *et al*, for what we need here.

The space-time metric (with no gravity) is in terms of a diagonal matrix $G = [g_{\mu\nu}]$ with entries $\{1, -1, \ldots -1\}$ for 1 time and $s-1$ space dimensions. The Lorentz invariant scalar product of space-time vectors x and y is $g_{\mu\nu}x^\mu y^\nu$ with Einstein summation convention understood on repeated indices. For example, in $s = 4$, Lorentz transformations can be denoted by $x' = \Lambda x$ where Λ is a 4×4 matrix satisfying $\Lambda^T G \Lambda = G$. General s is treated in [21].

The Poincaré group, whose elements are of the form (Λ, a), extends the Lorentz group, with space-time translations a. For $s = 4$ the restricted (proper, i.e. determinant $= 1$, orthochronous) Lorentz group is (universally) covered $2 \rightarrow 1$ by the $SL(2, \mathbb{C})$) group which consists of 2×2 complex matrices, denoted A, of determinant $= 1$. The image of the covering homomorphism is denoted by $\Lambda(A)$. Irreducible matrix representations of

[10] Separability corresponds to a countable infinity (at most) of dimensions.

A will be denoted by $S(A)$. Hence [42] the standard spinor representations $D^{(j/2,k/2)}$ of SL(2,$\mathbb{C}$) mentioned in Sec.2 are obtained. The Poincaré like group, called the *inhomogeneous* SL(2,$\mathbb{C}$) *group*, is the SL(2,$\mathbb{C}$) group together with translations a, and its elements can be denoted by (A, a).

The basic physical requirements [42] are the relativistic transformation law for states, spectral conditions, the transformation laws for fields, and microcausality.

States transform according to: $|\Psi'\rangle = U(A,a)|\Psi\rangle$ where $U(A,a)$ denotes a continuous unitary representation of the inhomogeneous SL(2,$\mathbb{C}$) group; the vacuum state exists and is invariant up a constant phase factor.

The spectral conditions are: The mass spectrum is assumed to be reasonable in the sense that momentum vectors p^μ lie in the open forward light cone, with time component $p^0 > 0$, except for the unique vacuum state having $p = 0$. (The electromagnetic and neutrino fields are supposed to be treated with a small positive mass epsilon, with zero limit taken later.)

The field operators, whose components are ϕ_α, transform according to appropriate unitary spin representations of the inhomogeneous $SL(2,\mathbb{C})$ group, for 3+1 space-time dimensions; and generally in s-dimensional space-time the field operators transform as spinors in s-dimensions.

Thus $U\phi_\alpha^{(i)}(x)U^{-1} = S_{\alpha\beta}^{(i)}(A^{-1})\phi_\beta^{(i)}(x')$ where U abbreviates $U(A,a)$, $x' = Ax + a$ and (i) distinguishes field types, which are not regarded as indices and over which there is no summation.

Because of translational invariance, the Wightman distributions are distributions in the set of difference (vector) coordinates:

$$\mathcal{W}_m(x_1, x_2, \ldots x_m) = \mathbf{W}_{m-1}(\xi_1, \xi_2, \ldots \xi_{m-1}) \tag{2}$$

where $\xi_i = x_i - x_{i+1}, i = 1, 2, \ldots m-1$.

It helps not to factor out (i.e. not to separate) the translational invariance; instead, we can use all m vector coordinates, rather than the $m - 1$ difference coordinates. Thus we introduce the complex space-time vectors $z_i, i = 1, 2, \ldots z_m$ such that $\Re z_i = x_i$ and $-\Im(z_i - z_{i+1})$ lie in the open forward light cone, V_+. Then because of the spectral conditions, the Wightman distributions $\mathcal{W}_m$ in (1) are boundary values of Wightman functions W_m as all $-\Im(z_i - z_{i+1}) \to 0+$.

Since the $\Re z$ are unrestricted and $\Im z$ are restricted, this domain for

$$(z_1, z_2, \ldots z_m) \tag{3}$$

is called a *tube domain*, namely $\mathcal{T}_m$.

Because these analytic functions are fundamental to the theory, one is led to computations of holomorphy domains for these functions over the space of several complex variables, $\mathbb{C}^n$. (The mathematical foundations for time-ordered and retarded transition amplitude functions are not as well established as for the vacuum expectation values at the present time.)

By the deep Hall-Wightman theorem the functions W_m, which are initially holomorphic in the tube domains $\mathcal{T}_m$, can be analytically continued into what are called the *extended tube domains* $\mathcal{T}'_m$. Thus $\mathcal{T}'_m$ is obtained by applying all proper complex Lorentz transformations to the vector complex variables in the tube domain $\mathcal{T}_m$. (Extended tubes are not tubes.) We note that the complex Lorentz group in s dimensions is just a physical view of the same complex orthogonal group in s dimensions.

We will call these extended tube domains $\mathcal{T}'_m$, *primitive domains of holomorphy*, because they have been shown in the literature, in different ways for different m, to be also natural domains of holomorphy. The domain boundaries are hypersurfaces which have been completely classifiied for all orders m of the W functions.

The primitive domains of holomorphy are basic to the proof of the CPT theorem [42]. The reason is that whereas there are no real points in the tube domains (because of the way tubes were defined), real points (called Jost points) do in fact exist in the extended tube domains. Assuming only what is called *weak local commutativity* in a real neighborhood of a Jost point, we have the consequence of CPT invariance [42].

3.2. The Problem WHOLO

With emphasis on the computational aspects, we will denote by WHOLO the (Wightman) problem for computing domains of holomorphy for W_m, and we split the problem into a few different parts which we need in this chapter:

A. First characterize the extended tube domains in suitable ways, such as finding their boundaries, which are in the form of hypersurfaces; see Sec. 4.

B. Next one uses microcausality, and analytically continues W_m into the union of permuted extended tube domains, i.e. find new boundaries; see Sec. 4.1.

C. Finally one tries to find the *envelope of holomorphy* of the union of permuted extended tube domains, i.e. find the furthermost boundaries possible; see Sec. 4.2.

Parts A, B, C happen to be also inter-related through values of n (the function index) and s (the space-time dimension); see Sec. 5 which addresses uniformity of computation over these values.

Thus the many complex numbers (or amplitudes) that need to be handled in quantum field computation were indeed tamed as complex variables in analytic functions, i.e. the Wightman functions.

One might ask why there is only one time dimension. It was only recently known, how to physically understand concepts like closed time-like loops in more than one time dimension [18], where the second time dimension is in a tiny loop of a Kaluza - Klein type brane universe theory. However, on non-tiny time scales, the concept of more than one time dimensions is difficult to reconcile with causality and we will restrict ourselves here to the conventional single dimension in time [20].

We use a general space-time dimension s for the sake of considering *uniformity* of computation (to approach *universality* of computation), for what appear to be computational problems in their own right; whereas certain values of s, such as $0, 1, 2, 3, 4, 5, 10, 11$ and 26 have turned out to be more appropriate for purely physics problems. (0 and 1 are very special cases which we do not need).

We will now abbreviate the notation by suppressing the explicit spinor indices: Let the (m-point) Wightman function, which has m complex vector variables, each vector being of length s, be denoted by $W(n; z)$ where z denotes the set of n complex s dimensional vector variables lumped together. Thus $n = sm$ where $s \geq 2$ is the space-time dimension; space-time will consist of 1-time and $(s-1)$-space dimensions. m is also called the function order (i.e. the number of fields in the vacuum expectation value in Eq.(1)), and n will be called the function index (the total number of complex variables).

Computation over $\mathbb{C}^n$ is common also in real computation. But, in the Wightman model, we could possibly have a deeper understanding of computation because of the use of holomorphic functions (over $\mathbb{C}^n$) of several complex variables. Not only the physics of quantum theory and special relativity, but also microcausality is utilized.

4. Analog Computation and Symbolic Computation

It is interesting that the strengths of analog and symbolic computation come into play as quantum field computation supplements and enhances quantum computation. We think that, it is sometimes debatable as to what is symbolic or analog computation when it comes to computing over the continuum. In real computation there seems to be a subtle re-emergence of the old analog computer in a new and powerful form. This new form is effectively digitally clamped [11] to avoid noise problems (such as voltage drifts in potentiometers) which plagued the old analog computer.

When $s = 2$, i.e. in 1-dimensional space and 1-dimensional time, deterministic exact analog computation [32] (computation over *cells* in the continuum of $\mathbb{C}^n$) is used to obtain what are called primitive extended tube domains of holomorphy for $W(n; z)$. The computation can be done with essentially reversible logic, as a *Horn clause satisfiability* problem (HORNSAT), and with simulation on a Turing machine. But HORNSAT is in the complexity class P (polynomial time) [37]. This is now a deterministic problem of complexity P, but (in a further problem) also implies non-deterministic polynomial time computation, in the complexity class NP, as discussed below, in Sec. 4.2.

We note a couple of points in this connection. First, we rely here on the *soundness theorem* and the converse theorem, namely, Gödel's *theorem of completeness of first order predicate calculus* [37]. Secondly, reversibility of computation is an asset because information content is maximized, or equivalently, the entropy increase is minimized.

Just as the classical computer, *Turing machine*, computes over $\mathbb{Z}$ or (up to polynomial time) equivalently over $\mathbb{Z}_2$ (the classical bit representation of numbers), we now have what can be called a *complex Turing machine*, in fact, a *severally complex Turing machine*.

The primitive extended tube domains have been fully classified. They are bounded by *analytic hypersurfaces*, namely several Riemann cuts, and other analytic hypersurfaces of types denoted by S, ..., F, which too play a role. These domains are in the form of *semi-algebraic sets* in the language used in real computation. Since the computation is symbolic, it is also exact [12], which is important in handling holomorphic functions and their domains of analyticity.

Because of Lorentz invariance properties of the physics involved, the domains have a structure referred to as *Lorentz complex projective spaces*. (These Lorentz complex spaces are different, but physical, "non-Euclidean" views of complex projective spaces which are well known in mathematics.) Related to this invariance are certain continuum *cells* over

[11] We recall that within the electronics of a digital computer, for example in *transistor transistor logic* (TTL), there is a *voltage gap* between logic 0 and logic 1 levels, which is like a no-man's land, guarantying safety from errors of confusing the two logic levels.

[12] Thus we are not computing approximately, up to a given $\epsilon > 0$, nor using probabilistic methods.

which the computation occurs. Thus this computation is also like analog computation which would otherwise be regarded as impossible to do exactly.

In this simple case, it is possible to think that (suitably encoded) pieces or whole continuous group orbits are being fed into the Turing machine. Hopefully there will be more possibilities like this in the future.

4.1. Analytic Extensions

In relativistic quantum field theory it is possible to implement the physical requirement of microcausality. There exists quantum microcausality i.e field operators commute or anti-commute at space-like separations: $[\phi_\alpha(x), \phi_\alpha(y)]_\mp = 0$, for $(x-y)^2 < 0$, where the $-$ and $+$ signs stand for commutation and anti-commutation respectively. The famous theorem on the connection of spin and statistics states that we have commutation for Boson fields and anti-commutation for Fermion fields [42].

Together with the consequence of permutation invariance of the domains, the so-called edge-of-the-wedge theorem provides enlargements of the original primitive domains of analyticity into analyticity in unions of permuted primitive domains.

Mapping these union domains creates some Boolean satisfiability problems. In fact, the novel methods of computation raise interesting issues of computability and complexity. Domains of analyticity are subject to a different type of entanglement which we can call *analytic combinatorial entanglement* [32]. The several complex variable analyticity domain diagrams exhibited in this reference illustrate this type of entanglement.

4.2. Non-Deterministic Holomorphic Extensions

By the nature of analytic domains in more than one complex variable, it is in general possible to further enlarge these domains (unions of permuted extended tubes) towards the maximal enlarged domains called *envelopes of holomorphy*.

The reasons are as follows: If we have a domain of analyticity for functions of one complex variable, there is always a function which is analytic inside the domain but is singular everywhere on the boundary of the domain, and so cannot be continued outside the domain. Thus every analyticity domain in $\mathbb{C}^1$, i.e. in one complex variable, is a *natural domain of holomorphy*. But for more than one complex variable, this is not true. We can have domains of analyticity in $\mathbb{C}^n$ for $n > 2$, for which every function analytic in the domain can be analytically continued beyond the domain. This is the situation for the union of permuted extended tubes; it is not a natural domain of holomorphy.

To make these analytic extensions of the union of permuted extended tube domains, one needs to identify points at the boundaries of the domains which cannot be points of singularity for any function analytic in the domain. This was first done by Källén and Wightman [26]. These points are found by looking at boundaries of the union of permuted extended tubes which are in the nature of hypersurfaces, i.e. semi-algebraic sets in the language of real computation. The process is non-deterministic because there is a guessing step at the beginning, as to what the analytic extension of the domain could be, and then one makes a deterministic verification of the guess. After the guessing step, the verification is by deterministic processes mentioned above (at the beginning of Sec. 4). Historically, this method was used by Källén and Wightman in computation, for the first time, of the holomorphy envelope [26] for $m = 3$.

Because HORNSAT is in P, [37], this results in an NP type problem, i.e. guessing the result and verifying in polynomial time [13]. So this part of the problem (for $s = 2$) is in the complexity class NP. (We note also that HORNSAT is P-complete.)

Built-in permutation invariance (because we have analyticity in the union of permuted extended tubes) has considerable power just as $n!$ rapidly dominates over 2^n for large n. In applying local commutativity, it might appear that we have to generate permutations of m objects; in fact, no algorithm is known to do this in polynomial time. But this is not a problem for us. Because of the power of non-deterministic computation [37], we are allowed to guess a candidate for a permutation; and then we can verify, in polynomial time, whether the guess is indeed a permutation, throwing out the candidate in case it is not a permutation.

5. Uniformity of Computation

Uniformity in the direction of universal computation has been discussed [5], in different contexts, including numerical analysis. We do indeed have certain types of uniformity here.

First we note that the computation is independent of any particular form of Lagrangian or dynamics, and is uniform in n, qualifying for a universal quantum machine over $\mathbb{C}^\infty$ which allows for an infinite number of complex variables [34]. The space $\mathbb{C}^\infty$ is defined in Appendix A.

5.1. Function Index Uniformity

When the logic program (mentioned in Sec.4) runs for $s = 2$, dynamic memory allocation is used through the operating system. Because n can be input as a variable, only part of the whole memory management cost is outside the program. The program itself is independent of $n = sm$ and therefore is uniform in n, which is unbounded above. We can call this *function index uniformity in* n^∞.

5.2. Space-Time Dimension Uniformity

In addition, there is uniformity in the dimension $s \geq 2$ of space-time, in the following manner, which is based on the theorem in Appendix B. Given a dimension $s \geq 2$ of space-time, looking at the semi-algebraic sets defining the primitive extended tube domains of holomorphy (with hypersurface boundaries) and at function orders, m, there are three different classes of orders. These classes comprise, a) lower order W functions, b) intermediate order W functions, and c) high order W functions [34]. Extended tube domains for all high order W functions have the same complicacy. For a) we have $m \leq s + 1$, and for c), $m > s(s-1)/2 + 2$. The remaining cases lie in class b). For example, there is no class b) for $s = 2$ (i.e. class b) is empty), the most complicated primitive domain being for the

[13] The method is one of exactly removing continuum chunks of removable singularities for analytic functions of several complex variables.

3-point function. If $s = 3$, then $m = 5$ is the only case in class b). When $s = 4$, we have in class b), the cases, $m = 6, 7$ and 8.

Since $s \geq 2$ is unbounded above, we can call this *space-time dimension uniformity in* s^{∞}.

5.3. Uniformity of WHOLO

We recall that although deterministic complexity classes are closed under complements, the non-deterministic complexity class NP is not necessarily closed under complements. In fact, it is known [37] that the complexity class P is a subset of both complexity classes co-NP and NP. Also the problem PRIMES ("given an integer, is it a prime?") belongs to both complexity classes co-NP and NP. But, until recently [19] it was not known whether PRIMES belongs to the complexity class P i.e. no polynomial time algorithm was known for PRIMES.

A most remarkable discovery has now been made [1], that the problem PRIMES belongs to P. (We take the given integer n, represented as a binary or decimal expansion with length of l digits, so that l can be regarded also as $O(\log n)$. Then the algorithm executes in a time which is a polynomial in l.)

These computer scientists, of whom two of them here (and two more in earlier work) were only undergraduates, were undeterred by centuries of obstacles encountered by expert number theorists, together with the greatest mathematical minds such as Euler, Gauss, Riemann and Ramanujan; and came up with an elegant polynomial time algorithm for PRIMES. This goes to show that a) there might be more wonderful algorithms to be discovered within the area of the P versus NP problem, and b) that if a problem belongs to P, it does not necessarily follow that the problem is trivial.

Moreover, through the prime number theory that is involved, the P versus NP problem [14] is also tied up with the Riemann Conjecture [15]. The P versus NP problem and the Riemann Conjecture (also known as "Hypothesis") are two of the greatest unsolved problems and for which the Clay Mathematical Institute offers a million dollars "Millennium" award for a solution of each [8].

At the present time, even if it can be known in polynomial time, that any given integer n is prime, or composite, there is no known polynomial time algorithm for factoring a composite number. This lack of knowledge (on factorization of large composite integers) is the basis for the success of trapdoor cipher type encryption algorithms like RSA, on which the world relies for banking and other security matters. But if we had a quantum computer (which we do not yet) then Shor's factoring algorithm [41] will factor a composite integer; the answer to the problem comes out in the form of a probability, as output of the quantum computer.

[14] By definition of NP, we have P $\subseteq$NP; so the question is: Is it true that P = NP? It would indeed be most extraordinary if this were to be true; most people think it is not so. If it were true that P = NP, then the hardest problems in NP, i.e. the NP-*complete* problems, would be solvable in polynomial time. Furthermore, all remaining 6 of the, 7 in all, million dollar Millennium award problems could become tractable, as pointed out by Cook [8].

[15] The Riemann Conjecture states that the non-trivial zeroes of the Riemann zeta function $\zeta(s)$ all have real part equal to 1/2. This has been verified up to billions of zeros, but there are known to be an infinite number of non-trivial zeros. Nevertheless it is generally believed that the Riemann conjecture is true.

Let us consider again the Wightman problem of computing holomorphy envelopes, named WHOLO. Thus we have seen above that the problem WHOLO has uniformity in n^∞ and s^∞.

The holomorphy envelopes for different orders m of Wightman functions are related; the holomorphy envelope for order m is contained in the intersection of holomorphy envelopes for lower order functions [32, 34].

For example, in $s = 2$, the 4-point function cannot be continued beyond the 2-point function Riemann cuts nor the (permuted) 3-point function Källén-Wightman domains of holomorphy.

This is a statement regarding analyticity that does not exist, and thus refers to the complements of domains of holomorphy; hence the use of the prefix *co-*. Because computations of analytic extensions of domains are non-deterministic (hence the notation *N*), we can say that we have *co-N* uniformity over s^∞, and in particular, co-NP complexity for $s = 2$.

In the case that the holomorphy domains are Schlicht (i.e. a several complex variable analog to single sheeted Riemann surfaces in one complex variable), which is the only case known at present in this quantum field model, then the domains of holomorphy under consideration [34] are closed under complements. This implies, in $s = 2$ for the relevant part of the WHOLO problem, that the succinct certificates (or polynomial witnesses) of co-NP complexity for higher order functions are contained in those for lower order functions. This result could have implications regarding general problems which are in co-NP and not in NP.

6. Discussion

We have not used the non-linear positive definiteness conditions for W- functions in Hilbert space. These conditions are required for the reconstruction theorem. On the other hand, we want to exploit the complexity conditions for the linear-program problem as computational problems in their own right.

The original problem posed [15] for a quantum field computer, was motivated by the existence of a great deal of mathematical physics relating to the case $s = 3$. In this 3-dimensional space-time, space itself is 2-dimensional, and there are a host of fruitful statistical mechanics and field theory problems in this case [21]. For example, instead of particles having to be Bosons or Fermions as in $s = 4$, we have *Anyons* [49] corresponding to braid-group statistics. There is also the fractional quantum Hall effect (FQHE), which not only has produced some of the most accurate experimental results to date, but is the fertile testing ground for new physical theories as well. In particular, Chern-Simons type gauge interaction terms in the Lagrangian [11] give more insight into field theories, including gravitation. In the future, we should expect such theories to be part of quantum field computation.

Relativistic physics for massive particles involves working on a mass hyperboloid in space-time. In the case here of 3 dimensional space-time, $s = 3$, hyperbolic geometry and 3-dimensional manifolds come into play. By Thurston's classification of 3-dimensional manifolds, most of them are hyperbolic [44]. Naturally therefore the knot problem and 3-dimensional hyperbolic manifolds studied as knot complements, show up here [25, 47, 33].)

In this connection we encounter another great unsolved problem, namely the Poincaré conjecture [16] which is also a Millennium problem [8]. The corresponding (generalized) problem was solved for 5 and higher dimensions by Smale, and for 4-dimensions by Freedman [17].

At the present time, it appears that Perelman [35] has solved this problem, but the proofs are still being verified by mathematicians. It is most interesting to note that Einstein's general relativity, namely the classical theory of gravitation enters here, in the form of Ricci tensors.

At the time of Turing, a *computer* was a human being doing calculations. In the present era, *computers* are machines on which humans are extremely dependent, not only for calculations but also for modeling natural phenomena. Quantum computers indeed have the potential of greater power than classical computers. Exploiting real computation methods and quantum field computation enhancements by invoking special relativity, gives an even deeper understanding of computational tools. In quantum cryptography, more powerful computation would mean stronger private code distribution and weaker public code methods. In the private code case, when Eve eavesdrops on the transmission of quantum information from Alice to Bob, the quantum data is disturbed so that Bob can decide it is so and discard those data items, requesting Alice to re-transmit. In the public code case, for example in the well-known RSA encryption and decoding algorithm, the code will be easier to break.

There is discrete translational invariance in quantum computation, compared to continuous translational invariance in quantum field computation. The discrete Fourier transform is of profound importance to the power of quantum computation. (See also the discussion of Lomonaco [27] regarding a continuous variable Shor algorithm.) In the early days of quantum field theory, it was usual to quantize over a finite, rather than an infinite, box. The finite box incorporates discrete translational invariance and allows discrete Fourier transforms. In this chapter, we go further by using generalizations of *real computation* in the form of exact continuous complex computation.

Since, in quantum field theory, particles with arbitrary spins can be annihilated and created, we can talk about *qubits, qutrits, ququads, ...*, and in general, about *quspinors*.

Relying on a fruitful set of models, we have related what appeared to be different models of quantum and classical computation based on relativistic and non-relativistic quantum mechanics and classical mechanics. Practically established exact deterministic and non-deterministic computation over continuous domains appear naturally. Furthermore there is uniformity in computation over, unbounded above, or arbitrarily high index n of $W(n; z)$ and arbitrarily high dimension s of space-time.

It is good to break up a complex problem into several parts and analyze the complexity of each part separately. Three parts of the problem WHOLO have been identified above. (There is a fourth part, namely, the representation of unions of domains, which has been possible to do only by human interaction.) In the case $s = 2$ the first part is in the complexity class P (and is P-complete), the second in NP, and the third in co-NP.

[16]The Poincaré conjecture states that every simply connected closed (meaning, in this situation, compact and without boundary) 3-dimensional manifold is homeomorphic to a 3-sphere.

[17]See the problem statement by J. Milnor [8]. If d denotes the dimension of the manifold, then all manifolds have been classified for $d = 2$, the problem is solved for all $d \geq 4$, but is most difficult for $d = 3$

Identification, within quantum field computation, of these methods of computation raise interesting issues of computability and complexity, and possibly could shed more light, not only on computability, but also on the description of Nature by fundamental physics theories themselves.

7. Conclusion

By *unity* between computation models we mean that the models are actually parts of a whole, higher (or broader) model of computation. Viewed from such a broader perspective it should be possible to better understand how the different parts, namely different computation models, fit together. The situation here is quite analogous to the situation in physics theories, where quantum field theory is the higher model (in this chapter), which contains quantum mechanics. Correspondingly we have quantum field computation as the higher level model which contains quantum computation.

Although some parts of the Wightman model of quantum field theory are exploited here, and in fact the only way employed up to the present of connecting up with the real computational model, these parts of the Wightman model should not be regarded as the only possible way of thinking in the future. The higher level model in physics is now quantum field theory, but this model might need to be expanded later (by including more symmetry groups such as non-abelian gauge symmetry, general relativity, topological fields, etc).

Each mathematical physics theory could possibly have some interesting, novel, computational and complexity ramifications [15]. Accordingly, within quantum field theory we have identified P versus NP consequences and certain uniformities of computation. These uniformities are helpful in thinking of universality of computation, a hopeful problem for the future.

Through Einstein's relativity, we have shown why there is unity between quantum field computation, real computation (computation over the continuum) and quantum computation. The Church Turing thesis for computation is supposed to be presently enhanced with the quantum field computation thesis we have proposed above. Thus the known ingenious methods in quantum computation, of dealing with discrete Fourier transforms, entangled states and fault-tolerant quantum error corrections could be profitably supplemented with concepts of infinite dimensional Hilbert spaces and (some) methods of computation over the continuum. Computation for the quantum field theory problem WHOLO is structured in layers, and each layer itself has a complexity structure.

From a more general standpoint we have approached, through relativistic quantum computation (QFC), common ground for the disciplines of physics, mathematics and computer science. This also gives us a, twenty first century, QFC view of three of the greatest unsolved problems of the physical sciences, namely the P vs NP problem, the Riemann hypothesis and the Poincaré conjecture.

A. The Complex Space $\mathbb{C}^\infty$.

This appendix gives a definition of notation we are using.

The complex space $\mathbb{C}^\infty$ is defined to be the infinite disjoint union $\bigsqcup_{m=1}^{\infty} \mathbb{C}^{sm}$. We have followed the type of definition used in real computation [5]. There is a certain lattice pattern in the values of n allowed in the subsequence $n = sm$. For example, since $s \geq 2, m \geq 2$, n is never a prime number. Of course $\mathbb{C}^\infty$ involves holomorphy in the variables, which is a much stronger condition than differentiability, so that the space is different from C^∞, the space of infinitely differentiable functions. Holomorphy of functions f of several (n) complex variables (z_i) can be expressed in terms of the Cauchy - Riemann conditions, namely as,

$$\frac{\partial f}{\partial \bar{z}_i}, i = 1, ...n$$

where $\bar{z}_i$ denotes the complex conjugate of z_i.

B. Relations Between Holomorphy Envelopes

This appendix states a theorem.

The holomorphy envelopes $H[D_m]$ for different orders m of Wightman functions are related in the following way.

For $0 < r < m$, and *relative to* $H[D_m]$,

$$H[D_m] \subset \bigcap_{\sigma \in \mathrm{P}_m} \{H[\sigma D_{m-r}] \times (\sigma \mathbb{C}^{sr})\},$$

where σ denotes permutations in P_m, the permutation group in the m points of the m-point W function. On the right side we have an intersection of permuted domains of holomorphy for lower order functions. This is a theorem which is referred to in [32]. In the case of *Schlicht* domains (analogous to single sheeted Riemann surfaces in $\mathbb{C}$, which is the case of functions of only one complex variable), the $\subset$ sign means set theoretic inclusion (but the concept is more subtle [30], in general, and is phrased in terms of (generalized) multi-sheeted *covering domains over* $\mathbb{C}^n$).

References

[1] Agrawal, M.; Kayal, N.; Saxena, N. (2002). PRIMES is in P. *http://www.cse.iitk.ac.in/news/primality.html*

[2] Bennett, C.H.; DiVincenzo, D. P.; Fuchs, C. A.; Mor, T.; Rains, E.; Shor, P. W.; Smolin, J. A.; Wootters, W. K. (1998). Quantum Nonlocality without Entanglement. *http://xxx.lanl.gov/archive/quant-ph/9804053*

[3] Bernstein, E.; Vazirani, U. *Siam. J. Comput.* 1997, 26, 1411-1473.

[4] Bethe, H. *Rev. Mod. Phys.* 1999, 71, No.2, S1-S5.

[5] Blum, L.; Cucker, F.; Shub, M.; Smale, S. *Complexity and Real Computation;* Springer Verlag: New York, NY, 1998.

[6] Blum, L.; Shub, M.; Smale, S. *Bul. Am. Math. Soc.* 21, 1-46 (1989).

[7] Brassard, G. (1998). Teleportation as a quantum computation. http://xxx.lanl.gov/archive/quant-ph/9605035

[8] Clay Mathematics Institute, Millennium Problems. http://claymath.org/millennium/

[9] Czachor, M.; *Phys. Rev. A* 1997, 55, 72-77.

[10] Childs A. M.; Cleve R.; Deotto E.; Farhi, E.; Gutmann S.; Spielman D. A. (2002). Exponential algorithmic speedup by quantum walk. http://xxx.lanl.gov/archive/quant-ph/0209131

[11] Deser, S.; Jackiw, R.; *Phys. Lett. B* 1999, 451, 73-76.

[12] Deutsch D. *Proc. R. Soc. Lond. A* 1985, 400, 97-117.

[13] Eliezer, C. J. *Rev. Mod. Phys.* 1947, 19, No. 3, 147-184.

[14] Feynman, R. P. *Int. J. Theor. Phys.* 1982, 21, 467-488 and *Found. Phys.* 1986, 16, 507-531.

[15] Freedman, M. H., *Proc. Natl. Acad. Sci.* 1999, 95, 98-101.

[16] Freedman, M. H.; Kitaev A.; Wang Z. *Commun. Math. Phys.* 2002, 227, 587 - 603.

[17] Gingrich, R. M.; Adami, C. *Phys. Rev. Lett.* 2002, 89, 270402.

[18] Gogberashvili, M. *Phys. Lett. B* 2000, 484, 124-128.

[19] Granville, A. *Bull. Am. Math. Soc.* 2005, 42, No. 1, 3-38.

[20] Hawking, S.; Penrose, R., *The Nature of Space and Time;* Princeton Univ. Press: Princeton NJ, 1996.

[21] Glimm, J.; Jaffe, A. *Quantum Physics, A Functional Integral Point of View, 2nd Ed.;* Springer Verlag: NY, 1987.

[22] Johnson, G. W.; Lapidus, M. L. *The Feynman Integral and Feynman's Operational Calculus;* Oxford Univ. Press.: Oxford, UK, 2002.

[23] Kaku, M. *Quantum Field Theory, a modern introduction;* Oxford Univ. Press,: Oxford, UK, 1993.

[24] Kauffman, L. H.; Lomonaco S.J. (2002). Comparing quantum entanglement and topological entanglement. http://xxx.lanl.gov/archive/quant-ph/0205137 and *New Journal of Physics* 2002, 4, 1.1-1.18, http://www.njp.org/

[25] Kauffman, L. H. *Knots and Physics;* 2nd Ed. World Scientific Publishing Co.: Singapore, 1993.

[26] Källén, G.; Wightman, A. S. *Mat. Fys. Skr. Dan. Vid. Selsk.* 1958, 1 (6), 1-58.

[27] Lomonaco, S. J.; Kauffman, L. H. (2004). A continuous variable Shor algorithm. http://xxx.lanl.gov/archive/quant-ph/0210141

[28] Lomonaco, S. J. in *Quantum Computation: A grand mathematical chanllenge for the twenty-first century and the millennium* , Lomonaco, S. J.; Ed.; *Proc. Symp. App. Math. (PSAPM)* 58; Am. Math. Soc.: Providence, RI, 2002; pp 3-65, 305-349.

[29] Mandel, L. *Rev. Mod. Phys.* 1999, 71, No.2, S274-S282.

[30] Manoharan, A. C. *J. Math. Phy.* 1967, 8, No.10, 2026-2029.

[31] Manoharan, A. C.; Manoharan, M. 1992, *Proc. Annual Computer Science Conference*, Association for Computing Machinery (ACM), 91-98.

[32] Manoharan, A. C. 1997, *Mathl. Comput. Modelling*, 26, No. 8-10, 227-254.

[33] Manoharan, A. C., SnapPea PC for Windows. http://home.att.net/~manoharan/ SnapPea/snappea.html

[34] Manoharan, A. C. (2001, 2003). The unity between quantum field computation, real computation, and quantum computation. http://xxx.lanl.gov/archive/quant-ph/0109015 and Beyond Quantum Computation and Towards Quantum Field Computation. http://xxx.lanl.gov/archive/quant-ph/0304136

[35] Morgan, J. W. *Bull. Am. Math. Soc.* 2005, 42, No. 1, 57-78.

[36] Nielsen, M. A.; Chuang, I. A. *Quantum Computation and Quantum Information;* Cambridge Univ. Press: Cambridge, UK, 2000.

[37] Papadimitriou, C. M. *Computational Complexity;* Addison-Wesley Pub. Co. Inc.: Reading, Mass, 1995.

[38] Penrose R. *The Emperor's New Mind;* Oxford Univ. Press.: Oxford, UK, 1989.

[39] Schweber, S. S. *QED and the men who made it: Dyson, Feynman, Schwinger and Tomonaga;* Princeton Univ. Press: Princeton, NJ, 1995.

[40] Shapiro, I. I. *Rev. Mod. Phys.* 1999, 71, No.2, S41-S53.

[41] Shor, P. W. *Siam. J. Comput.* 1997, 26, 1484-1509.

[42] Streater, R.F.; Wightman, A. S. *CPT Spin and Statistics and All That;* Addison-Wesley Pub. Co. Inc.: Reading, Mass,1989.

[43] Tarski, A. *A Decision Method for Elementary Algebra and Geometry;* Univ. of Calif. Press: CA, 1951.

[44] Thurston, W. *Three-dimensional Geometry and Topology;*, Vol. 1, Princeton Univ. Press: Princeton, NJ, 1997.

[45] Turing, A. M. *Proc. Lond. Math. Soc.* 1937, 42, 230-265.

[46] Veltman, M. *Facts and Mysteries of Elementary Particle Physics;* World Scientific Publishing Co.: Singapore, 2003.

[47] Weeks, J., SnapPea. http://thames.northnet.org/weeks/index/SnapPea.html

[48] Weinberg, S., *The Quantum Theory of Fields*, Vol I, II, III ; Cambridge Univ. Press: Cambridge, UK, 1995, 1996, 2000.

[49] Wilczek, F. *Phys. Rev. Lett.* 1982, 49, 957-959.

[50] Witten, E. *Commun. Math. Phys.* 1988, 121, 353-386.

[51] Zeilinger, A. *Rev. Mod. Phys.* 1999, 71, No.2, S288-S297.

In: Computer Science Research Trends
Editor: Casey B. Yarnall, pp. 93-150
ISBN: 978-1-60021-518-6

Chapter 4

SURVEY OF RELIABILITY EVALUATION TECHNIQUES IN DISTRIBUTED COMPUTING ENVIRONMENTS

Hossam Mahmoud Ahmad Fahmy*
Department of Computer Engineering and Systems Faculty of Engineering - Ain Shams. University Abdou Pacha Square – Abbassiah. Cairo - Egypt

Abstract

Studying distributed systems is a rich experience that involves many interacting hardware and software components, each component has its distinguishable characteristics and its own way of functioning and interacting. This chapter sheds light on major aspects of distributed systems and their reliability evaluation techniques. First, an insightful coverage, of all issues regarding distributed systems design and functioning, is presented. Then, a comprehensive investigation of different reliability definitions focuses on various complementary views of reliability. Subsequently, a thorough emphasis is accorded to innovative research work dealing with reliability evaluation techniques for distributed systems as a whole as well as for their hardware and software components. Some of the presented work may still need more elaboration but the issues and handling techniques they raise deserve careful follow up.

1. Introduction

This survey chapter focuses on recent innovative articles dealing with different aspects of reliability in distributed computing environments, it is not intended to be a substitute of the original work but rather a motivating insight on interesting topics and handlings distributed over the literature; some work may still need more elaboration but the raised issues deserve attention and follow up. It is intended by this chapter to get the reader involved in various definitions, terminologies, concepts and solution approaches; all required information is made available in a way that spares time which might otherwise be wasted in non directed search.

Distributed computing environments are large to the extent that they encompass several hardware and software components, while each of these components has a wide variety of

* E mail address: hossam.fahmy@ieee.org. Professor of Computer Engineering

classifications. Studies embodied in the literature either restrain to considering only the reliability of hardware systems or software systems, or widen their scope of interest to involve both hardware and software systems. Accordingly, the chapter organization is based on the research concern on the distributed systems components. Section 2 specifies the concepts and design considerations in distributed computing environments. Section 3 defines reliability from several view points, the traditional reliability definitions followed by the semantic reliability definition. Section 4 presents recent work that tackles reliability of distributed hardware systems, the choice was for a bi-criteria heuristic for scheduling data-flow graphs of operations onto parallel heterogeneous architectures, and for the *FARM* technique that increases reliability in large-scale storage systems. Section 5 is interested on work that studies reliability of distributed software systems, the Athena system is the model, it analyzes the factors related to reliability and real-time performance, collects information on the data files needed for program executions and their distributed status, and builds algorithms to evaluate the real-time performance of distributed software with reliability constraint. Section 6 is concerned with the research work that considers the reliability of distributed computing environments as a whole, more than one component are considered. Along this line, both, the grid computing system in Section 6.1, the recursive merge technique for the *BDD* in Section 6.2, and the *AHP* that evaluates the interaction between the various system components in Section 6.3, study the reliability of a distributed software system and that of the overall distributed system.

2. Distributed Computing Environments

This section presents the definitions of distributed systems, their main characteristics, and the issues that must be considered throughout their design and management processes. Distributed systems are the trend of an age, some thoughts are yet skeptically enthusiastic about them, they are not bypassed for the sake of scientific debate, a clear focus in this section brings them to light.

2.1. Concepts

There are two interpretive definitions for a *distributed system*:

- It is a system in which hardware and software components located at networked computers communicate and coordinate their actions only by message passing [1].
- It is a collection of independent computers that appear to its users as a single coherent system [2].

From these definitions, it is to be noticed that distributed systems provide global sharing of computational resources; in such environment, autonomous computers cooperate to solve a large problem or facilitate parallel execution of separate tasks. The network they use is always hidden from the user, it always look the same wherever the user is working. A network in distributed computing environment may vary from a *LAN* to a *WAN*, from an

Intranet to many Intranets linked by the Internet, from a network with wire links to a fully wireless network.

With distributed systems the notion of ubiquitous computing as signifying anytime/anyplace computing becomes meaningful. *Ubiquitous computing* integrates computation into the environment, rather than having computers as distinct objects. Another term for ubiquitous computing is *pervasive computing*. Promoters of this idea hope that embedding computation into the environment would enable people to move around and interact with computers more naturally than they currently do. One of the goals of ubiquitous computing is to enable devices to sense changes in their environment and to automatically adapt and act based on these changes and on user needs and preferences. Some simple examples of this type of behavior include GPS-equipped automobiles that give interactive driving directions and *Radio Frequency Identification (*RFID*)* store checkout systems. Ubiquitous computing is held by some to be the third wave of computing. The first wave was many people per computer, a mainframe. The second wave was one person per computer, a personal computer. The third wave will be many computers per person. Three key technical issues will accordingly arise: power consumption, user interface, and wireless connectivity. The idea of ubiquitous computing as invisible computation was first articulated by Mark Weiser [3] in 1988 at the Computer Science Lab at Xerox PARC [4].

Major applications rely on distributed systems, among them the following may be cited:

- Distributed file systems that allow users to create, read, write and delete files.
- Distributed database systems that are divided into separate cooperating databases where users will have access to local and remote data whilst using the database system.
- Distributed real-time systems like e-payments, real time process control and system monitoring.
- Distributed multimedia systems that can be used for network transmission of audio and video files.
- Distributed decision support systems to improve the human decision-making process. They also support several decision-markers with access to information from various sources.

Thus, several key characteristics of distributed systems may be observed:

- *Concurrency*, which means concurrent program execution and resource access. Protocols are implemented to coordinate between these concurrently acting programs.
- *No global clock*, this is due to the nature of distributed systems where each computer has its own physical clock. The deviation between these clocks makes it hard to accurately timestamp the events that occur on different nodes in the order they took place, which toughens finding the state of distributed programs as they execute and may jeopardize their correct execution on different nodes concurrently. The deviation between physical clocks is caused by two main factors: clock skew resulting from the instantaneous difference between the readings of any two clocks, and clock drift due

to the fact that clocks account time at different rates. Many synchronization algorithms are devised to overcome the lack of a global clock.

- *Independent failures*, each component of the system can fail independently, leaving the others still running. But it is essential that a distributed computing environment can answer questions such as: how to tell if the network has failed or become unusually slow? how to know if a remote server crashed immediately?

2.2. Design Issues

Multiple issues arise while ensuring that a distributed system properly connects all involved users as elaborated in the coming subsections [1],[2]. Before going through the details, [5] reminds that research is imagination, future exploration, that is what it exactly tries when presenting the challenges to be expected when distributed systems massively extend with the excessive use of embedded systems.

2.2.1. Heterogeneity

Heterogeneity spans all the distributed system components. Networks, computer hardware, operating systems and programming languages are widely different:

a)*Networks*, they are diverse to the degree that they are categorized according to many criteria, by range, by functional relationship, by network topology, and by specialized functions. Categorizations by range and by functional relationship are presented to emphasize such diversity. More on networks can be intensively found in [6].

- **Categorization by range:**
    - *Personal Area Network (PAN)*, a computer network used for communication among computer devices (including telephones and personal digital assistants) close to a person. The devices may or may not belong to the person in question. The reach of a *PAN* is typically a few meters. *PAN's* can be used for communication among the personal devices themselves (intrapersonal communication), or for connecting to a higher level network or to the Internet (an uplink). *PAN's* may be wired with computer buses such as USB and Firewire. Wireless PAN's can also be made possible with network technologies such as *Infrared Data Association* (IrDA*)* and Bluetooth.
    - *Local Area Network (LAN)*, a computer network covering a local area, like a home, office or small group of buildings such as a college. The topology of a network dictates its physical structure. The generally accepted maximum size for a *LAN* is 1000 m^2. *LAN's* are characterized by their high speed connections. Standardization efforts by the IEEE have resulted in the IEEE 802 series of standards. There are now two common wiring technologies for a *LAN*, Ethernet and Token Ring. When using *Ethernet* the computers are usually wired to a hub or to a switch, this constitutes the physical layer. The Spanning Tree *protocol* is often used to maintain a loop free network

topology within a *LAN*, particularly with Ethernet. *LAN's* can be interlinked through routers to form a *Wide Area Network (WAN).*

- Also, *Wireless LAN (WLAN)* technologies are evolving and are convenient for mobile computer users. Moreover, *Home Phoneline Networking Alliance (HomePNA)* is a relatively new technology, which allows to network home computers, like LAN, but using the existing telephone wiring. Internet access received by a single computer can be shared among several others without a router. Computers can access each other's peripherals such as printers, storage devices, files and play multiplayer games. Different frequencies are used to conduct data across the phone line. A frequency is reserved and prioritized for phone calls and fax so that they take precedence over all other data transfers.
- *Metropolitan Area Network (MAN)*, a large computer network usually spanning a campus or a city. *MAN's* typically use optical fiber connections to link their sites. For instance a university or college may have a *MAN* that joins together many of their local area networks *(LAN's)* situated around site of a fraction of a square kilometer, then from their *MAN* they could have several Wide Area Network *(WAN)* links to other universities or to the Internet. *Distributed Queue Dual Bus (*DQDB*)*, is the *MAN* standard for data communication, it is specified in the IEEE *802.6* standard. Using *DQDB*, networks can be up to 30 miles long and operate at speeds of 34 to 155 Mbps.
- *Wide Area Network (WAN)*, a computer network covering a wide geographical area, involving vast arrays of computers. This is different from *PAN's, MAN's* or *LAN's* that are usually limited to a room, building or campus. The best example of a *WAN* is the Internet. *WAN's* are used to connect local area networks together, so that users and computers in one location can communicate with users and computers in other locations.
- Many *WAN's* are built for one particular organization and are private, others, built by Internet service providers provide connections from an organization's *LAN* to the Internet. *WAN's* are most often built of leased lines, at each end of the leased line, a router connects to the *LAN* on one side and a hub within the *WAN* on the other. A number of network protocols may use the basic physical transport mechanism including TCP/IP, other protocols including X.25, ATM and Frame Relay can also be used for *WAN's*.

- **Categorization by functional relationship:**

  - *Client/Server*, a scalable architecture whereby each computer or process on the network is either a client or a server. Server software generally runs on powerful computers dedicated for exclusive use to running business applications. Client software on the other hand generally runs on common *PC's* or workstations. Clients get all or most of their information from the application server, they also rely on it for resources such as configuration files, stock quotes, business application programs. Clients can also offload compute intensive application tasks on the server to keep the client computer (and client computer user) free to perform other tasks.

- From the nature of its tasks, a server can be considered as being passive (slave) since it waits for incoming requests, serves them and sends replies. Servers can be stateless or stateful. A *stateless* server does not keep any information between requests, for instance an *HTTP* server for static *HTML* pages. A *stateful* server can remember information between requests, the scope of this information can be global or session based, an instance is *Tomcat*, the open-source implementation of *Java Servlet* and *JavaServer Pages* technologies developed at Apache Software Foundation.
- On the other hand a client is active (master) as it initiates requests and waits until replies arrive.
- *Three-Tier Architecture*, a client-server architecture in which the user interface, functional process logic ("business rules"), data storage and data access are developed and maintained as independent modules, most often on separate platforms. The *three-tier* model or *three layer* model is considered to be a software architecture and a software design pattern. Apart from the usual advantages of modular software with well defined interfaces, the three-tier architecture is intended to allow any of the three tiers to be upgraded or replaced independently as requirements or technology change
- Peer-to-Peer *(P2P)*, a network that relies on computing power at the edges (ends) of a connection rather than in the network itself. A pure peer-to-peer file transfer network does not have the notion of clients or servers, but only equal *peer* nodes that simultaneously function as both "clients" and "servers" to the other nodes on the network. This model of network arrangement differs from the client-server model where communication is usually to and from a central server. A typical example for a non peer-to-peer file transfer is an FTP server where one user uploads a file to the *FTP* server, then, many others download it, with no need for the uploader and downloader to be connected at the same time.
- Some networks and channels, such as Napster, OpenNap use a client-server structure for some tasks (e.g. searching) and a peer-to-peer structure for others. Networks such as Gnutella or Freenet, use a peer-to-peer structure for all purposes.

b) *Computer hardware,* several machines with different architectures are spread over the distributed environment; mainframes, personal computers, laptops, cell phones are contained in a distributed environment which implies many data representations for the same type whether it is integer, real, character, etc. Most computer scientists agree that till now there have been four distinct paradigms or eras of computing. These are: batch, time-sharing, desktop, and network.

Table 1 presents major characteristics of the different computing paradigms as associated with each decade of computing, starting from 1960 [7].

Table 1. Four decades of Computing

Feature	Batch	Time sharing	Desktop	Network
Decade	1960's	1970's	1980's	1990's
Location	Computer room	Terminal room	Desktop	Mobile
Users	Experts	Specialists	Individuals	Groups
Data	Alphanumeric	Text, numbers	Fonts, graphs	Multimedia
Objective	Calculate	Access	Present	Communicate
Interface	Punched card	Keyboard and *CRT*	See and point	Ask and tell
Operation	Process	Edit	Layout	Orchestrate
Connectivity	None	Peripheral cable	*LAN*	Internet
Owners	Corporate Computer Centers	Divisional *IS* shops	Departmental end users	Everyone

The most popular taxonomy of computer architecture was defined by Flynn [8], whose classification scheme is based on the notion of a stream of information. Two types of information flow into a processor: instructions and data. The *instruction stream* is defined as the sequence of instructions performed by the processing unit. The *data stream* is defined as the data traffic exchanged between the memory and the processing unit. According to Flynn's classification, either of the instruction or data streams can be single or multiple. Computer architecture can thus be classified into the following four distinct categories:

- *SISD (Single Instruction Stream, Single Data Stream)* is the conventional uniprocessor architecture employing a single instruction stream and a single data stream (Figure 1a). It is also known as von Neumann computer. This category includes the conventional scalar processors.
- *SIMD (Single Instruction Stream, Multiple Data Stream)* computers have several processing elements (*PE's*), which can perform the same operation simultaneously on different parts of the data stream (Figure 1b). This category includes the vector processors commercially available, such as *Thinking Machine CM-2* and *MasPar MP-2.*
- *MISD (Multiple Instruction Stream, Single Data Stream)* implies different operations by different *PE's* on the same data stream (Figure 1c). Examples of this type include pipelined and systolic machines.
- *MIMD (Multiple Instruction Stream, Multiple Data Stream)* indicates multiple *PE's* operating simultaneously on different parts of the data stream. (Figure 1d). This category includes most commercial parallel machines as *IBM SP-2*, *Thinking Machine CM-5* and *Cray T3D*. *MIMD* machines, although the most largely used, still offer limited scalability, since they rely on either a memory bus or a crossbar switch to allow its multiple processing elements to communicate. In order to solve these limitations [9] proposes and examines the potential of a new category of machines that is a hybrid between the *MISD* and the *MIMD* machines. Basically, by utilizing the unidirectional communication topology of an *MISD* machine in an *MIMD* machine, as illustrated in Figure 2, in order to overcome the scalability problem of the later.

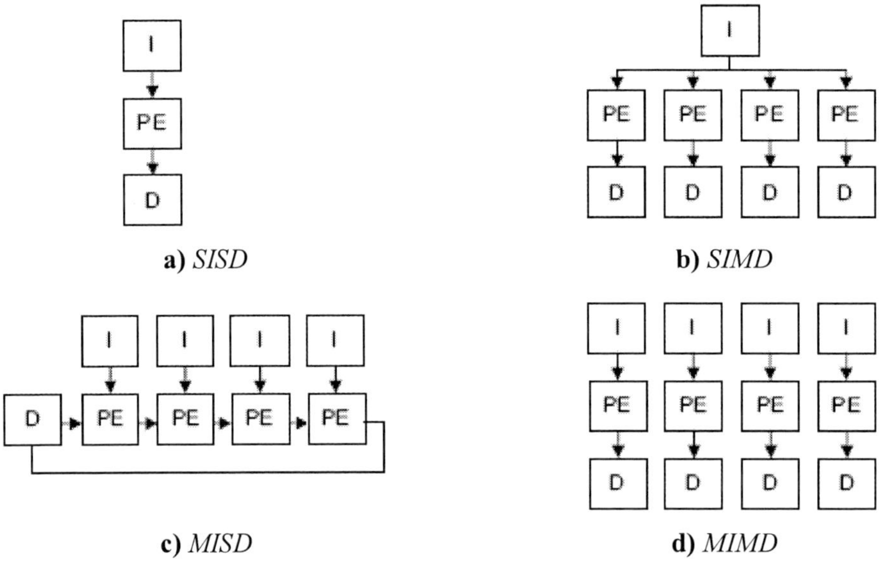

Figure 1. Flynn's taxonomy.

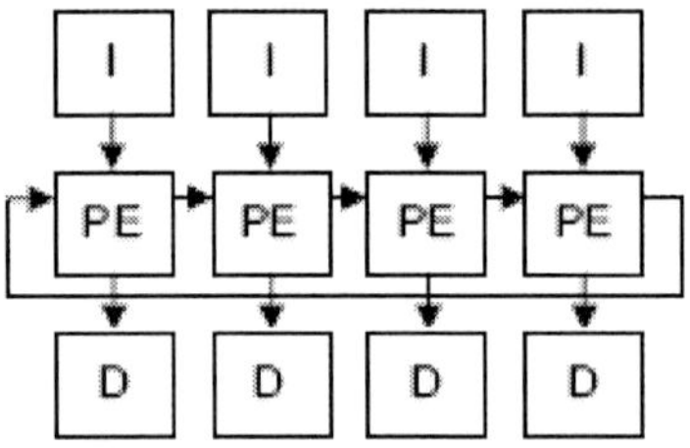

Figure 2. Hybrid *MIMD-MISD* machine.

c) *Operating systems*, *Unix*, *Linux*, *Windows*, *Macintosh* are some of a wide assortment of operating systems, each fits for a certain hardware and uses a specific task and resource management policy. The major operating systems in widespread use on general-purpose computers (including personal computers) have consolidated into two families: the Unix-like family and the Microsoft Windows family. Mainframe computers and embedded systems use a variety of different operating systems, many with no direct connection to *Windows* or *Unix*, such as *IBM's Z/OS* for mainframes and QNX, eCos, and PalmOS for embedded systems. As operating systems evolve, ever more services are expected to be common core. Nowadays, operating systems are required to provide network and Internet connectivity. They are also required to protect the computer's other software from damage by malicious programs, such as viruses. The *OS's* common core services are accessed by application programs through the *OS's* Application Programming Interfaces *(API's)*. In general, programs communicate with each other through *API's*, similar to how humans interact with programs through User Interfaces.

Operating systems may be distributed or networked. A *Distributed Operating System (DOS)* looks as a single coherent centralized *OS*, it is in fact distributed on many machines, invisible to the users, where its service procedures are mounted. In a *Network Operating*

System (NOS) the machines are holding all or some specific service procedures, a service procedure may be accessed locally or remotely, for instance an *ftp* may be executed on a local machine or on a remote one that holds the file to be transferred.

DOS may serve several multi-processors contained in one machine, each may have its private memory or may be sharing several memory modules. *DOS* also serves multi-computer systems where machines are distributed over a network. In multi-computer systems memory is not shared which shifts towards processor communication through message passing. *DOS* has to manage multi-computer synchronization since there are no system wide synchronization mechanisms, the *DOS* should also maintain a global memory map to manage virtual (distributed) shared memory, and has to allocate distributed resources among competing multi-computers.

Table 2. Comparison between operating systems

Item	**Distributed OS**		**Network OS**	**Middleware-based OS**
	Multiproc.	**Multicomp.**		
Degree of transparency	Very High	High	Low	High
Item	**Distributed OS**		**Network OS**	**Middleware-based OS**
	Multiproc.	**Multicomp.**		
Same OS on all nodes	Yes	Yes	No	No
Number of copies of OS	1	N	N	N
Basis for communication	Shared memory	Messages	Files	Model specific
Resource management	Global, central	Global, distributed	Per node	Per node
Scalability	No	Moderately	Yes	Varies
Openness	Closed	Closed	Open	Open

Table 2. presents a comparison between different operating systems [3].

d) *Programming languages,* hundreds of programming languages have been developed, some have decayed, others have adapted to a rapidly varying computing world and continue to exist. Each programming language can be thought of as a set of formal specifications concerning syntax, vocabulary, and meaning. These specifications usually include: data and data structures representation, instruction sets and control flow techniques, reference mechanisms and space re-use, motivating design philosophy. Most languages that are widely used, or have been used for a considerable period of time, have standardization bodies that meet regularly to create and publish formal definitions of the language, and discuss extending or supplementing the already extant definitions.

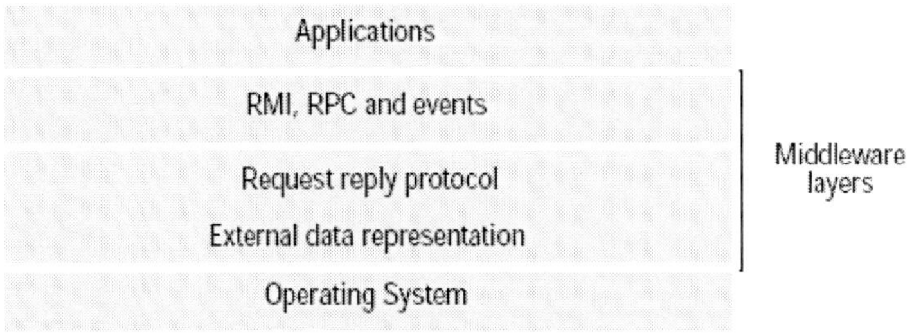

Figure 3. Middleware layers.

Middleware is the software layer that provides a programming abstraction as well as a masking of the heterogeneity in the underlying networks, hardware, *OS*, and programming languages; typical middleware systems include *Common Object Request Broker (CORBA)* and *Java Remote Method Invocation (RMI).* Middleware is thus the software that acts as the glue between two otherwise separate applications. In acting as an intermediary, it is in perfect position to provide a set of services to the end-applications. For instance, an order-entry *Java Web Application* may need to connect to a database. Instead of accessing the database directly, the order-entry application does so through an application server acting as middleware. The application server provides a set of common services to the application. These services could include security, transactions, load-balancing, failover and more. This means that the order-entry application programmer does not have to program these capabilities directly into her application (Figure 3 [1]).

2.2.2. Openness

Openness, signifies that the system can be extended and re-implemented in various ways, and new resource-sharing services can be added and made available for use by a variety of client programs. To achieve openness a detailed specification and documentation of key software interfaces must be published. The *WWW* is a typical open distributed system that can be extended and implemented in new ways without disturbing its existing functionality.

Open distributed systems should permit interoperability, portability, and flexibility. *Interoperability* characterizes the extent to which two heterogeneous systems can co-exist and work together by relaying on each other services as specified by a common standard. *Portability* indicates the scope an application developed for a distributed system can reach when executed in another distributed system that uses the same interface. *Flexibility* enables the possibility of configuring a system out of different components from various developers and the addition of new components or the replacement of existing ones without affecting the core components.

2.2.3. Security

Security, it has three components for information resources. *Confidentiality*, which implies protection against disclosure to unauthorized individuals. *Integrity*, to ensure safeguarding against alteration or corruption. *Availability*, to provide protection against denial of access caused by interferences with the means to access resources.

Many security mechanisms have been used to protect information resources; specifically, data encryption to prevent disclosure, authentication mechanisms like digital signatures and passwords, transmitting data via secure channels, using firewalls to prevent hackers from penetrating systems.

2.2.4. Scalability

Scalability, is the capability to increase resources and users to yield a linear (ideally) increase in service capacity. The key characteristic of a scalable application is that additional load only requires additional resources rather than extensive modification of the application itself. Although raw (basic) performance makes a difference in determining the number of users that an application can support, scalability and performance are two separate entities. In fact, performance efforts can sometimes be opposed to scalability efforts. *QoS* in a distributed environment imposes controls over the cost of added physical resources and on performance degradation due to expansions, prevents running out of system resources such as *IP* addresses due to the increase in users, and avoids resulting bottlenecks in the expanded system.

The scalability of a distributed system has three dimensions. The first is the *size scalability* where more users and resources can be easily added, the second is the *geographical scalability* in which users and resources lie apart, the third is the *administrative scalability* where a distributed system can still be managed even if it spans many independent administrations.

2.2.5. Failure Handling

Failure handling, is a serious task in distributed systems since components fail independently, which may produce incorrect results. There are several mechanisms that provide failure handling:

- *Fault detection (diagnoses)* mechanisms that can detect faulty components and their locations, such as the *heartbeat technique* where each node in the system sends a heartbeat to all others. If a node does not heartbeat then the failure is in the node or in its network connection.
- *Fault masking* mechanisms that hide some detected failures, this is particularly suitable for systems with high components redundancy.
- *Fault tolerance* mechanisms that allow distributed systems to continue functioning while some of their components are down.
- *Fault recovery* mechanisms. Two approaches are observable. *Backward recovery* techniques that use checkpoints to save the state of all processes in the system at a certain instant for later restoration if the system fails. *Forward recovery* techniques used in real time distributed systems where there is no time to rollback and restore a previous state.

2.2.6. Concurrency

Concurrency, indicates the capability of a distributed system to enable users to share resources at the same time. Since it endangers system integrity, data inconsistency is a major problem associated with concurrent access (invocation) of a data object. To avoid such inconsistency for shared memory distributed multi-processor systems, synchronizing techniques such as critical sections and semaphores are used. While for non-shared memory distributed systems, like distributed transaction based multi-computer systems, concurrency control techniques as time-stamping and data locking are widely used. The use of complex clock synchronization mechanisms makes synchronization harder in distributed systems than in non-distributed systems.

2.2.7. Transparency

Transparency, means that the system is perceived as a whole rather than as a collection of independent components, Table 3 illustrates the different forms of transparency [1].

Table 3. Different forms of transparency in distributed systems

Transparency	Description	Examples
Access	Hide whether the accessed data is local or remote through use of identical operations.	File System Operations in *NFS*, Navigation in the Web, *SQL* Queries.
Concurrency	Hide that a resource may be shared by several competitive users.	*NFS*, Automatic Teller Machine Network, Distributed *DBMS*.
Failure	Hide the failure and recovery of a resource allowing users and application programs to complete their tasks despite failure.	Distributed *DBMS*.
Location	Hide where a resource is located.	File System Operations In *NFS*, Pages in The Web, Tables in Distributed Databases.
Migration/Mobility	Hide the movement of resources and clients within a system.	*NFS*, Web Pages.
Performance	Hide that the system is reconfigured to improve performance as loads vary.	Distributed Make.
Replication	Hide from users and application programmers that a resource they are using may be replicated.	Distributed *DBMS*, Mirroring Web Pages.
Scaling	Hide that the system and applications have expanded in scale, which keeps unchanged the system structure and the application algorithms.	World-Wide-Web, Distributed *DBMS*.

2.3. Distributed Computing: Opportunity, Challenge, or Misfortune?

For over twenty years distributed computing has been the name of the game, it may be appropriate to stand back a bit with [10] and reflect on what has been achieved.

2.3.1. Introduction

Distributed computing may be defined as a computing in which a number of computers, usually connected by a network, perform calculations with a common goal and with some mutual dependence that varies very widely. Doing a job in a distributed manner makes it intrinsically more likely that undesired events will happen, through failures of communication, operating system, or computer. There are also complete impossibilities, such as determining in the case where no response is received to a remote request whether the request was lost on the way out, or whether the response was lost on the way back.

One might perhaps wonder why distributed computing is considered a good thing, there are several reasons:

- One reason is that it presents challenges to computer science. Some very ingenious theory has been done to show that some distributed algorithms do not exist and cannot exist, such as determining the currently active members of a class, or doing distributed transactions with no window at all for misfortune.
- Another reason is that there are enormous numbers of computers connected to networks that are themselves interconnected, and they constitute a powerful resource. The cheapest way to buy large numbers of cycles is by means of commodity machines. The economic motivation for distributed computing can be very strong, and was at one time often perceived as predominant.
- Yet another reason is generally referred to as scaling. Centralized solutions often have hard capacity limits, and it seems that distributed systems have more flexible scaling. But a matter is often ignored by computer scientists is that nothing scales indefinitely, and quite often the scale limit is known in advance.
- One more reason should not be missed, reliability and robustness. It is said that distributed systems are more reliable because their components do not all fail at once. It is indeed possible to arrange that distributed systems are very reliable; it is very possible for anyone to persuade himself that he has done so, but success is very far from being automatic.

This line of discussion leads to a central argument, centralized solutions are best where they are practicable. It is considerably easier to keep copies of information consistent when their number is one. It is easier to handle transactional integrity when all the data are in one place. It is easier to provide backup, hot standby, and so forth when it is known where the authoritative data is. Similar considerations apply to network management. The pioneers of internetworking took it as an article of faith that requiring any kind of *Galactic Central* was evil, and they were of course quite right. However, having central management of reasonably sized units can be much easier than extremes of distribution.

After all, using distributed techniques increases the chance that *something* will go wrong. There have been instances when attempts, to ensure availability of a service by heavy replication, simply made sure that an externally induced software fault destroyed *all* instances of the service that existed, as a result of doomed attempts to find an instance that would do what was wanted. To assume that failure is a random occurrence is not necessarily correct, systematic failures can be aggravated by distribution, rather than avoided.

2.3.2. What Has Failed and What Has Succeeded?

In the early days of distributed computing there was a pervasive idea. A large computation would be done by breaking it into pieces that would be scattered over a collection of machines, often machines that had other duties too. The pieces would be self-standing but cooperating processes, and they would migrate around the network to places where capacity was available for them to run.

That approach was part of a more general desire, to be able to use and to program a collection of computers as if they were one. A major manifestation of this was the invention of *Remote Procedure Calls (RPC's)*, which were intended to relieve the programmer from the grubbiness of handling the network directly, and to use a paradigm that was very familiar. In the context of very reliable short-range networks this worked reasonably well. It did, however, lead to a convoluted style of programming in the circumstance that the originator of an *RPC* did not want to await the result. As the geographical scale of distributed computing increased, with the consequent increase in the number of routers and other network components traversed, the latency began to hurt performance.

The fact, that flexible general purpose dynamic distributed computing has not worked out as hoped, should not obscure the evident other fact that vast amounts of computation today depend on collections of cooperating machines. Distributed computing is a way of life. It may accordingly be instructive to look at the differences of approach that make this possible:

1. Most multi-machine computation is done on configurations that are static while the work is going on, even if they depend on name and resource locators to find out where the services they depend on are purveyed. It does not matter where is the service a computation needs, and it is not necessary to cater for its movement while it is being used.
2. Much multi-machine computation is stylized. Dependencies tend to be in the form of chains or trees of very low degree, so any machine does not need to know very much about what may in total be a complex environment. However, the complex environment is pre-planned and recovers from faults on the basis of application semantics.
3. Probably most importantly, the grain of distribution has in some logical sense coarsened. Systems like *Component Object Module (COM)*, as extended to *Distributed Component Object Module (DCOM)*, make it easier to put distributed systems together, they lend themselves naturally to the application-level treatment of failures.

2.3.3. Distributed Computing and the Web

One of the current fallacies is that the Web is a triumph of distributed computing. In fact the Web has very little to do with distributed computing, which is not to deny that it is a work of genius. It has a naming scheme, supported by *DNS* name servers that are themselves a successful piece of distributed computing based on application-specific techniques. But, once a server is located, one has a simple client-server relationship.

2.3.4. Answers

Distributed computing: opportunity, challenge, or misfortune? The answer is: yes to opportunity, yes to challenge, yes to misfortune.

2.4. The Eight Fallacies of Distributed Computing

A great list of wishful thinking that clouds so much system design is first published by L. Peter Deutsch [11]. Essentially everyone, when first building a distributed application, makes the following eight assumptions. All prove to be false in the long run and all cause big trouble and painful learning experiences:

1. The network is reliable.
2. Latency is zero.
3. Bandwidth is infinite.
4. The network is secure.
5. Topology does not change.
6. There is one administrator.
7. Transport cost is zero.
8. The network is homogeneous.

3. Reliability

Many in the scientific community are absorbed by traditional reliability definitions, that is not enough though, mining for a recent survey would not abide by what everybody knows towards what must upgrade minds, even if its final shape is not yet attained or elaborated. Thus, the traditional reliability definitions will first be recalled, then in accordance with new innovative thoughts new definitions will be presented. Multiple reliability definitions, traditional and new, enhance each other, add mutual meanings and understandings, for the good of neat designs and performance.

3.1. Traditional Reliability

Traditionally, reliability has been described mathematically, with mathematical models it was possible to model hardware and software systems.

3.1.1. Mathematical Reliability

From a mathematical point of view, reliability is directly tied to the notion of failure. If random variable X is the lifetime (time to failure) of a system component, then the probability that the component survives (i.e. does not fail) to some time t is called the reliability $R(t)$ of the component and is defined:

$$R(t) = P(X>t) = 1 - F(t) \quad (1)$$

where $F(t)$ is the cumulative distribution function of the component lifetime X [12]. It is assumed that the component is working initially and will eventually fail (i.e.$F(t)$ will reach 1), hence the limit of $R(t)$ is 0 as $t \to \infty$. Furthermore, given individual component reliabilities, and assuming independence of component failure, the overall reliability of a system comprising these components can be determined.

Fault tolerance is a way to improve reliability, the effects of a fault-tolerant design strategy on system reliability can be expressed as follows [13]:

$$R_{system} = Pr\{no\ fault\} + Pr\{correct\ operation \mid fault\} \qquad (2)$$

The first term is the probability that no fault will occur; usually achieved by high-reliability components. Fault tolerance is represented by the second term of (Eq.2), it is the conditional probability that the system will continue to operate correctly given the occurrence of a fault. In the context of (Eq.2), the desired reliability can be obtained in spite of imperfect components as long as the fault tolerance techniques are up to the task. Unfortunately, failures may be induced not only by natural phenomenon, but by information attack and this goes beyond the scope of reliability.

3.1.2. Hardware Reliability

Hardware reliability implies the following characteristics for hardware components [14]:

- they degrade (wear out) with time;
- they are guaranteed to fail eventually;
- they usually have explicitly definable (and observable) failure characteristics;
- they are such that the assumption of independence of component failure is usually reasonable.

These characteristics, allow mathematical techniques to be applied. Sample testing of hardware components allows determination of such statistical parameters as *Mean Time to Failure* (*MTTF*), *Mean Time to Repair* (*MTTR*), and *Mean Time between Failures* (*MTBF*). With such figures for individual components, and assuming independence of components, it is possible to make probabilistic reliability predictions for aggregate systems. Empirically it has also been observed that for physical components the conditional failure rate *h(t)* exhibits the so called "bathtub shape" [12] of Figure 4.

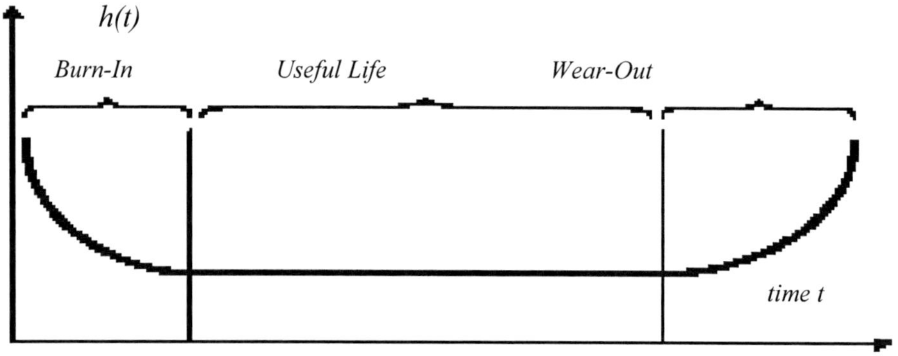

Figure 4. Conditional failure rate as a function of time (© 2005 IEEE).

The bathtub shape can be subdivided as follows:

- the early period ("burn-in") has an initially high but falling failure rate, these failures are predominantly of the endogenous type stemming from inherent defects in the manufacture or assembly of the component;
- a failure rate plateau ("useful life") is then reached where failures usually happen due to environmental conditions that place the components under severe and unusual stress, these failures are said to be of exogenous type;
- finally a period of increasing failure rate is entered due to components "wearing out" through abrasion, fatigue, tolerance creep, etc.

3.1.3. Software Reliability

Reliability of software components is not so easily quantified, and indeed it can be argued that reliability in the formal mathematical sense is not even applicable. This stems from the following facts [14]:

- software, being a logical construct, does not wear out as such with time;
- software may fail immediately, or if logically perfect may never fail at all (i.e. in the context of the system specification it is either incorrect or correct);
- what constitutes failure is usually hard to define unequivocally, for a continuum exists from minor cosmetic blemishes, through tolerable discrepancies (say rounding errors), to complete system crash.

Nonetheless, it can still be argued that the concept of reliability is still a valid and reasonable measure of software quality [15], [16]:

- This arises from the fact that software fails because its internal state causes behavior contrary to its requirements; moreover its internal state is a direct result of receiving and processing input sequences coming from an external stochastic environment, and as such errors will similarly manifest in stochastic manner.
- Further, software (treated as a black box) can be subjected to test input streams and the occurrence of errors observed. With such error data it is possible for reliability measures (within statistical confidence levels) to be determined. However, [15] demonstrates that such experimental quantification is infeasible (due to test times being in decades/centuries) for software required to operate at high and ultra-reliability levels (failure rate $<10^{-7}$ per hour). Technical experimentation is not thus consistent with the non-specialists view that some software is more reliable than other software, and that this can be assessed by the frequency and severity of the bugs observed.
- Also, with appropriate interpretation, it is possible to align software failure rates over time with the classic "bathtub" shape:

    - The initial "burn-in" period can be clearly associated with the debugging phase of software development and early alpha/beta trials, initially many software failures (bugs) are detected but these decrease over time.

- The plateau of "useful life" maps to the production code release period where most failures are a result of highly unusual input sequences from the environment (not tested for during development period) resulting in an internal state that causes behavior inconsistent with the requirements. It is to be noted that because of the logical nature of software artifacts the type of these failures is a moot point. Pedantically, they are of course endogenous; but if one could not reasonably have anticipated such input sequences it does seem reasonable to deem them to be of exogenous environmental origin.
- Finally, even though a logical construct cannot "wear out", it can over time increasingly fail to be in alignment with the organization's changing requirements. It should be noted that what is considered here as an entity called software is actually an artifact that evolves over time with new technologies.

3.2. Semantic Reliability

3.2.1. The Notion of Semantic Reliability

The notion of *semantic reliability* is re-adopted by [14] in line with the original use of the term [17] where it relates to "serious failures due to semantic variability of message content" even where the communicating "components as well as the interconnections are error free in the classical sense". Distributed computing systems work by exchanging information effectively. This exchange may be to achieve the goals of the individual participant systems or perhaps to achieve some larger overall system-wide goal. The key to the successful operation of distributed systems is that the messages between systems be interpreted in such way that the sender's desired effect is achieved. Desired effects include: to inform the receiver of a particular fact or belief held by the sender, to request that the receiver provide certain specified information to the sender, or that the receiver carry out certain actions. To achieve these effects the messages, when interpreted by the receiver, must necessarily be meaningful. More to the point, the meaning interpreted by the receiver must align with the meaning intended by the sender, if it does not then we have a *semantic mismatch or variance* and it is likely that the specific effect desired by the sender will not occur. When the extent of the mismatch is such that the effect achieved does not meet the core requirements of the sender then we have a system failure, and thus an unreliable system stemming from *semantic misinterpretation.*

Problems of semantic mismatch rarely occur in homogeneously developed single systems; even in most distributed systems the problem has not been significant to date because of what one could term the *low conceptual density* of the messages. Conceptual density could be defined as a measure of the complexity of the meaning lying behind the symbols passed in the message, and thereby the likelihood that misinterpretation of meaning will occur by recipients other than the creator of the symbol. Higher level of conceptual density arises in newly deployed distributed systems designed to enable interaction between programs with little human intervention, typical systems provide web services that use *XML* based messages as their primary form of communication, intelligent agent systems that fulfill roles such as service locators, brokers and negotiators. In considering such systems it may be reasonable to assume that:

a) the current very high reliability of physical message transmission will improve further with time, and
b) ongoing improvements in software engineering practices (object-orientation, componentization, fault tolerance through multi-versioning, etc.) will continue to improve conventional software reliability.

As such, lack of semantic reliability (through semantic mismatch) could assume a far higher profile in the cast of reasons for system failure; and might in extremis become, as noted, the "primary failure mode".

3.2.2. Relationship with Traditional Reliability Model

One cannot simply classify semantic reliability as a sub-type of software reliability. While it certainly impacts on overall system reliability, there are fundamental differences between semantic mismatch and normal software faults [14]:

- First, by definition semantic mismatches are inter-system not intra-system in nature. As such the designers and programmers of a given system (which is part of a larger distributed system) cannot in isolation determine that their usage of terms is anything other than correct. Putting this another way, semantic mismatches do not reside in implemented software but in different developers' differing understandings of what manipulated terms mean. Semantic variance, and hence mismatch, is a distributed system wide problem at the specification interpretation level, and not a detectable intra-system software fault in the conventional sense.
- There is also the valid question, "Can semantic variation be measured?" For the reasons noted above, the developers D_x of a given system X cannot measure the semantic variation of system X in isolation. However, a different set of developers, say D_y of system Y, could create a test stream which when applied to X would allow D_y to detect behavior at variance with that which D_y would expect, given D_y's interpretation of ontological terms. Thus measures of semantic variation, and hence semantic failure rates, could be measured on an inter-system basis; but for an overall distributed system comprising n independently developed systems their would be $n(n-1)$ sets of results.
- Further, would these inter-system semantic failure rates measured over time conform to the classic "bathtub" curve for conditional failure rates?

    - It seems more than reasonable to expect the failure rates to initially fall dramatically as different component system developers observe, communicate, and correct differences in term interpretation between the systems.
    - A plateau, could then be expected where the main cause of failure are inter-system messages that use terms in a manner, that although logically consistent with earlier uses, have not been anticipated in the design of the software.
    - Finally, would one expect the classic failure rate rise as systems "wear out"? This is more difficult to assess, and two points are noted:

1. semantic mismatches arise at the conceptual level and are not tied to particular code or technologies; and,
2. the primary goal of an ontology[1] [18] is to stabilize terminological use and ensure its long term invariance. As such one would reasonably expect an ontology to have a longer "useful life" than the software artifacts that use it. However, ontologies arise from our conceptualization of the world, and this conceptualization not only differs from one person to another but is itself an evolving entity effected by changes in world views, knowledge, and theories. With such evolution it is likely that an ontology (or some subset of it) may become obsolete. This being the case, unless there is significant ongoing maintenance to ensure ontology currency, we would inevitably see (in a manner similar to hardware and software failures) an increase in semantic failures at the end of some failure rate plateau. The full extent and rate of such rises could however only be assessed by the long term observation of ontologies in the field.

3.2.3. How to Improve Semantic Reliability

It is now appropriate to examine how semantic reliability may be improved: first, at the level of ontology interpretation by human developers; and then in terms of software techniques that may help detect and mitigate inter-system interpretational problems [14].

3.2.3.1. Improving Developer Interpretation

Two related ways establish and build meaning. These are: the accrual of meaning through sustained discourse, and an argued direct link between meaning and use.

- *Sustained Discourse.* Concise definitions of all ontological terms and the relations between these terms must necessarily be provided. However, it is also essential that extended commentary on these definitions also be available and considered if semantic variation is to be minimized. The use of such discourse is consistent with arguments saying that language-in-use (discourse) is intimately associated with "how people make and interpret meaning in specific social circumstances".
- *Meaning is Use.* The nexus between meaning and use is particularly associated with the "meaning-is-use" theory asserting that the meaning of a term or expression is simply a function of how the term or expression is used within a particular context. This in itself is not immediately useful, but it does suggest that possibly one of the most effective ways to communicate intended meaning is by providing extensive practical examples of the term in use in different contexts. This in fact, is a significant feature of all complete dictionaries.

---

[1] Ontologies are content theories about sorts of objects, properties of objects, and relations between objects that are possible in a specified domain of knowledge, they provide potential terms for describing our knowledge about the domain. An ontology is a representation vocabulary, translating its terms from one language to another does not change the ontology conceptually. The last point is important since it indicates that ontological terms are only symbols, carrying no meaning per se (other than relationships to other terms) and can readily be exchanged for other symbols. A consequence of this is that for an ontology to be useful, those using it must agree on the concepts represented by the arbitrary term

3.2.3.2. Relevant Software Engineering Techniques

There are possible steps software developers can take at the code level to deal with semantic reliability at the inter-systems level:

- *Software peer monitoring.* In general, the developers of the independent component systems need to increase the amount of system code devoted to monitoring, logging, and reporting the results of their message based requests with respect to conformance with expected application semantics. This constitutes a move to more autonomous systems. As noted earlier, the level of semantic conformance detected will be dependent on which system is observing which other system, as there are $n(n-1)$ possibilities.
- *Decomposition into multiple smaller steps.* Where performatives that effect observable change in the domain are issued, consideration should be given to decomposition of a performative into smaller performative steps so that all parties, sender and receiver(s), have an opportunity to assess conformance with expected outcomes at each step in the process. If the performative steps are reversible in nature, this allows systems to backout of processes, where significant semantic variance is detected, before reaching the point of actual semantic failure. Thus correction as well as detection is available.
- *Multi-versioning.* It should also be noted that classic software multi-versioning with voting techniques could also be applied at the semantic level of message interpretation.
- It is important to note that a critical feature of the above software techniques is that they all require a significant increase in the complexity of the system code. This has two effects: first it will reduce performance, and second it could potentially decrease the reliability of the system in the conventional software sense. Thus we have a trade-off: by trying to monitor and reduce semantic variation, we might actually increase the number of conventional software faults. Getting the balance correct is critical to improving overall system reliability.
- *Interoperability test beds.* When an ontology is developed, it is possible to develop not only a series of standard usage patterns with expected results, but also a software system that can embody these standards as tests. Such a test bed has application not only during initial development of systems, but also as part of the production systems' lives to check for ontological drift as systems and requirements evolve.

4. Reliability Evaluation of Distributed Hardware Systems

This section is concerned with research work that tackles distributed hardware systems. Section 4.1 presents a latest bi-criteria heuristic for scheduling data-flow graphs of operations onto parallel heterogeneous architectures according to two criteria: first the maximization of the system reliability, and second the minimization of the schedule length. To reduce the time needed to deal with disk failure and importantly to improve reliability of large-scale storage systems, Section 4.2 illustrates *FARM,* a technique that treats fast the consequences of failures and limits the chance of additional failures during the period of vulnerability.

4.1. A Bi-Criteria Scheduling Heuristic for Distributed Embedded Systems under Reliability and Real-Time Constraints

4.1.1. System Models

Multi-criteria scheduling problems involve optimization of more than one criterion. This work [19] presents a new bi-criteria heuristic for scheduling data-flow graphs of operations onto parallel heterogeneous architectures according to two criteria: first the maximization of the system reliability, and second the minimization of the schedule length. The aim is to automatically produce a *reliable distributed static schedule* of a given algorithm onto a given distributed architecture which satisfies these two criteria, while replicating operations. Active replication of operations is used. There are two techniques for the replication of services and objects: the *active replication technique* and the *primary-backup technique* [20]. In the active replication technique, also called *state-machine approach*, all replicas play the same role: there is no centralized control, whereas in the primary-backup technique one of the replicas, called the primary, plays a special role: it receives the invocations from the client process, and sends the response back.

The problem is difficult to solve because the two criteria are *antagonistic*: the reliability is usually improved by replicating the operations, which has a negative impact on the schedule length, and hence on the system's run-time. Replication has the advantage of increasing locality of operations which may reduce schedule length. Specifically, the following data are given as input to the proposed *Reliable Bi-criteria Scheduling Algorithm* (*RBSA*):

- a specification (*Alg*) of the algorithm to be distributed (Figure 5a),
- a specification (*Arc*) of the target distributed architecture (Figure 5b),
- some distribution constraints (*Dis*),
- some information about the execution times of the algorithm blocks on the architecture processors, and the communication times of the algorithm data-dependencies on the architecture communication links (*Exe*),
- some information about the reliability characteristics of each component of the architecture (*Rel*),
- a parameter θ provided by the user to compromise between the reliability decrease and the schedule length increase due to replication,
- a reliability objective (Rel_{obj}),
- and a run-time objective (Rt_{obj}).

The goal is thus to build out of *RBSA* a static schedule of *Alg* on *Arc*, satisfying both objectives Rel_{obj} and Rt_{obj}, with respect to *Exe*, *Dis*, and *Rel* (Figure 6).

The algorithm to be distributed is modeled by a *data-flow graph, Alg,* where each vertex is an *operation* and each edge is a *data-dependency* (Figure 5a). The algorithm is executed repeatedly for each input event from the sensors (operations without predecessors) in order to compute the output events for actuators (operations without successors). This periodic sampled model is commonly used for embedded systems and automatic control systems.

The architecture is modeled by a graph *Arc*, where each vertex is a processor, and each edge is a communication link (Figure 5b). Classically, a processor is made of one computation unit, one local memory, and one or more communication units, each connected to one communication link.

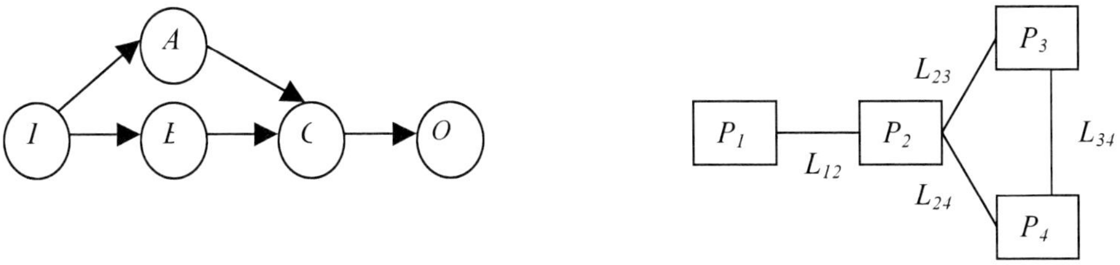

Figure 5. Example graphs (© 2005 IEEE).

Legend: Operations: *I* sensor; *O* actuator; *A,B,C* computations. Data dependencies: $A \Longrightarrow C$, $B \Longrightarrow C$, a) Algorithm graph (*Alg*) b) Architecture graph (*Arc*)

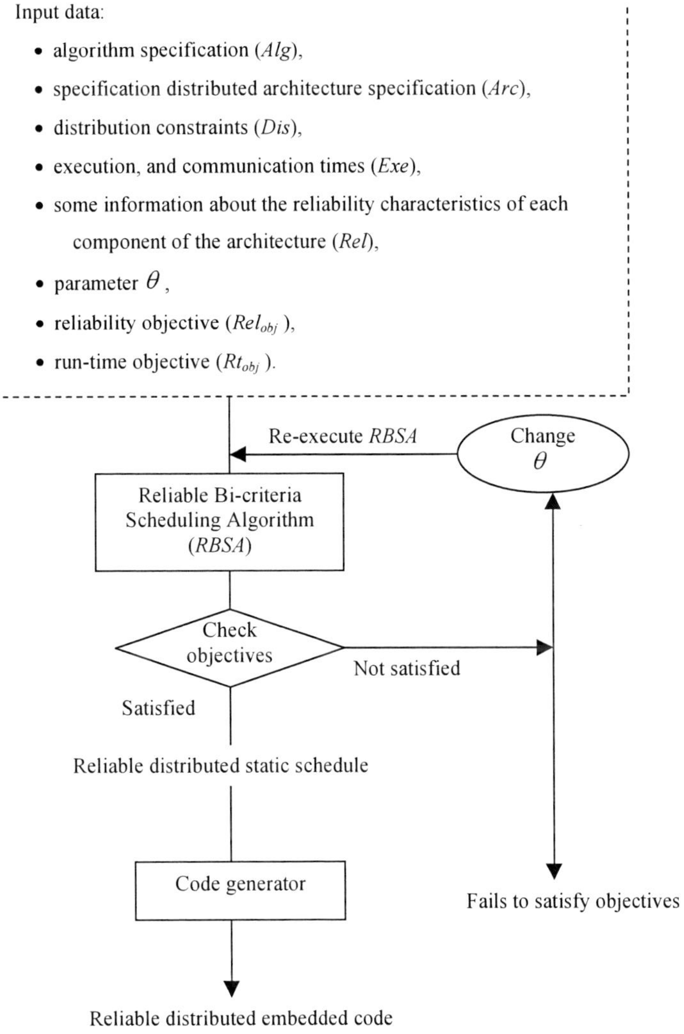

Figure 6. Methodology to generate reliable distributed code (© 2005 IEEE).

In a table *Exe* each entry *<o, p>* is the *Worst Case Execution Time* (*WCET*) of the operation *o* of *Alg* on the processor *p*, expressed in time units. Since the target architecture is heterogeneous, the *WCET* for a given operation can be distinct on each processor. Similarly, in another table *Exe*, each entry *<d, l>* is the *Worst Case Transmission Time* (*WCTT*) of the data dependency *d* of *Alg* on the communication link *l*, again expressed in time units. Since the target architecture is heterogeneous, the *WCTT* for a given data-dependency can be distinct on each communication link. The distributed constraints *Dis* determine on the *Exe* tables which processors are to execute which operations and on which links flow the data dependencies.

4.1.2. The Bi-Criteria Problem

In the proposed model, only failures of hardware components (processors and communication links) are considered, failures are independent and have exponential distributions. It is assumed that the algorithm is correct and formally validated. To find a static schedule of *Alg* on *Arc*, two criteria are to be satisfied:

Real-time criterion such that the schedule Rt_{sched} completes in less then Rt_{obj} time units. The schedule length Rt_{sched} is computed as follows:

$$Rt_{sched} = \max_{\forall p_j \text{ where } o_i \text{ can be executed}} \{ \max_{o_i \text{ on } p_j} E(o_i, p_j) \} \tag{3}$$

where $E(o_i,p_j)$ is the time at which operation o_i terminates its execution on processor p_j (Figure 7a and Figure 8a).

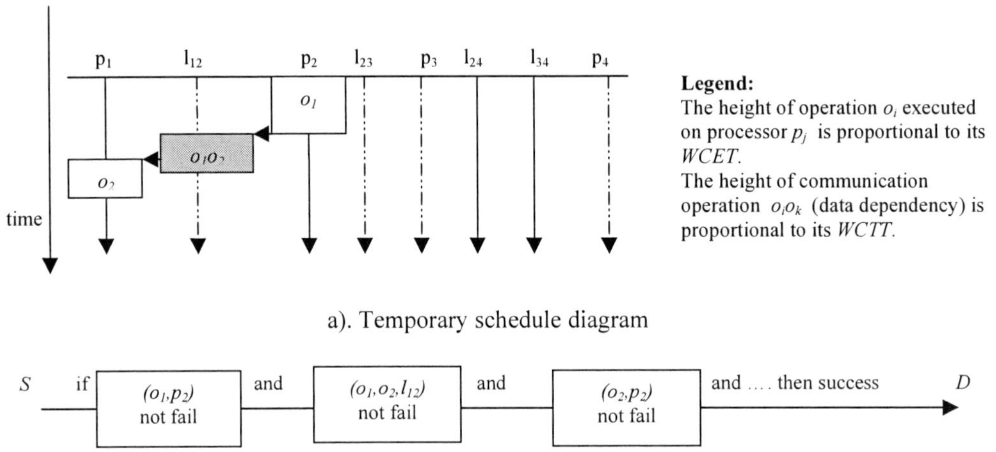

a). Temporary schedule diagram

b) Reliability block diagram

Figure 7. Sample temporary schedule and reliability block diagrams without replication (© 2005 IEEE).

Reliability criterion such that the system reliability Rel_{sched} must be greater than Rel_{obj}. *Reliability Block Diagrams* (*RBD's*) [21],[22] are used for representing and analyzing the reliability of systems (Figure 7b and Figure 8b). A system is operational if there is a path from the source *S* to the destination *D* in its *RBD*. Each block $\{o_i, c_j\}$ of an *RBD* is assigned the reliability cost in time units of executing the operation/communication o_i on the processor/link c_j. The system reliability in an *RBD* is based on the reliability of each of its components. The computation of the component blocks reliability $Rel_{sched}(o_i, c_j)$ value is given as follows [23]:

$$Rel_{sched}(o_i, c_j) = e^{-\lambda_{c_j} Exe(o_i, c_j)} \tag{4}$$

where the time $Exe(o_i,c_j)$ is obtained from the *Exe* tables for *WCET* and *WCCT*.

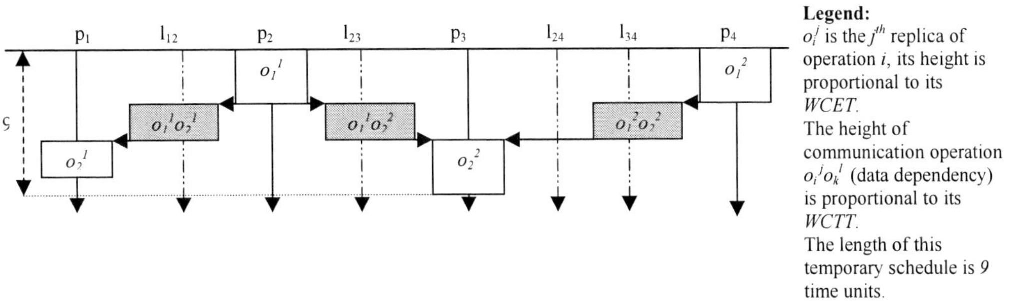

a). Temporary schedule diagram

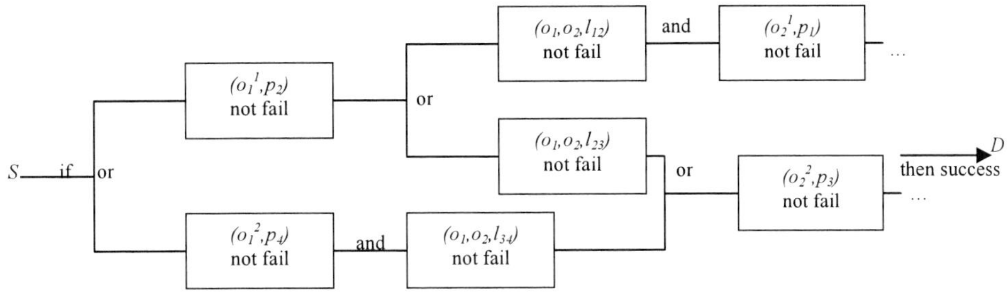

b). Reliability block diagram

Figure 8. Sample temporary schedule and reliability block diagrams with replication (© 2005 IEEE).

Using Eq.4 the overall system reliability Rel^*_{sched} may be obtained:

- In systems without replication, the *RBD* of the schedule has a serial structure (Figure 7b); its reliability can therefore be obtained in linear time by multiplying the reliability of each block of the *RBD*.
- In systems with replication, the *RBD* of the schedule does not have a serial/parallel structure (Figure 8b); its exact reliability can only be obtained in exponential time. However, we can compute an *upper bound* of the reliability Rel_{sched} in polynomial time, using the *Minimal Cut Sets* (*MCS*) method [24]. The *MCS* allows to compute

the upper bound of the system's reliability in a linear time when processors/links failures are assumed to be independent:

$$Rel^{*}_{sched} \le \prod_{i=1}^{k}(1 - \prod_{(o,c)\in M_i}((1 - Rel_{sched}(o,c)) \tag{5}$$

where M_i is an *MCS*.

4.1.3. The Reliable Bi-Criteria Scheduling Algorithm (RBSA)

The proposed algorithm is a greedy list scheduling heuristic [25], called *Reliable Bi-Criteria Scheduling Algorithm* (*RBSA*), which uses a *bi-criteria compromise function* (*Bcf*) as a cost function to introduce priority between operations to be scheduled. It is based on two functions:

The first function $L^{(n)}(o_i, \{p_1, \ldots, p_j\})$ computes, at each step n of the algorithm, the loss on reliability resulting from the scheduling of the j replicas respectively on the j processors $p_1, \ldots, p_j$ (Figure 9b):

$$L^{(n)} = \frac{Rel^{(n)}_{sched}(o_i,\{p_1,\ldots,p_j)\} - Rel^{(n-1)}_{sched}(o_i,\{p_1,\ldots,p_j)\}}{Rel_{obj} - Rel^{(n-1)}_{sched}} \tag{6}$$

The second function $G^{(n)}(o_i, \{p_1, \ldots, p_j\})$ computes, at each step n of the algorithm, the gain on the schedule length resulting from the scheduling of the j replicas respectively on the j processors $p_1, \ldots, p_j$ (Figure 9a):

$$G^{(n)} = \frac{Rt^{(n)}_{sched}(o_i,\{p_1,\ldots,p_j)\} - Rt^{(n-1)}_{sched}(o_i,\{p_1,\ldots,p_j)\}}{Rt_{obj} - Rt^{(n-1)}_{sched}} \tag{7}$$

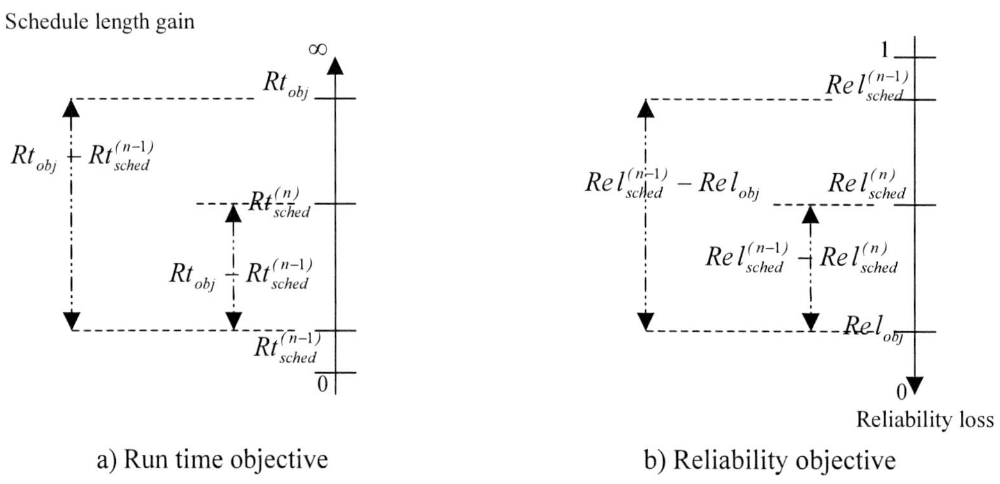

Figure 9. Run time and reliability objectives (© 2005 IEEE).

To minimize the loss on reliability and maximize the gain on schedule length, the cost function *Bcf* computes the bi-criteria compromise value between normalized $L^{(n)}$ and $G^{(n)}$. At each step *n*, *Bcf* selects for each operation o_i, the best subset $\{p_1, \ldots, p_j\}$ which gives the smallest compromise value $Bcf^{(n)}(o_i, \{p_1, \ldots, p_j\})$ between $L^{(n)}(o_i, \{p_1, \ldots, p_j\})$ and $G^{(n)}(o_i, \{p_1, \ldots, p_j\})$. If the processor subset has more than one element, then the chosen operation o_i is replicated on them.

For the computation of *Bcf*, a parameter θ is provided by the user and set by default to $45°$ (Figure 10):

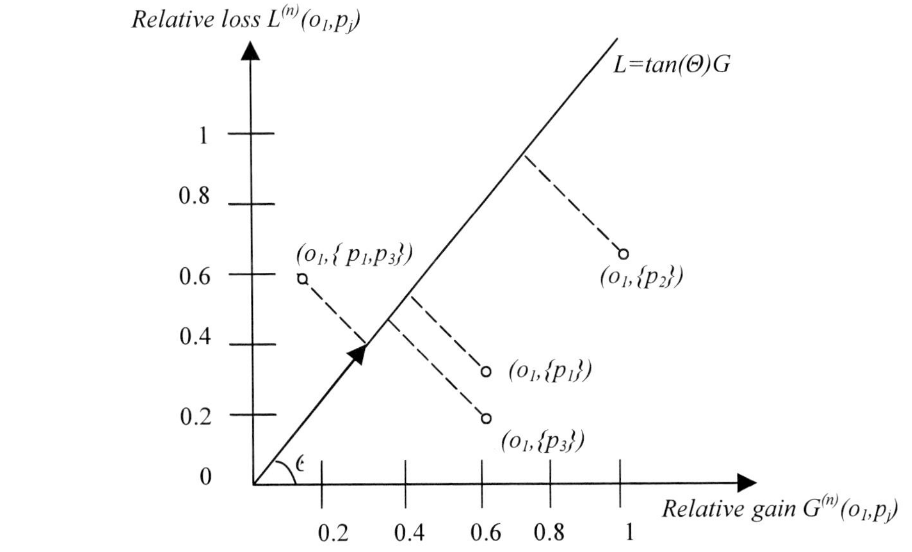

Legend: Subset p_1, p_3 gives the best *Bcf* for the execution of o_1.

Figure 10. Example selection of the best *Bcf* for an operation o_1 at step *n* (© 2005 IEEE).

$$Bcf^{(n)} = cos(\theta)L^{(n)} + sin(\theta)G^{(n)} \tag{8}$$

RBSA maintains two lists of operations for *Alg.* $O^{(n)}_{sched}$ a list of scheduled operations, it is initially empty (at step *0* of *RBSA*); and $O^{(n)}_{cand}$ a list of candidate operations, it initially contains the operations without predecessors. At each step *RBSA* computes the compromise function for each pair (*candidate operation*, *processor set*), and chooses the best compromise function *Bcf*; if it fails to obtain one of the objectives Rel_{obj} or Rt_{obj} or both, then the user has to either loosen the unattained objective or change θ. *RBSA* stops at the step where all candidate operations are scheduled on a processors subset (empty $O^{(n)}_{cand}$).

Simulation results show that *RBSA* slightly outperforms other scheduling algorithms with replication on both criteria [26], [27].

4.2. Evaluation of Distributed Recovery in Large-Scale Storage Systems

4.2.1. Fast Recovery Mechanism (FARM)

Advances in storage technology have reduced cost and improved performance and capacity; however, disk drive reliability has improved slowly. In a typical environment for large supercomputing systems data loss is intolerable. Moreover, the time to rebuild a failing single disk is becoming longer as increases in disk capacity outpace increases in bandwidth. The work presented in this section [28] proposes *Fast Recovery Mechanism (FARM)* for *petabyte-scale*[2] storage systems with thousands of disk drives. *FARM* uses declustering to reduce the time needed to deal with disk failure and importantly to improve reliability, it treats fast the consequences of failures and thus limits the chance that additional failures might lead to data loss during the period that precedes recovery, period of vulnerability. *Declustering* distributes the mirrored copies or redundancy groups across the disk array, so that after a disk failure, the data needed to reconstruct the lost data is distributed over a number of drives in the disk array. In *FARM* failure and recovery are transparent to users.

In order to achieve high reliability in large systems, user data is stored redundantly using either replication or some form of erasure correcting code such as storing the parity of a group of blocks. A *redundancy group* is a group of data blocks composed of user data and their associated replicas or parity/erasure blocks. The size of a redundancy group is the total user data in the group, excluding the replicas or parity blocks.

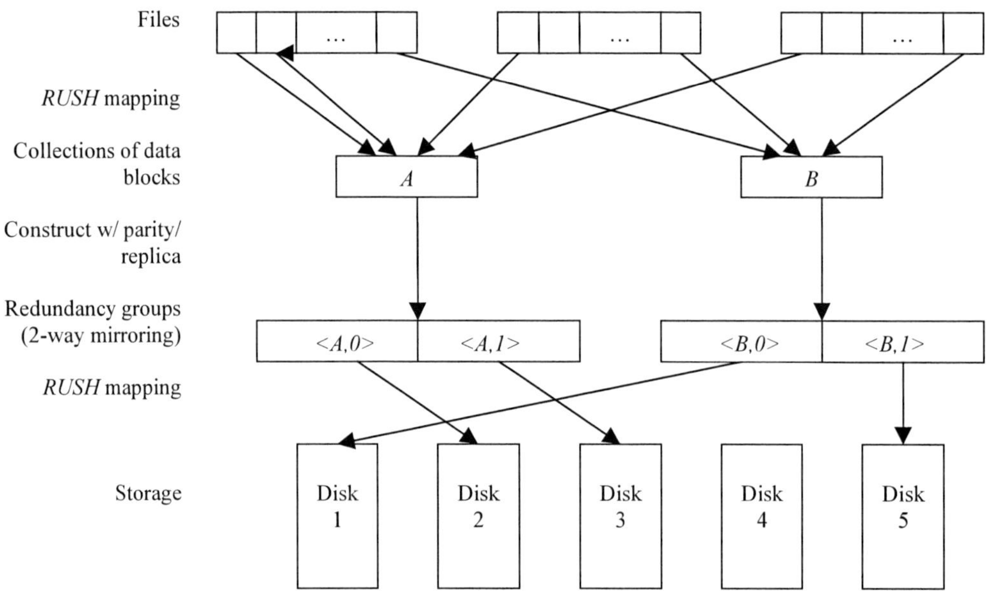

Legend: Each data block is marked <*grp_id*,, *rep_id*>, where, *grp_id* is the identifier of the group to which it belongs, and *rep_id* is its identifier in the group. Data blocks that reside in the same redundancy group share one *grp_id* with various values of *rep_id*.

A *n*-way mirroring keeps *n* copies of each user data block, each block on a different disk.

Figure 11. Redundancy group construction (© 2005 IEEE).

[2] A petabyte is 2^{50} bytes, it is equal to 1,024 terabytes.

There are several redundancy schemes. An *n-way mirroring* scheme maintains *n* copies of each user data block, each block residing on a different disk; it is the simplest redundancy scheme. Alternatively, a *parity scheme* adds a block containing the *(XOR)* parity of the user data blocks. For higher fault tolerance, *Erasure Correcting Codes (ECC's)* are used to generate more than a single parity block, they are called *m/n* schemes, such that $n=m+k$, where m is the number of user data blocks and k is the number of parity blocks [29], [30]. An *m/n* scheme gives m-availability but must update all k parity blocks whenever a data block changes.

In the proposed petabyte-scale system, files are broken into fixed-size *1 MB blocks*. A number of blocks are gathered in a *collection* with the mapping of block to collection done by *Replication under Scalable Hashing (RUSH)* [31]. A collection is then assigned to a *redundancy group* by, the afore mentioned, redundancy schemes such as replication or adding parity blocks. Collection of blocks enable efficient data management and redundancy groups provide enhanced reliability. *RUSH* is used again to allocate redundancy groups to storage devices (Figure 11).

4.2.2. Disks Failure and Recovery in FARM

The traditional recovery approach, in the *Redundant Array of Independent (or Inexpensive) Disks (RAID)* architectures, replicates data on a failed disk to one dedicated spare disk upon disk failure. Such a scheme works properly for small systems consisting of up to hundred disks, but fails to provide acceptable reliability for large systems with thousands of disks.

Besides surpassing *RAID* in scale, the system envisioned in *FARM* is also dynamic: batches of disk drives will be deployed to replace failed or old disks and to provide additional capacity. A *RAID* is declustered if parity data and spare space are evenly distributed throughout the disk array. *FARM* is declustering at a much higher scale, with a primary focus on reliability, though performance also benefits, as will be illustrated in the simulation results.

Figure 12 illustrates the principles of *FARM* as compared to traditional *RAID* in a *2*-way mirroring system. *FARM* distributes all new replicas to different disks. In a system with thousands of disks, replication can proceed in parallel reducing the period of vulnerability from the time needed to rebuild an entire disk to the time needed to create one or two replicas of a redundancy group, reducing thus the probability of data loss.

- The reliability of a large storage system employing *FARM* depends on:
- the size and structure of redundancy groups,
- the size of the blocks,
- the latency of disk failure detection,
- the bandwidth utilized for recovery,
- the amount of data stored on disks,
- the number of disks in the system,
- the way disks are replaced.

Two inherent factors affect the probability of data loss; the total number of the redundancy groups across the system, and the size of a single redundancy group.

Disk 0	Disk 1	Disk 2	Disk 3	Disk 4
<A,0>	*<A,1>*	*<B,0>*	*<E,0>*	*<E,1>*
<B,1>	*<C,0>*	*<D,0>*	*<C,1>*	*<D,1>*

a) The system works normally

Disk 0	Disk 1	Disk 2	Disk 3	Disk 4
<A,0>	*<A,1>*	*<B,0>*	*<E,0>*	*<E,1>*
<B,1>	*<C,0>*	*<D,0>*	*<C,1>*	*<D,1>*

b) Disk 3 fails after a while

Disk 0	Disk 1	Disk 2	Disk 3	Disk 4	Disk 5
<A,0>	*<A,1>*	*<B,0>*	*<E,0>*	*<E,1>*	*<E,2>*
<B,1>	*<C,0>*	*<D,0>*	*<C,1>*	*<D,1>*	*<C,2>*

c) Traditional *RAID* replicates data to a spare disk

Disk 0	Disk 1	Disk 2	Disk 3	Disk 4
<A,0>	*<A,1>*	*<B,0>*	*<E,0>*	*<E,1>*
<B,1>	*<C,0>*	*<D,0>*	*<C,1>*	*<D,1>*
...	...	*<E,2>*	...	*<C,2>*

d) *FARM* distributes data replicas

Figure 12. Upon disk failure, different behaviors with/without *FARM* (© 2005 IEEE).

4.2.3. Simulation Assumptions and Results

The following assumptions are made:

- two petabyte storage system *(2 PB)*,
- up to *15,000* disk drives, each with extrapolated capacity of *1 TB* and extrapolated sustainable bandwidth of *80 MB/sec*,
- recovery can consume up to *20%* of the available disk bandwidth,
- each device reserves no more than *40%* of its total capacity, at system initialization, for recovered data,
- the size of a redundancy group is the amount of user data stored on it, it varies from *1 GB* to *100 GB*,
- disk drives have a typical *End of Design Life (EODL)* of six years and follow Elerath [32] for the failure rates.

Interesting results are obtained out of the conducted simulation using *PARSEC* [33]:

- *Reliability* always increases with *FARM*, this is marked by a decrease in the probability of data loss during the six years test interval. Six types of redundancy groups are constructed for test with and without *FARM*: *2*-way mirroring *(1/2)*, *3*-way mirroring *(1/3)*, two *RAID 5* Schemes *(2/3* and *4/5)*, and two *ECC* configurations *(4/6* and *8/10)*. The results also show that the size of the redundancy groups has little impact on the systems using *FARM*.

- After a disk fails, it is needed to identify the failed disk and then reconstruct the data that was on it. The period of vulnerability consists of the time to detect a failure and the time to rebuild the data. *Latency of failure detection* is noticeable on systems with small redundancy group sizes since it takes less time to reconstruct smaller sized groups, which makes a constant failure detection latency occupy a relatively larger portion of the period of vulnerability. It was found that the *ratio* of failure detection latency to actual data recovery time determines the probability of data loss.
- Data rebuild time can be shortened by allocating a higher portion of *disk bandwidth to recovery*. The obtained results show that the probability of data loss decreases as recovery bandwidth increases. It is also shown that high recovery bandwidth (in *MB/sec*) increases reliability for systems without *FARM*. The advantage of higher recovery bandwidth is to reduce the data rebuild time, but *FARM* has already cut recovery time which lessens further reduction from higher bandwidth.
- *FARM* distributes both data and redundancy information across the whole system. As disks fail, data stored on them is redistributed to the rest of the system, never to a single disk. This approach may unbalance the actual amount of data stored on each individual disk, however with proper *disk space utilization* such shortcoming is avoided. The unevenness in data distribution is caused by the relatively large ratio of redundancy group size to disk size. It was found from the simulation that reducing redundancy group size would alleviate this problem and balance disk utilization, but at the cost of lower reliability.
- Large scale storage systems are dynamic, old disk drives are removed when they fail or retire, and new disk drives are added to satisfy the demands of *disk replacement* and data capacity growth. It is infeasible to add disk drives one by one as it may be done daily, instead a *batch* of disk drive is added. Large batch sizes may have a bad impact on the system reliability since they introduce a large number and more failure-prone disks into the system. Experimentation was carried by replacing failed disk drives when the system has lost *2%*, *4%*, *6%*, and *8%* of the total number of disk drives. It was found that the number of disks, in each replacement batch, and the replacement frequency have a small effect on system reliability.
- Experimentation shows that the probability of data loss increases linearly as *system scale* varies throughout chosen test sizes ranging from *0.1 PB* to *5 PB*. It is also seen that when the failure rate of individual disks doubled while the rest of the configuration stayed the same, the probability of data loss more than doubled.

Simulation results show that *FARM* provides high-performance high-capacity reliable petabyte scale storage systems, compared to traditional redundancy techniques.

5. Reliability Evaluation of Distributed Software Systems

In this section the Athena system is introduced. Athena analyzes the factors related to reliability and real-time performance, it then collects information on the data files needed for program executions and their distributed status, finally, it builds algorithms to evaluate the real-time performance of distributed software with reliability constraint. More interest is accorded to the reliability evaluation of distributed software. The reliability of a distributed program in a grid computing system is among the concerns of Section 6.1, while Section 6.2 uses a recursive merge technique based on the *BDD* to evaluate the reliability of dependable distributed computing systems.

5.1. Athena: A Real-Time Performance Evaluation for Distributed Software with Reliability Constraints

The evaluation of the *Real-time Performance of Distributed Software* (*RTPDS*) with reliability constraint is a new and complex research topic. There are many influencing factors, such as the status of available programs and data files on nodes, the network topology, the transmission time, and the bandwidth [34]. Three approaches are available for the evaluation of *RTPDS*: fine-grained benchmarks, simulation, and application-oriented benchmarks [35], [36], [37]; noticeably, they are only concerned with real-time performance without reliability constraint.

In Athena [38], the factors related to reliability and real-time performance are analyzed, then information on the data files needed for program executions and their distributed status is collected. Finally, algorithms are built to evaluate *RTPDS* with reliability constraint.

The execution time of a program is the sum of two components: the data transmission time from the nodes containing the files needed for the program execution to the node where the program resides, and the program running time. The running time is negligible compared to the transmission time. The Athena system is based on calculating the transmission time of each file needed for the execution of a given program while satisfying a predetermined reliability constraint.

A distributed system is defined as follows:

$$G = (V, E, F, P) \tag{9}$$

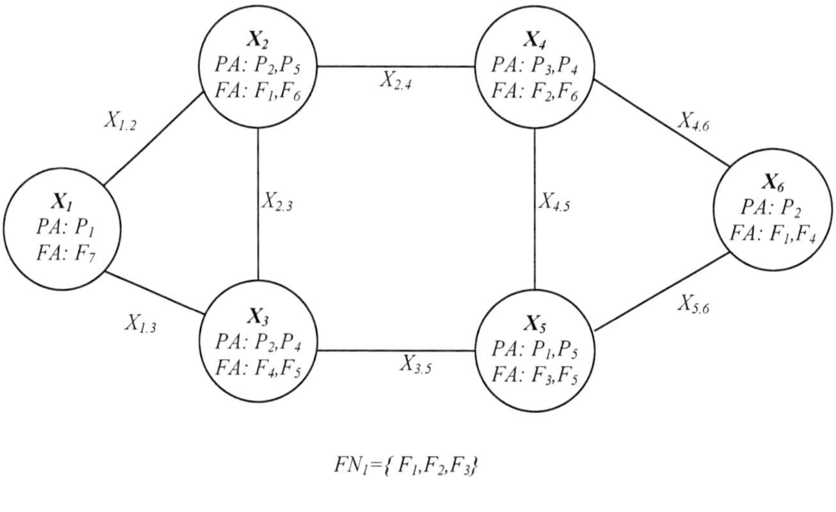

Figure 13. A simple distributed system with different file distributions (© 2005 IEEE).

G is an undirected graph including four parameters. ***V*** is a set of nodes on which the processing elements run. ***E*** is a set of edges between nodes and each edge represents a communication link between two nodes. ***F*** is a set of available data files. ***P*** is a set of available programs. Figure 13 is an example of a simple distributed system. There are six circles. Each circle represents a node and every node has a processing element. Every node communicates with others by communication links. For example, node x_1 has one data file, F_7. It could perform program P_1, which directly communicate with other nodes (x_2, x_3) by two links $(x_{1,2}, x_{1,3})$. From the figure we have:

$$\boldsymbol{G} = (\boldsymbol{V}, \boldsymbol{E}, \boldsymbol{F}, \boldsymbol{P})$$
$$\boldsymbol{V} = \{x_1, x_2, x_3, x_4, x_5, x_6\}$$
$$\boldsymbol{E} = \{x_{1,2}, x_{1,3}, x_{2,3}, x_{2,4}, x_{3,5}, x_{4,5}, x_{4,6}, x_{5,6}\}$$
$$\boldsymbol{F} = \{F_1, F_2, F_3, F_4, F_5, F_6, F_7\}$$
$$\boldsymbol{P} = \{P_1, P_2, P_3, P_4, P_5\}$$

$\boldsymbol{FA_k}$ denotes the set of data files available on node x_k, $\boldsymbol{PA_k}$ is the set of programs available on node x_k, $\boldsymbol{FN_j}$ is the set of dada files needed for program P_j. Each program can be performed on more than one node, it accesses data files from other nodes if needed. Each program or available data file may have more than one copy in the whole distributed system. For file transmission, data file are independent of each other.

Among several paths available for the transmission of file *i* to the node where a program *j* is to be run, the one that satisfies the minimum transmission time under predefined reliability constraint is chosen, $T^j_{i,b(j,i)}$), where $b(j,i)$ is the index of the transmission path whose transmission time satisfies the reliability constraint $P(F_i)$ of file *i*, such that:

$$\frac{b(j,i)}{n(j,i)} \geq P(F_i) \tag{10}$$

then,

$$b(j,i) \geq n(j,i) \times P(F_i) = \lceil n(j,i) \times P(F_i) \rceil \tag{11}$$

where $n(j,i)$ is the number of transmission paths of file *i* from the network nodes to the node where a program *j* is to be run.

The set of transmission times Γ of file *i* needed for the execution of program *j* over $n(j,i)$ paths is:

$$\Gamma = (T^j_{i,1}, T^j_{i,2}, \ldots, T^j_{i,b(j,i)}, \ldots, T^j_{i,n(j,i)}) \tag{12}$$

where Γ is sorted in ascending order of transmission times from $T_{i,1}$ up to $T_{i,n(j,i)}$.

Such path selection is performed for all files required for the program execution. Since the files are transmitted in parallel to the node where the program is to be run, the *Real-Time-Performance of a Distributed Software (RTPDS)* is thus:

$$max(T^{j}_{1,b(j,1)},\ldots,T^{j}_{i,b(j,i)},\ldots,T^{j}_{m,b(j,m)}) \tag{13}$$

where m is the number of files required for the execution of program j.

Illustrative results are obtained out of this study, a different determination of $b(j,i)$ may yield a different outcome.

6. Global Reliability Evaluation of Distributed Systems

This section presents research work dealing the distributed computing environment as a whole, the reliability of such system is built upon the reliability of the composing components. The grid computing system in Section 6.1 and the recursive merge technique for the *BDD* in Section 6.2 study the reliability of a distributed software system and that of the whole distributed system. In Section 6.3 the *AHP* is used to evaluate the effect of the interaction between the different distributed system components on the overall reliability.

6.1. Reliability Analysis of Grid Computing Systems

6.1.1 Grid Computing Systems

Grid computing systems have emerged as an important new field, distinguished from conventional distributed systems, by their focus on large-scale resource sharing, they are a kind of wide-area distributed systems [39], [40]. The real and specific problem that underlies the Grid concept is coordinated resource sharing and problem solving in dynamic multi-distributed programs. The sharing that the grid computing is concerned with is not primarily file exchange but rather "direct access" to remote resources such as computers, printers, data, software as required by a range of collaborative problem-solving and resource-brokering strategies. Thus, the communication between computing programs and resources significantly affects the grid computing system reliability.

From the viewpoint of a grid computing program, the program reliability can be defined as the probability of its successful execution when running on multiple nodes and exchanging information with the remote resources of other nodes. From the system point of view, the reliability of the grid system can be defined as the probability of all the grid computing programs to be executed successfully in the grid computing environment. In fact, the grid program reliability and grid system reliability are typical cases of distributed program and distributed system reliabilities.

The work presented in this section [41] tries to assess the reliability of grid programs and grid computing systems by according care to the large size of communicated data and the processing times of grid programs. Figure 14 shows a sample grid computing system.

The communication time $T_c(i,j)$ between nodes i and j can be derived from the total size of information $D(i,j)$ exchanged through the link $L(i,j)$ between the two nodes:

$$T_c(i,j) = \frac{D(i,j)}{S(i,j)} \tag{14}$$

where $S(i,j)$ is the mean speed of the link. It can be assumed that failures of nodes and links satisfy the Poisson process [42]. Communication fails if any failure occurs either on the link or on the two connected nodes. Knowing that the failure rate of a node *k* is λ_k and that of a link *L(i,j)* is $\lambda_{i,j}$, the probability for the successful communication between nodes *i* and *j* through link *L(i,j)* can be expressed as:

$$R_c(i,j) = e^{\{-(\lambda_i+\lambda_j+\lambda_{i,j})\times T_c(i,j)\}} \tag{15}$$

where $T_c(i,j)$ can be calculated from Eq.14.

Similarly, a program fails while executed if the node where it is processed fails. Thus, the probability for a program P_m to be executed successfully during its processing time $t(m)$ on node *n* is:

$$R_p(m,n) = e^{\{-\lambda_n \times t(m)\}} \tag{16}$$

6.1.2 Reliability Evaluation

The *Minimal Resource Spanning Tree (MRST)* is to be sought for the reliability calculation of the grid computing systems. A *Resource Spanning Tree (RST)* is defined as a spanning tree that connects the node that executes the program under consideration to other nodes such that its vertices hold all the required resources for exchanging information with the given program. In Figure 14, if G_1 executes program P_1 with resources R_1 and R_2, it is required to access the remote resource R_3 resident at nodes G_2 or G_4. The following are some *RST's* that make P_1 run successfully on G_1:

{G_1,G_2, *L(1,2)*}; { G_1, G_2, G_3, *L(1,2)*,*L(2,3)*}; { G_1, G_2, G_4, *L(1,2)*,*L(2,4)*};
{ G_1, G_2, G_3, *L(1,3)*,*L(2,3)*};{ G_1, G_3, G_4, *L(1,3)*,*L(3,4)*};
{ G_1, G_2, G_3, G_4, *L(1,2)*,*L(2,3)*,*L(3,4)*};{ G_1, G_2, G_3, G_4, *L(1,2)*,*L(2,4)*,*L(3,4)*};
{ G_1, G_2, G_3, G_4, *L(1,3)*,*L(2,3)*,*L(2,4)*}; {G_1,G_2, G_3, G_4, *L(1,3)*,*L(2,4)*,*L(3,4)*}.

On the other hand, the notion of *Minimal Resource Spanning Tree (MRST)* is to be defined. For a given program executed by a certain computing node, an $MRST_i$ is an RST_i such that there exists no other resource spanning tree, say RST_j, which is subset of RST_i, i.e.,

$$\neg(\exists j)RST_j \subseteq RST_i) \tag{17}$$

Continued to the above example, the *RST* composed of {G_1, G_2, G_3, *L(1,2)*, *L(2,3)*} is not an *MRST* for P_1 executed by G_1 because it has the *RST* constituted of {G_1,G_2, *L(1,2)*} as a subset.

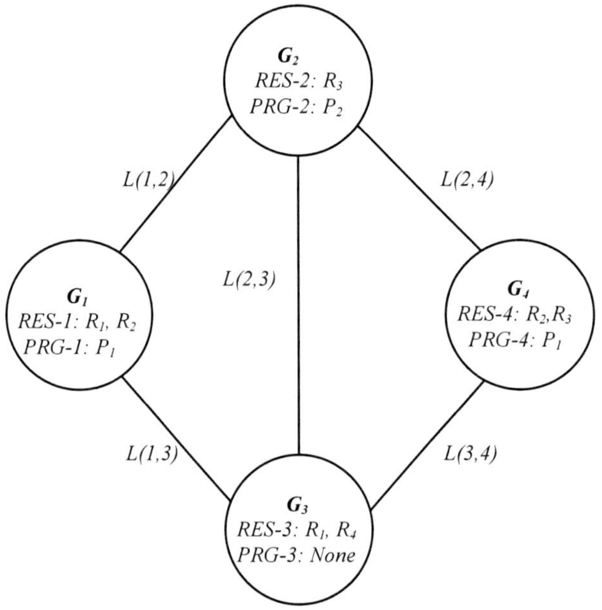

Legend: Program P_1 can run successfully on either computing node G_1 or G_4 and is able to reach the required resources R_1, R_2, R_3.

Figure 14. A four nodes sample grid computing system (© 2005 IEEE).

The reliability R_{MRST} of an *MRST* is defined as the probability of the *MRST* to be operational to execute the given program. It has three components:

1). reliability of all the links contained in the *MRST* during the communication;
2). reliability of all the nodes contained in the *MRST* during the communication;
3). reliability of the root node that executes the program during its processing time.

The reliability of link *L(i, j)* for exchanging the information can be expressed by:

$$R_L(i,j) = e^{\{-\lambda_{i,j} \times T_c(i,j)\}} \tag{18}$$

where $T_c(i,j)$ can be calculated from Eq.14. Thus the total communication time of node G_j is:

$$T(j) = \sum_{i \in D_j} T_c(i,j) \tag{19}$$

such that $\boldsymbol{D_j}$ is the set of nodes communicating with node G_j in the *MRST*.

The reliability function of node G_j for communication is:

$$R_c(j) = e^{\{-\lambda_j \times T(j)\}} \tag{20}$$

Finally, the reliability of a program P_m to be executed successfully during the processing time *t(m)* on node *n* can be obtained from Eq.16.

Thus, the reliability of the *MRST* can be derived from Eq.16, Eq.18, Eq.20:

$$
\begin{aligned}
R_{MRST} &= R_P(m,n) \times \prod_{L(i,j)\in MRST} R_L(i,j) \times \prod_{G_j \in MRST} R_c(j) \\
&= e^{-\lambda_n \times (t(m)+T(n))} \times \prod_{l(i,j)\in MRST} e^{-\lambda_{i,j} \times T_c(i,j)} \times \prod_{\substack{G_j \in MRST \\ j\neq n}} e^{-\lambda_j \times T(j)}
\end{aligned} \tag{21}
$$

Finding all *MRST's* permits the calculation of the grid programs and grid computing systems reliabilities.

There are many algorithms to search the *Minimal File Spanning Trees (MFST's)* for conventional distributed systems [43], [44]. However, *MRST* is different from *MFST* because of the working time (communication time or node processing time). The same program executed by different root nodes may cause different working times on the same elements (links or nodes). For example, revisit Figure 14, the *MFST's* (obtained by replacing the resources in the figure with files) searched without considering the working times of the elements should be four trees:

1) $\{G_1, G_2, L(1,2)\}$;
2) $\{G_1, G_2, G_3, L(1,3), L(2,3)\}$;
3) $\{ G_3, G_4, L(3,4)$;
4) $\{G_2, G_3, G_4, L(2,4), L(2,3)\}$.

But the *MRST's*, considering the working time of the elements, should be separated into two groups:

a) P_1 is executed by G_1 with three *MRST's*:
  1) $\{G_1, G_2, L(1,2)\}$;
  2) $\{G_1, G_2, G_3, L(1,3), L(2,3)\}$;
  3) $\{ G_1, G_3, G_4, L(1,3), L(3,4)\}$.

b) P_1 is executed by G_4 with three *MRST's*:
  4) $\{G_3, G_4, L(3,4)\}$;
  5) $\{G_2, G_3, G_4, L(2,3), L(2,4)\}$;
  6) $\{ G_1, G_2, G_4, L(1,2), L(2,4)\}$.

The total number of *MRST's* for this case is six trees, in which the third and the sixth trees would have been omitted by *MFST's* because the first tree dominates the sixth tree and the fourth tree dominates the third tree, if the working times are not to be considered.

After finding an *MRST*, its reliability can be calculated (Eq.21). If all the *MRST's* for a program executed by a node can be identified, they will build the foundation of the algorithms developed in this work to analyze the grid program reliability and the grid system reliability. Thus, an algorithm is built to search all the *MRST's* for a given program executed by a given node meanwhile it obtains the working time of each element in the *MRST's*. This algorithm can be briefly described as:

1). start from the given node to search the required resources on the other nodes along the possible links;
2). record each element that forms the searching route and its working time, when all the required resources are reached an *MRST* is found and recorded;
3). try other routes to search other *MRST's* (repeat steps 1, 2) until all the *MRST's* are searched.

6.1.2.1. Grid Program Reliability

Any one of the *MRST's* can provide a successful execution of the given grid program if all of its elements are operational when working. Thus, given a grid program, its reliability *GPR* can be described as the probability of having at least one of its *MRST's* reliable:

$$GPR=Pr(\text{at least one MRST of a program is reliable}) \tag{22}$$

Let $N(P_m)$ be the total number of *MRST's* for the given program P_m. E_j represents the event in which $MRST_j$ is reliable to successfully execute the given program, ($j=1,2,\ldots,N(P_m)$). Thus, the grid program reliability of P_m can be written as:

$$GPR(P_m)=Pr(\bigcup_{j=1}^{N(p_m)} E_j) \tag{23}$$

Using conditional probability, the events in Eq.23 can be decomposed:

$$\begin{aligned} GPR(P_m) &= Pr(E_1)+Pr(E_2)\times Pr(\overline{E}_1|E_2)+\cdots \\ &+ Pr(E_{N(P_m)})\times Pr(\overline{E}_1\cap\overline{E}_2\cap\cdots\cap\overline{E}_{N(P_m)-1}|E_{N(p_m)}) \end{aligned} \tag{24}$$

where $Pr(\overline{E}_1|E_2)$ is the conditional probability that $MRST_1$ fails given that $MRST_2$ is in the operational state.

Hence, the grid program reliability expression of Eq.24 can be evaluated in terms of the probability of two distinct events. The fist event indicates that $MRST_i$ is in the operational state while the second event indicates that all of its previous trees $MRST_j$ ($j=1,2,\ldots,i-1$) are in the failure state given that $MRST_i$ is in the operational state. The probability of the first event, $Pr(E_i)$, is straightforward and can be calculated through (Eq.21). The probability of the second event $Pr(\overline{E}_1\cap\overline{E}_2\cap\cdots\cap\overline{E}_{i-1}|E_i)$ can be computed using another proposed algorithm. The brief description of such algorithm is that at first, identify the conditional elements that can fail any tree of $MRST_j$ ($j=1,2,\ldots,i-1$) while keeping $MRST_i$ operational. Then seek the possible combinations of these identified elements and compute the probabilities of those combinations, the summation of their probabilities gives $Pr(\overline{E}_1\cap\overline{E}_2\cap\cdots\cap\overline{E}_{i-1}|E_i)$.

6.1.2.2. Grid System Reliability

For the grid computing system, it is important to obtain a global reliability measure that describes how reliable the grid system is for a given distribution of programs and resources. Since the grid system reliability *GSR* is defined as the probability that all the computing programs are executed successfully, it is thus the probability of the intersection of the set of *MRST's* of all programs:

$$GSR = Pr(\bigcap_{m=1}^{M} MRST(P_m)) \tag{25}$$

where $MRST(P_m)$ denotes the set of all the *MRST's* associated with program P_m .

After finding all the intersected *MRST's*, similarly to the calculation of grid program reliability, if any one of these intersected *MRST's* is operational all the computing programs in the grid computing system are executed successfully. Thus, the grid system reliability can be written as:

$$GSR = Pr(\bigcup_{j=1}^{N} E_j) \tag{26}$$

where N is the total number of the intersected *MRST's* and E_j represents the event in which the intersected $MRST_j$ is reliable, ($j=1,2,\ldots, N$). By using conditional probability, the events considered in Eq.26 can be decomposed into mutually exclusive events as:

$$\begin{aligned} GSR = {} & Pr(E_1) + Pr(E_2) \times Pr(\overline{E}_1 | E_2) + \cdots \\ & + Pr(E_N) \times Pr(\overline{E}_1 \cap \overline{E}_2 \cap \cdots \cap \overline{E}_{N-1} | E_N) \end{aligned} \tag{27}$$

The probability of the first event $Pr(E_i)$ is straightforward, and can be calculated through Eq.21. The probability of the second event $Pr(\overline{E}_1 \cap \overline{E}_2 \cap \cdots \cap \overline{E}_{i-1} | E_i)$ can be calculated using the second algorithm as previously mentioned.

As the number of nodes and links increases in the grid computing system, the usability of the proposed algorithms becomes under severe questioning which lays down the way for future research towards a better performance.

6.2. Reliability Evaluation of Dependable Distributed Computing Systems Based on Recursive Merge and BDD

6.2.1. DPR, DSR and DCS

The development of computer networking and embedded *VLSI* processing devices has led to an increasing interest in *Distributed Computing Systems* (*DCS*) in which the computations are distributed among many processing elements (*PE's*). Distributed systems provide cost effective means for resource sharing and extensibility, and obtain potential increases in performance, reliability, and fault tolerance. A distributed program usually requires one or more of the resources for successful execution, such as *PE's*, data files, etc. For successful completion of a program, the local hosts (the *PE's* that contain the required files) and the interconnection links must all function correctly. Therefore, the distribution of data files can affect the overall reliability of the system.

Many researchers are interested in studying the *Distributed Program Reliability* (*DPR*) and the *Distributed System Reliability* (*DSR*) [45], [46], [41], [47]. The work presented in this section [48] proposes a *BDD*-based algorithm, to compute the reliability of a *DCS* with both perfect and imperfect nodes. There are several features that make the algorithm more efficient than previous work:

- The *Binary Decision Diagram (BDD)* representing the Boolean reliability expression of a *DCS* can be constructed by avoiding the redundant computation of the isomorphic sub-graphs during the merging process. Therefore, the reliability can be quickly derived from the *BDD*.
- In addition, the proposed method can be integrated with the methodologies that use the *BDD* to analyze the dependability of a system, such as system availability, system failure frequency, importance measures and sensitivity analysis [49].
- Moreover, using the *BDD*, the proposed method has the capability of dealing with large number of Boolean variables, which makes it suitable for large scale *DCS*.

A *DCS* is an undirected graph in which the nodes represent the hosts and the edges represent the communication links (Eq.9). Figure 15 presents the sample *DCS* to be studied. A *File Spanning Tree (FST)* is defined as a spanning tree that connects the root node (the host node that runs the program under consideration) to some other nodes such that its nodes contain all the required files for the successful execution of the program. An *FST* is a *Minimal File Spanning tree* (*MFST*) if there exists no other *FST* that is a subset of this *FST*. For

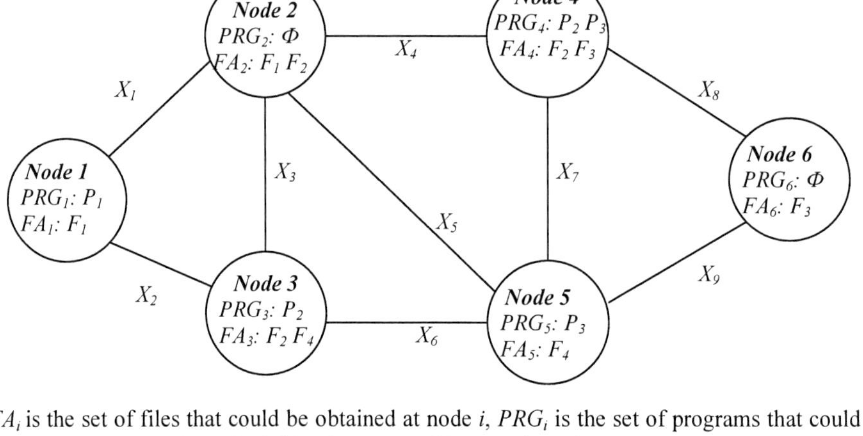

Legend: FA_i is the set of files that could be obtained at node *i*, PRG_i is the set of programs that could be run at node *i*,FN_j is the set of required files for successful execution of program *j*.$FN_1= F_1\ F_2\ F_3$, $FN_2= F_2\ F_4$, $FN_3= F_1\ F_3$.

Figure 15. An example *DCS* (© 2005 IEEE).

instance, program P_2 in Figure 15 will function if it can run at node n_3 or n_4, and can access files $\{F_2, F_4\}$. Therefore, $\{n_3\}$ and $\{n_4, x_4, n_2, x_3, n_3\}$ are two *FST's* of P_2, but the later one is not a *MFST* since $\{n_3\}$ is a subset of $\{n_4, x_4, n_2, x_3, n_3\}$. The set of *MFST's* of the program P_2 are: $\{n_3\}$, $\{n_4, x_4, n_2, x_5, n_5\}$, $\{n_4, x_7, n_5\}$, $\{n_4, x_8, n_6, x_9, n_5\}$.

From the definition of *MFST* [45], the *Distributed Program Reliability* (*DPR*) for program *j* and the *Distributed System Reliability (DSR)* are defined respectively as:

$$DPR_j = Pr\{\bigcup_{1}^{n_{mfst}} MFST_i = 1\} \tag{28}$$

$$DSR = Pr\{\bigcup_{1}^{m_{mfst}} MFST_i = 1\} \tag{29}$$

where n_{mfst} is the number of *MFST's* belonging to program *j* and m_{mfst} is the number of *MFST's* over all programs.

6.2.2. Binary Decision Diagram (BDD)

BDD [50] is based on a disjoint decomposition of a Boolean function called the *Shannon expansion*. Given a Boolean function $f(x_1,\ldots,x_n)$, then for any $i \in (1,\cdots,n\}$:

$$f = x_i \cdot f_{x_i=1} + \overline{x}_i \cdot f_{x_i=0} \tag{30}$$

In order to express the Shannon decomposition concisely, the *if-then-else (ite)* format is defined as:

$$f = ite(x_i, f_{x_i=1}, f_{x_i=0}) \tag{31}$$

From the above equation *if* x_i*=1 then* $f_{x_i=1}$ is executed *else* $f_{x_i=0}$ is to be executed. Eq.31 can also be written as:

$$f = x_i \rightarrow f_{x_i=1}, f_{x_i=0} \tag{32}$$

A useful property of *BDD* is that all the paths from the root to the leaves are mutually disjoint. If f represents the Boolean expression of the system availability, based on the property of the disjoint decomposition of *BDD*, the reliability (or availability) of a system can be recursively evaluated by Eq.30 as:

$$Pr\{f\} = Pr\{x_i\} \cdot Pr\{f_{x_i=1}\} + Pr\{\overline{x}_i\} \cdot Pr\{f_{x_i=0}\} \tag{33}$$

If $Pr\{x_i\}$ is the availability A_i of component *i* and U_i is the unavailability of component *i*, then the system availability *A* is:

$$A = Pr\{f\} = A_i \cdot A_{x_i=1} + U_i \cdot A_{x_i=0} = A_i \cdot A_{x_i=1} + (1 - A_i) \cdot A_{x_i=0} \quad (34)$$

where $A_{x_i=1}$ and $A_{x_i=0}$ represent $Pr\{f_{x_i=1}\}$ and $Pr\{f_{x_i=0}\}$ respectively.

6.2.3. Proposed Merging Algorithm for Perfect Nodes

The proposed algorithm for computing the *DPR* begins the merging procedure from a host node *s* where the program can run, it then produces sub-graphs by recursively merging the adjacent nodes one by one into the source set (*SS*). Each sub-graph has its corresponding *SS*. An *SS* is the set of nodes such that the host node $s \in SS$ and *SS* are connected. Therefore, if the *SS* of a sub-graph satisfies the requirement (i.e. contains all the required files), the merging with adjacent nodes stops. Two sub-graphs derived from different merging procedures are isomorphic if their *SS's* are identical, since the follow-up traversing path for the rest of the required files will be the same. Consequently, isomorphic sub-graphs have the same Boolean reliability expression *BF(.)*, i.e. the same *BDD*. This property is used to avoid redundant computations.

Figure 16 illustrates the recursive merge procedure as would be applied in the proposed algorithm to evaluate the DPR_1 of Figure 15. The traversed path, which includes the branches from the top-root graph to any one of the bottom-leaf sub-graphs in Figure 16 represents a *FST*. It can be transformed into the *BDD* representation by the proposed algorithm. Then taking the advantage of the disjoint property of *BDD*, the *DPR* can be efficiently calculated.

Each graph has its own Boolean reliability expression *BF*(·), i.e. *BF*(*G*) represents the Boolean reliability expression of *G*. Therefore, the recursive relationship of *BF*(·) between graph *G* and its sub-graph *G*n* is obtained as:

$$BF(G) = \bigoplus_{n \in N_{ss}} [BF(G * n) \otimes (\bigoplus_{i \in E_{ss:n}} x_i)] \quad (35)$$

where,

n is a node of G,

N_{ss} is the set of nodes that are adjacently connected to *SS*,

$E_{ss:n}$ is the set of edges that connect n and *SS*,

$G*n$ is the sub-graph of G obtained by merging adjacent node $n \in N_{ss}$ into *SS* and deleting any edge connecting n and *SS*,

$x_i / \bar{x}_i$ is the Boolean edge variable indicating if edge i is functional/failed (i.e. $x_i = 1 / \bar{x}_i = 1$),

$\oplus$ is the Boolean *OR* operation *BDD_or()*,

$\otimes$ is the Boolean *AND* operation *BDD_and()*.

For example, in Figure 16,

$$BF(G_1) = [BF(G_2) \otimes (x_2 \oplus x_3)] \oplus [BF(G_3) \otimes x_4] \oplus [BF(G_4) \otimes x_5]$$

By the bottom-up procedure, the *BDD* of the top-root graph representing the Boolean reliability expression of the *DPR*, is constructed. An example step by step follow up of the

BDD formation for DPR_1 as would be obtained by the proposed algorithm (Figure 18) is as follows:

$$BF(G)= [\ BF(G_3)\ (X_4) \oplus [\ BF(G_7)\ (X_4) \oplus [BF(G_{11})\ (X_4 \oplus X_7) \oplus BF(G_{12})\ (X_9)]\ (X_5 \oplus X_6)\ ]\ (X_2 \oplus X_3) \oplus [\ BF(G_9)\ (X_4 \oplus X_7) \oplus BF(G10)\ (X_9) \oplus [BF(G_{11})\ (X_4 \oplus X_7) \oplus BF(G_{12})\ (X_9)]\ (X_2 \oplus X_3 \oplus X_6)\ ]\ (X_5)\ ]\ (X_1) \oplus [\ [\ BF(G_{13})\ (X_7) \oplus BF(G_{14})\ (X_9) \oplus [BF(G_{11})\ (X_4 \oplus X_7) \oplus BF(G_{12})\ (X_9)]\ (X_1 \oplus X_3 \oplus X_5)\ ]\ (X_6) \oplus [BF(G_7)\ (X4) \oplus [BF(G_{11})\ (X_4 \oplus X_7) \oplus BF(G_{12})\ (X_9)]\ (X_5 \oplus X_6)\ ]\ (X_1 \oplus X_3)]\ (X_2) \tag{36}$$

This leads to the following:

$$\begin{aligned} BDD= {} & X_4\ (\underline{X_5 X_2 X_1 \oplus X_5 X_3 X_1 \oplus X_6 X_2 X_1 \oplus X_6 X_3 X_1} \oplus X_2 X_1 \oplus X_3 X_1 \oplus X_1 \\ & \oplus X_2 X_3 \underline{\oplus X_5 X_6 X_2 \oplus X_5 X_6 X_1 \oplus X_5 X_1 \oplus X_6 X_3 X_2)} \\ & \oplus X_7\ (\underline{X_5 X_2 X_1 \oplus X_5 X_3 X_1 \oplus X_6 X_2 X_1 \oplus X_6 X_3 X_1 \oplus X_5 X_1 \oplus X_5 X_6 X_1} \\ & \underline{\oplus X_5 X_6 X_2 \oplus X_6 X_3 X_2} \oplus X_6 X_2) \\ & \oplus X_9\ (X_5 X_2 X_1 \oplus X_5 X_3 X_1 \oplus X_6 X_2 X_1 \oplus X_6 X_3 X_1 \oplus X_5 X_1 \oplus X_5 X_6 X_1 \\ & \oplus X_5 X_6 X_2 \oplus X_6 X_3 X_2 \oplus X_6 X_2) \end{aligned} \tag{37}$$

where the underlined represents redundant polynomial portions. Then the BDD for the graph can be rewritten as:

$$BDD= X_4\ T1 \oplus X_7\ T2 \oplus X_9\ T3 \tag{38}$$

From Eq.37, it is noticed that T2 = T3, then Eq.38 can be rewritten as:

$$BDD= X_4\ T1 \oplus X_7\ T2 \oplus X_9\ T2 \tag{39}$$

$$\begin{aligned} T2= {} & X_5\ (\underline{X_2 X_1 \oplus X_3 X_1} \oplus X_6 X_1 \oplus X_6 X_2 \oplus X_1) \\ & \oplus X_6\ (\underline{X_2 X_1 \oplus X_3 X_1} \oplus X_2 X_3 \oplus X_2) \end{aligned} \tag{40}$$

Once more, there are redundant parts (T4) as underlined in Eq.40:

$$T2= X_5\ (T4 \oplus T5 \oplus X_1) \oplus X_6\ (T4 \oplus X_2 X_3 \oplus X_2) \tag{41}$$

Using Shannon expansions:

$$T4= X_2 \rightarrow X_1, (X_3 \rightarrow X_1, 0) \tag{42}$$

$$T5= X_6 \rightarrow (X_2 \rightarrow 1, X_1), 0 \tag{43}$$

$$X_1= X_1 \rightarrow 1,0 \tag{44}$$

$$X_2 X_3 = X_2 \rightarrow X_3, 0 \tag{45}$$

$$X_2= X_2 \rightarrow 1, 0 \tag{46}$$

Assuming the following heuristic ordering of variables: $x_4 < x_7 < x_9 < x_5 < x_6 < x_2 < x_3 < x_1 < x_8$ and drawing the BDD for the equations from Eq.42 to Eq.46 release Figure 17 a-e.

From Eq.37, Eq.38, Eq.40, Eq.41:

$$T1 = T2 \oplus T4 \oplus X_2 X_3 \oplus X_1 \tag{47}$$

where it is clear that all terms are redundant. The complete *BDD* for DPR_1 can thus be drawn as shown in Figure 17 f.

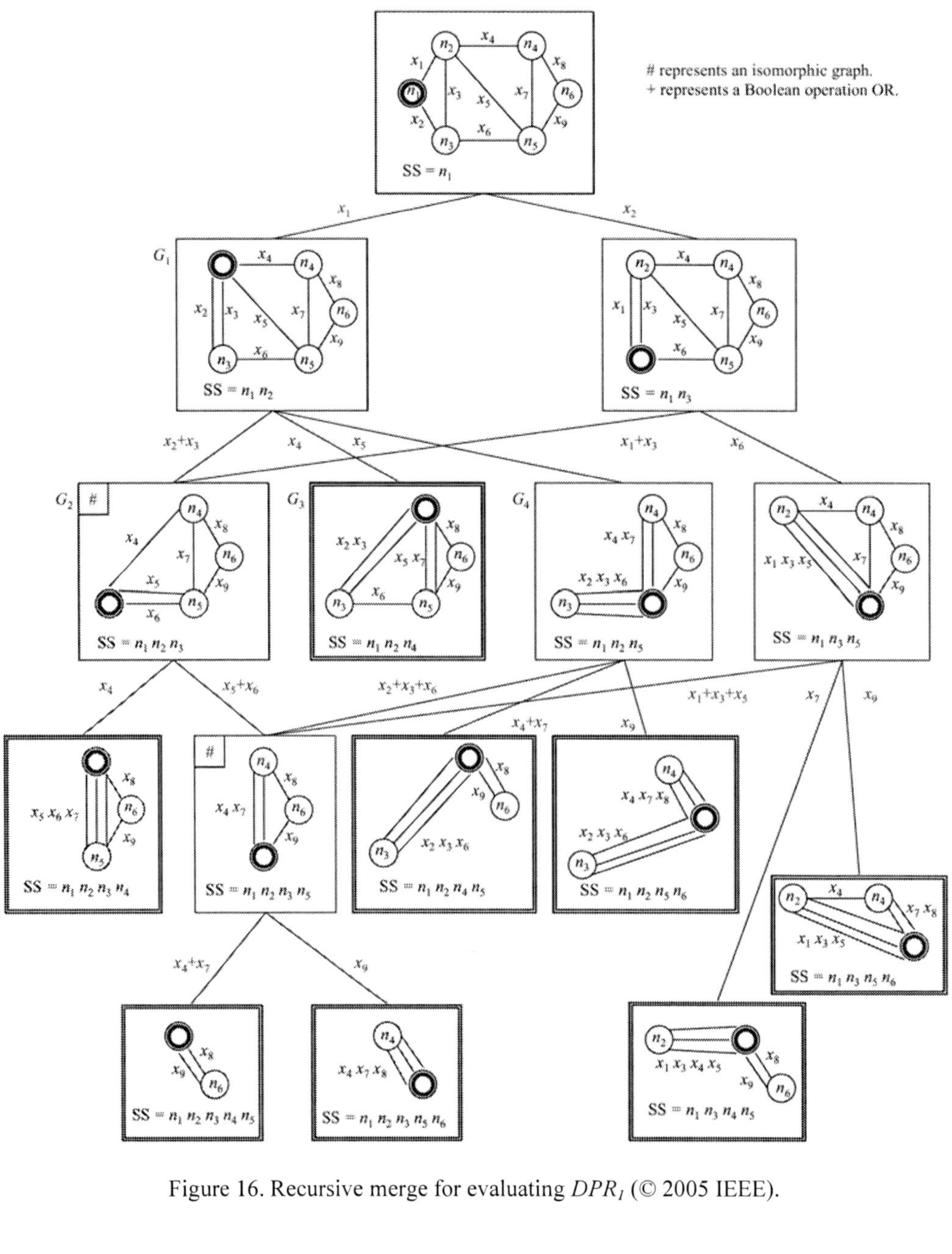

Figure 16. Recursive merge for evaluating DPR_1 (© 2005 IEEE).

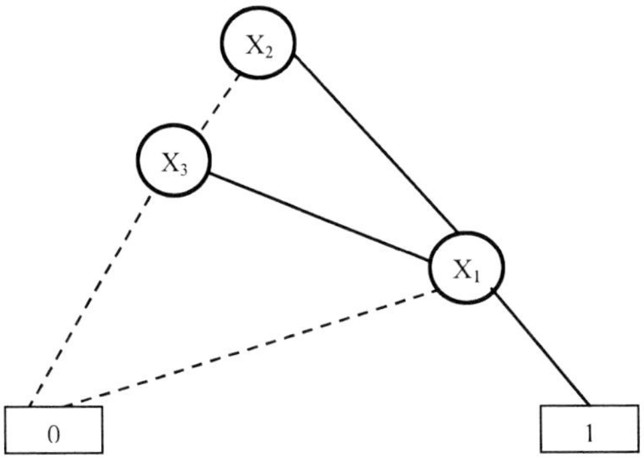

a) Eq.42 , Eq.44

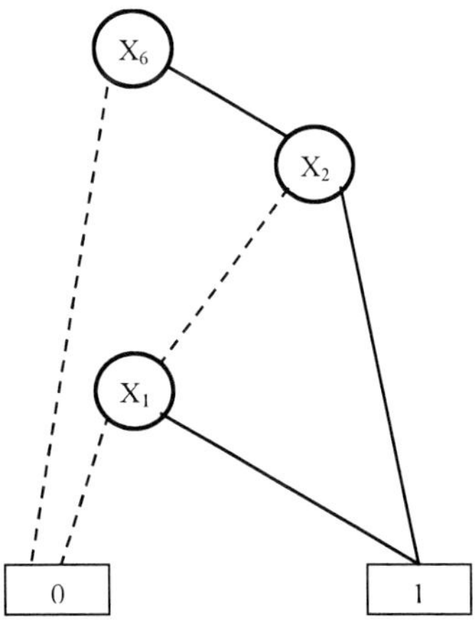

b) Eq.43

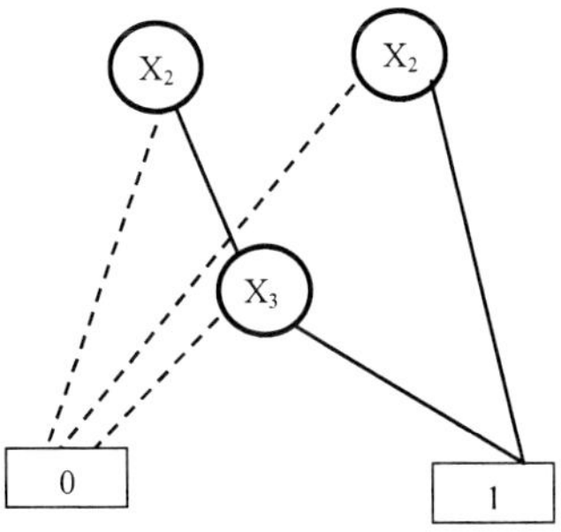

c)Eq.45, Eq.46

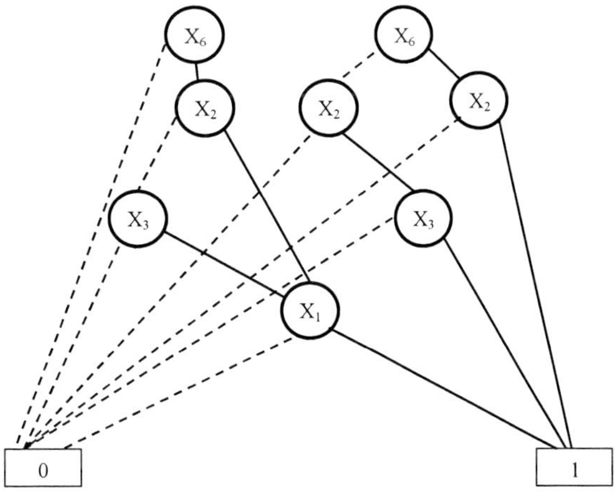

d) Eq.42, Eq.44, Eq.45, Eq.46 plus the *BDD* for the right hand side of *T2*

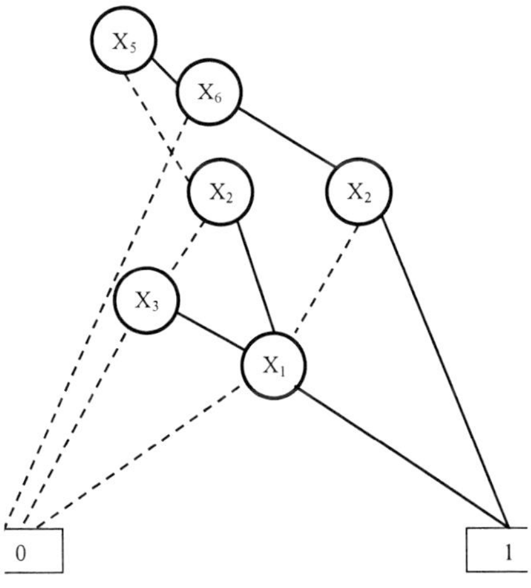

e) *BDD* for Eq.42, Eq.43, Eq.44 plus the *BDD* for the left hand side of *T2*

Figure 17. continued on next page.

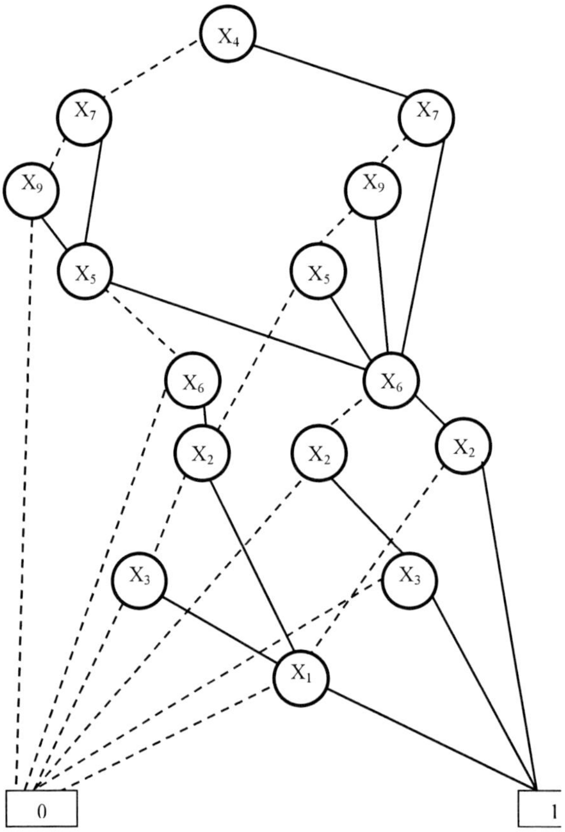

f) Final *BDD*

Figure 17. A step by step build up of the *BDD* for DPR_1

Simulation results, for perfect and imperfect nodes, show that the proposed algorithm has a reduced *BDD* size and is about 20% execution time efficient when compared to other methods [51], [52], [53], [54].

```
Initialize SS [N]=n, Sub_G[N]=G, p =0, L =0, r = -1,  k=0;
// N is the upper bound expected for SS or G, n is the node of executed program
Recursive_Merge (Sub_G[0], SS[0], n)
{
    for (j =k; L, j++)
    {
      for (each n_i adjacent to SS[j] )
      {
        p = p +1;   r = r +1;
        if (SS[j] contains all the required files)
              tmp2[p]= BDD_one;
              else
                 {
                  SS[p]=SS[j]+ n_i;
```

Figure 18. Continued on next page.

```
                If ( SS[p] gets hit in the hash table) result[j] = getBDD_table;
                else
                  {
                    tmp2[p] = BDD_or (all edges connected to n_i);
                    result1[j] =BDD_and(tmp2[p]; tmp2[j]);
                    result[j] = BDD_or (result[j] , result1[j]);
                  }
              }
            insert_table(SS [p], result[p])
      }
  }
  L = p;  k = p – r;  r = -1;
  for ( j =k; L, j++)
  {
   If (  SS[j] does not contains all the required files)
     {
       if ( SS[j] contain all the nodes)
           tmp2[j]=BDD_zero;
       else  Recursive_Merge (Sub_G[j], SS[j], n_i);  }
   return result[j];
  }

  }
```

Figure 18. The recursive merge algorithm for constructing the *BDD* with perfect nodes.

6.3. Reliability Evaluation In Distributed Computing Environments Using The AHP

6.3.1. The Analytic Hierarchy Process (AHP)

In this study of distributed system reliability using *AHP* [55], it is possible to involve the reliability of hardware elements such as network nodes, and computer systems, along with the reliability of the software applications. A better insight into the interaction between the different system components is, thus, attained. According to the suggested reliability evaluation, it is possible to determine the effect, on system performance, of any component. This method also allows the identification of critical paths and may be adopted to obtain an optimized reliability function for a typical distributed system configuration. Such in-depth study can be obtained at affordable time and space costs.

Without the *AHP* many crucial details regarding a distributed computing environment may be missing. Typically, which computer systems are installed in each node? Which system programs are included in which computer system? How are computer systems compared? How are system programs distributed? How would the network be affected if a node fails? Furthermore, which of the network nodes have more effect on the overall network reliability? What is the composite effect of each network node, computer system and system program on the overall network performance?

The *AHP* deals with complex structures that can be broken into top-down levels. It makes understandable and clear the study of the cumulative effects transmitted from higher to lower levels [56]. As shown in Figure 19, each of the hierarchy levels is divided into components that perform the same function. For instance, in a distributed environment, the network nodes form a level, the computer systems form a second one, and the system programs (software) constitute a third level. Each component is characterized by an *absolute weight*, a *local weight* and a *global weight* as will be detailed in Sub-section 6.3.3.

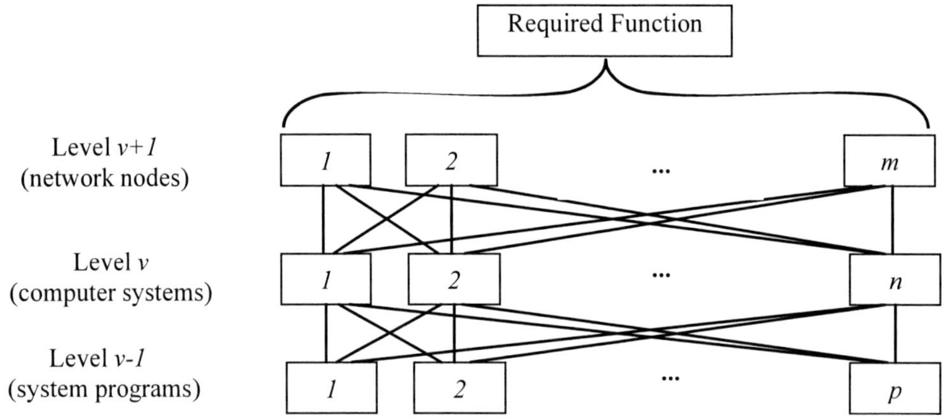

Legend: *m, n, p* are the number of components in levels *v+1*, *v* and *v-1* respectively.

Figure 19. A three-level hierarchical structure for a distributed environment[3].

The general form of the *AHP* is represented as follows:

$$WG^{v-1} = WG^{v} . \begin{vmatrix} WL_1^{v-1} \\ WL_2^{v-1} \\ \vdots \\ WL_m^{v-1} \end{vmatrix} \tag{48}$$

where,

WG^v is the vector of global normalized weights of the m components (blocks) in level *v*,

WG^{v-1} is the vector of global normalized weights of the *n* components in level *v-1*,

WL_i^{v-1} (for *i* = *1, ..., m*) is the vector of pair-wise local weights between component *i* in level *v* and each component in level *v-1*.

In expanded form we get:

$$\begin{vmatrix} wg_1^{v-1} & wg_2^{v-1} & \cdots & wg_n^{v-1} \end{vmatrix} = \begin{vmatrix} wg_1^{v} & wg_2^{v} & \cdots & wg_m^{v} \end{vmatrix} . \begin{vmatrix} wl_{1,1}^{v-1} & wl_{1,2}^{v-1} \cdots & wl_{1,n}^{v-1} \\ wl_{2,1}^{v-1} & wl_{2,2}^{v-1} \cdots & wl_{2,n}^{v-1} \\ & \vdots & \\ wl_{m,1}^{v-1} & wl_{m,2}^{v-1} \cdots & wl_{m,n}^{v-1} \end{vmatrix} \tag{49}$$

[3] Reprinted from Computer Networks, Vol.36, Fahmy, H.M., Reliability Evaluation in Distributed Computing Environments Using the AHP, p.600, Copyright 2005, with permission from Elsevier.

where,

$wl_{j,i}^{v-1}$ is the local weight of component *i* at level *v-1*, when connected to component *j* at level *v*, it is zero if there is no connection,

wg_k^v is the global weight of component *k* installed at level *v* of the *AHP*.

It is obvious from Eq.49, that moving downwards transfers to a lower level the effects accumulated from all the levels above. Thus, based on the particular interest, the required function at any level can be computed.

6.3.2. The Proposed AHP Model

6.3.2.1. Model Components

In the presented *AHP*, three network elements are considered, specifically, the nodes, the computer systems and the system programs. Additional levels or elements may be comprised in the *AHP*, if found more representative of a typical network structure than the hierarchy proposed in this work. The network nodes, at the top level of the *AHP* hierarchy, are the connection points that constitute the computer network, they create, receive, or repeat a message, each node contains one or more computer systems.

A computer system is a complete computer installation, including the peripherals. Computer systems reside in the second level of the hierarchy.

At the bottom level of the *AHP* hierarchy, reside the system programs. A program may be contained in a single computer system or may be distributed over several computer systems.

6.3.2.2. Distributed Environment Structure

The network nodes are connected by links according to a determined topology. It is assumed that the network is divided into clusters. If clusters perform different applications, reliability is studied individually for each one. But, if several clusters perform the same application, it is possible to compare their obtained reliability measures.

6.3.3. Weights of the AHP Components

The reliability of a network element is not just a stony numeric figure, but it must exhibit the weight of the element in the network. Thus, a centrally located node with four emanating links, has an effect on the network performance higher than that of a remotely placed node connected to a single link. Also, a parallel computer system with high execution rate is more influential than a slower, less modern computer system. A system program distributed over five nodes has a tangible effect far beyond that of a program spanning two nodes.

Determining the weight of a network element does not follow specific predetermined rules, but, it varies from network to another with regard to the design considerations, the network topology, the diversity of computer systems architecture and the types of system programs.

6.3.3.1. Absolute Weights

The *absolute weight* is a numeric figure that represents the merit of an *AHP* component per se, it may be evaluated using one or more subjective evaluation parameters. A high grading is accorded to the parameter if it is an asset to the component evaluation. More parameters may be added, and different ranking grades may be adopted if found more interpretive for components evaluation than those suggested in this work.

The absolute weight of component *k* at level *v* of the *AHP* can be represented as follows:

$$wa_k^v = \sum_{j \in P^v} r_j \tag{50}$$

where,

P^v is the set of evaluation parameters used in the calculation of wa_k^v at level *v*,

$r_j \in \Gamma^v$ is the numeric ranking of evaluation parameter *j*,

$\Gamma^V = \{1,2,3,4,5\}$ is the set of numeric rankings for the level *v* components.

Table 4-Table 6 show the proposed parameters considered in the evaluation of the absolute weights of the nodes, computer systems and system programs. A Highest ranking is given numeric value 5, while Lowest is given a numeric value 1.

The evaluation parameters (P^3) included in the suggested absolute weight of a network node, are its location, the number of emanating links, the sum of the links capacities and installation costs. The absolute weight of a computer system (P^2) involves its architecture, speed and cost. In the estimation of the absolute weight of a system program (P^1), are considered the number of nodes participating in its execution, its function and cost.

6.3.3.2. Local Weights

The *local weight* of an element is its subjectively calculated figure of merit, it reflects the relative effect of its absolute weight with regard to the environment in which it is installed. To determine the local weight of each element, the hierarchy must first be defined. A hierarchy that interprets the order of putting-up a network is proposed. At the top level are the network nodes, the next lower level is that of the computer systems, followed downwards by the system programs (Figure 19).

The local weight of component *k* at level *v-1* when contained in component *i* al level *v* is given by:

$$wl_{i,k}^{v-1} = \frac{wa_k^{v-1}}{\sum_{j \in \Lambda_i^v} wa_j^{v-1}} \quad , \quad \forall k \in \Lambda_i^v \tag{51}$$

such that,

$$\sum_{\forall k \in \Lambda_i^v} wl_{i,k}^{v-1} = 1 \tag{52}$$

where,

Λ_i^v is the set of level *v-1* components contained in component *i* installed at level *v*,

m^v is the number of level *v* components,

$m_i^v = |\Lambda_i^v|$ is the number of level *v-1* components installed in component *i* at level *v*.

Table 4. Absolute weight of a node[4]

Evaluation parameters (P^3)	RANKING (Γ^3)				
	Highest (5)	**High (4)**	**Medium (3)**	**Low (2)**	**Lowest (1)**
Location	✓				
Number of emanating links		✓			
Sum of the links capacities			✓		
Installations cost ($)				✓	

Minimum value:4, maximum value:20 Node absolute weight: 5+4+3+2=14

Table 5. Absolute weight of a computer system[4]

Evaluation parameters (P^2)	RANKING (Γ^2)				
	Highest (5)	**High (4)**	**Medium (3)**	**Low (2)**	**Lowest (1)**
Clock speed (Mhz)	✓				
Memory size	✓				
Cost ($/MIPS or $/MFLOPS)	✓				

Minimum value:3, maximum value:15 Computer system absolute weight: 5*3=15

Table 6. Absolute weight of a system program[4]

Evaluation parameters (P^1)	RANKING (Γ^1)				
	Highest (5)	**High (4)**	**Medium (3)**	**Low (2)**	**Lowest (1)**
# of sharing computer systems	✓				
Function			✓		
Cost ($)					✓

Minimum value:3, maximum value:15 System program absolute weight: 5+3+1=9

6.3.3.3. Global Normalized Weights

The *global normalized weight* determines the relative effect of an *AHP* component as compared to other components in the same level of the hierarchy when connected to

[4] Reprinted from Computer Networks, Vol.36, Fahmy, H.M., Reliability Evaluation in Distributed Computing Environments Using the AHP, p.602, Copyright 2005, with permission from Elsevier.

(contained in) components from the levels above. Such measure assembles the effects of components from higher levels of the hierarchy on the local weights of low level components.

At the top level v, the global normalized weight wg_k^v of component k is given by:

$$wg_k^v = \frac{wa_k^v}{\sum_{j \in \Lambda^v} wa_j^v} \quad , \quad \forall k \in \Lambda^v \tag{53a}$$

where, Λ^v is the set of level v components. It is clear that, for these components, the global normalized weight is the same as its local weight.

To determine the normalized weight of component k at level v-1, we have:

$$wg_k^{v-1} = \sum_{i \in \Pi_k^v} wg_i^v \cdot wl_{i,k}^{v-1} \quad , \quad \forall k \tag{53b}$$

where,

Π_k^v is the set of level v components connected to component k installed at level v-1.

Thus, the vector WG^{v-1} of global normalized weights of level v-1 components is:

$$WG^{v-1} = (wg_1^{v-1} \quad wg_2^{v-1} \quad \cdots \quad wg_{m^v}^{v-1}) \tag{54}$$

such that $\sum_{1=1}^{m^{v-1}} wg_i^{v-1} = 1$, where, m^{v-1} is the number of level v-1 components.

6.3.4. Measures of Reliability

The node reliability may be defined in terms of the emanating links reliabilities to be the probability of having at least n functional links out of m emanating links. Similarly, for a computer system, it is the probability of having at least n working computer systems out of m computer systems. Also, for a system program, it is the probability of having n correctly executing copies (partitions) out of m.

From the *AHP* previously introduced in Figure 19, it is seen that a cluster of nodes (subnet) is composed of paths extending from level *3* to level *1*. Thus, define the *reliability function* F_k of cluster k to be:

$$F_k = \sum_{t=1}^{s_k} rh_{k,t} . wh_{k,t} \tag{55a}$$

$$= \sum_{t=1}^{s_k} (\prod_{\substack{i \in \Psi_{k,t} \\ v \in \Omega}} rel_i^v \cdot wg_i^v) \tag{55b}$$

where,

$rh_{k,t}, wh_{k,t}$ are the reliability and weight of path *t* in cluster *k*,

$\psi_{k,t}$ is the set of vertices forming path *t* in cluster *k*,

Ω is the set of hierarchic levels forming the *AHP*,

$=\{1,2,3\}$ in the *AHP* of a distributed computing environment,

rel_i^v is the reliability of vertex *i* installed at level *v*, it is a given or known characteristic of vertex *i*. It may be determined by dividing the period of time a vertex fails by a predetermined period of system operation.

s_k is the number of paths in cluster *k*, such that:

$$rh_{k,t} = \prod_{\substack{i \in \psi_{k,t} \\ v \in \Omega}} rel_i^v \tag{56}$$

$$wh_{k,t} = \prod_{\substack{i \in \psi_{k,t} \\ v \in \Omega}} wg_i^v \tag{57}$$

As previously stated, the global weight of a lower level vertex is loaded with the effects transferred from higher levels, which effect its reliability.

From Eq.55 define the ratio R_k to be:

$$R_k = \frac{F_k}{s_k} \tag{58}$$

if $R_k > R_h$, then cluster (subnet) *k* is "globally" more reliable than cluster *h*.

The *nominal reliability function* FN_k for a cluster *k* of nodes is the reliability function F_k, when all components weights are set to *1*:

$$FN_k = \sum_{t=1}^{s_k} rh_{k,t} \tag{59}$$

The *weighted reliability effect* $e_{k,i}$ of a path *i* in a cluster *k* of nodes is defined to be:

$$e_{k,i} = \frac{rh_{k,i} \cdot wh_{k,i}}{F_k} \tag{60}$$

where, $rh_{k,i}, wh_{k,i}$ are the reliability and weight of path *i* in cluster *k*.

A path *h* is more "reliability effective" than a path *i* in a cluster *k* if $e_{k,h} > e_{k,i}$.

Also, define *the weighted reliability effect* $q_{k,x}$ of a node x in a cluster k of nodes to be:

$$q_{k,x} = \frac{\sum_{j \in m_{k,x}} rh_{k,i} \cdot wh_{k,j}}{F_k} \tag{61}$$

where, $m_{k,x}$ is the set of paths going through node x in cluster k.

To increase the reliability effect of the paths in a cluster k of nodes, a linear optimization model is proposed in Eq.62-Eq.64. Such model calculates the weights $wh_{k,i}$ for the given reliability values $rh_{k,i}$. An increased weight $wh_{k,i}$ may imply modifying the network topology to enhance the node weights, upgrading the used computer systems, or redistributing the system programs. These boosting alternatives could be partially attainable in an installed network, but may be easily achievable while at the design stage. The suggested optimization may be carried either over all paths in cluster k, or it may be concerned only with the paths having a low reliability effect.

Thus, the proposed model may be formulated as follows:

$$max_{wh_{k,i}} \sum_{i=1}^{s_k} rh_{k,i} \cdot wh_{k,i} \tag{62}$$

subject to

$$rh_{k,i} \cdot wh_{k,i} \leq 1 \tag{63.1}$$

$$rh_{k,s_k} \cdot wh_{k,s_k} \leq 1 \qquad (63s_{k)}$$

$$wh_{k,1}, wh_{k,2}, \cdots, wh_{k,s_k} > 0 \tag{64}$$

Lower limits may also be added to the set of constraints Eq.63.

Typical case studies illustrate how better is the *AHP* insight into the interaction between the different system components; it is possible to determine the effect, on system performance, of any component and to identify the critical paths that might exist. The *AHP* can be used at the design or management phases of a distributed computing environment.

7. Conclusion

This chapter focuses on the reliability evaluation techniques in distributed computing environments. To reach the point of surveying the reliability evaluation techniques, it was necessary to stop first by the definitions of distributed systems, their aspects and the underlying design issues. Afterward, for the sake of complete acquaintance, a necessity stop is a must at different complementary reliability definitions. The way laid down, comprehensive understanding of several recent reliability evaluation techniques becomes a less complicated task. Techniques regarding software and hardware components are presented besides those that evaluate the overall reliability of distributed computing systems.

References

[1] Coulouris, G.; Dollimore, J.; Kindberg, T. *Distributed Systems: Concepts and Design.* Addison-Wesly, 3rd Edition, 2001.

[2] Tanenbaum, A.; Steen, M. *Distributed Systems: Principles and Paradigms.* Prentice Hall, 2002.

[3] http://www.ubiq.com/hypertext/weiser/weiser.html. Last visited May 7, 2005.

[4] Weiser, M. Some Computer Science Problems in Ubiquitous Computing. *Communications of the ACM,* vol.36, July 1993, pp.74-83.

[5] Nessett, D. Massively Distributed Systems: Design Issues and Challenges. *Proceedings of the Embedded Systems Workshop*, Cambridge, Massachusetts, USA, March 29–31, 1999.

[6] Tanenbaum, A. *Computer Networks.* Prentice Hall, 4rd Edition, 2003.

[7] El-Rewini, H.; Abd-El-Barr, M. *Advanced Computer Architecture and Parallel Processing.* John Wiley & Sons, Inc, 2005.

[8] Flynn; M. Some Computer Organizations. *IEEE Transactions on Computers*, vol. C-21, 1972, pp. 948-960.

[9] Lima, C.; Sano, K.; Khondkar, P.; Nakamura, T. Hybrid Parallel Machines. *Proceedings of the 2nd International Conference on Information Technology for Application (ICITA 2004)*, Harbin, China, January 9-11, 2004, pp.358-363.

[10] Needham, R.M. *Distributed Computing: Opportunity, Challenge, or Misfortune?* Millennial Perspectives in Computer Science: Proceedings of the 1999 Oxford-Microsoft Symposium in Honor of Sir Tony Hoare, *edited by Jim Davies, Bill Roscoe,* and Jim Woodcock, Palgrave Macmillan Publishing, 2000.

[11] Deutsch, P.L. The Eight Fallacies of Distributed Computing, http://www.virtualtravelog.net/entries/system_design/, March 20, 2003. Last visited May 7, 2005.

[12] Trivedi, K.S. *Probability and Statistics with Reliability, Queuing, and Computer Science Applications.* Prentice Hall, Englewood Cliffs, New Jersey, 1982.

[13] Nelson, V.P. Fault-Tolerant Computing: Fundamental Concepts. *Computer*, *IEEE,* July 1990, pp.19-25.

[14] Linn, C. Semantic Reliability in Distributed Systems: Ontology Issues and System Engineering. *Proceedings of the IEEE/WIC International Conference on Web Intelligence (WI'03),* Halifax, Canada, October 2003, pp. 292.

[15] Butler, R.W.; Finelli, G.B. The Infeasibility of Quantifying the Reliability of Life-Critical Real-Time Software. *IEEE Transactions on Software Engineering*, vol. 19, January 1993, pp.3-12.

[16] Torres-Pomales, W. Software Fault Tolerance: A Tutorial. *NASA /TM-2000-210616*, October 2000.

[17] Sundresh, T.S. Semantic Reliability in Distributed AI Systems. *Proceedings of the IEEE International Conference on Systems, Man, and Cybernetics*, Tokyo, Japan, October 12-15, 1999, vol.3, pp. 798-803.

[18] Chandrasekaran, B.; Josephson, J.R.; Benjamins, V.R. What Are Ontologies, and Why Do We Need Them? *IEEE Intelligent Systems*, vol. 14, Jan/Feb 1999, pp. 20-26.

[19] Assayad, I.; Girault, A.; Kalla, H. A Bi-Criteria Scheduling Heuristic for Distributed Embedded Systems under Reliability and Real-Time Constraints. *Proceedings of the 2004 International Conference on Dependable Systems and Networks (DSN'04)*, Florence, Italy, June 2004, pp.347-356.

[20] Guerraoui, R.; Schiper, A. Fault-Tolerance by Replication in Distributed Systems. *Conference on Reliable Software Technologies*, Springer-Verlag, 1996, pp.38–57.

[21] Figiel, K.D.; Sule, D.R. A Generalized Reliability Block Diagram (RBD) Simulation. *Proceedings of the 22nd Conference on Winter simulation*, New Orleans, Louisiana, USA, 1990, pp.551–556.

[22] Abd-allah, A. Extending Reliability Block Diagrams to Software Architectures. *Technical report*, Center for Software Engineering, Computer Science Department, University of Southern California, Los Angeles, CA90089 USA, 1997.

[23] Shatz, S.; Wang, J.; Goto, M. Task Allocation for Maximizing Reliability of Distributed Computer Systems. *IEEE Transactions on Computers*, vol.41, September 1992, pp.156–168.

[24] Chen, Y.; Yuang, M. A Cut-Based Method for Terminal-Pair Reliability. *IEEE Transactions on Reliability*, September 1996, pp. 413–416.

[25] Yang, T.; Gerasoulis, A. List Scheduling with and without Communication Delays. *Parallel Computing*, vol.19, December 1993, pp.1321–1344.

[26] Girault, A.; Kalla, H.; Sighireanu, M.; Sorel, Y. An Algorithm for Automatically Obtaining Distributed and Fault-Tolerant Static Schedule. *Proceedings of the International Conference on Dependable Systems and Networks*, San Francisco, California, USA, June 2003.

[27] Hashimoto, K.; Tsuchiya, T.; Kikuno, T. Effective Scheduling of Duplicated Tasks for Fault-Tolerance in Multiprocessor Systems. *IEICE Transactions on Information and Systems*, vol. E85-D, March 2002, pp.525-534.

[28] Xin, Q.; Miller, E.L.; Schwarz, T. Evaluation of Distributed Recovery in Large-Scale Storage Systems. *Proceedings of the 13th IEEE International Symposium on High Performance Distributed Computing (HPDC'04)*, Honolulu, Hawaii, USA, June 2004, pp.172-181.

[29] Plank, J.S. A tutorial on Reed-Solomon Coding for Fault-Tolerance in RAID-like Systems. *Software-Practice and Experience (SPE),* vol. 27, September 1997, pp.995-1012. Corrections in: Plank, J.S.; Ding; Y. *Technical Report UT-CS-03-504,* University of Tennessee, 2003.

[30] Blaum, M.; Brady, J.; Bruck, J.; Menon, J. EVENODD: An Efficient Scheme for Tolerating Double Disk Failures in RAID Architectures. *IEEE Transactions on Computers,* vol. 44, February 1995, pp.192-202.

[31] Honicky, R.J.; Miller, E.L. Replication under Scalable Hashing: A Family of Algorithms for Scalable Decentralized Data Distribution. *Proceedings of the 18th International Parallel* & Distributed Processing Symposium (IPDPS 2004), Santa Fe, New Mexico, USA, April 2004.

[32] Elerath, J.G. Specifying Reliability in *the Disk Drive Industry: No More MTBF's. Proceedings of the 2000 Annual Reliability and Maintainability*, Los Angeles, CA, USA, January 2000, pp.194-199.
[33] Meyer, R.A.; Bagrodia, R. PARSEC *User Manual, release 1.1,* http://pcl.cs.ucla.edu/projects/parsec.
[34] Lin, M.S.; Chang, M.S.; Chen, D.J.; Ku, K.L. The Distributed Program Reliability Analysis on Ring-type Topologies. *Computer & Operations Research*, vol.28, 2001, pp.625-635.
[35] Weideman, N.H.; Kamenoff, N.I. Hartstone. Uniprocessor Benchmark: Definitions and Experiments for Real-Time Systems. *The Journal of Real-Time System*, vol.4, 1992, pp.282-353.
[36] Drummond, J. Establishing a Real-Time Distributed Benchmark. *Proceedings of the 4th* International Workshop on Parallel and Distributed Real-Time Systems, Honolulu, Hawaii, USA, April 1996, pp.198-201.
[37] Kamenoff, N.I. One Approach for Generalization of Real-Time Distributed Systems Benchmarking. *Proceedings of the 4th International Workshop on Parallel and Distributed* Real-Time Systems, Honolulu, Hawaii, USA, April 1996, pp.204-207.
[38] Jin, H.; Xie, X.; Li, Y.; Han, Z.; Chen, H. Athena: A Real-time Performance Evaluation for Distributed Software with Reliability Constraints. *Proceedings of the 18th International Parallel and Distributed Processing Symposium (IPDPS'04) - Workshop 14,* Santa Fe, New Mexico, USA, April 2004, p.247a.
[39] Foster, I.; Kesselman, C.; Tuecke, S. The Anatomy of The Grid: Enabling Scalable Virtual Organizations. *International Journal of High Performance Computing Applications,* vol. 15, 2001, pp. 200-222.
[40] Foster, I.; Kesselman, C. *The Grid: Blueprint for a New Computing Infrastructure*, Morgan-Kaufmann, 1998.
[41] Dai, Y.S.; Xie, M.; Poh, K.L. Reliability Analysis of Grid Computing Systems. *Proceedings of 2002 Pacific Rim International Symposium on Dependable Computing (PRDC'02),* Tsukuba, Japan, December 2002, pp.97-104.
[42] Lyu, M.R. Handbook of Software Reliability Engineering. *IEEE Computer Society Press*, McGraw-Hill, 1996.
[43] Chen, D.J.; Chen, R.S.; Huang, T.H. A Heuristic Approach to Generating File Spanning Trees for Reliability Analysis of Distributed Computing Systems. *Computers and Mathematics with Application,* vol.34, November 1997, pp.115-131.
[44] Kumar, A.; Agrawal, D.P. A Generalized Algorithm for Evaluating Distributed-Program Reliability. *IEEE Transactions on Reliability*, vol.42, September 1993, pp.416-424.
[45] Kumar,V.K.; Hariri, S.; Raghavendra, C.S. Distributed Program Reliability Analysis. *IEEE Transactions Software Engineering*, vol. 12, January 1986, pp.42-50.
[46] Lai, C.D.; Xie, M.; Poh, K.L.; Dai, Y.S.; Yang, P. A Model for Availability Analysis of Distributed Software/Hardware Systems. *Information and Software Technology*, vol. 44, 2002, pp.343-350.
[47] Minato; S. Streaming BDD Manipulation. *IEEE Transactions on Computers*, vol. 51, May 2002, pp.474-485.
[48] Chang, Y.; Lin, H.; Kuo; S. Reliability Evaluation of Dependable Distributed Computing Systems Based on Recursive Merge and BDD. *Proceedings of 10th IEEE*

Pacific Rim International Symposium on Dependable Computing (PRDC'04) , Papeete, Tahiti, French Polynesia , March 2004, pp.197-206.

[49] Chang, Y.R.; Amari, S.V.; Kuo; S.Y. Computing System Failure Frequencies and Reliability Importance Measures Using OBDD. *IEEE Transactions on Computers*, vol.53, January 2004, pp.54-68.

[50] Bryant, R.E. Graph-Based Algorithms for Boolean Function Manipulation. *IEEE Transactions on Computers*, vol. 35, August 1986, pp.677-691.

[51] Chen, D.J. ; Huang, T.H. Reliability Analysis of Distributed Systems Based on a Fast Reliability Algorithm. *IEEE Transactions on Parallel and Distributed Systems*, vol. 3, March 1992, pp.139-154.

[52] Chen, D.J.; Chen, R.S.; Huang, T.H. A Heuristic Approach to Generating File Spanning Trees for Reliability Analysis of Distributed Computing Systems. *Computers and Mathematics with Application*, vol. 34, November 1997, pp.115-131.

[53] Ke, W.J.; Wang, S.D. Reliability Evaluation for Distributed Computing Networks with Imperfect Nodes. *IEEE Transactions on Reliability*, vol. 46, September 1997, pp.342-349.

[54] Zang, X.; Sun, H.; Trivedi, K.S. Dependability Analysis of Distributed Computer Systems with Imperfect Coverage. *Proceedings of 29th Annual International Conference on* Fault-Tolerant Computing (FTCS-29), Madison, Wisconsin, USA, June 1999, pp.330-337.

[55] Fahmy, H.M. Reliability Evaluation in Distributed Computing Environments Using the AHP. *Computer Networks*, vol.36, August 2001, pp.597-615.

[56] Harker; P.T. *The Art and Science of Decision Making: The Analytic Hierarchy Process.* in the Analytic Hierarchy Process: Applications and Studies, edited by B.L. Golden, E.A. Wasil, and P.T. Harker , Springer-Verlag, Berlin, 1989, pp.2-38.

In: Computer Science Research Trends
Editor: Casey B. Yarnall, pp. 151-180

ISBN: 978-1-60021-518-6

Chapter 5

SELF-RECONFIGURATION IN ADAPTIVE WIRELESS SENSOR NETWORKS

Peter K. K. Loh*[*] *and A. B. Premkumar
School of Computer Engineering Nanyang Technological University, Singapore

Abstract

A deployed wireless sensor network is prone to disruptions to communications, degradation and failure of sensor nodes as well as due to limited energy reserves. The network requires a degree of adaptiveness in order to reconfigure itself to sustain operations. Except for extreme environmental conditions, spare sensor nodes pose a significant cost overhead. A wireless sensor network, however, already has some inherent redundancy in terms of the number of nodes as well as the possible communication channels existing between neighbouring nodes. An alternative approach is therefore to exploit software control of this inherent redundancy to detect and reconfigure the network to adapt to node failures and communication disruptions. This research presents two variations of a novel protocol, called SOS, that provide a sensor network with self-reconfigurability as well as selective path redundancy to adapt to network failures and disruptions. Simulations show that SOS compares favourably with existing protocols in terms of performance, reliability and energy efficiency.

1. Introduction

Smart environments represent the next evolutionary stage in buildings, homes, outdoor environments and transportation systems. The smart environment relies on sensory data from the real world. Sensory data comes from multiple sensors that are often distributed spatially. The smart environment needs information about its surroundings as well as about its internal workings in order to function reliably and efficiently. The information needed is provided by a wireless sensor network (WSN). The importance of such sensor networks is highlighted by the number of recent funding initiatives, including the DARPA SENSIT program, military programs, and NSF Program Announcements [11].

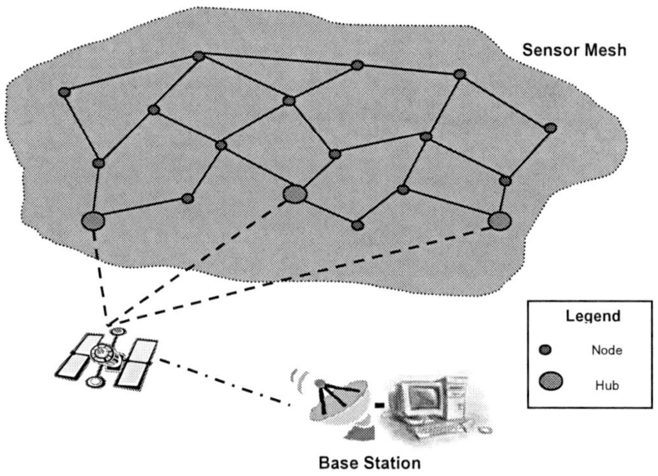

Figure 1. A Wireless Sensor Network.

A WSN is made up of a several sensor nodes and one or more base station nodes known as hubs or sinks. A hub acts as a gateway to connect the WSN to end users. A hub is a special node equipped with additional longer-range radio or satellite transceiver for communication with the base station. Each sensor node (also known as a mote) is embedded with a tiny sensor, battery pack, radio frequency (RF) communications and microprocessor with memory. Recent advances in radio and micro-electro mechanical technologies have significantly reduced the cost of manufacturing these nodes. Hence, these sensor nodes are cheap, small, and portable and have the capabilities of sensing, computing, as well as wireless communications [10, 2]. These characteristics make the sensor nodes suitable to be scattered spatially in large numbers in various environments to collect interesting and/or important data. Figure 1 shows a WSN with sensor nodes arranged in a mesh-like configuration.

Applications based on WSNs are numerous and growing, examples include natural disasters detection, performance measurements of manufacturing machinery, building safety monitoring, and even covert military applications. An even wider spectrum of future applications is likely to follow, including the monitoring of highway traffic, pollution, wildfires, and even an individual's well-being. Typically, however, WSNs are often deployed in dynamically changing and inhospitable environments, exacerbated with limited energy, battery-operated sensor motes. Under such conditions, communication among network nodes may be disrupted by noise and/or sensor motes may cease to operate due to low battery levels or faults causing the WSN configuration to change [8].

These conditions pose severe constraints for maintaining a stable configuration within the sensor network to allow existing work to continue. Typically, a *routing protocol* handles communication and coordination of work in a WSN and all nodes execute the same routing protocol. Many routing protocols have been designed for WSNs. However, several of these protocols cannot cope well with changes in network configuration due to node failures and noise. For example, if a node next to a hub fails, large sections of network nodes further away may not be able to relay important data to the hub if there is no available mechanism to re-

* E-mail address: askkloh@ntu.edu.sg

route this data via alternative routes. This could prove crucial, especially in safety-critical or covert operations. As a WSN is also an unattended system, there is a need to make this system "long-lived" and able to operate for prolonged periods with efficient use of the limited battery power in the sensor motes. As such, the "re-routing" strategy must also be energy efficient [5, 6, 9].

To realise these objectives, the WSN must be managed by an efficient and reliable routing protocol that will enable the network to maintain its configuration and hence, operations in the presence of environmental disruptions and distortions. The challenge then is to have a routing protocol that can achieve self-reconfiguration of the network while meeting the conflicting requirements of minimizing communications and energy overheads. Our work contributes to the field of WSNs in the following ways:

- We have identified key performance measures of a WSN that reflects operational requirements. This allows design of protocol solutions that have measurable practical benefits.
- We have proposed a novel self-reconfiguring routing protocol for WSNs that can sustain reliable operations with reasonably efficient energy requirements even under adverse environmental and network conditions.
- We have analysed and evaluated the performance of our protocol against four other existing protocols using simulation. The results reveal useful behavioural characteristics and anomalies of existing protocols under adverse scenarios.
- Our design could serve as a framework for further research and study into high performance and effective self-reconfiguration protocols.

The rest of the paper is organised as follows - Section 2 presents a survey of four existing self-reconfiguring routing protocols for WSNs. Section 3 presents the design details of the two variations of our proposed routing protocol while Section 4 presents the detailed observations and evaluation of the simulation results under both ideal and non-ideal conditions. The paper concludes with Section 5 followed by the References.

2. Related Work

In this section, we present a concise survey of four routing protocols with self-reconfiguration capability. They are the Periodic, Event-Driven and Query-Based protocol (PEQ) [3-4], Efficient and Reliable protocol (EAR) [12], Gradient-Based Routing protocol (GBR) [15], and Gradient Broadcast protocol (GRAB) [13, 16]. These routing protocols are similar in the sense that they make use of some path length metric expressed as hops or distance costs for reconfiguration decisions. Each protocol has its own strengths and weaknesses. It is apparent that achieving performance, reliability and energy efficiency are often conflicting objectives.

2.1. PEQ

The PEQ (Periodic, Event-Driven and Query-Based) routing protocol uses an ACK (acknowledgement)-based scheme to identify node failures or weak signal conditions. To set up route distance information, a flooding algorithm is used to initialise each network node with a hop count to the hub. The hub is initialised with a hop count of 0. If a node receives hop information from more than one neighbour, only the lowest value is stored. Each node will only send data to the next node that is of a lower hop value. Hence, a single, shortest path for each node is created to deliver its data to the hub. To tolerate node failures and noisy links, self-reconfiguration consists of two phases: (i) failure detection at receiver node and (ii) location of a new neighbour. When a sender node forwards data to its neighbouring node, it will set a timeout and then wait for the acknowledgement from its neighbour. The ACK message will only be received after the neighbour has forwarded the packet. Thus, the sender node receiving its neighbour's ACK, knows that its neighbour is alive and that its packet has also been forwarded to the next node. No retransmission of packet will be needed. However, if no ACK message is being received, the neighbour node is deemed to have failed and the sender node will select another neighbour as its new intermediate destination. To do this, the sender node broadcasts a search message to its neighbours. Neighbours will reply to the sender with a message containing their hop count (the level in the hop tree set up during initialisation) and identification. The sender will choose among the neighbours, a lower hop count (hop count difference of 1), and the first one to reply becomes the new intermediate destination node. The routing table of the sender will be updated for forwarding subsequent packets. The sender node then sets its own hop count to be the intermediate node's hop count plus one. This can also avoid the problem of looping in paths.

2.2. EAR

EAR achieves self-reconfiguration with minimal compromise of latency and energy efficiency. Re-routing decisions in EAR are based on two metrics: hop-count and a weighted combination metric. This second metric is a weighted combination of energy levels and transmission success history used alongside hop-count to determine optimal routes during reconfiguration. A "sliding-window" concept that keeps track of the last N successful transmission attempts via a specified link is used to compute transmission success history. An optimal route in EAR is not necessarily the shortest but represents the best combination of distance, energy requirements and link quality. Control packets are minimized by "piggy-backing" reconfiguration information onto MAC-layer protocol packets. EAR deals well with communication disruptions and distortions in WSNs with low to moderate traffic volumes, mostly due to more-informed and therefore accurate reconfiguration decisions. However, in WSNs with a high-volume of network traffic, the more complex reconfiguration decisions incur a more appreciable overhead affecting its performance.

2.3. GBR

GBR achieves self-reconfiguration by distributing traffic load evenly among all nodes using stochastic measures. This also prevents traffic overloading a portion of the network. A gradient is set up from the nodes to the hub and all messages will flow in that direction towards the hub. The hub will broadcast an interest message that is flooded throughout the network. Each node upon receiving the interest message will record the number of hops taken by the interest message. Each node then knows the number of hops it needs to reach the hub. A node will forward a message to a neighbour nearer to the hub than itself. When there are multiple neighbours with the same hop count to the hub, one is randomly chosen. Random choice of the next hop has a good effect of spreading traffic over time as well as achieving re-configuration to adapt to communication disruptions and distortions. However, in WSNs where RF transmission varies from one pair of nodes to the next even on an optimal route, the routing protocol may require a mechanism to select the better links instead of a random choice for re-routing the message.

2.4. GRAB

GRAB exploits the inherent redundancy in a WSN to achieve self-reconfiguration. GRAB is designed for reliability by routing redundant copies of messages in a mesh from a source node to the hub. A cost field is set up in the network and the value of a node in the field is the minimum cost to reach the hub from that node. The cost field has a value of 0 starting from the hub and the value at each node increases with the distance from the hub. Messages will flow through the cost field in the direction of decreasing cost, that is, towards the hub. Messages will travel from the originating nodes to the hub using the minimum cost path. When a node generates a message, it initialises a message header field with its cost to the hub and also assigns a credit value to that message before broadcasting it. When neighbouring nodes receive the message, only those nodes that have a lower cost (i.e. those nodes nearer to the hub than the sender) will enter a decision process of whether to route or drop that message. The decision process involves the concept of credit consumption by nodes in routing a message. When a message has enough credit, the node will route the message or else the message will be dropped. A message's credit is therefore consumed at each intermediate node on the path to the hub. When a message has insufficient credit, it can only be routed on a single path - the minimum cost path. By assigning an appropriate amount of credit to each message, duplicate copies of that message will travel in multiple paths from the source node to the hub thus forming a mesh. This mechanism provides flexible self-reconfiguration at the expense of higher energy consumption and message latency due to the existence of duplicate messages.

3. Protocol Design Details

In this section, we detail the design of the SOS and SOS_d self-reconfiguring routing protocols. The basic design of SOS assumes standard, cost-effective sensor motes with non-variable radio range. SOS (SOS_d) supports single or multiple hubs in a multi-hop WSN based on IEEE 802.11 Medium Access Control (MAC) protocol [17]. SOS can also be easily modified to support either query or event-detection based WSNs. The design comprises 3 phases: route discovery phase, data forwarding phase and failure recovery phase.

3.1. Route Discovery Phase

This phase determines the WSN's configuration and builds appropriate routing tables at each node. Route discovery consists of two parts. In the first part, a hop-level distribution from the hub is established in each node during network initialisation. This is achieved with constrained flooding of the network with 'hop' messages. The hub starts this by broadcasting a message with a hop level of 0, received by all its neighbours. Each node initially has a hop level of 0xfffffffa (representing a very large value). When a node receives the 'hop' message from its neighbours, it will broadcast this message only when the received hop level is smaller than its own hop level. These 'hop' messages, which record the number of hops from the hub taken, will be used by each node to discover its minimum hop-level to the hub. A node will use its hop-level to identify the next possible neighbour(s) to forward the data. If the hop level received is lower than the receiving node's hop level by more than one, the receiving node updates its own hop level by adding one to the received hop level and retransmitting the 'hop' message with its own hop level to its neighbour node(s). If the difference between hop levels is otherwise, there will no updating of hop levels and the 'hop' message will be discarded. The retransmission of 'hop' messages is repeated until all nodes are initialised with a minimum hop level to the hub. Figure 2 shows an example of a hop-level distribution in a WSN.

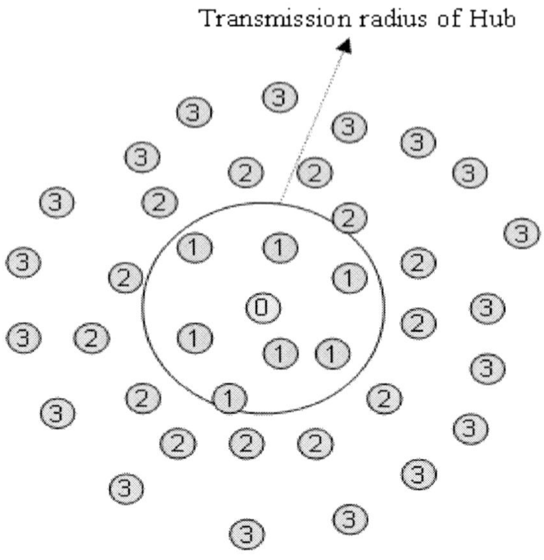

Figure 2. Hop Gradient in WSN.

Each node may store up to three possible routes to enhance fault-tolerance to route failures due to noise or faulty nodes. To minimise the probability that an important node may not be discovered or a link that could have failed due to interference between two neighbouring nodes, each node retransmits the 'hop' message twice, with each message separated by a random delay to prevent collision of messages. The hub, however, only broadcasts the 'hop' message once to avoid energy wastage as in periodic flooding.

3.2. Data Forwarding Phase

This phase enables forwarding of data from each node to the hub, and vice versa. The data will be forwarded from the nodes to the hub using the best available route, in terms of energy consumption and packet latency, at the point of time. Each node maintains a routing table that has up to three different routes to the hub that can be used. Each table entry is a 5-tuple: *<hub address, neighbour node ID, route status, number of times route failed, route usage counter>*. *Hub address* is the node ID of the hub in the WSN, *neighbour node ID* is the node ID of the intermediate node to which a data packet is to be sent en-route to the hub, *route status* indicates the route availability, *number of times route failed* tracks the number of times the route have failed and will be removed from the routing table if it reaches the specified maximum number of retries, *route usage counter* is used to keep track of the number of times the route has been used.

During the forwarding of data packets, a node will choose the route with the lowest usage. This helps distribute network traffic more uniformly among all available routes in the routing table. As a consequence, network lifetime can be increased with probability of node failure due to insufficient energy reduced. Another advantage is that different data packets of a message will be forwarded along different routes. This will reduce the chance that a fault in one route causes loss of the entire message. As in Figure 3, when node 7 receives a data packet, it will choose the next route by checking its route table. As shown in the 'Route Table of node 7', although the route to neighbour node 8 has the smallest route usage of 1, the route status indicates it has failed. Thus, the next suitable route is to node 6, an active route with the lowest route usage.

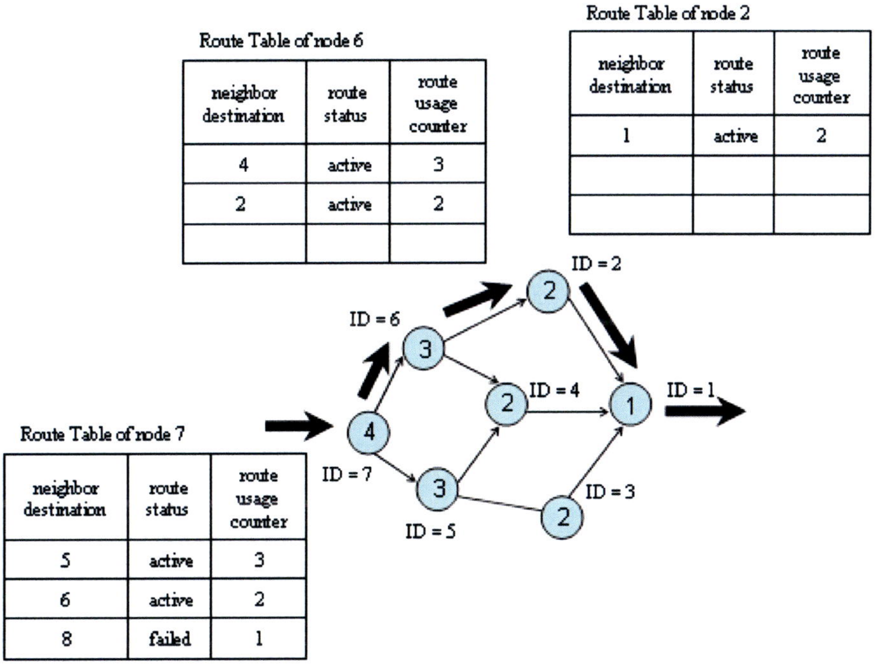

Figure 3. Illustration of data packet forwarding in SOS.

After forwarding the data packet to node 6, the route usage value of this route will increase by 1. Hence, its usage value will be the same as the route to node 5. The route to node 5 will be chosen the next time round as the forwarding algorithm will always select the node that first appears in the routing table, all else being equal. Thus, data packets will be forwarded from node 7 to node 6 to node 2 (and node 4). Then, from nodes 2 and 4 to node 1 until the hub is reached.

3.3. Failure Recovery Phase

In this phase, a node may detect link or node failures and update its routing table based on configuration changes in the WSN. Failure recovery ensures that a node will have a route to the hub by locating new neighbours. In this phase, fast recovery is achieved by minimizing the exchange of information among neighbour nodes.

A node *x* on receiving a data packet will forward it to a neighbour *y* by first sending an RTS. If after a specified number of retries, node *x* still has not received a CTS, or ACK from node *y*, node *x* then reports that the route to node *y* or node *y* itself (or both) has a problem. Node *x* then updates its routing table by deleting the problematic node, decrementing its 'number of routes to hub' counter value and broadcasting the problematic node ID with an 'error' message to its neighbouring nodes. The neighbouring nodes on receiving this 'error' message, will also remove the ID of this problem node *y* if it appears in their routing tables (see Figure 4).

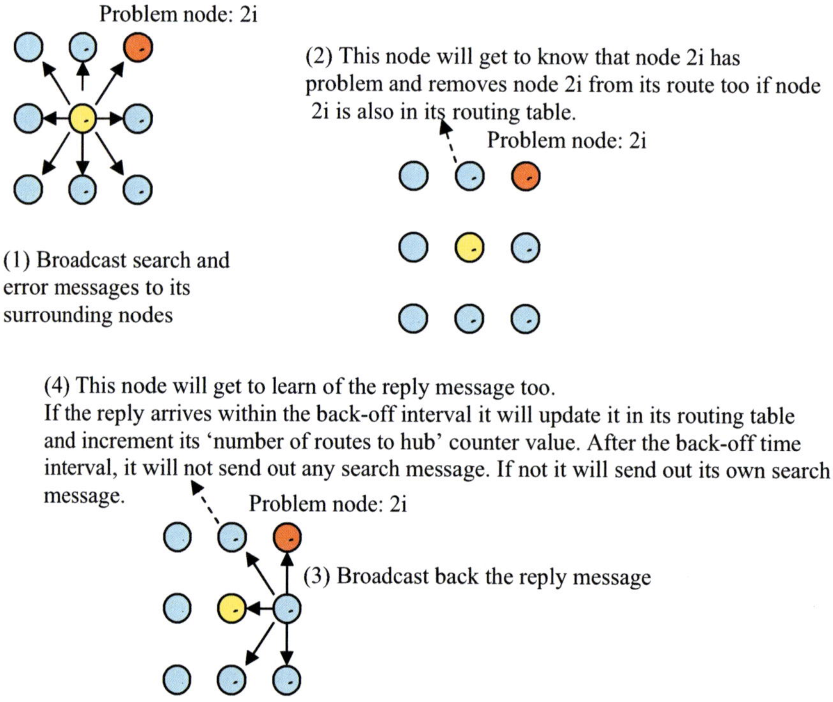

Figure 4. Failure Recovery Phase in SOS.

If there is at least one route to the hub after removal of the problematic node, it will be selected as the next appropriate route to forward the data packet. Hence, the presence of more than one route to the hub will increase the chance of the data packet being forwarded when route failures occur. At the same time, the node detecting the failure will also broadcast a 'search once' message to see if any neighbouring node with identical hop level to the removed problematic node is available for replacement. The message is so named as the node will only do a search once regardless of whether there will be replies from any suitable neighbours. Each time the node receives a reply, it checks to ensure the replying node is not already in its routing table before accepting it.

In the extreme situation where all routes in the routing table have failed, the 'number of routes to hub' counter is reset to zero. The node will then broadcast a 'search' message to its neighbours to search for a new route to reconfigure the WSN. If this node does not learn of new neighbours after a specified time interval, the node will resend the 'search' message a specified number of times. After which, it will proceed to search for neighbours with the same hop level as its own instead of one level lower. This is shown in Figure 5. If a suitable neighbour node has replied, the node will increment its hop level to the replying node's hop level plus one if the replying node is not of lower hop level. This ensures that there is no looping as data packets will always be forwarded to a node of lower hop level. After a specified number of retries, if the node has still not found a neighbour, it will backtrack to accept neighbours of higher hop level. There could be cases where a node becomes an isolated node after its neighbours have all failed. Hence, if after the last searching stage, there is still no neighbour node identified, the searching process will terminate. Its neighbour nodes of higher hop level now know that this node has no more routes to the hub. Its neighbouring nodes will then check to see if this problematic node is in their routing tables and remove it. A node will only respond to a 'search' or 'search once' message when it has at least one route to the hub. The reply message includes its hop level and ID and is sent after a random delay to minimize collisions when more than one available node wants to reply.

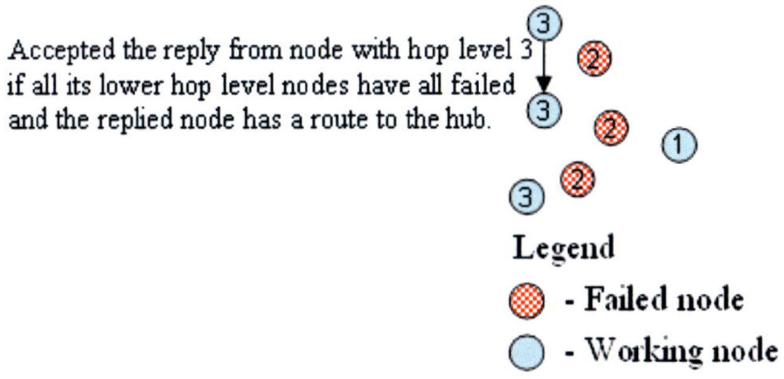

Figure 5. Accepting reply packet from same hop level.

3.4. SOS Double Path - SOS_d

Presence of node failures and/or noise along some routes in a WSN can jeopardize data packet delivery by altering the network configuration. SOS aims to achieve a degree of fault tolerance in WSNs with restricted redundancy. The SOS double path algorithm, SOS_d, incorporates limited route redundancy by utilizing an additional path to bypass node failures and avoid packet loss while forwarding data packets. A protocol that uses multiple paths to forward data packets from the source to the hub will have a higher chance of ensuring that data packets will be delivered to the hub. However, the cost in terms of energy usage will be higher especially in the case of large networks. The limitation of a double instead of multiple paths is to avoid excessive redundancy, which can cause significant increases in packet collisions and network congestion, and may result in wastage of limited energy resources. Only the source node will send the data packet to two different neighbouring nodes. Subsequent intermediate nodes will just forward the data packet along a single path. This is illustrated in Figure 6.

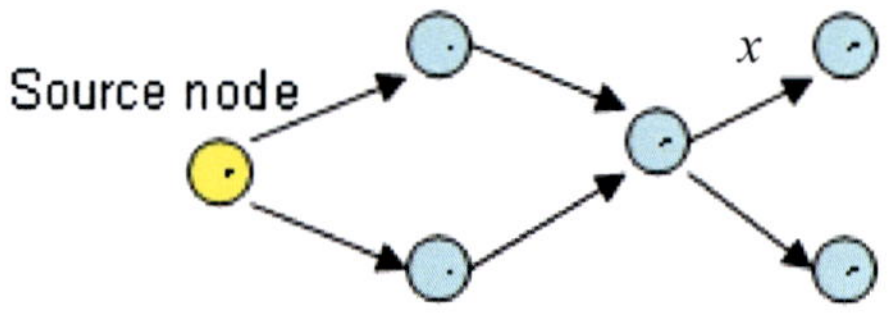

Figure 6. Illustration of a double path.

If both data packets sent out by the source node happened to reach the same node *x*, node *x* will still be able to send out the data packet to two different nodes due to routing control imposed by the route usage counter value. The first transmission from node *x* will make use of the route with the lowest usage counter value. The second transmission will use the route with the next lowest usage counter value. Recall that each node stores up to three routes to a hub in its routing table.

3.5. Analysis of SOS Design

In this section, an analysis of the SOS protocol will be presented. The following analysis will demonstrate the fundamental correctness of the SOS design framework.

Fact 1:

With the presence of at least one hub in the connected network, every node in the network will have at least one route to the hub. The sequence of such a route will be in decreasing order of hop level.

Discussion:

Consider the sequence of nodes: $Ak \rightarrow \cdots \rightarrow A7 \rightarrow A6 \rightarrow \cdots \rightarrow A1 \rightarrow Hub$, where Ai $(1 \leq i \leq k)$ denotes an arbitrary node and k denotes the number of hops needed to reach the hub from Ak. When the neighbouring nodes of the hub receive the 'hop' message, they have a hop-level of 1. And when these nodes with hop-level of 1 propagate the 'hop' message; their neighbouring nodes that are not within the radio range of the hub will have a hop-level of 2, which is the least number of hops to the hub. This process is repeated until the farthest node from the hub is also assigned a hop-level.

Fact 2:

The tree graph formed by the propagation of 'hop' messages from the hub is acyclic.

Discussion:

Recall that every node updates its hop-level based on the smallest hop-level received. Each node is associated with only one hop-level, which is the smallest of all hop-levels received plus one. Hence, a loop or cycle cannot be formed due to the propagation of the 'hop' message along the tree edges and each node has the shortest route, in terms of hops, to the hub.

Fact 3:

The route from a node to the hub is loop-free.

Discussion:

This follows from *Fact 2*.

Fact 4:

SOS is deadlock- free.

Discussion:

According to Facts 1 to 3, there are no loops during initialization and operation, hence SOS is deadlock-free.

Fact 5:

SOS will deliver data packets generated by the nodes to the hubs successfully in a noiseless and fault-free environment in a connected network.

Discussion:

From *Fact 1*, since every node will have an uninterrupted route to the hub, the packet forwarded on this route will eventually reach the hub.

4. Simulation

The UCLA's Global Mobile Simulation Systems Library (GloMoSim) [1] was employed to simulate a WSN where the nodes are modelled after the crossbow MICA2 mote [7]. The MICA2 mote is a popular hardware platform, which is widely deployed for sensor network research and systems testing. This simulator provides a high degree of simulation accuracy for wireless communication with detailed MAC, propagation, radio, and network layer components. Evaluations of SOS and SOS_d were made by comparing their behaviours and performances with PEQ, EAR, GBR and GRAB in both ideal and non-ideal environmental conditions.

In the simulations, the MAC protocol was implemented using the distributed coordination function (DCF) of IEEE 802.11. Radio transmission range for each node was 56 meters. Radio model was signal-to-noise (SNR) bounded. Propagation model was ground reflection (two-ray). Frequency used was 433 MHz and the bandwidth used was 76800 kbps. These settings are fixed throughout each simulation experiment conducted. Each simulation was executed for 60 minutes and the size of data payload was 24 bytes.

4.1. Performance Metrics

The performance of each protocols was analyzed using the following performance metrics.

(a) Packet Delivery Ratio (PDR): the percentage ratio between the number of data packets received by the hub and those generated by the source nodes.

$$\frac{\text{Total number of data packets received}}{\text{Total number of data packets sent}} \text{ X } 100\%$$

PDR will be low if the data packets drop rate is high. PDR thus reflects the routing reliability and effectiveness of a protocol.

(b) Packet Latency: the average time from when the source nodes produce the data packet to when the hub receives it.

$$\frac{\text{? Individual data packet latency}}{\text{Total number of data packets delivered}}$$

It includes processing times at various layers of each node, route recovery and repair, retransmission, queuing, propagation, transfer times etc.

(c) Energy Consumption: the energy consumed per packet that is successfully delivered.

$$\frac{\text{Total energy consumed}}{\text{Total number of packets delivered}}$$

where Total energy consumed = ∑ Individual node's expended energy

The node energy consumption model in GloMoSim is utilized, where energy used by a node for each packet transmission at the radio layer/ received at the MAC layer is calculated as follows:

Energy expended (J) = Voltage (V) X Current draw (A) X Transmission/Receive Duration = 3.0V X 0.0052A X ((packet size X 8) / bandwidth)

Only energy consumed during transmission and reception by each node's RF transceiver is considered. Transmission energy will increase proportionally with the number of packets sent. Hence, energy consumption can also indirectly reflect the total overhead cost of a protocol.

(d) Packet Collisions: the total number of packet collisions that occurred during the simulation

It includes collisions by both control and data packets.

(e) Number of nodes that consumed more than 2J of energy: tally the total number of nodes that have consumed more than 2J of energy during the simulation experiments.

The practical range for battery capacity of a sensor node is from 2J to 2KJ [14]. Thus, this metric can be used to find out whether the protocols evaluated can be used for sensor nodes equipped with just the minimum available battery capacity.

4.2. Ideal Conditions Simulation Experiments

The first experiment conducted simulates the protocols in an ideal environment with no noise or faults. The objective was to evaluate the performance of the protocols operating in ideal conditions to later show that performance variations in non-ideal conditions are due to the protocols' ability or inability to tolerate specified levels of noise and fault. The simulations were carried out for network sizes that ranged from 50 to 500 nodes with 10% and 50% active source nodes. An active source node will generate the data to be transmitted to the hub(s). For example, with a network size of 500 nodes, 10% active source nodes will mean 50 out of 500 nodes will generate the data to be transmitted to the hub(s). This enables the scalability of the protocols to be compared for an increasing number of active nodes and also increasing traffic volume. Active source nodes are randomly chosen from among the available nodes. The total data packet generated per source node was 120 at a rate of 1 packet every 30 seconds. Results for 20 runs with different seed numbers for each network size were collected and averaged. The results obtained are shown in Figure 7.

Packet Delivery Ratio (PDR)

The PDR of GBR, EAR and SOS are close to 100% on average for both 10% and 50% active source nodes. This shows that GBR, EAR and SOS can reliably deliver data packets under a noise- and fault-free environment where routes are stable and little or no network reconfiguration occurs. All three protocols make use of a single route for each data packet.

The PDR for PEQ is close to 100% for 10% active source nodes but its PDR drops drastically when active source nodes increase to 50%. With increased number of active source nodes, there are more data packets as well as control packets. Recall that PEQ employs an ACK-based scheme for data packet transmissions. This results in an increase in packet collisions, causing more packets to be dropped and thus reducing the PDR. Packet collisions will also initiate more retransmissions and therefore consume more energy.

A similar trend is observed for SOS_d due to the additional path used by each source node. Duplicate data packets transmitted from each source node increases collision rates as in PEQ but performance is increasingly better with more active source nodes as path redundancy in SOS_d is restricted to only source nodes.

The PDR for GRAB is the lowest for both 10% and 50% active source nodes. GRAB uses flooding to forward the data from source nodes to the hub; this generates a significantly large number of data packets in the network and results in over-utilization of bandwidth. This also explains that the average PDR of 10% active source nodes is better than that for 50% active source node. As the volume of traffic for 50% active source nodes is very much higher than 10% source nodes, considerably more packet collisions and packet loss occur as evident in Figure 7. This large volume of data traffic also resulted in GRAB having higher packet latency and energy consumption than other protocols (please refer to graphs in Figures 8 and 9).

Packet Latency

SOS has the lowest packet latency for both 10% and 50% active source nodes on average. Performance of SOS_d is competitive with EAR due to restricted path redundancy. SOS's simple data forwarding technique enables data packets to be quickly transmitted from source to hub using the shortest route. In EAR, the need to continuously process piggybacked control information increases the processing time of data packets. This processing overhead increases the packet latency as shown in Figure 8. SOS informs its neighbouring nodes that a change has occurred only when necessary. With PEQ, fairly low latency can be achieved by the use of shortest routes, provided the data traffic in the network is low as evinced in smaller networks. With higher proportions of active source nodes in larger WNSs, increased data packet transmissions are accompanied by increased acknowledgements. Packet drop rate increases significantly leading to more retransmissions - this significantly increases the latency. GRAB's use of flooding by source nodes generates large quantities of redundant message copies, resulting in unacceptable levels of packet collisions (also, see Figure 10). This severely degrades its latency to beyond the graphs' axes scales.

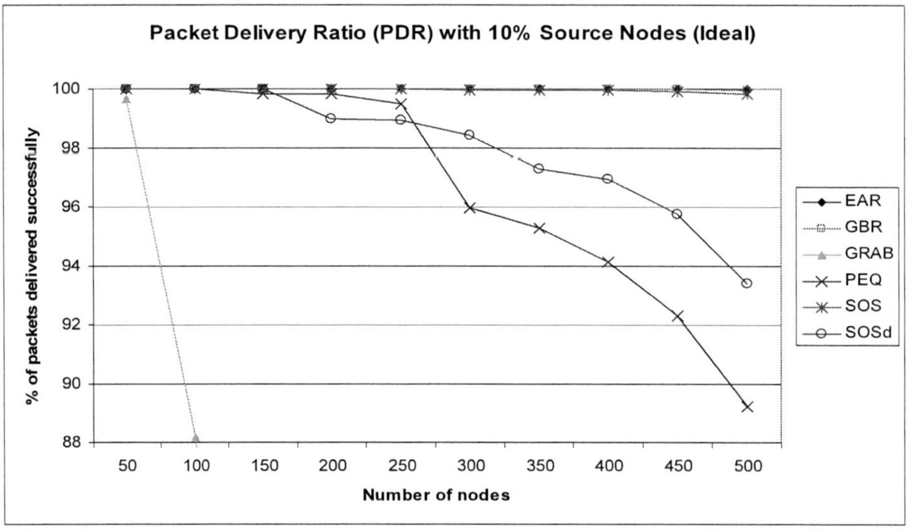

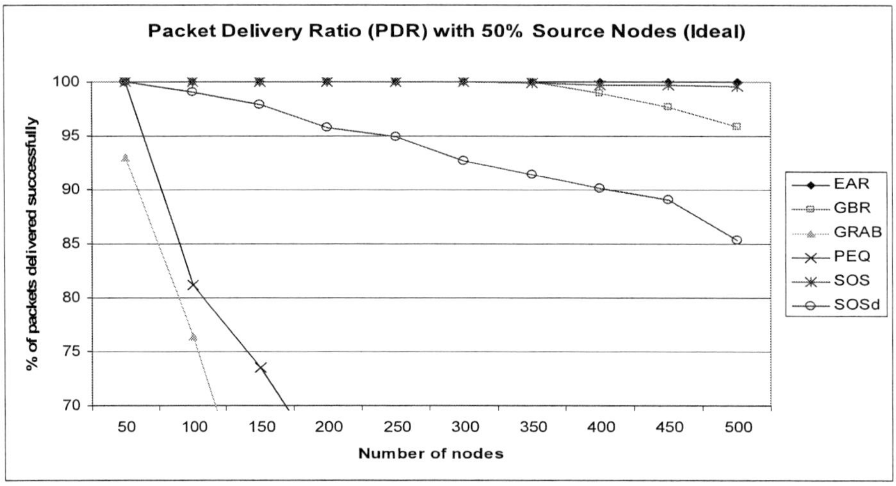

Figure 7. Packet Delivery Ratio in Ideal Conditions.

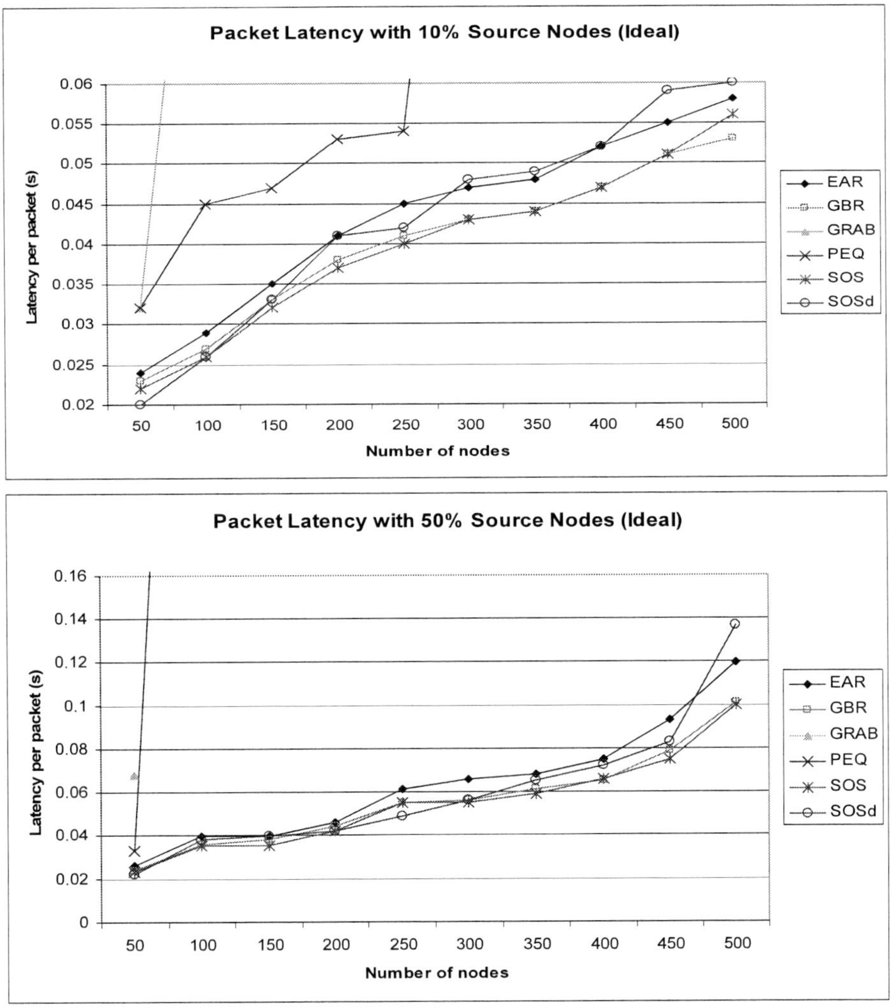

Figure 8. Packet Latency in Ideal Conditions.

Energy Consumption

SOS has the lowest energy consumption for both 10% and 50% active source nodes. It is lower than EAR even though EAR uses piggybacked control information at the MAC layer to inform nodes of the latest neighbourhood information. In an ideal environment where the WSN is subjected to less changes and reconfiguration, this constant update of information by EAR reduces energy efficiency. SOS also has the lowest number of nodes that consume more than 2J of energy for 50% source nodes as shown in the 3rd graph of Figure 9. SOS spreads data traffic evenly among its available routes so that the average energy consumed by each node is reduced, lengthening its operation lifetime. Traffic load distribution will reduce the chance of any section of the WSN consuming far more energy then the rest and disrupting operations for the entire network. For this 3rd graph, the results for 10% active source nodes are not available as all nodes did not consume more than 2J of energy with all protocols. This is due to the relatively small number of data packets with just 10% active sources transmitting.

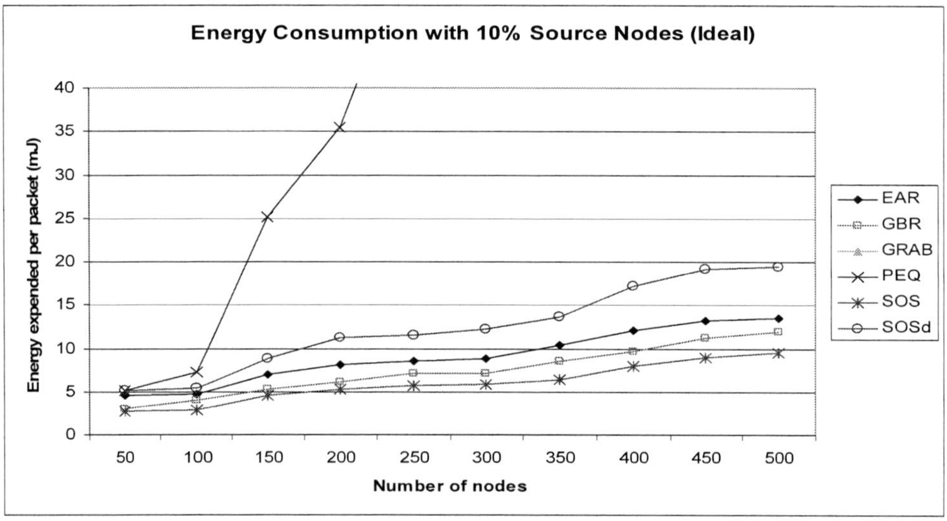

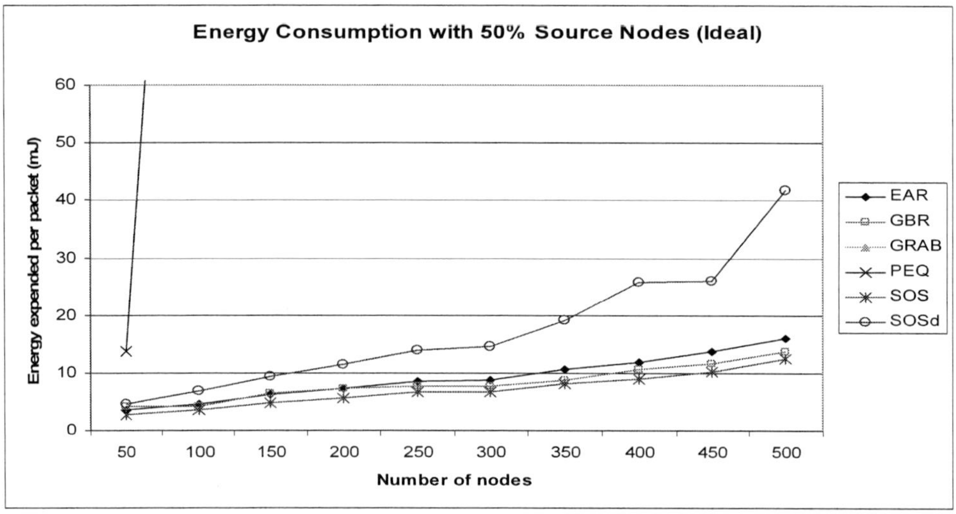

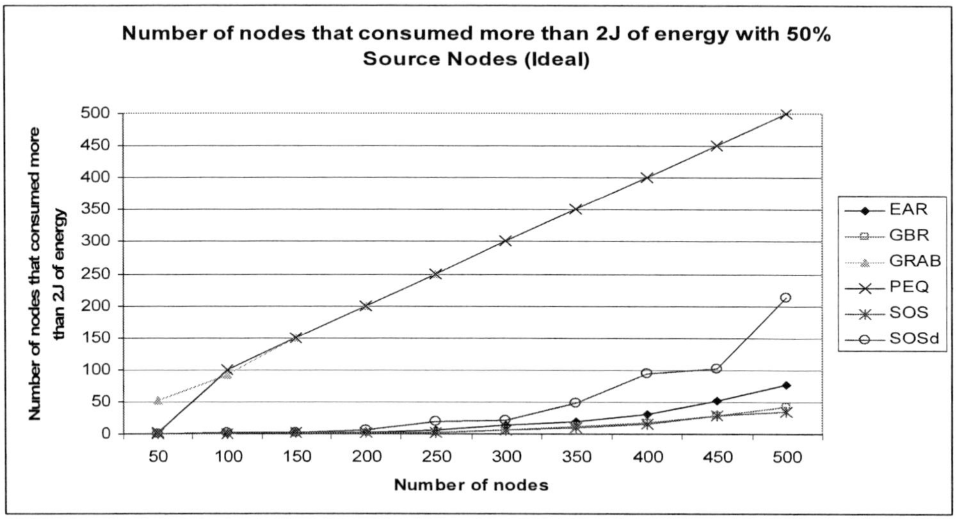

Figure 9. Energy Consumption in Ideal Conditions.

Since PEQ utilises an acknowledgement for each data packet forwarded, these additional transmissions also require expenditure of energy. This is significantly more evident when there are 50% active source nodes. GRAB has the highest energy consumption for both 10% and 50% source nodes. GRAB is designed to achieve reliability through the flooding of data packets through multiple paths. During this process, a large amount of redundant data packets will be generated. Thus, the energy consumption levels will be very much higher than the other protocols being compared. GRAB's energy consumption values fall outside the specified graph scales.

Packet Collisions

As the number of active source nodes increase, collisions will become a significant factor that will affect the performances of all routing protocols. Extra overhead will be involved in dealing with collisions.

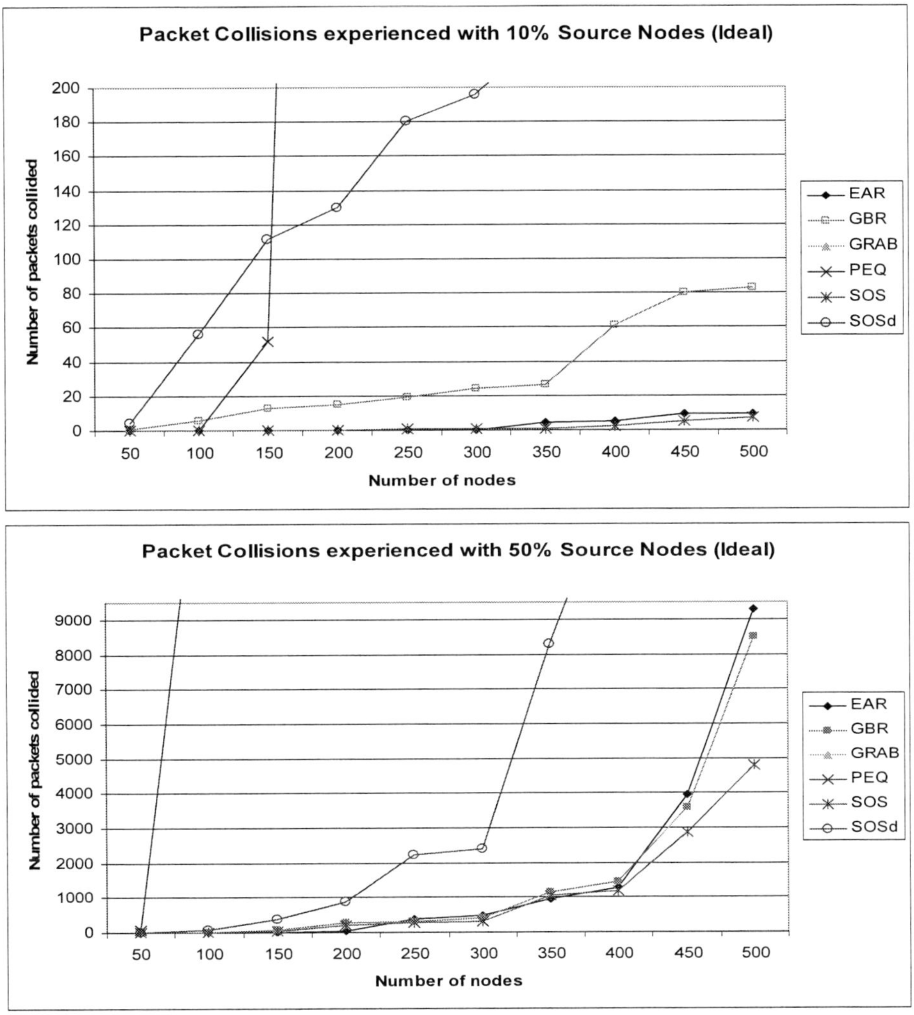

Figure 10. Packet Collisions in Ideal Conditions.

As evidenced in Figure 10, SOS has the lowest packet collisions for both 10% and 50% active source nodes. SOS involves minimum amount of messages to be exchanged between nodes during the setting up of routes to hub and sending the data packets in ideal situation. Also, SOS does not make use of duplicate transmissions that cause the higher rate of collisions experienced by SOS_d and GRAB. In SOS_d, this is moderated to an extent as the path redundancy is restricted to only source and not intermediate nodes.

With PEQ, packet collisions result as a consequence of the ACK-based scheme it employs. The requirement of frequent exchange of ACK messages between nodes during data transmissions in PEQ generates a lot of additional control packets in the network. Thus, there will be high packet collisions, as well as congestion, leading to packet drops even in ideal environment. With larger proportion of active source nodes (as found in larger WSNs), this becomes more evident allowing the performance of SOS to better it. This also explains the significant PDR degradation in high load conditions with 50% active sources.

PEQ is also able to achieve reliability, fast path recovery in situations of node failure while providing energy efficiency. Not many protocols are able to achieve these three requirements at the same time. PEQ uses only a few messages to set up paths and propagate events. Hence, it will have better packet delivery as there will be fewer cases of packet collisions. The amount of information (basically the hop level and routing table) kept in each node is small. The route table only stores one neighbouring node ID for each hub. Hence, the routing table size will be independent of network size. Thus, processing done by the nodes will be fast. The ACK-based scheme used to provide fault tolerance helps to save energy compared to protocols that used periodic flooding mechanism to reconfigure broken paths.

4.3. Non-ideal Conditions Simulation Experiments

To evaluate the fault tolerance and reconfiguration effectiveness of the routing protocols, they were simulated in practical network situations where the wireless medium will experience (i) interferences or low quality / failed connectivity caused by noise and (ii) node failures. The routing protocols must be able to reconfigure and re-route packets around the network gaps caused by noise and faulty nodes and adapt to the changes in network topology.

The ideal condition simulation experiment environment described in Section 4.2 was used and a noise model and a fault model were added to the simulation. A noise model where every node in the network except the hub takes on a random noise factor between 10% and 50% was used. The noise factor of a node indicates the probability that a packet received by the node is assumed to be corrupted or lost in transmission.

A fault model where 50% of the nodes, except the source nodes in the network, were randomly selected to fail at a random time within the simulation duration was used. 20 runs with different seed numbers for each of the network sizes were conducted and the collected results were averaged over the 20 runs. The results obtained are shown in Figures 11 - 14.

Packet Delivery Ratio (PDR)

Expectedly, the PDR for 10% and 50% source nodes show decreases for all protocols as the number of nodes increase. As the number of nodes increase, the number of neighbours within transmission range of a node also increases. Thus, the probability of any pair of neighbours not receiving packets from each other also increases due to increased collisions. There is also the increased probability of neighbors having bad RF links due to noise. PDR graph in Figure 11 shows that both SOS and EAR are able to maintain a reasonable data delivery rate of above 85% even in the presence of a high percentage of noise and node failures. This shows that both these protocols can still operate effectively in a noisy environment coupled with non-operational network components.

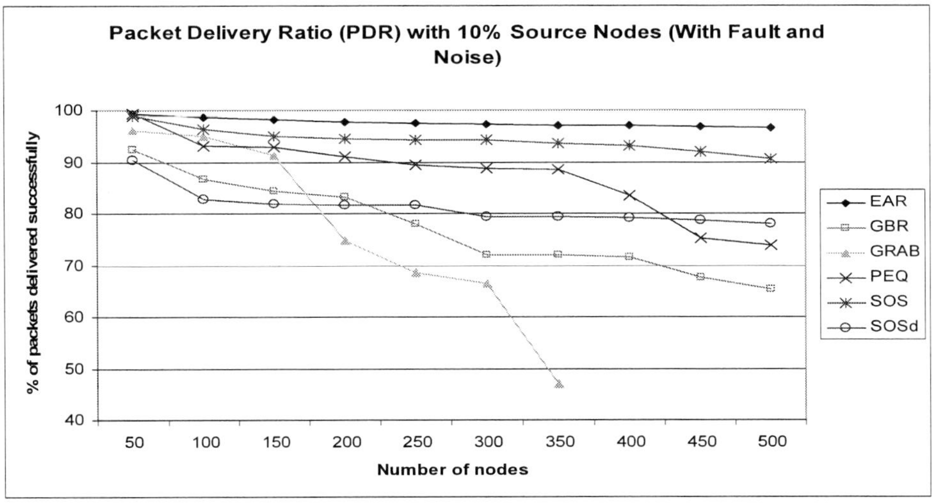

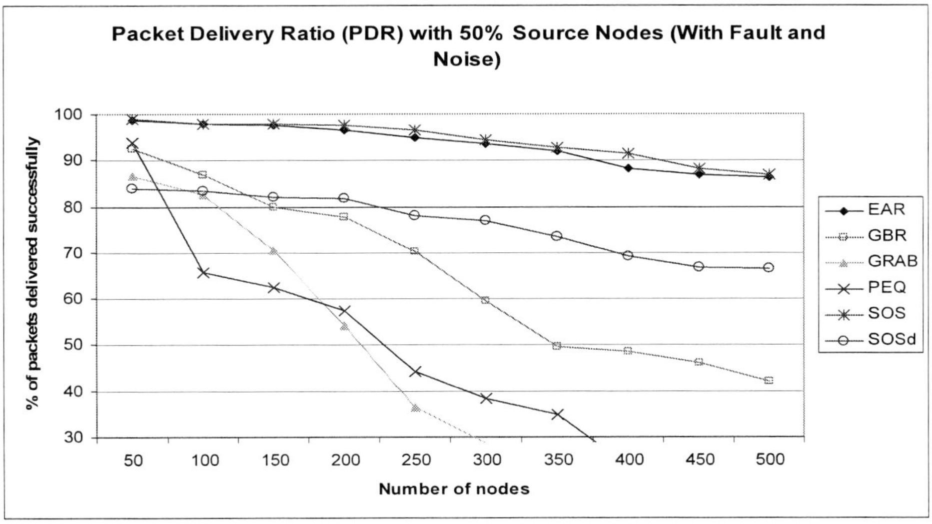

Figure 11. Packet Delivery Ratio in Non-Ideal Conditions.

With 10% source nodes, PDR of PEQ averages above 80% for networks of 400 nodes or less. This shows that it is able to maintain a reasonable PDR even at the high node failures of 50%. However, as the load in the traffic increased by increasing the number of source nodes in the network to 50%, PEQ soon loses its capability to maintain its high PDR in an environment with noise and faulty nodes. This is due to increasing routing overhead, especially the acknowledgement packets, under high traffic volumes. The resultant increase in packet collisions causes more packets to be dropped and PDR reduces significantly.

This experiment also highlights the situation where the reliability of data delivery is not necessarily proportional directly to the degree of redundancy exploited e.g. by having multiple paths from the source to the hub. Both GRAB and SOS_d attempt to achieve resilience to noise and node failures by sending duplicate copies of data packets along different routes. However, as shown in Figure 11, the PDR of SOS_d (using limited path redundancy) for both 10% and 50% source nodes scale better with network size, even exceeding GBR for large networks with in excess of 400 nodes. For GBR, reconfiguration decisions do not take into account link quality when selecting alternative routes randomly.

Packet Latency

As the network size increases, the packet latency also increases due to more hops a data packet has to travel from the source to the hub. Also, in order to reconfigure to find alternate routes due to the occurrence of node failures or noise, the new path being configured will typically be longer than the original shortest path and hence explains the higher latency experienced by all routing protocols. Packet latency will also increase with the data traffic volume in the network. If there are more packets in the network, there will be more congestion and hence the longer waiting time and processing time before the packets can be transmitted.

GBR is able to maintain relatively low packet latency for both 10% and 50% source nodes. GBR has the lowest packet latency for 50% source nodes. GBR uses a fast and simple data forwarding approach which does not account for whether the packet is being delivered successfully. In larger networks, GBR's random selection process has increased probability of locating an active link. However, this does not guarantee that a complete route from source to a hub is available. Also, GBR will only update the nodes with network configuration changes during its periodic broadcasting. Thus, although GBR has low packet latency, its PDR is appreciably lower than SOS, SOS_d and EAR.

EAR has a lower latency than SOS for 10% source nodes as shown in Figure 12. EAR piggybacks the route information of a node on both RTS and CTS packets at the MAC layer. This enables a node to obtain the latest route information of its surrounding nodes during the RTS/CTS packets transmission. Thus, a node may rapidly update the necessary changes to its routing table even before a data packet is routed to the node. As such, there will be little delay in forwarding the data packet when node failures and/or disruptions are occurred.

In the case of SOS, reconfiguration is only performed when it detects that a problem has occurred with its intended receiver node. This can help to save memory and bandwidth, but comes at the cost of slowing down the packet delivery; hence, a higher packet latency in the face of dynamic network conditions. SOS needs time to do route restructuring and recovery. With larger networks in excess of 350 nodes and 50% active nodes, the situation reverses. EAR has to contend with significant bandwidth consumption by its considerably increased proportion of control packets.

For networks of less than 450 nodes with 10% active source nodes, SOS_d has lower packet latency than both SOS and EAR. Having a double path will allow one of the data packets to reach the hub first even when reconfiguration is being carried out in the other failed path. Hence, the reconfiguration process will have a reduced effect on the packet latency of SOS_d. However, with 50% active source nodes, the trend changes. EAR's packet latency increases to become higher than SOS and SOS_d. The piggybacking advantage of EAR mentioned early is no longer significant with network sizes in excess of 350 nodes. With an increase in network size, the control information processing overhead becomes considerable and compromises packet latency. SOS also reverses its trend against its double path counterpart since, with larger networks, the probability of avoiding a failed path increases with more neighbours available. In such cases, the double packet transmissions at each source node for SOS_d becomes an overhead.

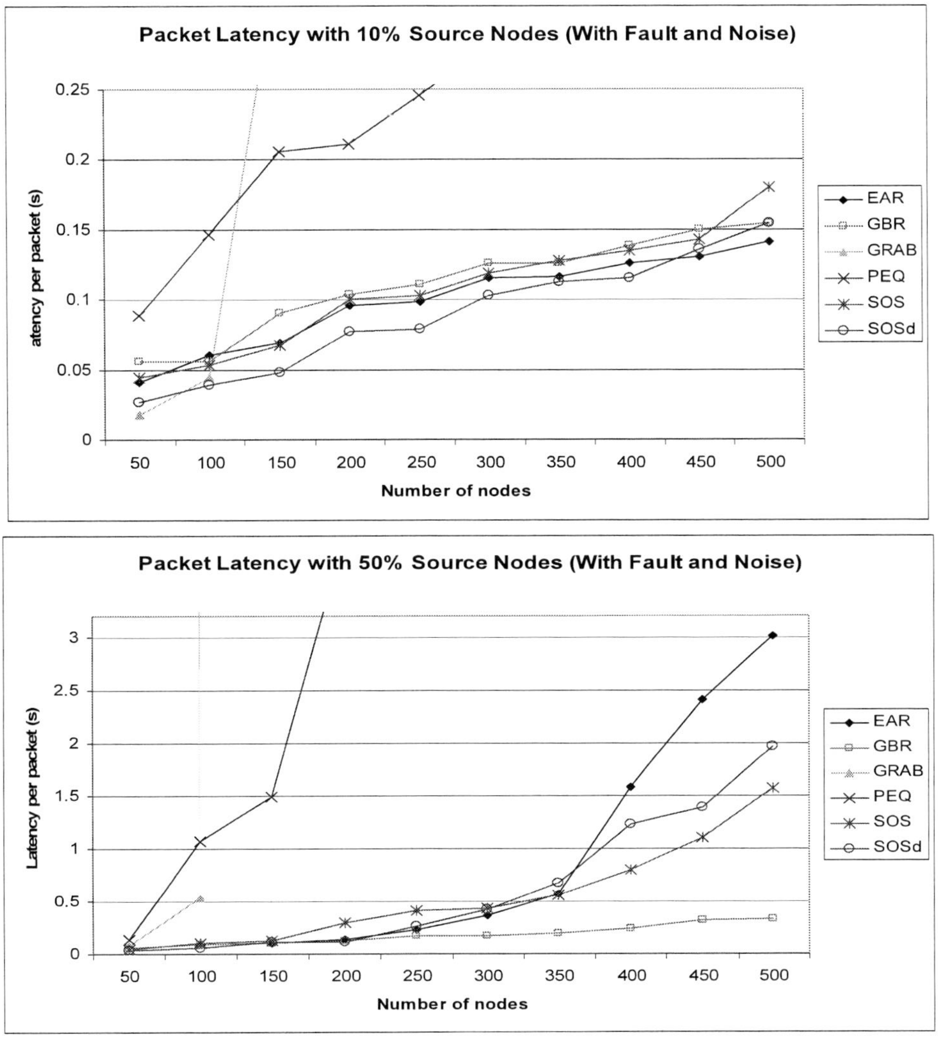

Figure 12. Packet Latency in Non-Ideal Conditions.

PEQ has higher packet latency than GBR, EAR, SOS and SOS_d because PEQ has to wait for an acknowledgement message timeout interval to realize that there was a problem with its receiver node before the path repair process begins. However, the data packet will already have been lost. The next data packet will have to wait for PEQ to find a new path before it can be forwarded. The PEQ packet latency results in Figure 12 also show that having a routing table that contains more than one route to the hub will significantly reduces the packet latency for the case of SOS, SOS_d, EAR and GBR. Less time is spent in finding a new route while another alternate route is readily available in the routing table. Thus, PEQ packet latency is higher primarily due to no available alternative routes when packet transmission fails.

GRAB's use of broadcasts to do packet transmissions results in an unacceptably high rate of packet collisions and hence, retransmissions (also, see Figure 14). Hence, packet latencies measured exceed the graph scales specified for the other routing protocols.

Energy Consumption

Utilizing multiple paths may come at the expense of increased energy and packet collisions. Sending multiple copies of the same data packet over multiple paths will consume extra energy and increase traffic loads in the network resulting in more collisions and loss of data packets, as in the case for GRAB and SOS_d in Figure 13. Hence, SOS_d consumes more energy and experiences more collisions than SOS, EAR and GBR, which use only a single path per transmission.

GRAB has the highest energy consumption for both 10% and 50% active source nodes. The large energy consumption is one of the drawbacks of GRAB's flooding-based strategies to achieve reliability. However, despite incurring this significant energy cost, GRAB is still not able to achieve the high PDR of SOS and EAR in an environment with faulty nodes and noise.

PEQ's use of acknowledgement per packet forwarded raises the transmissions incurred two-fold and reduces its energy efficiency to below that of protocols like SOS, EAR, SOS_d and GBR, which are not acknowledgement-based.

GBR has the lowest number of nodes that consumed more than 2J of energy. However, this is due to its lower data packets available in the network as can be shown from its PDR results (Figure 11). The next lowest is SOS. However, its energy efficiency and load distribution strategy increase the average life time of each node and that of the network without compromising PDR.

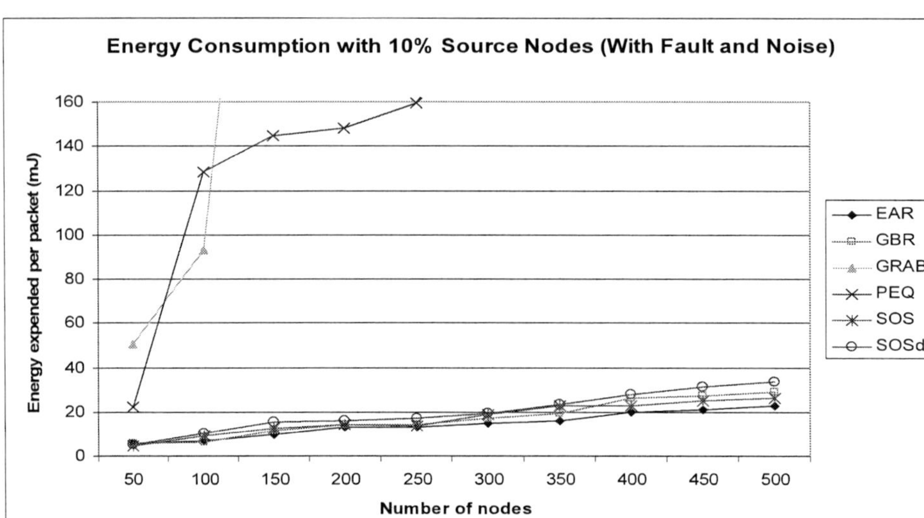

Figure 13. continued on next page.

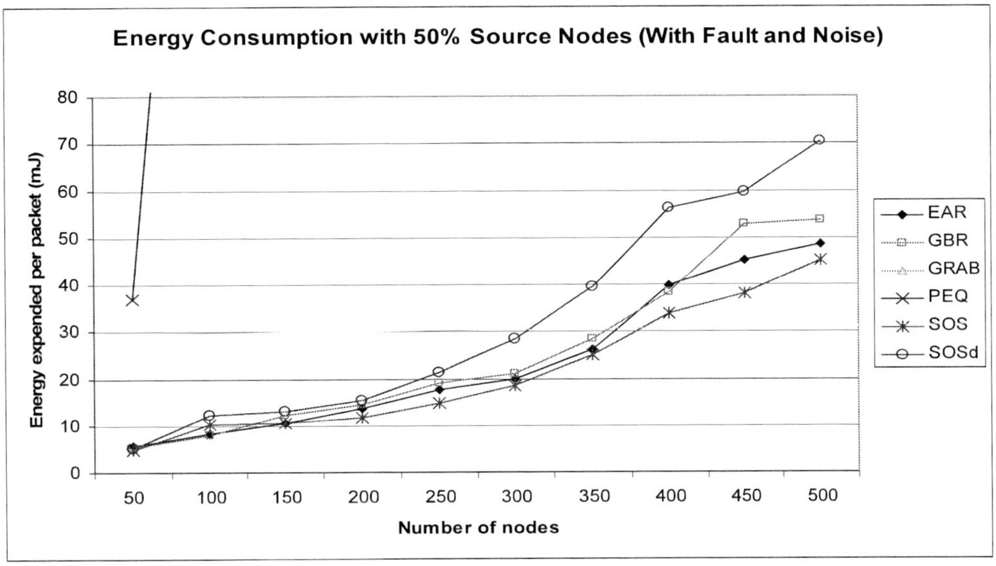

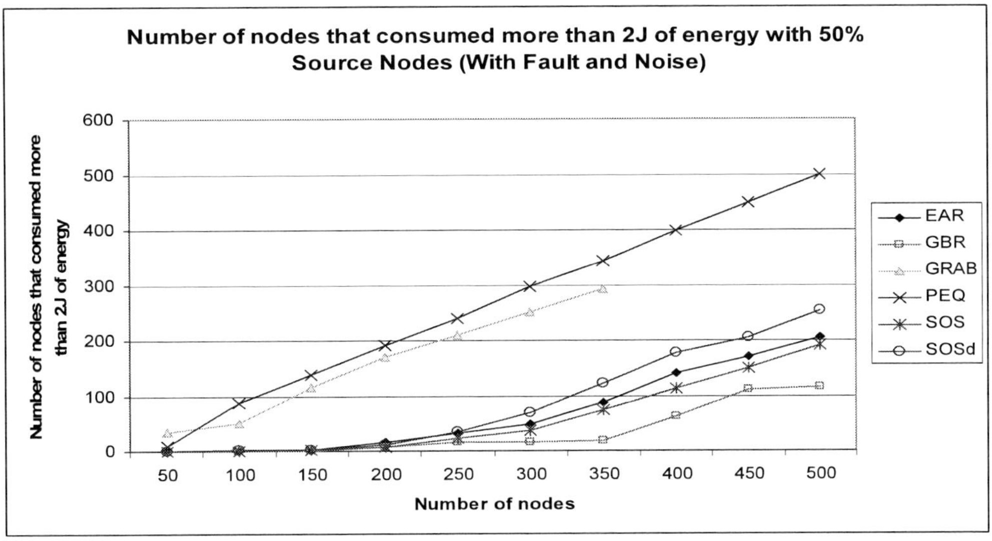

Figure 13. Energy Consumption in Non-Ideal Conditions.

Packet Collisions

As can be seen in Figure 14, packet collisions experienced for both 10% and 50% active source nodes with the network size and number of data packets to be transported. Hence, this results in less packets being delivered successfully. Packet collisions will also cause unnecessary retransmissions of packets and will have an impact on the latency and energy efficiency performances of the protocols as well. Thus, protocols, PEQ and GRAB, which experience high levels of packet collisions, also experience large latencies and high energy consumption figures.

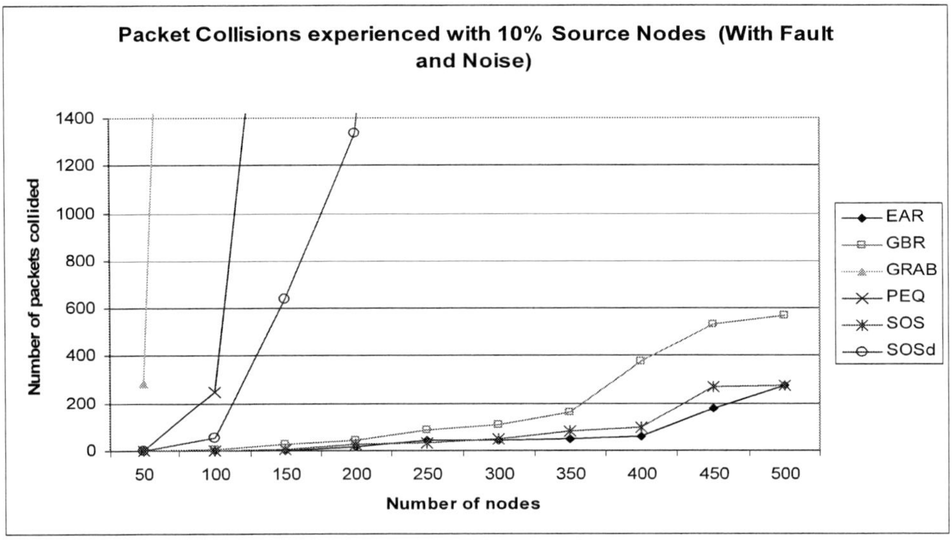

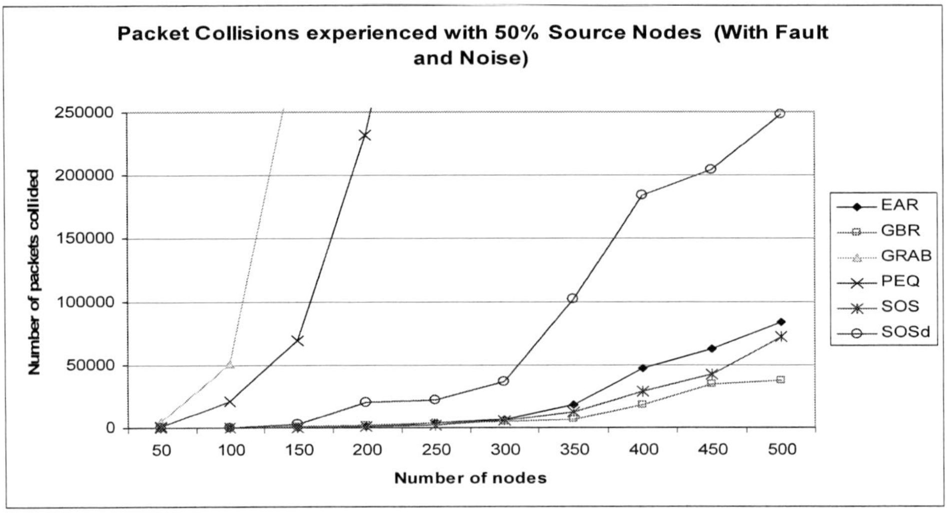

Figure 14. Packet Collisions in Non-Ideal Conditions.

Both EAR and SOS have smaller number of packet collisions compared to other protocols. EAR uses piggybacked information from RTS/CTS packets to detect node failures that has occurred. Hence, for lower data traffic levels with 10% active source nodes, EAR experiences the least number of packet collisions. However, as the level of data traffic increase with 50% active source nodes, more failed transmissions will be experienced by EAR. Since EAR will send out its "help" messages when a node detects that there is a problematic neighbouring node, this results in it generating more control packets exacerbating the level of packet collision.

SOS, on the other hand, only sends out reconfiguration messages after error detection during data packet transmission. Hence, the situation reverses with SOS experiencing lower packet collisions than EAR with 50% active source nodes. SOS_d experiences higher packet collisions than SOS, EAR and GBR as it exploits an additional path to transmit data packets at each source node.

With 10% active source nodes, GBR experiences more packet collisions than SOS and EAR. The situation reverses with 50% active source nodes. With more active sources transmitting, the levels of packet collisions are higher for every protocol. This is evidenced from Figure 14. However, this congestion of data traffic has slightly less effect on GBR due to its stochastic random route selection, enabling it to avoid more collisions with "well-spaced" transmissions. However, it must be noted that a randomly selected path may not translate to eventual successful delivery due to failed nodes. This is evidenced from GBR's comparatively low PDR values in Figure 11.

With PEQ, the additional acknowledgement packets exacerbate the packet collision level it would otherwise face with just data packet transmissions. It is evident, as mentioned previously, that unrestricted use of redundant paths for packet flooding in GRAB is detrimental to performance.

4.4. Multiple Hubs Simulation Experiment

Instead of deploying only a single hub in the entire WSN, a few hubs can be selectively deployed in distributed parts of the WSN. This multiple hub scenario will provide better resilience and higher system availability in the case of occurrence of hub failure. As will be shown later in the discussion, the advantages of this scheme is that it will cut down on traffic in the network, reduce energy usage, packet collision and packet latency.

To evaluate the ability of the routing protocols to support multiple hubs, simulations were performed within the non-ideal environment described in Section 4.3 with 50% active source nodes. The experiment is performed with 4 and 9 hubs in the network. 20 runs with different seed numbers for each of network size were conducted and the collected data was averaged over the 20 runs. The results obtained are shown in Figure 15.

Packet Delivery Ratio (PDR)

As shown in Figure 15, PDR of routing protocols in WSNs with multiple hubs are better than the PDR with single hub as in Figure 11. A data packet travelling in a multi-hub network will typically need fewer hops on average to reach a nearer hub as compared to a network where only one hub is available. Thus, data packet will have a lower chance of being dropped along the way before reaching the hub. This also explains why the PDR of 9 hubs is better than the PDR of 4 hubs for all protocols.

SOS, EAR and PEQ achieved PDRs of close to 90%, on average, with multiple hubs. This is a significant improvement for PEQ, which managed to achieve a PDR of less than 50% in a single hub network with 50% active source nodes. This can be attributed to the significant decrease in the number of packet collisions experienced by PEQ with multiple hubs.

The performance of GRAB is much better with multiple hubs too. This is because with multiple hubs, the flooding of data packets to a hub is now being restricted to a smaller region in the network and hence this leads to an overall better PDR with lower packet drops and collisions. However, the average amount of energy consumption and packet latency experienced by GRAB are still very much higher as compared to the rest of the other protocols. These are due to the presence of still relative large number of redundant packets being forwarded in the network as compared to other routing protocols.

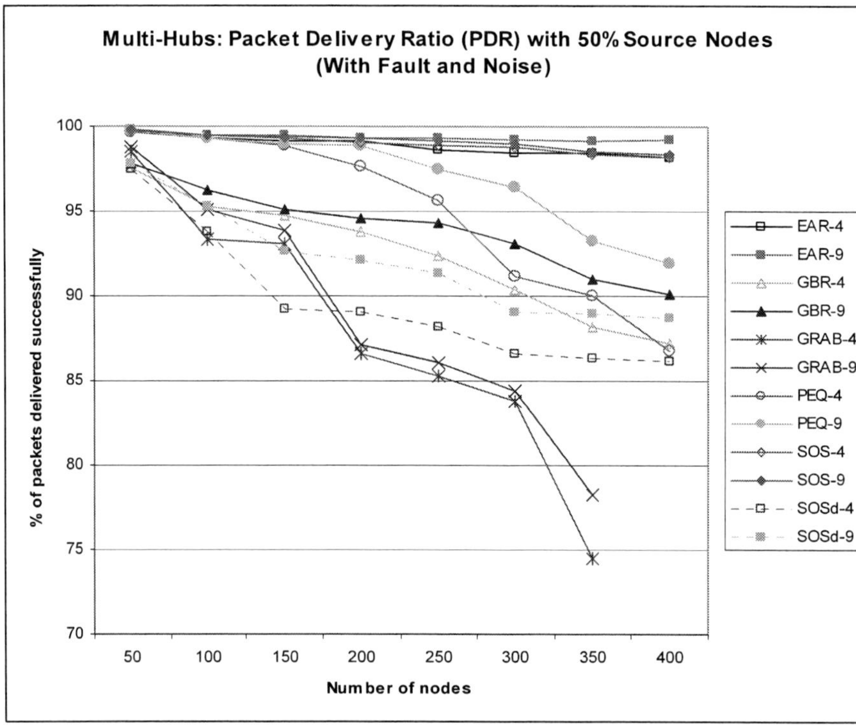

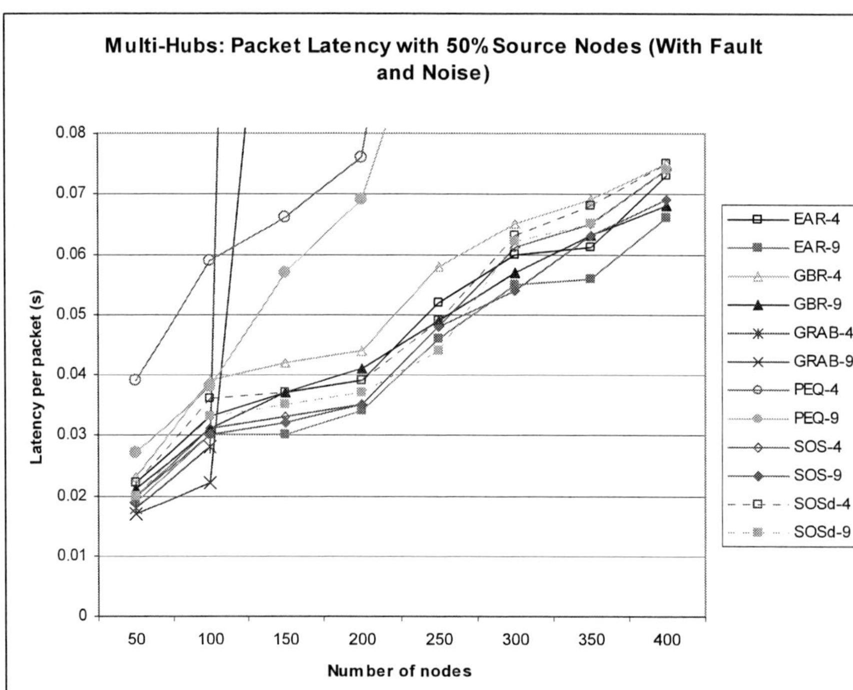

Figure 15. PDR and Packet Latency in Non-Ideal Conditions (Multi-Hub).

Packet Latency

Partitioning of the network through the use of multiple hubs clearly avoids a large increase in latency in the network situation where there is only one hub while the number of nodes increase. With more than 1 hub distributed throughout the network, the data packet can make fewer hops to reach the closer hub and hence results in lower packet latencies.

Energy Consumption

The energy consumptions of all the protocols in Figure 16 have also decreased as compared to Figure 13. The cases where retransmission of packets occurred due to packet loss as a result of packet collisions will be reduced. Also with more hubs to share the data traffic in the network and with less hopping done by the data packet, all the factors have contributed towards the saving of energy.

Packet Collisions

Having multiple hubs in a given network segregates packet transmissions to different regions in the WSN. This clearly makes it easier to avoid collisions between transmissions of nodes as shown in Figure 16. This is in contrast with having only one hub, which will experience frequent packet collisions since packet transmissions from different network sections have to eventually merge at the same location.

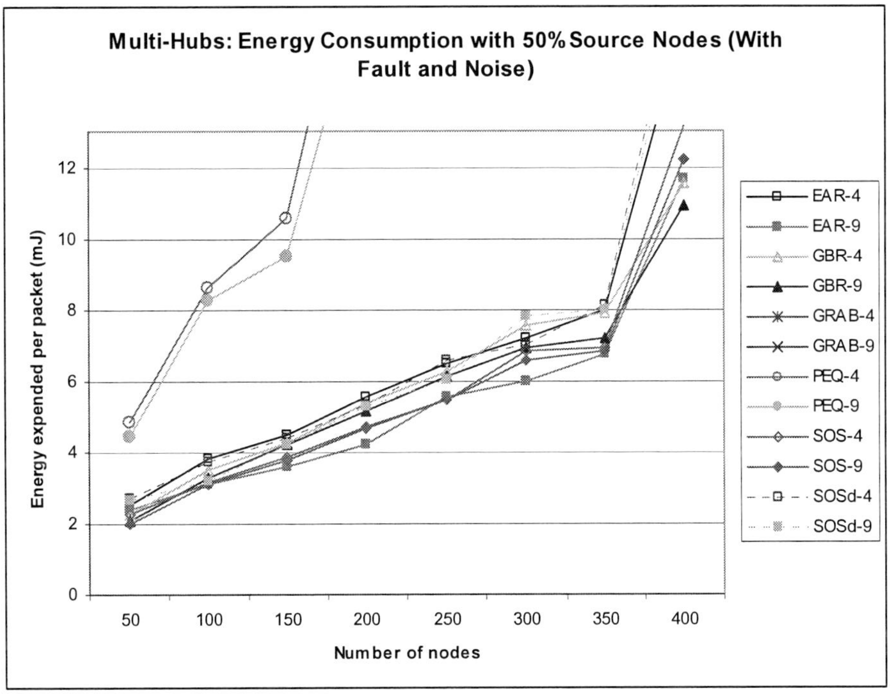

Figure 16 continued on next page.

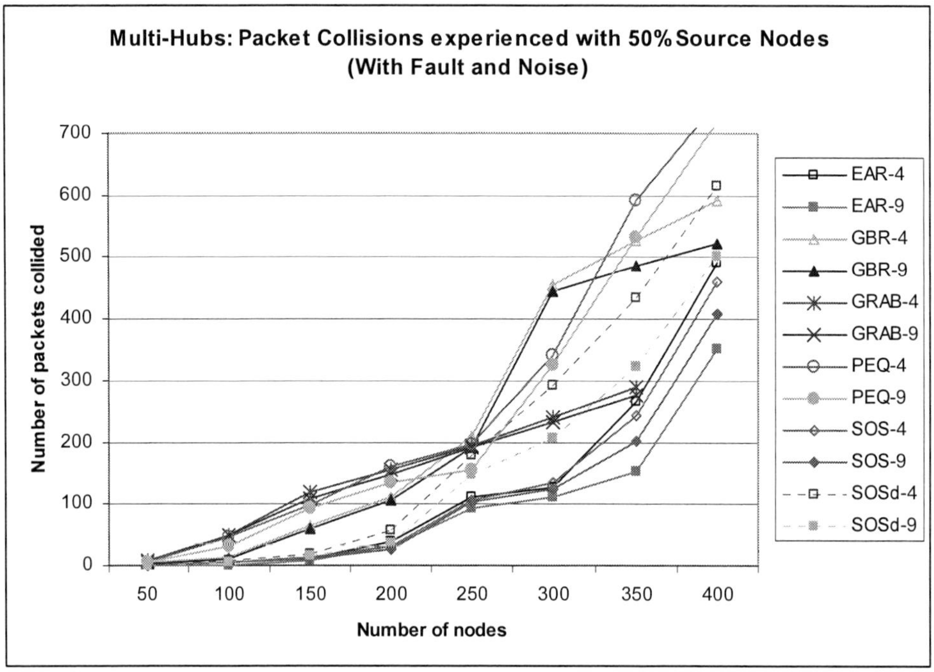

Figure 16. Results of multiple hubs simulation.

5. Conclusions

Several self-reconfiguration routing protocols were evaluated against two variations of SOS. The simulation experiment results illustrate the effectiveness of both protocols' localized self-reconfiguration approaches. SOS is preferred over SOS_d in WSNs with moderate to heavy data traffic while SOS_d, with restricted redundancy, serves as a viable alternative in lightly loaded networks. The results showed that SOS is able to achieve high levels of PDR, low energy consumption and packet latency, and experiences comparatively fewer packet collisions in a WSN environment. The multi-hub experiments have shown that by having more uniformly scattered hubs, the network traffic loads can be better distributed and hence, improve the performance of the routing protocols.

The following limitations have been identified from the simulations:

- **Poor performance in having unrestricted multiple data delivery paths:**
  Reliability achieved through unconstrained exploitation of a WSN's inherent redundancy does not augur well and instead more energy is wasted and higher packet collisions are experienced. The simulations show that having only a single path with alternate routes in the route table is better than having multiple paths.
- **The use of acknowledgement control overheads of PEQ:**
  The high acknowledgement packet overheads prevent PEQ's performance from scaling well with the number of active sources as well as network size. Thus, it is necessary to minimize the number of control packets disseminated in the WSN.

EAR requires a modification to the MAC layer to be made in order to perform its routing algorithm. Thus, effort will be incurred in rewriting the components of the upper MAC layer during practical implementation. SOS does not require any changes to the upper MAC layer and is able to achieve a competitive performance to EAR. Practical realization of SOS will be more easily achieved as only the network layer needs to be implemented.

References

[1] Ahuja R., Bagrodia R., Bajaj L., Gerla M., Takai M., "GloMoSim: *A Scalable Network Simulation Environment*", Technical report 990027, UCLA, Computer Science Dept, 1999.

[2] Akyildiz I.F., Cayirci E., Sankarasubramaniam Y., Su W., "A Survey on Sensor Networks", *IEEE Communications*, Pages 102-114, 2002.

[3] Bourkerche A., *"Performance Evaluation of Routing Protocols for Ad Hoc Wireless Networks"*, Mobile Networks and Applications, Volume 9, Issue 4, pp 333-342, 2004.

[4] Boukerche A., Werner R., Pazzi N., de Araujo R.B., *"A fast and reliable protocol for wireless sensor networks in critical conditions monitoring applications"*, pp 157-164, MSWiM 2004.

[5] Broch J., Maltz D. A., Johnson D. B., Hu Y-C., Jetcheva J., *"A Performance Comparison of Multi-Hop Wireless Ad Hoc Network Routing Protocols"* Proceedings of ACM/IEEE International, Conference on Mobile Computing and Networking, pp 85-97, October 1998.

[6] Bulusu N., Estrin D., Girod L., Heidemann J., *"Scalable Coordination for Wireless Sensor Networks: Self-Configuring Localization Systems"* Proceedings of 6th International Symposium on Communication Theory and Applications (ISCTA'01), July 2001.

[7] CrossBow MICA 2 motes specification http://www.xbow.com

[8] Estrin D., Girod L., Pottie G., Srivastava M., *"Instrumenting The World With Wireless Sensor Networks"*, Proceedings of International Conference on Acoustics, Speech and Signal Processing (ICASSP 2001), Salt Lake City, Utah, USA, May 2001.

[9] Estrin D., Govindan R., Heidemann J., Kumar S., *"Next Century Challenges: Scalable Coordination in Sensor Networks"*, International Conference on Mobile Computing and Networks (MobiCOM'99), Seattle, Washington, United States, August 1999.

[10] Kahn J. M., Katz R. H., Pister K. S. J., *"Next Century Challenges: Mobile Networking for "Smart Dust""* Proceedings of the 5th Annual ACM/IEEE International Conference on Mobile Computing and Networking, Pages 271-278, Seattle, Washington, USA, 1999.

[11] Lewis F.L., *"Wireless Sensor Networks"*, Smart Environments: Technologies, Protocols, and Applications, John Wiley, New York, 2004.

[12] Loh K.K., Long S. H., Yi Pan, "A New, Efficient and Reliable Routing Protocol", *IEEE International Symposium on a World of Wireless, Mobile and Multimedia Networks* (WOWMOM 2005), 2005.

[13] Lu S., Ye F., Zhang L., Zhong G., "GRAdient Broadcast: A Reliable Data Delivery Protocol for Large Scale Sensor Networks" *ACM Wireless Networks* (WINET), Vol 11, No.2, March 2005.

[14] Min R., Chandrakasan A., “Energy-Efficient Communication for Ad-Hoc Wireless Sensor Networks” Signals, *Systems and Computers Thirty-Fifth Asilomar Conference*, Vol. 1, Nov. 2001, pp.139-143.

[15] Schurgers C., Srivastava M. B., “Energy Efficient Routing In Wireless Sensor Networks” In *MILCOM Proceedings on Communications for Network-Centric Operations: Creating the Information Force*, McLean, VA, 2001.

[16] Ye F., Zhong G., S. Lu, and Zhang L., "GRAdient Broadcast: A robust data delivery protocol for large scale sensor networks," *ACM Wireless Networks*, Vol. 11(2), March 2005.

[17] Ye W., Heidemann J., Estrin., D., “An Energy-Efficient MAC Protocol for Wireless Sensor Networks” In Proceedings of the 21st International Annual Joint Conference of the IEEE Computer and Communications Societies (INFOCOM 2002).

In: Computer Science Research Trends
Editor: Casey B. Yarnall, pp. 181-188
ISBN: 978-1-60021-518-6

Chapter 6

A PARALLEL IMPLEMENTATION OF AN ITERATIVE RECONSTRUCTION ALGORITHM USING A SPACE-BASED PROGRAMMING MODEL

P. Knoll*[*] *and S. Mirzaei
Dept. of Nuclear Medicine, Wilhelminenspital, Montleartstr. 37, 1171 Vienna, Austria

Abstract

Iterative algorithms to reconstruct single photon emission computerized tomography (SPECT) data are based on the mathematical simulation of the acquisition process. The reconstruction times of these methods are much longer than that of routinely used reconstruction methods (such as filtered back projection). Java, a platform independent programming language changed the way of software design by using Jini and JavaSpaces, new technologies that have been introduced recently. By applying JavaSpaces, a *space* is used to store objects persistently which can be used also for effective parallel processing. In this paper, we report a novel approach for iterative reconstruction of SPECT data by means of JavaSpaces, which uses only a standard personal computer equipment and results in significant improvement of reconstruction time due to the fact that several layers of the object are computed in parallel.

Key words: space-based programming model, iterative reconstruction, distributed computing, JavaSpaces

I. Introduction

Nuclear medicine is a medical speciality that applies small amounts of radioactive materials or radiopharmaceuticals, which are attracted to specific organs, bones, or tissues to diagnose and treat disease. Nuclear medicine imaging is unique because it documents organ function and structure, in contrast to diagnostic radiology, which is based upon anatomy. Nuclear medicine imaging techniques often identify abnormalities very early in the progression of the

[*] E mail address: peter.knoll@wienkav.at

disease – long before some medical problems are apparent with other diagnostic tests [1]. This early detection allows a disease to be treated early in its course when there may be a more successful prognosis. A radioactive tracer is intravenously injected and transported into the organ of interest from which the emitted photons pass through the body of the patient. These photons can be detected externally by a gamma camera. The radionuclides used for gamma cameras emit only a single photon and therefore a special "lens" known as a collimator, which is placed between detector surface and the patient, has to be used to select a ray orientation. The resulting scintigram represents the two-dimensional projection of the three-dimensional activity distribution and therefore the tomographic information is lost if only a single planar acquisition is performed. Rotating Anger gamma cameras have been developed to utilize this information and the single photon emission computed tomography (SPECT) acquisition technique is widely used. During a standard SPECT acquisition the head of the gamma camera rotates around the patient. In order to determine the three-dimensional activity distribution mathematical reconstruction algorithms are applied. The filtered back projection (FBP) algorithm currently is the standard reconstruction method in nuclear medicine [2]. The FBP involves projecting the acquired data back across the reconstruction matrix. At each angle, the counts from each ray sum are evenly distributed between each element on the ray. Applying this method results in reconstructed transaxial slices (cross sections of the object) [3], which are usually blurred by the presence of noise. These image artefacts of the reconstructed slices can only be partly controlled by a filter function but not totally eliminated [4]. Instead of back projecting the acquired projection data, iterative algorithms update an estimate of the image until calculated ray sums and measured projection data match adequately. Iterative algorithms have the advantage that a-priori information can be incorporated at each step of the reconstruction process [5]. Although different iterative solutions already exists, the clinical application is altered by the following fact: the mean square error between reconstructed and true activity improves in early iterations, but then degrades due to increasing noise [6]. The Java platform developed by Sun Microsystems [1] represents a new means of computation specially designed for network computing and based on the idea that computer software should run on different available computer hardware and operating systems. Software written in Java and compiled with the commercially available Java Development Kit 1.2 [2] runs different kinds of computers due to the Java virtual machine which enables the Java platform to host applications on any computer without rewriting the programming code. Java applications are already used in medicine, but mainly to distribute clinical information [3, 4]. However, it does not seem reasonable to translate already existing programs written in C/C++ into Java. A new programming language rather should influence the way of software designing. The Jini concept which is 100 % pure Java, is a brand new technology that can be used to create homogeneous distributed systems. The JavaSpaces technology kit (JSTK 1.0) [5] , which has to be installed together with the Jini application programming interface (API) provides a fundamentally different programming model. This model considers application as a collection of processes cooperating via the flow of objects into and out of one or more *spaces*. In this context, these spaces are used as a shared and network accessible repository for data objects [4]. Therefore, the space-based model of distributing computing can also be elegantly used to solve computing-intensive problems faster by means of parallel application patterns.

Single photon emission computed tomography (SPECT) data can be reconstructed either by filtered back projection (FBP) or iterative methods. Instead of filtering and backprojecting the projection data, iterative algorithms try to simulate the acquisition process itself and minimize the difference between measured and simulated data [4]. This process is repeated until a "final" image is found. Due to the time-consuming iterative calculations, the reconstruction time of these methods are much longer than that of the FBP even if very simple acquisition models (no scatter, no attenuation, etc.) are applied. Therefore, the FBP is still the standard reconstruction method in nuclear medicine. By separating the algorithm into independent tasks, it is possible to shorten the computation time but existing methods mostly require either specialized hardware [7,8] or network computing [9]. Instead of using dedicated hardware or peer-to-peer network communication we present a new approach of successful parallel implementation of an iterative algorithm for reconstructing of SPECT data using a truly distributed system and a space-based programming model.

II. Methods

To accelerate iterative reconstruction, it is possible to decompose this computing intensive problem into smaller independent tasks that then can be computed simultaneously. Recently, Sun Microsystems introduced Jini and JavaSpaces which are new technologies that changed the way of software design fundamentally [6, 10].

Jini, built on top of Java, provides a homogeneous view of the network and does not require any centralized administration of available services as opposed to already existing communication patterns. JavaSpaces uses the Jini programming model and provides a simple mechanism for sharing objects in network resources based on Java technology[4]. As for any other Jini service it is necessary to run

- A HTTP server
- The Remote Method Invocation daemon (RMID)
- A lookup service
- A transaction manager [10, 11]

when applying Java Spaces. The Jini API includes a simple *HTTP server* which is necessary for exporting the code. The *RMID* uses a log file to keep track of the on demand activation and persistent service registration. Once a service has already been registered, it does not have to re-register after each reboot. Instead, RMID will restart it upon start-up [12]. *Lookup services* keep track of all services that have joined a Jini community. Jini services broadcast its presence by dropping a multicast packet to a certain IP/Port (4160) as defined in the Jini specification. Furthermore the Jini service also establishes a TCP server socket, that awaits incoming connections (Fig.1). The multicast request relies upon the User Datagram Protocol (UDP) which allows multicast (one-to-many) networking to function properly. Lookup services monitor IP/Port 4160 for incoming requests that provide information about the Jini service such as the IP/Port number. The lookup service uses this information to contact the Jini service directly using UDP, and receives and registers a proxy object of the Jini service (Fig. 2). The Jini client contacts the Jini lookup service, downloads the proxy object reference and uses that proxy to communicate directly with the Jini service (Fig. 3). Transactions are effective ways to organize a series of related operations resulting in only two possible outcomes: either all operations succeed or fail. Transactions, coordinated by a centralized *transaction manager*, are executed as if they were a single ("atomic") operation.

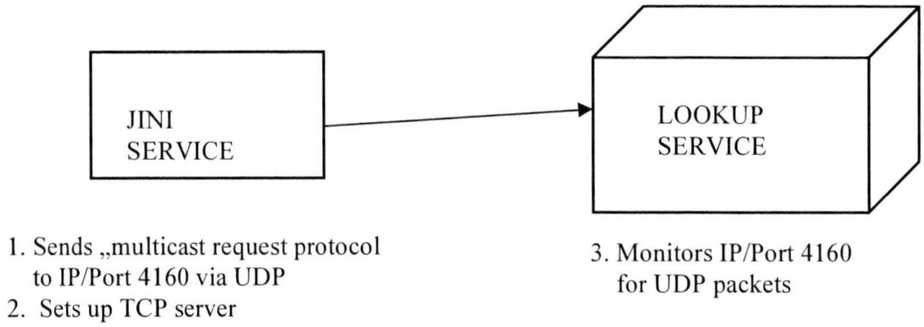

Figure 1. Registering a Jini service I.

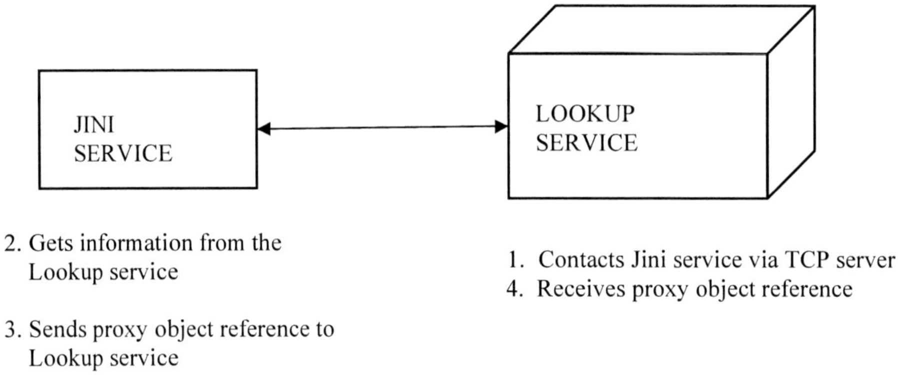

Figure 2. Registering a Jini service II.

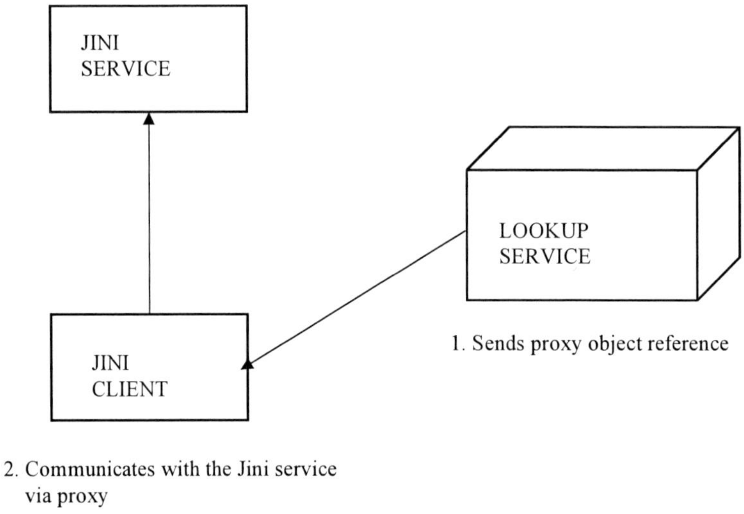

Figure 3. Use of a Jini service.

The Jini API introduces a "leasing concept" that is able to clean up the whole system without human intervention if components have failed. Leasing is based on the idea that the resource is loaned to clients only for a fixed period of time. If this time interval expires, the resource is automatically removed.

If all these processes (HTTP server, RMID, lookup service and transaction manager) run on the host, a *space* can be created. In a distributed application, JavaSpaces act as virtual spaces between providers and users of Java objects. When applying this programming model, processes are loosely coupled because in this case processes interact indirectly through a *space* and not directly with other processes. One of the most common application pattern used for parallel computing is the replicated worker pattern. This pattern involves a master process along with a number of workers [6]. An iterative reconstruction algorithm based on the error back propagation method which is used in artificial neural networks [13, 14] was implemented and applies the space-based model with one master process and five reconstruction workers. The reconstruction software package was installed on 6 personal computers (PCs) routinely available in our department. The master process which runs on computer A simply writes the slice numbers and the projection data to be reconstructed into the *space using* a template matching mechanism. Each of the reconstruction workers which run on Computers B-F, takes one of the tasks, removes it from the space, and reconstructs only the slice that corresponds to this specific task. Since the task is removed from the *space*, exclusive access to this job is guaranteed. After reconstruction, the worker writes the reconstructed transaxial slice back into the space from where it will be collected by the master process. After the worker has finished his work, he looks into the *space again* for more available tasks. If successful, the worker starts to reconstruct the next slice. At the same time, the other workers reconstruct other slices and write them into the *space*. When all slices are reconstructed, the master process collects and views the reconstructed slices using a self developed Java slice viewer. The parallel implementation of this iterative reconstruction method shortens the reconstruction time significantly by a factor of approximately 20 as compared to a single processor.

III. Results

Reconstruction of In-111 Octreotide SPECT Images

SPECT raw data of a routine receptor study using In 111 octreotide in a patient with SCLC were used for reconstruction. After injection of 150 MBq In-111 octreotide a 360° SPECT was performed (acquisition. parameters: 64x64 matrix, 6°/step and 30 sec. per angular position) using a MEGP collimator. Acquired data were distributed among the workers by the master process and iteratively reconstructed. An iterative algorithm, based on the learning methods used by artificial neural networks [13, 14] needs approximately 15 seconds to reconstruct the whole object using the presented JavaSpaces implementation. When applying the same iterative reconstruction algorithm (and the same number of iterations), it takes approximately 3 minutes to reconstruct the data if a single processor implementation is used. The iteratively reconstructed slices were compared with those reconstructed with FBP. The iteratively reconstructed image (Fig. 4a) demonstrates a lesion (confirmed by CT) in the left suprarenal gland which is not shown by FBP (Fig. 4b).

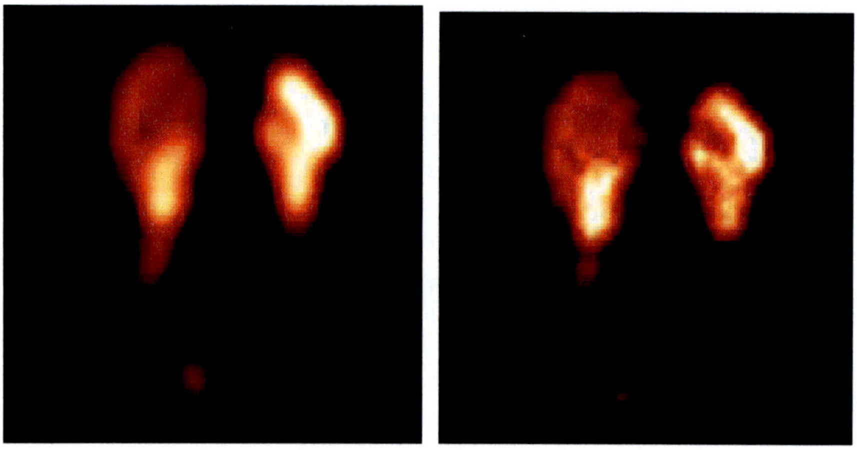

a) b)

Figure 4. In 111 Octreotide image of the abdomen: a) Iterative reconstruction demonstrates a lesion in the left suprarenal gland. b) The lesion is not detected by FBP

IV. Discussion

Distributed applications are - despite their advantages - difficult to design due to the complexity of the distributed environment which does not concern when writing standalone applications[15]. In the past, the variety of existing machine architectures and software platforms has prevented the development and proliferation of distributed applications [10]. JavaSpaces is a high-level coordination tool for combining processes into a distributed application by means of a network-accessible "space". This recently introduced technology [5, 6] can also be elegantly used to solve computational intensive tasks. In this paper, a new approach of the parallel implementation of an iterative reconstruction algorithm using Jini and JavaSpaces is presented, which reduces the computation time by several orders of magnitude. Although other attempts of parallel implementation for tomographic reconstruction methods using networking and/or dedicated hardware has been described before [7-9], a truly distributed system applying only standard PC equipment to reconstruct SPECT data has not been presented before. Applying JavaSpaces, the SPECT acquisition data are distributed by a master process between five reconstruction workers, which reside on different computers of our department's Intranet. Each reconstruction worker computes specific layers of the object. After successful computation of all the layers, the master process collects and views the reconstructed slices. The parallel implementation results in a significant acceleration of the reconstruction time, thus providing the possibility for additional implementation of physical properties (e.g. gamma camera resolution, scatter) into the algorithm, which further improves the quality of the reconstructed images. Use of an improved mathematical model will not necessarily lengthen the overall computation time, since the number of reconstruction workers can be incremented very easily. The significant acceleration of processing time is due to:

- Parallel implementation
- Loading of auxiliary data in advance

- Correct balance between computation and communication
- Processing and transfer time

The *parallel implementation* of the iterative algorithm enables reconstruction of several layers of the object at the same time. Reconstruction workers are able to *load auxiliary data*, needed for iterative reconstruction, in advance. A *correct balance between computation and communication* is difficult to achieve with other software design models [8]. Using a JavaSpaces implementation, the reconstruction workers stay busy and compute tasks in relation to their availability and ability to work. Consideration of both, the *processing and transfer time* is important for application in a clinical routine environment. The applied platform independent technology allows the use of hardware, which already exists in any department, thus avoiding communication bottlenecks since transfer time over the network connection is minimized. JavaSpaces technology does not only improve tomographic reconstruction but may also be used as a platform-independent, cost-effective means to shorten the computation time of other time-consuming computational tasks.

References

[1] http://www.sun.com

[2] http://java.sun.com/products/jdk1.2

[3] Malameteniou F., Vassilacopoulos G., Mantas J.: A search engine for virtual patient records. *Int. J. Med.* Inf. 1999 Aug;55(2):103-15

[4] Slomka P.,Elliot E., Driedger A.: Java-Based Remote Viewing and Processing of Nuclear Medicine Images: Toward "the Imaging Department without walls" *J. Nucl. Med.* 2000;41:111-118

[5] http://www.sun.com/jini/index.html

[6] Freeman E., Hupfer S., Arnold K.: JavaSpaces. *Principles, Patterns and Practice* Addison-Wesley, Massachusetts, USA 1999

[7] Passeri A., Formicioni A. R, de Cristofaro M., Pupi A. Meldolesi U.: High-performance computing and networking as tools for accurate emission computed tomography reconstruction. *Eur. J. Nucl. Med.* (1997) 24:390-397

[8] Comtat C., Defrise M., Morel C., Townsend D.: The FaVor Algorithm for 3D Pet Data and its Implementation using a Net of Transputers. *Phys. Med. Biol.*, Vol. 38; pp 929-944, 1993

[9] Kontaxakis G., Strauss L. G., vanKaick G.: Optimized Implementation and Perfromance Evaluation of Iterative Image Reconstruction Algorithms for PET on Distributed Pentium Systems and a Web-Based Interface. (Abs.) *J. Nucl. Med.* 1998; 39:8P

[10] Arnold K., Sullivan B., Scheifler R., Waldo J., Wollrath A.*: The Jini Specification Addison Wesley*, Massachusetts, USA, 1999

[11] Edwards K.: *Core Jini Prentice Hall*, NJ, USA, 1999

[12] Horstmann C, Cornell G.: Core Java 1.2: *Fundamentals Prentice Hall*, NJ, USA, 1999

[13] Knoll P., Mirzaei S., Müllner A., Koriska K., Köhn H., Neumann M.: An Artificial Neural Net and Error Backpropagation to Reconstruct Single Photon Emission Computerized Tomography Data. *Med. Phys.* 1999;26:244-248

[14] Knoll P, Mirzaei S., Krotla G., Koriska K., H, Köhn: Improvement in *Image Quality Using a Single Layered Artificial Neural Network to Reconstrcut SPECT data. Proceedings of the International Conference on Imaging Sciences*, Systems and Technology (CISST '98), LasVegas, USA 1998

[15] Farley J.: *Java Distributed Computing O'Reilly Associates Inc.*, CA, USA 1998

In: Computer Science Research Trends
Editor: Casey B. Yarnall, pp. 189-237
ISBN 978-1-60021-518-6

Chapter 7

DESIGNING PROOF PROCEDURES FOR LOGIC PROGRAMS BY REASONING WITH CHAIN PROGRAMS

David A. Rosenblueth and Julio C. Peralta*
Instituto de Investigaciones en Matemáticas Aplicadas y en Sistemas
Universidad Nacional Autónoma de México
Apdo. 20-726, 01000 México D. F., México

Abstract

Substitutions are typically pervasive in proof procedures for logic programs. This chapter presents a technique relegating the role played by substitutions, thereby simplifying the design of both the inference systems and the search strategies of such proof procedures. Our method converts logic programs into "chain" form, whose proof trees have (nontrivial) substitutions only at the leaves. Existing parsers for context-free grammars can then in principle be converted into sound inference systems for chain programs simply by adding unification to the treatment of terminals.

Just as proof trees are simplified in chain programs, so are derivations. Hence, chain programs are also useful for describing search strategies requiring an explicit representation of the derivation tree. We apply our technique to the design of deterministic metainterpreters.

Keywords: Logic programming, Proof procedures, Inference systems, Context-free parsing, Search strategies, Deterministic metainterpreters.

1. Introduction

Logic programming, as embodied by Prolog, has long relied on a simple proof procedure consisting of SLD resolution as its inference system and a top-down, left-to-right discipline as its search strategy. It is important, however, to be able to develop other, more sophisticated proof procedures.

*E-mail address: drosenbl@servidor.unam.mx

Logic programs resemble context-free grammars. The multiplicity of context-free parsers makes it all the more important to study possible connections between logic programs and context-free grammars, allowing us to develop proof procedures inspired by parsers. The lack of substitutions in context-free grammars suggests considering first a restricted kind of logic program, similar to context-free grammars, where an inference system would not have to apply a substitution at every step.

At the same time, substitutions are a source of complexity in the design of search strategies for logic programs. Such ubiquity of substitutions in search strategies also invites concentrating on logic programs where substitutions play a secondary role.

This chapter argues that "chain" programs can simplify not only the design of inference systems, but also the traversal of search spaces for logic programs. Both these applications of chain programs must then be accompanied by conversion methods transforming logic programs that do not have chain form, into equivalent programs in chain form. We give two such transformations: one for "moded" programs [1], where each argument place is used either as "input" (instantiated) or "output" (uninstantiated), and another one for arbitrary definite programs. Although many of the results presented here have already appeared in [26, 27, 28], we think it is advantageous to have all these results uniformly presented. Moreover, we now have a better understanding of the conception of deterministic metainterpreters.

1.1. Proof Trees

The similarity between context-free grammars and logic programs is no coincidence. A motivation for the design of Prolog was that of having a programming language suitable for natural-language processing.

This resemblance is important because myriad parsing methods have been developed, that avoid recomputing some partial results as well as entering some nonterminating loops. In principle, then, parser-inspired inference systems would preserve the advantages of the originating parsers. Few inference systems for logic programs, however, have been designed with a parser in mind. To be sure, some researchers have indeed devised such inference systems: an example is Pereira and Warren's generalization [24] of Earley's parsing algorithm [9].

As we will see in Section 2., "proof trees" for logic programs play the role of parse trees for context-free grammars. A possible reason for this scarcity of parser-inspired proof procedures is that proof trees are not similar enough to parse trees as to enable us to readily obtain logic-program inference systems from parsers. This suggests reviewing the relationship between context-free grammars and logic programs.

1.1.1. Difference Lists

Logic programs can be thought of as a generalization of context-free grammars. Therefore, logic programs can be restricted to "coincide" with context-free grammars. An important restriction is that of "difference lists" [8]. A difference list represents a string $c_1 \ldots c_n$ as a pair of terms

$$([c_1, \ldots, c_n|X], X)$$

where X is a variable which may or may not be instantiated. Here and throughout, we adhere to the convention of using names starting with a lower-case letter for function and predicate symbols, and names starting with an upper-case letter for variables. We will assume some familiarity with logic programming [21].

A production:

$$A_0 \rightarrow A_1\ A_2 \ldots A_m$$

can then be represented by the clause:

$$a_0(X_0, X_m) \leftarrow a_1(X_0, X_1),\ a_2(X_1, X_2),\ \ldots,\ a_m(X_{m-1}, X_m) \qquad (1)$$

where each $a_i(X, Y)$ denotes the string represented by the difference list (X, Y). This representation has of course only the expressive power of context-free grammars. To increase such expressive power, definite-clause grammars [8] generalize the difference-list representation of context-free grammars with additional argument places. Once this addition is performed, however, the syntactic similarity with context-free grammars is lost.

1.1.2. Chain Programs

This chapter follows another path for increasing the expressiveness of the difference-list representation. The main idea is that we allow the a_i's denote arbitrary binary relations. This enables us to preserve the form of the nonunit clauses (1).

Having dealt with nonunit clauses, let us now consider unit clauses. The difference-list representation of context-free grammars has unit clauses of the form:

$$a([c|X], X) \leftarrow \qquad (2)$$

When we allow the a_i's denote arbitrary binary relations, we are in fact giving up this simple syntax for unit clauses. Unit clauses must now be allowed to be arbitrary, provided that the predicate symbol is binary:

$$a(t, t') \leftarrow \qquad (3)$$

where t and t' are any term.

1.1.3. Parser-Based Inference Systems for Chain Programs

Consider now a parser for context-free grammars. Evidently, such a parser is an inference system for a logic program consisting of clauses of the form (1) and (2). Since we are generalizing the clauses of the form (2) to (3), it is natural that the treatment of terminals, which occur at the leaves of parse trees, must be modified. The treatment of nonterminals, however, may remain untouched. The reason is that the substitutions in internal nodes of proof trees for chain programs are trivial. We will see that in principle, by adding unification to the treatment of the terminals in a context-free parser, we obtain an inference system for chain programs.

This chapter will argue that the resulting inference system is sound, but not necessarily complete. Completeness is not guaranteed because unlike strings, which have a linear structure, the sequences of terms defined by a chain program have a branching structure. Context-free parsers deal with the usual nondeterminism appearing from several productions having the same left-hand side. This other kind of nondeterminism is also dealt with by parser-based inference systems for chain programs. However, there is a nondeterminism of a different nature, resulting from the possibility of extending a computation in more than one way. Our method does not apparently suggest how to remove or decrease this kind of nondeterminism, and we have to leave this problem as a possible avenue of future research.

1.1.4. Transformations into Chain Form

Clearly, knowing how to convert parsers into inference systems for chain programs is not enough. Unlike definite-clause grammars, which have predicates with an arbitrary number of argument places, chain programs have a rigid syntax, especially for nonunit clauses. Such a syntax is awkward for programming. We must therefore provide transformations taking a logic program not having chain form and producing an equivalent program in chain form. A chain-program inference system, together with a transformation into chain form would then constitute an inference system (for programs that do not necessarily have chain form) based on a parser.

As we will see, even with transformations producing programs in chain form the situation may remain unsatisfactory. When we "convert" a parser into an inference system, we naturally wish an inference system having similar advantages to those of the corresponding parser. For example, Pereira and Warren's "Earley deduction" [24], just as Earley's parsing algorithm [9], reuses some partial results, and is less prone to falling into nonterminating loops, compared with Prolog. Once we have coupled a transformation of logic programs into chain form with a parser-based inference system for chain programs, we apparently have a sound inference system for the kind of logic program to which the transformation is applicable. However, the original advantages of the parser may no longer be present in the obtained inference system, as a result of the conversion to chain form.

We will illustrate this phenomenon with inference systems obtained from "chart" parsers. This is an example of such a situation because the original advantages of the parsers are lost as a result of adding the transformation into chain form. It is possible, however, to recover the lost benefits in this particular case by slightly modifying the resulting chart-based inference system. In general, however, it is not clear how to retrieve such properties if they disappear when adding a transformation into chain form. This is a second candidate for future research.

1.2. Derivation Trees

Proof trees are simplified in chain programs because (nontrivial) substitutions only appear at the leaves. Now, a derivation is a sequence of goals, each of which is the frontier of a proof tree. Thus, derivations are also simplified in chain programs. Such a simplification allows us to describe search strategies on the derivation tree without considering substitutions but for unit clauses.

1.2.1. Applications of Search Strategies

An application of explicit representations of derivation trees is that of counting the number of steps in the search for a proof, as opposed to the number of steps in the proof. Kowalski [19] advocates reconciling reactive agents [5], with rational agents [13] through a metainterpreter behaving in this manner.

Another application where a simplified derivation tree is useful is that of search-strategy implementations in imperative programming languages [22]. Prolog's search strategy comes to mind, but other strategies may be desirable.

Yet another area in which we wish to describe search strategies for logic programs is that of committed-choice processors [32, 34]. Such processors are deterministic. Hence, traversals of the (nondeterministic) search space for a logic program and a goal must be performed by either a deterministic metainterpreter or a deterministic, compiled version of the original nondeterministic logic program. This application is important for us, as the methods of Ueda [34] and Tamaki [32] compiling a nondeterministic program into a deterministic version have an implicit transformation of a restricted kind of logic program into *chain* form.

1.2.2. Chain-Form Transformations Implicit in Committed-Choice Methods

These methods for executing nondeterministic programs in committed-choice processors have two limitations, however. On the one hand, they are compiled in the sense of transforming a given program into another program which, under Prolog, deterministically traverses the search space of the original program. Such a compiled nature obscures the use of chain programs. On the other hand, these methods were originally restricted to moded programs (in which each argument place of each predicate is assigned a role of either instantiated or uninstantiated) [1].

As for the first of these limitations, the compilative nature of these techniques, we have given a metainterpreter reconstruction [27] of the methods of Ueda and Tamaki. Our metainterpreter reconstruction makes manifest not only the implicit use of chain programs but also the needed transformation of moded programs into chain form.

1.2.3. Extending the Implicit Transformation

We have overcome the second drawback, namely the restriction to moded programs as follows. First, we observe that chain programs also appear in Clark and van Emden's descriptions [7] of flowcharts with logic programs. Next, note that Prolog implementations (in imperative programming languages) are describable with flowcharts. The close connection between imperative and chain programs, together with the existence of Prolog implementations suggest that it should be possible to extend the moded transformation to arbitrary definite programs. We have developed such a transformation in [27].

This second, "unmoded" transformation extended the original committed-choice traversal methods to arbitrary definite programs. Such a transformation enabled us, in addition, to apply chain programs to the design of deterministic metainterpreters.

The first, moded transformation is still important, nevertheless, for efficiency reasons, because inference can be performed from the resulting chain programs using "matching" (one-side unification) instead of full unification.

2. Chain Programs

This section motivates chain programs by first reviewing difference lists as a fundamental connection between context-free grammars and logic programs. Difference lists, however, only have the expressive power of context-free grammars. We next consider, as a source for increasing expressiveness, Clark and van Emden's results relating flowcharts to logic programs. (Clark and van Emden's programs will appear again when we extend the moded transformation to one applicable to arbitrary definite programs.) Then we will be in a position to see how proof trees and derivation trees are simplified in chain programs; we conclude this section with such simplifications.

2.1. Difference Lists

A difference list uses the "quotient" representation of a formal language as follows. Let Σ be an alphabet. A language over Σ is any subset of Σ^*. We define the *quotient representation* of a language L over Σ as:

$$\mathcal{Q}_L = \{(xw, w) \ : \ x \in L \text{ and } w \in \Sigma^*\}$$

This representation is suitable for modeling productions of context-free grammars with clauses of logic programs.

A production

$$A_0 \rightarrow A_1 A_2 \dots A_n \tag{4}$$

is traditionally interpreted as a *rewriting* of the left-hand side into the right-hand side. However, sometimes it is useful to view each symbol A_i in a production as a *language* over Σ. In this case, it can be proved that a production (4) means that the *product* of the languages for $A_1, A_2, \dots, A_n$, respectively, is contained in the language for A_0.[1] If we denote by $A \cdot B$ the product of the languages for A and B, then (4) means that

$$A_0 \supseteq A_1 \cdot A_2 \cdot \ \dots \ \cdot A_n$$

If P and Q are binary relations, then we denote by $P \circ Q$ the *composition* of P and Q.[2] One can easily verify that if A and B are languages, then $\mathcal{Q}_A \circ \mathcal{Q}_B = \mathcal{Q}_{A \cdot B}$; and that $A \supseteq B$ iff $\mathcal{Q}_A \supseteq \mathcal{Q}_B$. Thus, (4) also means that

$$\mathcal{Q}_{A_0} \supseteq \mathcal{Q}_{A_1} \circ \mathcal{Q}_{A_2} \circ \dots \circ \mathcal{Q}_{A_n}$$

Let us now consider clauses. A binary predicate denotes a binary relation. Thus, if a predicate $p_i(X, Y)$ denotes the relation P_i, then the clause

$$p_0(X_0, X_n) \leftarrow p_1(X_0, X_1),\ p_2(X_1, X_2),\ \dots,\ p_n(X_{n-1}, X_n) \tag{5}$$

[1]The product of languages L and M is defined as: $L \cdot M = \{xy : x \in L \text{ and } y \in M\}$.

[2]The composition of relations P and Q is defined as: $P \circ Q = \{(x, z) : (x, y) \in P \text{ and } (y, z) \in Q\}$.

means that

$$P_0 \supseteq P_1 \circ P_2 \circ \ldots \circ P_n$$

Consequently, if P_i is the quotient representation of A_i, then (4) and (5) mean the same relational equation.

We find two contrasting situations. First, arbitrary definite logic programs, although similar to context-free grammars, are not similar enough to them to establish a close connection. Second, logic programs can be restricted, using the difference-list representation of formal languages, to coincide with context-free grammars. Such programs, however, are only as expressive as those grammars. Assuming that we are interested in having a programming language, this suggests taking these restricted programs and generalizing them so that we can compute every computable function without losing the strong similarity with context-free grammars.

2.2. Logic-Based State-Oriented Programs

We shall look at state-oriented programs, such as flowcharts, for this generalization. The reason is that such programs have been connected both with formal grammars and with logic programs.

On the one hand, various authors [2, 10, 16, 29] have observed that state-oriented programs can be regarded as grammars with primitive instructions as terminal symbols.

On the other hand, flowcharts have been described [7] with logic programs in such a way that a flowchart and its associated logic program define the same set of computations. A state of a flowchart is represented by a variable-free (ground) term denoting an ordered tuple, with one coordinate for each variable of the flowchart. A primitive instruction is modeled as a predicate denoting a set of pairs of states, that is, a binary relation over a set of states. Clauses of the logic programs of [7] describing flowcharts have the form

$$p(X, Z) \leftarrow c(X, Y),\ q(Y, Z) \tag{6}$$

where c is a symbol of a predicate denoting a primitive command that transforms state X into state Y, and p and q are symbols of predicates associated with labels of the flowchart. These clauses are similar to (5). A difference is that predicates in (6) may denote arbitrary binary relations, whereas those of (5) denote the quotient representation of a language.

2.3. Chain Programs

Both these connections, (i) flowcharts with grammars and (ii) flowcharts with logic programs, suggest generalizing the difference-list representation of a context-free grammar by allowing predicates of (5) denote *arbitrary* binary relations. With programs so generalized we can compute every computable function (since such programs can describe flowcharts) while preserving a close similarity with grammars. In principle, we need only consider derivations having a single-subgoal initial goal with a ground term in its first argument and a variable in its second argument. However, we will be interested in relaxing this groundness condition, so as to be closer to the usual spirit of logic programming.

The occurrences of variables in the body of (5) make each subgoal reminiscent of a chain link. Thus, we shall refer to programs with clauses of such a form as chain programs.

Our chain programs are similar to, but different from, certain programs occurring in the deductive-database literature under the same name; a difference is that we allow function symbols other than constants.

We define a *chain program* as a logic program consisting only of clauses of the form:

$$p(X_0, X_n) \leftarrow q_1(X_0, X_1),\ q_2(X_1, X_2),\ \ldots,\ q_n(X_{n-1}, X_n) \quad n > 0 \tag{7}$$

$$\text{or } p(t, t') \leftarrow \tag{8}$$

where the X_i's are distinct variables, and t and t' are any term. The first argument place of a predicate will be called its *input*, and the second argument place its *output*. A *chain goal* is a goal of the form:

$$\leftarrow q_1(t, X_1),\ q_2(X_1, X_2),\ \ldots,\ q_n(X_{n-1}, X_n) \tag{9}$$

where t is any term not containing any occurrence of any X_i.

It will be useful to single out a kind of chain program where all answers for such a program and a goal with a leftmost ground input are ground, assuming a leftmost computation rule. If $\mathrm{var}(t) \supseteq \mathrm{var}(t')$ in every unit clause (8), then the program will be called an *M chain program* (for "moded"). Here, and throughout the sequel, we use $\mathrm{var}(t)$ to denote the set of variables in expression t.

It will also be useful to identify another type of chain program, where each predicate occurring in the head of a nonunit clause (7) denotes a subset of the identity relation (i.e. an atom $p(t, t')$ can only hold if t is t'). Such a chain program will be called an *I chain program* (for "identity").

2.4. Proof Trees for Chain Programs

Let us now see how proof trees and derivation trees are simplified for chain programs. We will assume a single-subgoal goal (as proof trees are only defined for such goals):

$$\leftarrow p(t, Z)$$

In the case of an M chain program, we will assume that t is ground. In the case of an I chain program, we will assume that Z does not occur in t, and that p denotes a subset of the identity relation.

First we need to observe that if the program is either an M chain program or an I chain program, then it suffices to compute the substitution received by the *output* of such a subgoal.

In the case of an M chain program, the M goal has an input t which is a ground term, so that t does not receive any substitution. Therefore, we are only interested in the substitution received by the output of the topmost subgoal.

In the case of an I chain program, the predicate of the topmost subgoal denotes a subset of the identity relation. Therefore, for every answer, both the input and the output of such a subgoal are instantiated to the same term. Hence, we can also restrict ourselves to computing the output substitution of the original goal.

Proof trees did not play an important role in the advent of logic programming theory; for instance, they do not appear in Lloyd's book [21]. However, their relevance is at present

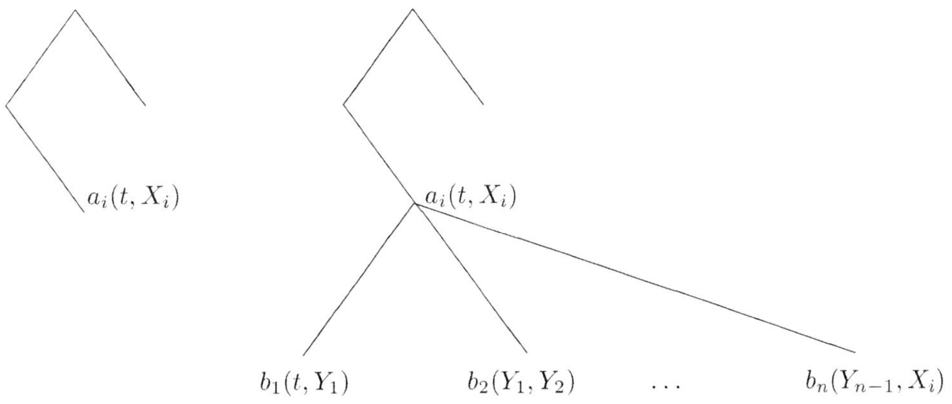

Figure 1. Extending a proof tree for a chain program with a nonunit clause.

well established [31, 33]. In our case, proof trees serve to connect inference systems for logic programs with parsers for context-free grammars.

A *proof tree* for a definite program P is a tree of atoms defined as follows:

1. An *open* single atom is a *proof tree*.

2. Let A be an open leaf of a proof tree T and $B \leftarrow B_1, \ldots, B_n$ $(n \geq 0)$ a variant of clause in P with no variables in common with T, such that A and B unify with most general unifier θ. Let T' be the tree obtained by adding $B_1, \ldots, B_n$ as children of A. Then $T'\theta$ is also a *proof tree*. If $n = 0$, then $A\theta$ is *closed*; otherwise $B_1\theta, \ldots, B_n\theta$ are *open*.

A proof tree with all its leaves closed is called a *closed proof tree*.

2.4.1. Chain Programs

When extending a proof tree with the inductive part of the above definition, we may have to apply the unifier θ, in the worst of cases, to all the nodes of the tree T'. However, when constructing proof trees for chain programs following the definition above, and extending every time the leftmost open leaf, two simplifications occur.

First, nonunit clauses (7) have no function symbols (or constants), and the argument places of their heads are distinct variables. This implies that extending a proof tree at a node $A_i = a_i(t, X_i)$ with a nonunit clause $C = a_i(Y_0, Y_n) \leftarrow b_1(Y_0, Y_1),\ b_2(Y_1, Y_2),\ \ldots,\ b_n(Y_{n-1}, Y_n)$ translates to copying t to the input of the first subgoal of C and renaming the output of the last subgoal of C. We depict this situation in Fig. 1.

Second, when closing a leaf $A_i = a_i(t, X_i)$ we do need to compute the substitution received by the output X_i but not the substitution received by the input t of such a leaf.

To see this, recall that we are ultimately interested in the substitution acting on the output of the topmost subgoal. Next, note that X_i does not occur in t. Hence, closing A_i

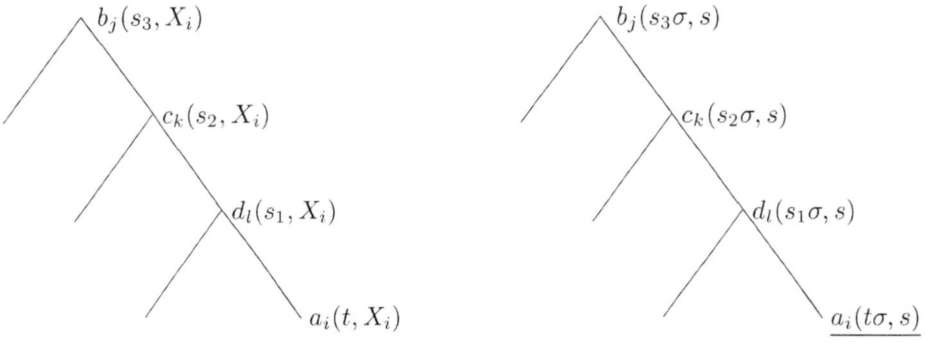

Figure 2. Closing a rightmost leaf in a proof tree for a chain program.

results in the application of a substitution σ to the input t as well as the application of a substitution θ to the output X_i of A_i, such that σ and θ are disjoint. Observe that σ may have an effect on many nodes of the tree, but not on the output of the topmost subgoal. By contrast, θ can instantiate the output of interest. This may happen if A_i is the rightmost leaf. We illustrate this possibility in Fig. 2. In this and other proof trees, closed leaves are underlined.

As a consequence of these two simplifications, if we build a proof tree following a top-down, left-to-right discipline, then we can forget all terms of intermediate proof trees except for the last term resulting from closing a leaf.

A context-free parser building parse trees following this regime can then be used to build proof trees, provided that the leaves are closed with unification, instead of simply advancing a pointer one symbol, as happens in such parsers. Moreover, it is easy to see that in the construction of proof trees for M chain programs, unification is reduced to matching (one way unification).

We will see in Sect. 4. an example of a parser following a different strategy for constructing parse trees. Such a strategy affixes an incomplete parse tree (corresponding to a proof tree with open leaves) with a complete parse tree (corresponding to a closed proof tree). When converting such a parser into an inference system we will then need to record *two* terms for every proof tree (which is still preferable to recording all terms of a proof tree built with arbitrary definite clauses).

2.5. Derivation Trees for Chain Programs

Having mentioned some properties of chain programs streamlining the construction of their proof trees, we will now observe that derivation trees for chain programs are likewise simplified. The reason is that an SLD derivation can be viewed as a sequence of frontiers of proof trees.

Derivations are often defined by allowing an arbitrary subgoal to be selected. However, since the position of the selected subgoal plays no role in our discussion, we will simplify the notation by writing such a subgoal first.

Let G be $\leftarrow A_1, \ldots, A_k$ and C be $B \leftarrow B_1, \ldots, B_q$ with no variables in common. Then G' is *derived* from G and C using mgu θ if the following conditions hold:

1. θ is an mgu of A_1 and B, restricted to $\mathrm{var}(A_1) \cup \mathrm{var}(B)$
2. G' is the goal $(\leftarrow B_1, \ldots, B_q, A_2, \ldots A_k)\theta$

G' is said to be the *resolvent* of G and C.

Let P be a definite program and G a definite goal. An *SLD derivation* for $P \cup \{G\}$ consists of a (finite or infinite) sequence $G_0 = G, G_1, \ldots$ of goals, a sequence $C_1, C_2, \ldots$ of variants of program clauses of P, and a sequence $\theta_1, \theta_2, \ldots$ of mgus such that each G_{i+1} is derived from G_i and C_{i+1} using θ_{i+1}.

Let P be a definite program and G a definite goal. A *computed answer* θ for $P \cup \{G\}$ is the substitution obtained by restricting the composition $\theta_1 \ldots \theta_n$ to the variables of G, where $\theta_1, \ldots, \theta_n$ is the sequence of mgus used in an SLD refutation of $P \cup \{G\}$.

2.5.1. Chain Programs

Consider now chain programs. First, observe that the resolvent of a chain goal resolved with a chain clause (be it unit or nonunit), is also a chain goal.

Let us now determine the resolvent goal. If the variant of the program clause is nonunit, then the resolvent goal will have, instead of the leftmost subgoal, all the subgoals of the variant of the program clause, and a substitution applied to it. Such an application (1) copies the input of the first subgoal of the previous goal to the input of the first subgoal of the program-clause variant, and (2) renames the output of the last subgoal of the program-clause variant to the input of the second subgoal of the previous goal. We depict this resolution step in Fig. 3 (a).

If the variant of the program clause is unit, by contrast, we do need to perform a unification and compute an mgu. However, in the resolvent the application of the mgu only has an effect on the input of the next subgoal. Furthermore, no subgoals are affixed in front of the goal to obtain the resolvent, as unit clauses have no body. Finally, recall that we are only interested in the substitution received by the output of a single-subgoal initial goal. Thus, we need not compose the mgu of a resolution step with a unit clause with any substitution to obtain the answer substitution. We illustrate in Fig. 3 (b) this operation.

In the particular case in which we have an M chain program, we can evidently use matching instead of full unification.

3. Conversion of Logic Programs Into Chain Form[3]

In this section, we will review two transformations into chain form. The first such transformations is in fact implicit in two existing exhaustive, deterministic traversal algorithms [32, 34] for committed-choice processors. This first transformation, just as these traversal algorithms, is limited to moded programs. It would then be desirable to have a more general transformation without such a restriction.

[3]This section is drawn, with revisions, From [27].

$$(a)\quad \begin{array}{l} \leftarrow a_1(t, X_1),\ a_2(X_1, X_2),\ \ldots,\ a_k(X_{k-1}, X_k) \\ \quad\Big| \\ \leftarrow b_1(t, Y_1),\ \ldots,\ b_q(Y_{q-1}, X_1),\ a_2(X_1, X_2),\ \ldots, a_k(X_{k-1}, X_k) \end{array}$$

$$(b)\quad \begin{array}{l} \leftarrow a_1(t, X_1),\ a_2(X_1, X_2),\ \ldots,\ a_k(X_{k-1}, X_k) \\ \quad\Big| \\ \leftarrow a_2(X_1\theta, X_2),\ \ldots,\ a_k(X_{k-1}, X_k) \end{array}$$

Figure 3. A step in the construction of a derivation tree: nonunit clause (a) and unit clause (b).

This second, unmoded transformation is strictly more general than the moded version. It might seem appropriate, therefore, to omit the more limited, moded variant. However, from an efficiency point of view, the moded transformation is preferable to the more general one, as terms are not copied during execution. At the same time, we find the moded transformation illustrative in explaining the second, more elaborate version. Thus, we will start with the moded transformation.

3.1. Conversion of Moded Programs

We will describe our transformation of moded programs into chain form in two steps. First we will deal with a simpler case, for which the transformation is straightforward. We will therefore refer to such programs as "quasi-chain programs." Next we will focus on arbitrary moded programs.

3.1.1. Quasi-Chain Programs

Consider the following *sum* program:

$$\begin{array}{l} sum(0, Y, Y) \leftarrow \\ sum(s(X), Y, s(Z)) \leftarrow sum(X, Y, Z) \end{array}$$

where $sum(X, Y, Z)$ is intended to hold if $X + Y = Z$ using successor notation.

Let us use this program for decomposing a given number into two addends. We will rearrange the argument places, so as to have only two argument places. The number to be decomposed will appear as the first argument place, and the addends will appear as the second argument place. In this example and throughout, we will use ":" as a distinguished function symbol for grouping input and output argument places. We do this so as to have binary predicates.

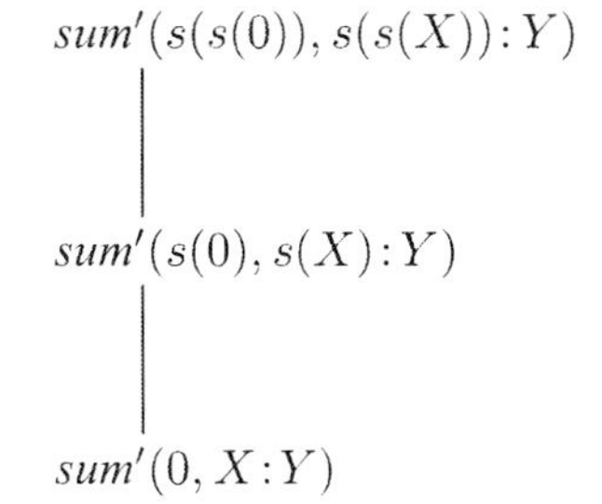

Figure 4. A proof tree for a non-chain program.

$$sum'(Y,\ 0:Y) \leftarrow \tag{10}$$
$$sum'(s(Z),\ s(X):Y) \leftarrow sum'(Z,\ X:Y) \tag{11}$$

Clause (10) is already in chain form, but not so (11). Hence, let us deal with the problem of transforming (11) into chain form. We know that in the transformed program all nontrivial unifications must occur at the leaves of the proof trees.

Figure 4 shows an intermediate proof tree requiring only the closure of its leaf to become a closed proof tree. Note that the application of the mgu $\{X/0, Y/0\}$ in this last a step has an effect on all nodes. The reason is that the outputs are constructed in a top-down manner through partially instantiated terms (nonvariable terms with variables), so that both X and Y occur in all nodes. This suggests constructing the outputs bottom-up *after* the subgoal with predicate symbol *sum′* has succeeded. Hence, we would have leaves for performing the input unifications before such a subgoal is selected, and leaves for performing the output unifications after such a subgoal is selected. These leaves would then be:

$$l_0(s(Z),\ Z) \leftarrow \tag{12}$$
$$l_1(X:Y,\ s(X):Y) \leftarrow \tag{13}$$

Clause (11) would then be transformed into:

$$sum'(U_0, U_3) \leftarrow l_0(U_0, U_1),\ sum'(U_1, U_2),\ l_1(U_2, U_3) \tag{14}$$

We have chosen subscripted l's as symbols for these introduced predicates (for “leaf”). However, some predicates not having such symbols may also be leaves of proof trees, as is the case of the original unit clause (10). An intermediate proof tree for the transformed program appears in Fig. 5.

Having suggested an equivalent chain program, we would like now to justify logically such a transformation. Throughout, we will use the least Herbrand model semantics. Clearly, if we resolve (14) with (12) and (13), we obtain (11). However, to prove correctness, we would need to perform the inverse process, namely, derive (14) from (11), (12), and (13). We will see that it is possible to do so with an appropriate equality theory.

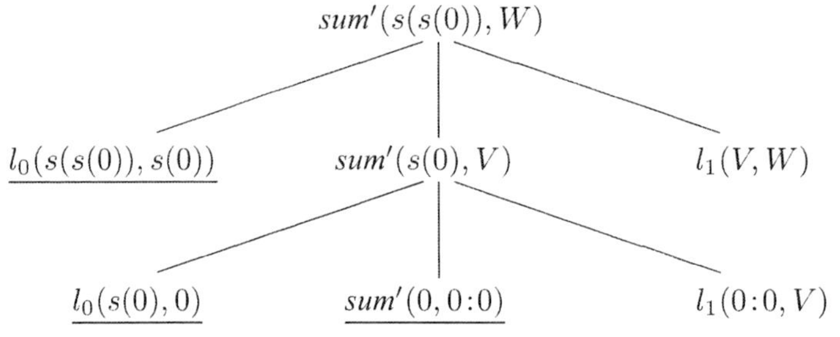

Figure 5. A proof tree for an M chain program.

The fact that the chain clause (14) has variables as arguments invites replacing each argument t of the original clause (11) by a variable X. To preserve the semantics, we can add the equation $X = t$ to the body of the new clause for each such replacement. Having added equations, we will eliminate them by the introduction of new predicates (the l_i's).

We will use the *standard equality theory*. Given a program P, this theory consists of the following axioms:

$$X = X \leftarrow$$
$$X = Y \leftarrow Y = X$$
$$X = Z \leftarrow X = Y,\ Y = Z$$
$$\{f(X_1, \ldots, X_{n_f}) = f(Y_1, \ldots, Y_{n_f}) \leftarrow X_1 = Y_1,\ \ldots,\ X_{n_f} = Y_{n_f} : \text{f is a function symbol occurring in } P\}$$
$$\{p(X_1, \ldots, X_{n_p}) \leftarrow X_1 = Y_1,\ \ldots,\ X_{n_p} = Y_{n_p},\ p(Y_1, \ldots, Y_{n_p}) : \text{p is a predicate symbol occurring in } P\}$$

which are called, reflexivity, symmetry, transitivity, function substitutivity, and predicate substitutivity, respectively.

Resolving predicate substitutivity for *sum*′:

$$sum'(U, V') \leftarrow U = A,\ V' = B,\ sum'(A, B)$$

with (11), we get:

$$sum'(U, V') \leftarrow U = s(Z),\ V' = s(X){:}Y,\ sum'(Z, X{:}Y)$$

We again apply predicate substitutivity:

$$sum'(A, B) \leftarrow A = V,\ B = U',\ sum'(V, U')$$

and obtain:

$$sum'(U, V') \leftarrow U = s(Z),\ V' = s(X){:}Y,\ Z = V,\ X{:}Y = U',\ sum'(V, U')$$

Next, we apply symmetry to the third and fourth subgoals, and rearrange the resulting subgoals:

$$\begin{aligned} sum'(U, V') \leftarrow\ & U = s(Z),\ V = Z, \\ & sum'(V, U'), \\ & U' = X{:}Y,\ V' = s(X){:}Y \end{aligned} \tag{15}$$

We would like now to substitute the subgoal $l_0(U, V)$ for the subgoals $U = s(Z)$, $V = Z$, and similarly for $l_1(U', V')$ and $U' = X{:}Y$, $V' = s(X){:}Y$. It is possible to do so by first resolving predicate substitutivity for l_0 and l_1 with (12) and (13), respectively:

$$\begin{aligned} l_0(U, V) &\leftarrow U = s(Z),\ V = Z \\ l_1(U', V') &\leftarrow U' = X{:}Y,\ V' = s(X){:}Y \end{aligned}$$

and then applying the "folding" operation developed in the logic-program transformation [25] literature. This operation essentially replaces subgoals matching the body of a clause with substitution θ by the head of such a clause after applying θ to such a head. In our case, both folding applications have the identity substitution ϵ as θ. We thus arrive at:

$$\begin{aligned} sum'(U, V') \leftarrow\ & l_0(U, V), \\ & sum'(V, U'), \\ & l_1(U', V') \end{aligned}$$

Although we will not go into much detail about such a folding operation here, some observations will be relevant for us. (We refer the reader to [27] for a more formal treatment of our transformations.)

Let $\tilde{Q}$ and $\tilde{R}$ be sequences of subgoals. A clause $C = A \leftarrow \tilde{Q}\theta, \tilde{R}$ can be folded using a variant $D = B \leftarrow \tilde{Q}$ of a clause sharing no variables with C, obtaining a folded clause $C' = A \leftarrow B\theta, \tilde{R}$. There are, however, two sufficiency syntactical conditions for preserving the least Herbrand model. First, it is easy to see that D must be the only variant of a clause whose head, after standardizing apart, unifies with $B\theta$. To see this, let us fold

$$C = a \leftarrow q,\ r \tag{16}$$

using

$$D = b \leftarrow q \tag{17}$$

obtaining:

$$C' = a \leftarrow b,\ r \tag{18}$$

If there is another clause defining b, say

$$b \leftarrow c \tag{19}$$

then by resolving (18) with (19) we obtain

$$a \leftarrow c,\ r$$

which is not equivalent to (16) and (17) under any reasonable semantics.

There is a second, more delicate condition. Consider for example the following folding application, given by Tamaki and Sato [33]. Let us fold

$$C = a(X) \leftarrow q(X, Y),\ r(Y) \tag{20}$$

using

$$D = b(U) \leftarrow q(U, V) \tag{21}$$

obtaining:

$$C' = a(X) \leftarrow b(X),\ r(Y) \tag{22}$$

If we resolve this resulting clause (22) with (21), we derive a generalization of the original clause (20):

$$a(X) \leftarrow q(X, Y'),\ r(Y)$$

which is also unsound under any reasonable semantics.

We can prevent such situations by requiring θ to map the variables which occur in $\tilde{Q}$ but not in B into distinct variables that do not occur in C'. A weaker condition was first given by Tamaki and Sato [33]; this stronger version was later given by Gardner and Shepherdson [11]. We will thus refer to this as the Gardner–Shepherdson condition. These two conditions allow us to replace C by C' while preserving the least Herbrand model of the program.

It is also possible to remove a clause C through resolution while preserving the least Herbrand model by resolving C with all possible clauses of the program. Such an operation is often called *unfolding* [11, 25, 33].

We are now ready to define a clause in *quasi-chain form* as:

$$p(s_0, s'_n) \leftarrow q_1(s'_0, s_1),\ q_2(s'_1, s_2),\ \ldots,\ q_n(s'_{n-1}, s_n) \qquad n \geq 0 \tag{23}$$

where:

1. $\mathrm{var}(s'_i) \subseteq \mathrm{var}(s_i)$ for $i = 0, \ldots, n$; and
2. $\mathrm{var}(s_i) \cap \mathrm{var}(s_j) = \emptyset$, for $i, j = 0, \ldots, n$ and $i \neq j$.

Requirement 1 causes every input to be ground if the input of the initial goal is also ground and we use a leftmost computation rule. At the same time, requirement 1 allows us to satisfy the Gardner–Shepherdson condition when obtaining a chain clause. When a subgoal succeeds, requirement 2 causes the constructed term to have an effect only on the input of other subgoals, thus avoiding speculative bindings.

By repeatedly following the process we used for clause (11), it is possible to convert any clause of the form (23) in quasi-chain form into:

$$p(U_0, U'_n) \leftarrow l_0(U_0, U'_0),\ q_1(U'_0, U_1),\ l_1(U_1, U'_1),\ q_2(U'_1, U_2),\ \ldots,\ q_n(U'_{n-1}, U_n),\ l_n(U_n, U'_n)$$

where the l_i's are defined as:

$$l_1(s_0, s_0') \leftarrow$$
$$l_2(s_1, s_1') \leftarrow$$
$$\vdots$$
$$l_n(s_n, s_n') \leftarrow$$

3.1.2. Moded Programs

Let us now turn our attention to moded programs that do not necessarily have quasi-chain form. Consider the following *append* program used for splitting lists.

$$s(L,\ [\,]{:}L) \leftarrow \tag{24}$$
$$s([A|N],\ [A|L]{:}M) \leftarrow s(N,\ L{:}M) \tag{25}$$

The predicate $s(N,\ L{:}M)$ is intended to hold if N is L affixed in front of M. Clause (25) does not have quasi-chain form (23) because the variable A occurs in $s_1' = [A|L]{:}M$ and not in $s_1 = L{:}M$, thus violating requirement 1.

As a result, if we follow the transformation process we used for *sum*$'$, we will infringe the Gardner–Shepherdson condition. To see this, let us apply predicate substitutivity and symmetry as we did before, arriving at:

$$\begin{aligned} s(U, V') \leftarrow\ & U = [A|N],\ V = N, \\ & s(V, U'), \\ & U' = L{:}M,\ V' = [A|L]{:}M \end{aligned} \tag{26}$$

The l_i's would be:

$$l_0(U, V) \leftarrow U = [A|N],\ V = N \tag{27}$$
$$l_1(U', V') \leftarrow U' = L{:}M,\ V' = [A|L]{:}M$$

However, if we fold (26) using a variant of (27), we will fail to satisfy the Gardner–Shepherdson condition, as θ would map a variable occurring in the body and not in the head of the variant of (27) into a variable A which occurs in the folded clause.

Since we know how to convert quasi-chain clauses into chain form, one way of converting (25) into chain form would be to convert such a clause first into quasi-chain form. We will informally perform such a conversion in the following steps. Later we will formally reconstruct such a process.

Observe now that to achieve quasi-chain form, we have to manipulate the occurrences of the variable A in both the input s_0 and the output s_1' of the head. Currently, we are infringing requirement 1, which says that we must have all variables of the output of the subgoal s_0' occurring also in the input of the head s_0, and similarly for s_1' and s_1. This suggests adding a component both to the input and to the output of the subgoal, holding the value of A. Let us call this new predicate s', which we use at this point in the subgoal only.

$$s(\underbrace{[A|N]}_{s_0},\ \underbrace{[A|L]{:}M}_{s_1'}) \leftarrow s'(\underbrace{A{:}N}_{s_0'},\ \underbrace{A{:}L{:}M}_{s_1})$$

However, we would have to rename occurrences of A so as to satisfy requirement 2 of quasi-chain clauses (that s_0 and s_1 share no variables):

$$s([A_0|N],\ [A_1|L]:M) \leftarrow s'(A_0:N,\ A_1:L:M)$$

To return to an inductive definition of our predicate, we would have to add such a component to the head as well.

$$s'(B:[A_0|N],\ B:[A_1|L]:M) \leftarrow s'(A_0:N,\ A_1:L:M)$$

This last clause unfortunately violates requirement 1 again. This invites grouping together (in the subgoal) both the component added to the head and the component added to the subgoal (we will arbitrarily use the list-constructor function symbol):

$$s'(B_0:[A_0|N],\ B_1:[A_1|L]:M) \leftarrow s'([A_0|B_0]:N,\ [A_1|B_1]:L:M) \tag{28}$$

which finally has quasi-chain form.

Having established the desired clause, let us now logically justify such a conversion process. It is easy to derive from (25) the following clause through the standard equality theory

$$s([A_0|N],\ [A_1|L]:M) \leftarrow A_0 = A_1,\ s(N,\ L:M) \tag{29}$$

To arrive at quasi-chain form, we will use an auxiliary list, which we introduce in the following predicate:

$$\hat{s}(As_0:X,\ As_1:Y:Z) \leftarrow As_0 = As_1,\ s(X,\ Y:Z) \tag{30}$$

Resolving (29) with (30) and switching the equations, we obtain:

$$\hat{s}(As_0:[A_0|N],\ As_1:[A_1|L]:M) \leftarrow A_0 = A_1,\ As_0 = As_1,\ s(N,\ L:M)$$

Next, we fold using function substitutivity for the list constructor:

$$[X|Y] = [X'|Y'] \leftarrow X = X',\ Y = Y'$$

and derive:

$$\hat{s}(As_0:[A_0|N],\ As_1:[A_1|L]:M) \leftarrow [A_0|As_0] = [A_1|As_1],\ s(N,\ L:M)$$

We are now in a position to fold using a variant of (30):

$$\hat{s}(As_0:[A_0|N],\ As_1:[A_1|L]:M) \leftarrow s([A_0|As_0]:N,\ [A_1|As_1]:L:M)$$

Now that we have quasi-chain form, we can arrive at chain form through the following l_i's predicates:

$$l_0(As_0:[A_0|N],\ [A_0|As_0]:N) \leftarrow$$
$$l_1([A_1|As_1]:L:M,\ As_1:[A_1|L]:M) \leftarrow$$

deriving:

$$\hat{s}(U_0, U_3) \leftarrow l_0(U_0, U_1),\ \hat{s}(U_1, U_2),\ l_1(U_2, U_3) \qquad (31)$$

This technique allows us to convert into chain form clauses similar to those in quasi-chain form, but satisfying a weaker version of requirement 1.

A clause

$$p(t_0, t'_n) \leftarrow q_1(t'_0, t_1),\ q_2(t'_1, t_2),\ \ldots,\ q_n(t'_{n-1}, t_n) \qquad n \geq 0 \qquad (32)$$

is called *moded* if:

1. $\mathrm{var}(t'_i) \subseteq \mathrm{var}(t_0) \cup \cdots \cup \mathrm{var}(t_i)$, for $i = 0, \ldots, n$; and
2. $\mathrm{var}(t_i) \cap \mathrm{var}(t_j) = \emptyset$, for $i, j = 0, \ldots, n$ and $i \neq j$.

A program is called *moded* if it consists only of moded clauses.

A *moded goal* has the form:

$$\leftarrow q_1(t, t_1),\ q_2(t'_1, t_2),\ \ldots,\ q_n(t'_{n-1}, t_n) \qquad n \geq 0$$

where:

1. $\mathrm{var}(t'_i) \subseteq \mathrm{var}(t_1) \cup \cdots \cup \mathrm{var}(t_i)$, for $i = 1, \ldots, n$;
2. $\mathrm{var}(t_i) \cap \mathrm{var}(t_j) = \emptyset$, for $i, j = 1, \ldots, n$ and $i \neq j$; and
3. t is a ground term.

By generalizing the above method, we can convert an arbitrary moded clause into chain form, as stated by the following theorem (a variant of which appears in [27]).

Theorem 1 *Let C be a moded clause:*

$$p(t_0, t'_n) \leftarrow q_1(t'_0, t_1),\ q_2(t'_1, t_2),\ \ldots,\ q_n(t'_{n-1}, t_n) \qquad n \geq 0$$

and let

$$\Pi_i = \big(\mathrm{var}(t_0) \cup \cdots \cup \mathrm{var}(t_{i-1})\big) \cap \big(\mathrm{var}(t'_i) \cup \cdots \cup \mathrm{var}(t'_n)\big) \qquad i = 0, \ldots, n+1$$

Let P be a program having C, the standard equality theory, and the following definitions:

$$\hat{p}(As\!:\!X,\ As\!:\!Y) \leftarrow p(X, Y)$$
$$\hat{q}_i(As\!:\!X,\ As\!:\!Y) \leftarrow q_i(X, Y) \qquad i = 1, \ldots, n$$
$$l_i(\Lambda_i\!:\!t_i,\ \Lambda_{i+1}\!:\!t'_i) \leftarrow \qquad i = 0, \ldots, n$$

where Λ_i is any list of the form $[X_{1,i}, \ldots, X_{d_i,i}|As]$, such that $\{X_{1,i}, \ldots, X_{d_i,i}\} = \Pi_i$, if $\Pi_i \neq \emptyset$, and Λ_i is As if $\Pi_i = \emptyset$, for $i = 0, \ldots, n+1$, and the l_i's are predicate symbols not occurring in C.

Then the program obtained by replacing C in P by:

$$\hat{p}(U_0, U'_n) \leftarrow l_0(U_0, U'_0),\ \hat{q}_1(U'_0, U_1),\ l_1(U_1, U'_1),\ \hat{q}_2(U'_1, U_2),\ \ldots,\ \hat{q}_n(U'_{n-1}, U_n),\ l_n(U_n, U'_n)$$

has the same least Herbrand model as P.

We have chosen the name "Π" for "pass-on variables," which is the term used in [32] for a compiled version of this transformation, and "Λ" for "list."

Let us apply Theorem 1 to (25), of the list-splitting example.

$$\underbrace{s}_{p}\,(\underbrace{[A|N]}_{t_0},\ \underbrace{[A|L]:M}_{t'_1}) \leftarrow \underbrace{s}_{q_1}\,(\underbrace{N}_{t'_0},\ \underbrace{L:M}_{t_1})$$

$$\begin{array}{lcl} \Pi_0 &=& \emptyset \ \cap\ \left(\mathrm{var}(t'_0) \cup \mathrm{var}(t'_1)\right) \ =\ \emptyset \\ \Pi_1 &=& \mathrm{var}(t_0)\ \cap\ \mathrm{var}(t'_1) \ =\ \{A\} \\ \Pi_2 &=& \left(\mathrm{var}(t_0) \cup \mathrm{var}(t_1)\right)\ \cap\ \emptyset \ =\ \emptyset \end{array}$$

So, $\Lambda_0 = As$, $\Lambda_1 = [A|As]$, and $\Lambda_2 = As$. The resulting clause in chain form is (31). The definitions of the l_i's are as before, up to variable renaming.

3.2. Conversion of Arbitrary Definite Programs

Having shown how to convert moded programs into chain form, we will now turn our attention to arbitrary definite programs.

Let us now consider the possibility of this extended transformation's existence. Recall first the fact that Prolog implementations can construct refutations from unmoded programs. At the same time, Prolog implementations can be described with flowcharts. Finally, Clark and van Emden's [7] connections relating flowcharts with programs having chain form would allow us to describe Prolog implementations with chain programs. Such chain-program descriptions of Prolog implementations suggest the possibility of transforming unmoded programs into chain form.

We will again employ two stages, the first one of which will deal with a simpler case, where all variables occur in all atoms of the clause.

3.2.1. All Variables Occur in All Atoms

The first apparent obstacle we find in trying to convert an arbitrary, *unmoded* clause into chain form, is that arguments of predicates in such a clause do not have predetermined input/output roles. The fact that any argument of a predicate may play the role of either input or output suggests treating all arguments uniformly. One way of doing so and yet have binary predicates could be to replicate the arguments of each predicate so as to have two copies of each set of arguments: one copy behaving as a single input (possibly having variables when the subgoal is selected), and the other copy behaving as a single output. Such predicates *denote a subset of the identity relation*. Naturally, we now have to give up the groundness property of runtime terms, which translates to having to use full unification instead of matching.

Consider the following unmoded *sum* program:

$$sum(0:Y:Y) \leftarrow \quad (33)$$

$$sum(s(X):Y:s(Z)) \leftarrow sum(Z:X:Y) \quad (34)$$

Let us convert this program into quasi-chain form, from which it is straightforward to obtain chain form. As usual, we will first develop the desired program informally, and we will then formally justify such a transformation. Taking the suggestion of the previous paragraph, we would prefer over *sum* a binary predicate $\widehat{sum}(X\!:\!Y\!:\!Z,\ X\!:\!Y\!:\!Z)$, intended to hold when $Z = X + Y$. Duplicating the definition of *sum* (writing one copy for each argument place), we would get:

$$\widehat{sum}(0\!:\!Y\!:\!Y,\ 0\!:\!Y\!:\!Y) \leftarrow \tag{35}$$

$$\widehat{sum}(s(X)\!:\!Y\!:\!s(Z),\ s(X')\!:\!Y'\!:\!s(Z')) \leftarrow \widehat{sum}(X\!:\!Y\!:\!Z,\ X'\!:\!Y'\!:\!Z') \tag{36}$$

To obtain this program through program transformation, we can first write the intended meaning for $\widehat{sum}$ in terms of *sum*:

$$\widehat{sum}(X\!:\!Y\!:\!Z,\ X\!:\!Y\!:\!Z) \leftarrow sum(X\!:\!Y\!:\!Z) \tag{37}$$

The clause (35) is readily derived by resolving (37) with (33). Let us derive now (36). Using the standard equality theory, from (37) we can easily infer:

$$\widehat{sum}(X\!:\!Y\!:\!Z,\ X'\!:\!Y'\!:\!Z') \leftarrow \\ X = X',\ Y = Y',\ Z = Z',\ sum(X'\!:\!Y'\!:\!Z') \tag{38}$$

Subsequently, we instantiate (38) so as to have the desired head:

$$\widehat{sum}(s(X)\!:\!Y\!:\!s(Z),\ s(X')\!:\!Y'\!:\!s(Z')) \leftarrow \\ s(X) = s(X'),\ Y = Y',\ s(Z) = s(Z'),\ sum(s(X')\!:\!Y'\!:\!s(Z'))$$

which we convert to:

$$\widehat{sum}(s(X)\!:\!Y\!:\!s(Z),\ s(X')\!:\!Y'\!:\!s(Z')) \leftarrow \\ X = X',\ Y = Y',\ Z = Z',\ sum(s(X')\!:\!Y'\!:\!s(Z')) \tag{39}$$

using function substitutivity. Next, we resolve (39) with (34):

$$\widehat{sum}(s(X)\!:\!Y\!:\!s(Z),\ s(X')\!:\!Y'\!:\!s(Z')) \leftarrow \\ X = X',\ Y = Y',\ Z = Z',\ sum(X'\!:\!Y'\!:\!Z') \tag{40}$$

which puts us in a position to fold (40) using (38):

$$\widehat{sum}(s(X)\!:\!Y\!:\!s(Z),\ s(X')\!:\!Y'\!:\!s(Z')) \leftarrow \widehat{sum}(X\!:\!Y\!:\!Z,\ X'\!:\!Y'\!:\!Z')$$

arriving at (36). We can now immediately obtain chain form by introducing the l_i's predicates.

3.2.2. Definite Programs

We will now consider a more general example with the standard definition of *append*:

$$ap([\,]\!:\!L\!:\!L) \leftarrow \tag{41}$$

$$ap([A|L]\!:\!M\!:\![A|N]) \leftarrow ap(L\!:\!M\!:\!N) \tag{42}$$

This example has the additional difficulty that the A variable only occurs in the head. As in the list-splitting example, we will add a list holding the values of such a variable. We can include such a list in the predicate denoting a subset of the identity relation:

$$\widehat{ap}(As\!:\!X\!:\!Y\!:\!Z,\ As\!:\!X\!:\!Y\!:\!Z) \leftarrow ap(X\!:\!Y\!:\!Z) \tag{43}$$

Using a process similar both to that of the list-splitting example and to that of unmoded *sum*, it is possible to derive a quasi-chain clause. A decision we have to make, however, is which variables to hold in the added list. In fact, we could hold all variables of the clause, but we will be more economical by holding only the variables not occurring in all atoms of the clause. The obtained clause would then be:

$$\begin{aligned}\widehat{ap}(As_0\!:\![A_0|L_0]\!:\!M_0\!:\![A_0|N_0],\ As_1\!:\![A_1|L_1]\!:\!M_1\!:\![A_1|N_1]) \leftarrow&\\ \widehat{ap}([A_0|As_0]\!:\!L_0\!:\!M_0\!:\!N_0,\ [A_1|As_1]\!:\!L_1\!:\!M_1\!:\!N_1)&\end{aligned}$$

The following theorem (a variant of which appears in [27]) allows us to transform an arbitrary definite clause.

Theorem 2 *Let C be a definite clause:*

$$p(t_0) \leftarrow q_1(t_1),\ q_2(t_2),\ \ldots,\ q_n(t_n) \qquad\qquad n \geq 0$$

and let

$$\Pi = \big(\mathrm{var}(t_0) \cup \cdots \cup \mathrm{var}(t_n)\big) \setminus \big(\mathrm{var}(t_0) \cap \cdots \cap \mathrm{var}(t_n)\big)$$

Let P be a program having C, the standard equality theory, and the following definitions:

$$\begin{array}{ll}\hat{p}(As\!:\!X_{1,0}\!:\!\ldots\!:\!X_{r_0,0},\ As\!:\!X_{1,0}\!:\!\ldots\!:\!X_{r_0,0}) \leftarrow p(X_{1,0}\!:\!\ldots\!:\!X_{r_0,0}) & \\ \hat{q}_i(As\!:\!X_{1,i}\!:\!\ldots\!:\!X_{r_i,i},\ As\!:\!X_{1,i}\!:\!\ldots\!:\!X_{r_i,i}) \leftarrow q_i(X_{1,i}\!:\!\ldots\!:\!X_{r_i,i}) & i = 1, \ldots, n \\ l_0(As\!:\!t_0,\ \Lambda\!:\!t_1) \leftarrow \qquad (i = 0) & \\ l_i(\Lambda\!:\!t_i,\ \Lambda\!:\!t_{i+1}) \leftarrow \qquad i = 1, \ldots, n-1 & \\ l_n(\Lambda\!:\!t_n,\ As\!:\!t_0) \leftarrow \qquad (i = n) & \end{array}$$

where Λ is any list of the form $[X_1, \ldots, X_d|As]$, such that $\{X_1, \ldots, X_d\} = \Pi$, if $\Pi \neq \emptyset$, and Λ is As if $\Pi = \emptyset$.

Then the program obtained by replacing C in P by:

$$\begin{aligned}\hat{p}(U_0, U'_n) \leftarrow l_0(U_0, U'_0),\ \hat{q}_1(U'_0, U_1),\ l_1(U_1, U'_1),\ \hat{q}_2(U'_1, U_2),\ \ldots,&\\ \hat{q}_n(U'_{n-1}, U_n),\ l_n(U_n, U'_n)&\end{aligned}$$

has the same least Herbrand model as P.

3.3. Multiple Chain Versions of a Clause

We will finish this section by observing that in general a clause may by transformed into any of various chain clauses. This multiplicity of chain clauses may result in a paradox, which requires an explanation.

Note that the conversion of a definite clause into chain form depends on the order in which we write the subgoals of such a clause. Therefore, we would have as many chain versions of this clause as there are permutations of its subgoals. At first sight, Theorem 2 seems to imply that all such chain clauses are equivalent (in the sense of the least Herbrand model) to each other. However, such an assertion is clearly wrong, as

$$p(X_0, X_2) \leftarrow q_1(X_0, X_1),\ q_2(X_1, X_2)$$

say, is not equivalent to

$$p(X_0, X_2) \leftarrow q_2(X_0, X_1),\ q_1(X_1, X_2)$$

Theorem 2 is instead asserting equivalence of the initial clause and one of its chain-form clauses, together with the definitions of the l_i's, which depend on the order the subgoals had before the transformation.

4. Inference Systems Based on Context-Free Parsers[4]

Now that we know how to convert moded and unmoded clauses into chain form, let us consider the possibility of obtaining an inference system for logic programs from context-free parsers via chain programs. Here we will only consider chart parsers [26], but refer the reader to [28] for inference systems based on LR parsers.

4.1. Chart Parsers

Chart parsers [12] are methods for parsing strings of context-free languages, which can be viewed as a generalization of Earley's algorithm [9]. These parsers normally assume, with no loss of generality, that the grammar has been rewritten so that it only contains productions of the form:

$$A \rightarrow B_1 B_2 \dots B_n$$
$$A \rightarrow c$$

Here, and throughout the chapter, unless otherwise noted, we adhere to the convention of using lower-case letters for terminals, and upper-case letters for nonterminals. In addition, we denote by Σ the alphabet of terminals.

The main idea in chart parsing is the construction of successive directed graphs, each of which is called a "chart." Each node in a chart is labeled with a symbol c_i of the string $c_1 \dots c_m c_{m+1}$ to be parsed, where c_{m+1} is a distinguished symbol which is not part of the string itself, but rather an end marker. Edges are added to a chart according to certain rules.

[4]This section is drawn, with revisions, from [26].

Each edge is labeled with a "partially applied production" $A \to B_k \ldots B_n$. Intuitively, the meaning of an edge going from c_i to c_{j+1} and labeled with $A \to B_k \ldots B_n$ corresponding to a production $A \to B_1 \ldots B_{k-1} B_k \ldots B_n$ is that the prefix $B_1 \ldots B_{k-1}$ of the right-hand side of the production has already been applied to $c_i \ldots c_j$, and it remains to apply the suffix $B_k \ldots B_n$. In particular, if such a suffix is empty, then the edge from c_i to c_{j+1} asserts that the string $c_i \ldots c_j$ belongs to the language generated by A.

To state this meaning formally, it will be convenient to refer to the language generated by a nonterminal. Let $A' = \{x \in \Sigma^* : A \overset{*}{\Rightarrow} x\}$ and $B_i' = \{x \in \Sigma^* : B_i \overset{*}{\Rightarrow} x\}$. Then an edge going from c_i to c_{j+1} and labeled with

$$A \to B_k \ldots B_n \tag{44}$$

means that

$$A' \supseteq \{c_i \ldots c_j\} \cdot B_k' \cdot B_{k+1}' \cdot \ldots \cdot B_n' \tag{45}$$

If $k > n$ in (44), we write the label $A \to \epsilon$, and $B_k' \cdot B_{k+1}' \cdot \ldots \cdot B_n' = \{\epsilon\}$.

Having established the meaning of an edge, we can rephrase the fact that a string $c_1 \ldots c_m$ belongs to the language generated by a grammar with start symbol S as an edge going from c_1 to c_{m+1} and labeled with $S \to \epsilon$.

Figure 6 shows a chart constructed with the rules we explain below. We will use this same example to illustrate how chart parsing augmented with unification can be regarded as an inference system for chain programs, where we will split the list $[1, 2]$ into $[1]$ and $[2]$. We have therefore had to violate our notational conventions for grammars. Here, terms constructed with ":" denote terminals and lower-case letters denote nonterminals.

In this example, the input string is $[\,]{:}[1,2]$ $[1]{:}[2]$ $[1]{:}[\,]{:}[2]$ $[\,]{:}[1]{:}[2]$, where $[\,]{:}[1]{:}[2]$ is the end marker, and the grammar has the productions:

$$\begin{aligned} \hat{s} &\to l_0\ \hat{s}\ l_1 \\ \hat{s} &\to [1]{:}[2] \\ l_0 &\to [\,]{:}[1,2] \\ l_1 &\to [1]{:}[\,]{:}[2] \end{aligned}$$

Let us now give rules for adding edges to a chart. We shall concentrate on "top-down" chart parsing, but refer the reader to [12, 17] for more comprehensive explanations of chart parsing.

4.1.1. The Fundamental Rule

The operation sometimes called "fundamental rule" takes two edges and produces a third edge. Given (1) an edge going from c_i to c_j and labeled with $A \to B_d \ldots B_n$, and (2) an edge going from c_j to c_k and labeled with $B_d \to \epsilon$, the *fundamental rule* adds (3) an edge going from c_i to c_k and labeled with $A \to B_{d+1} \ldots B_n$. Figure 7 depicts this operation. Intuitively, this rule can be viewed as the application of one symbol to the partially applied production represented by the first edge.

An example of an application of the fundamental rule is in the addition of the edge from $[\,]{:}[1,2]$ to $[1]{:}[\,]{:}[2]$ and labeled with $\hat{s} \to l_1$ in Fig. 6.

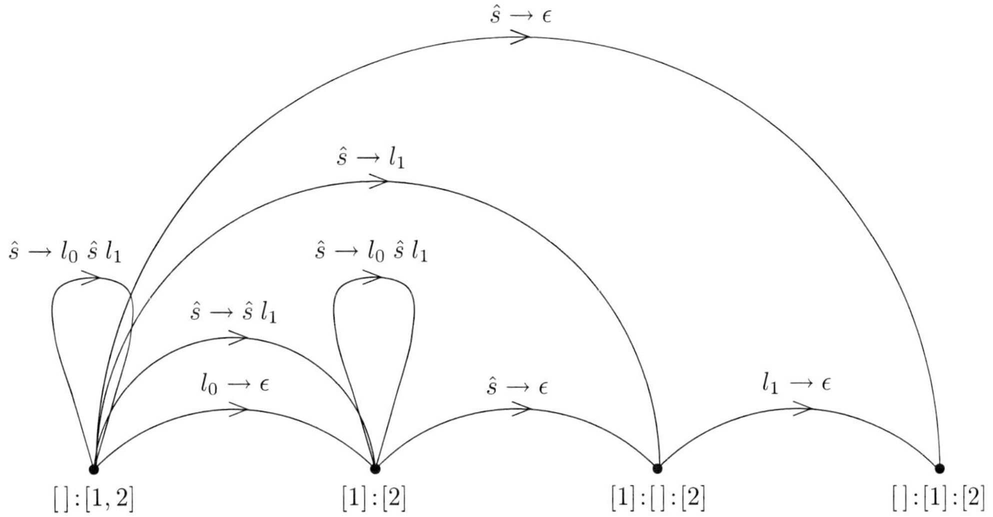

Figure 6. *A chart constructed with the top-down rule.*

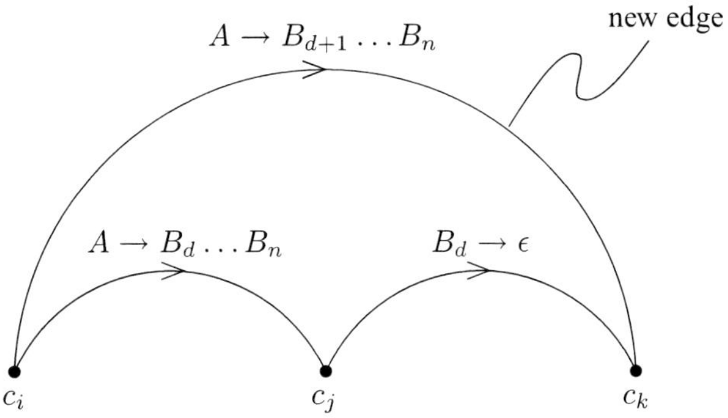

Figure 7. The fundamental rule.

4.1.2. The Top-Down Rule

The fundamental rule produces a new edge from existing edges. Thus, we need a rule that takes into account the productions of the grammar. The *top-down rule* generates, from (1) an edge going from c_i to c_j and labeled with $A \to B_d \ldots B_n$, and (2) a production $B_d \to C_1 \ldots C_r$, (3) an edge going from and to c_j and labeled with $B_d \to C_1 \ldots C_r$. Note that the edges added by the top-down rule are vacuously true. Intuitively, the reason for adding these edges, is to allow for the possible future application of B_d to the edge going from c_i to c_j labeled with $A \to B_d \ldots B_n$. This rule is depicted in Fig. 8 (a).

Given a parse tree with a leaf B_d, this rule starts the expansion of B_d by creating an edge labeled with a pair having B_d on its left-hand side. Hence a parse tree is built by expanding the leaves with nonterminals, which is a construction of parse trees from the root towards the leaves.

The chart in Fig. 6 was constructed with the top-down rule, applied for instance, by

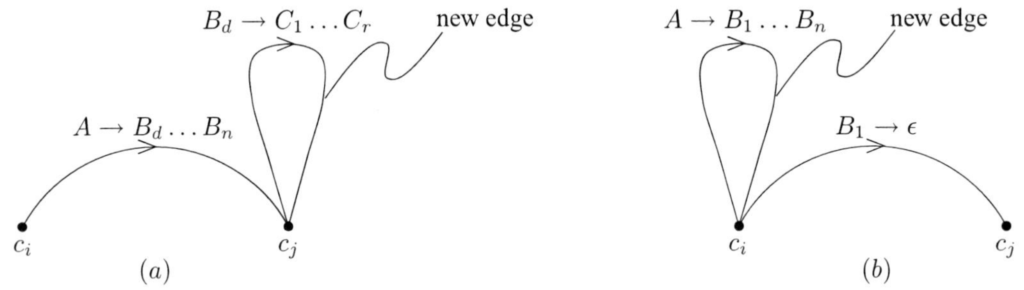

Figure 8. The top-down rule (a) and the bottom-up rule (b).

adding the edge from and to $[1]\!:\![2]$ and labeled with $\hat{s} \to l_0\ \hat{s}\ l_1$.

4.1.3. The Initialization Rules

There are usually rules for creating the first edges of a chart. For the top-down parser, one such rule adds to the chart an edge going from and to c_1 and labeled with $S \to A_1 \ldots A_n$ for each production $S \to A_1 \ldots A_n$.

In addition, we must take care of productions of the form $S \to c_1$ by adding an edge going from c_1 to c_2 and labeled with $S \to \epsilon$ for each such production.

4.1.4. The Base-Extension Rule

Finally, observe that, except for productions of the form $S \to c_1$, we have no rule considering the productions having a terminal on their right-hand side. Such productions are normally used to generate a set of edges often called the *base* of the chart, consisting of one edge labeled with $A \to \epsilon$ and going from c_i to c_{i+1} for each production $A \to c_i$.

Some chart parsers create the base in its totality at initialization, and require the whole string before parsing starts. It is also possible, however, to create the base incrementally as the chart is built. For us, a parser that builds the base incrementally is preferable. The reason is that in our inference systems, terms play the role of terminals, so that we will use a transformed parser for *computing* a sequence of terms. Such a sequence is the analogue to the input string. In particular, we are interested in the last term of the sequence, corresponding to the end marker, as depicted in Fig. 6. Hence, a parser which builds the base incrementally will allow us to use the part of the chart already constructed as a guide for extending the base.

A common base-extension rule for such chart parsers [17] (1) takes an edge going from c_i to c_j and labeled with $A \to B_d \ldots B_n$, and (2) for each production $B_d \to c_j$ this rule adds an edge going from c_j to c_{j+1} and labeled with $B_d \to \epsilon$.

4.1.5. Agenda

Note that a rule may produce more than one edge, so that nondeterministic choices may appear. Normally, chart parsers contain, in addition to the chart being built, an auxiliary data structure, called the *agenda*, storing all the edges to which the rules have not yet been applied. Hence, when the rules generate edges, these are added to the agenda, from which they are removed one by one. The discipline with which the edges are added to and removed from the agenda determines a search strategy in the space produced by the nondeterministic choices. For instance, if the agenda is represented by a stack, then depth-first traversal is obtained; if represented by a queue, breadth-first traversal is obtained instead.

Observe also that whenever an edge is removed from the agenda, such an edge may already exist in the chart. Thus, a test for membership is needed to prevent the parser from going into a nonterminating loop.

4.1.6. The Bottom-Up Rule

Parse trees are built from the leaves towards the root when the so-called *bottom-up rule* is used instead of the top-down rule. From (1) an edge going from c_i to c_j and labeled with $B_1 \rightarrow \epsilon$ and (2) a production $A \rightarrow B_1 \ldots B_n$, this rule adds (3) an edge going from and to c_i and labeled with $A \rightarrow B_1 \ldots B_n$. Figure 8 (b) shows the bottom-up rule.

Given a parse tree T with root B_1, this rule creates an edge labeled with $A \rightarrow B_1 \ldots B_n$, thus adding an elementary subtree with root A on top of T. This is a construction from the leaves towards the root.

4.2. Converting Chart Parsers Into Inference Systems for Chain Programs

Having described chart parsing, we now turn our attention to obtaining inference systems based on these parsers. By virtue of the difference-list representation of context-free grammars, we can regard a chart parser as an inference system for logic programs having clauses of the form:

$$a(X_0, X_n) \leftarrow b_1(X_0, X_1),\ b_2(X_1, X_2),\ \ldots,\ b_n(X_{n-1}, X_n)$$
$$a([c|X], X) \leftarrow$$

by rewriting these clauses into the productions:

$$A \rightarrow B_1 B_2 \ldots B_n$$
$$A \rightarrow c$$

4.2.1. Modification of Parsing Rules

We now address the problem of dealing with chain programs. We observed in Sect. 2. that when we generalize unit clauses to

$$a(t, t') \leftarrow$$

we can preserve the fragment of the parser handling nonterminals, and need only incorporate unification to the treatment of terminals, provided that we build parse/ proof trees following a top-down, left-to-right regime. As we obtain an inference system from a chart parser we will see that we can indeed use verbatim the rules employing productions with nonterminals on the right-hand side, namely the top-down rule, one of the initialization rules, the base-extension rule, and even the bottom-up rule. These rules will now operate nonunit clauses. At the same time, the rules employing productions with terminals can be

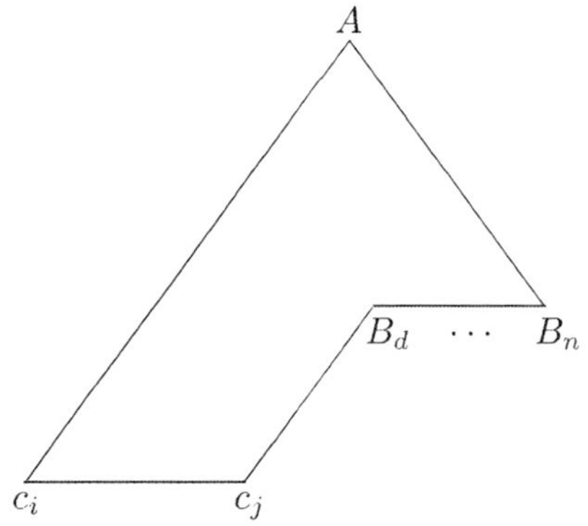

Figure 9. Parse tree represented by an edge.

used as inference rules when unification is incorporated. The fundamental rule, which does not employ productions, will be a second case in which unification must be used. The reason is that the fundamental rule behaves in a manner similar to that of the base-extension rule.

4.2.2. The New Fundamental Rule

To see why the fundamental rule requires unification, let us first determine the parse tree represented by an edge. Each edge going from c_i to c_j and labeled with $A \rightarrow B_d \ldots B_n$ represents a possibly incomplete parse tree with root A and frontier partitioned into a prefix $c_i \ldots c_j$ of terminals, and a suffix of $B_d \ldots B_n$ nonterminals, as depicted in Fig. 9.

The top-down rule adds a parse tree in which its frontier is entirely composed of nonterminals. The base-extension rule, in turn, corresponds to closing a leaf. Hence, the reasoning in Subsect. 2.4. concluding that it suffices to add unification to the treatment of terminals is valid. The fundamental rule, however, constitutes an exception because such a rule does not extend a tree in a top-down manner. Instead, the fundamental rule affixes an incomplete parse tree to a complete parse tree. This rule is illustrated in Fig. 10.

Note that the right, complete parse tree could be thought of as extending the base of the left, incomplete parse tree. This explains the need for including unification in the inference rule corresponding to the fundamental rule.

We will start with the input t_1 of the subgoal of the top-level goal $\leftarrow s(t_1, Z)$, playing the role of the first symbol c_1 of the string to be parsed. *Unification will serve to determine the next term in the frontier of the proof tree being constructed. Such a term will be the counterpart of the next symbol of the string.* This suggests having charts in which each node is labeled with a term instead of a symbol of the string being parsed.

4.2.3. The New Initialization Rule

Let us now turn to the rules for operating edges. There are two rules where terminals appear. The first one is the initialization rule that adds edges labeled with $S \rightarrow \epsilon$ going from c_1 to c_2. This rule can be translated by computing the term corresponding to c_2 through unification.

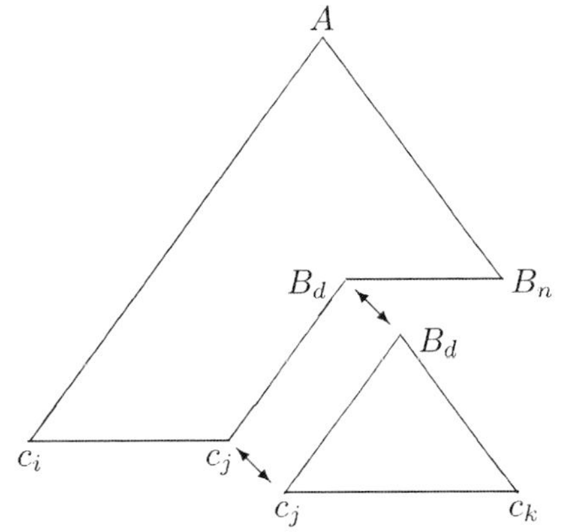

Figure 10. The fundamental rule as an operation on parse trees.

4.2.4. The New Base-Extension Rule

The second one is the base-extension rule, which adds an edge labeled with $B_d \rightarrow \epsilon$, going from c_j to c_{j+1}, for every production $B_d \rightarrow c_j$ and every edge going from c_i to c_j and labeled with $A \rightarrow B_d \ldots B_n$. Given the term t_j playing the role of c_j, we must *construct* the term t_{j+1} corresponding to c_{j+1} with unification. Now for every variant of a program clause

$$b(u, u') \leftarrow$$

such that t_i unifies with u with mgu θ we add a node $u'\theta$ and an edge labeled with $B \rightarrow \epsilon$ from $u\theta$ to $u'\theta$. Observe that unlike the parsing of a given string, which has a linear structure, constructing a sequence of terms may result in a branching structure, as there may be more than one $u'\theta$. This is tantamount to utilizing a parser as a generator of strings. In the case of a chart parser, the nondeterminism resulting from the branching structure can be easily dealt with. We can simply use the already-existing mechanism for handling the nondeterminism of having more than one edge to operate with the current chart, namely the agenda.

As we concluded earlier, the fundamental rule also requires unification. We will only affix a nonclosed proof tree T_1 (corresponding to an incomplete parse tree) to a closed proof tree T_2 (corresponding to a complete parse tree) if the rightmost term of the frontier of T_1 unifies with the leftmost term of the frontier of T_2.

4.2.5. The Resulting Inference System

Let us now recapitulate and phrase the modified chart rules as inference rules. To do so, we must view each production as a chain clause. Hence, each nonterminal will stand for the name of a binary predicate. A possibility for the meaning of an edge going from t to t' and labeled with $A \rightarrow B_1 B_2 \ldots B_n$ would be the clause:

$$a(t, X_n) \leftarrow b_1(t', X_1),\ b_2(X_1, X_2),\ \ldots,\ b_n(X_{n-1}, X_n) \qquad n \geq 0$$

We can abbreviate clauses of this form as:

$$edge(t, t', a, [b_1, b_2, \ldots, b_n])$$

We will only use this shorthand for clauses inferred by the inference system.

Let P be a chain program, and $\leftarrow s(t_1, Z)$ a chain goal. Then, the fundamental rule becomes:

$$\frac{edge(t, t', a, [b_i, b_{i+1}, \ldots, b_n]) \qquad edge(u, u', b_i, [\,])}{edge(t\theta, u'\theta, a, [b_{i+1}, \ldots, b_n])}$$

where θ is the mgu of t' and u.

The top-down rule would be:

$$\frac{edge(t, t', a, [b_i, \ldots, b_n]) \qquad (b_i(X_0, X_k) \leftarrow c_1(X_0, X_1),\ \ldots,\ c_k(X_{k-1}, X_k)) \in P}{edge(t', t', b_i, [c_1, \ldots, c_k])}$$

The initialization rules, in turn, result in:

$$\frac{(s(X_0, X_n) \leftarrow a_1(X_0, X_1),\ \ldots,\ a_n(X_{n-1}, X_n)) \in P}{edge(t_1, t_1, s, [a_1, \ldots, a_n])}$$

for nonunit clauses, and

$$\frac{(s(t, t') \leftarrow) \in P}{edge(t\theta, t'\theta, s, [\,])}$$

where θ is the mgu of t_1 and t, for unit clauses.

The base-extension rule employs unification:

$$\frac{edge(t, t', a, [b_i, \ldots, b_n]) \qquad (b_i(u, u') \leftarrow) \in P}{edge(u\theta, u'\theta, b_i, [\,])}$$

where θ is the mgu of t' and u.

Finally, the bottom-up rule would be:

$$\frac{edge(t, t', b_1, [\,]) \qquad (a(X_0, X_n) \leftarrow b_1(X_0, X_1),\ \ldots,\ b_n(X_{n-1}, X_n)) \in P}{edge(t, t, a, [b_1, \ldots, b_n])}$$

If the program is an M chain program, and the goal an M goal, then the unifications in the unit-clause initialization, and base extension rules reduce to matching; the unification in the fundamental rule reduces even more, to syntactic equality between ground terms.

4.2.6. An Inference-System Edge as a Proof Tree

It might be illuminating to determine the proof tree represented by an edge of the resulting inference system. In the case of a pure top-down, left-to-right construction of proof trees, we could dispose of all terms but the rightmost term of the frontier.

Now, however, because we have the additional operation joining two proof trees, we must also record the leftmost term of a proof tree. Hence, we can view an inference-system edge going from t to t' and labeled with $A \rightarrow B_1,\ \ldots,\ B_n$ as a proof tree with root a and with frontier partitioned into a left sequence of closed leaves with leftmost term t and rightmost term t', and a right sequence of open leaves with predicate symbols $b_1, \ldots, b_n$.

4.2.7. Example

A portion of the chart created by an inference system using the top-down rule for the program:

$$\hat{s}(U_0, U_3) \leftarrow l_0(U_0, U_1),\ \hat{s}(U_1, U_2),\ l_1(U_2, U_3)$$
$$\hat{s}(As\!:\!L,\ As\!:\![\,]\!:\!L) \leftarrow$$
$$l_0(As\!:\![A|N],\ [A|As]\!:\!N) \leftarrow$$
$$l_1([A|As]\!:\!L\!:\!M,\ As\!:\![A|L]\!:\!M) \leftarrow$$

and the goal $\leftarrow \hat{s}([\,]\!:\![1,2],\ Z)$ was shown in Fig. 6. For simplicity, we have not drawn the complete chart, which can be thought of as having several planes, where the other answers for the program and the goal would appear.

4.3. Coupling the Chart-Based Inference System to the Transformations

The inference system we have so far, although sound and complete, only avoids the recomputation of a few partial results, when given a program resulting from our transformation. To illustrate this phenomenon, consider the following program for computing permutations. The predicate $perm(L, M)$ is intended to hold iff M is a permutation of the list L. This predicate uses an auxiliary predicate, $del(L, X\!:\!M)$, which is intended to hold iff M is the list L with the element X removed.

$$perm(L,\ [X\,|\,Ys]) \leftarrow del(L,\ X\!:\!Xs),\ perm(Xs,\ Ys)$$
$$perm([\,],\ [\,]) \leftarrow$$

$$del([X\,|Xs],\ Y\!:\![X\,|\,Ys]) \leftarrow del(Xs,\ Y\!:\!Ys)$$
$$del([X\,|Xs],\ X\!:\!Xs) \leftarrow$$

The chain form of this program appears in the URL:

`http://leibniz.iimas.unam.mx/~drosenbl/chain_chapter`

Since we have implemented the term added by the transformation as a list, and such a list follows a first-in, first-out discipline, we will call such a term the *stack*.

When computing the permutations of a 4-element list, say $[a, b, c, d]$, some partial results are computed many times. The reason is that only edges having exactly the same partial result (including the stack) are considered equal. For instance, among the created edges, there are two edges:

$$edge(\boxed{[a,b]}\!:\![c,d],\ \boxed{[a,b]}\!:\![c,d],\ \widehat{perm},\ [\,])\ \text{and}$$
$$edge(\boxed{[b,a]}\!:\![c,d],\ \boxed{[b,a]}\!:\![c,d],\ \widehat{perm},\ [\,]),$$

that are syntactically identical to each other, except for the terms added by the transformation, which are enclosed in a rectangle. (Both edges assert that $[c, d]$ is a permutation of $[c, d]$.)

We will therefore make some changes to our inference system so far. Observe that moded programs converted into chain form have, by definition, the property that predicates with symbols $\hat{p}$ hold only over pairs of terms having the same stack. We will call this the *constant-stack property*.

We can exploit the constant-stack property by replacing the fundamental rule by:

$$\frac{edge(As_1\!:\!t,\ As_2\!:\!t',\ \hat{p}_0,\ [\hat{p}_i, l_i, \ldots, \hat{p}_n, l_n]) \qquad edge(As_3\!:\!u,\ As_3\!:\!u',\ \hat{p}_i,\ [\,])}{edge((As_1\!:\!t)\theta,\ (As_2\!:\!u')\theta,\ \hat{p}_0,\ [l_i, \ldots, \hat{p}_n, l_n])}$$

where θ is the mgu of t' and u. Thus, the partial result that was computed with stack As_3 is used by the edge having stacks As_1 and As_2.

We must keep, however, the original fundamental rule for the predicates with symbols of the form l_i:

$$\frac{edge(As_1\!:\!t,\ As_2\!:\!t',\ \hat{p}_0,\ [l_i, \hat{p}_{i+1}, \ldots, l_n]) \qquad edge(Bs_1\!:\!u,\ Bs_2\!:\!u',\ l_i,\ [\,])}{edge((As_1\!:\!t)\theta,\ (Bs_2\!:\!u')\theta,\ \hat{p}_0,\ [\hat{p}_{i+1}, \ldots, l_n])}$$

where θ is the mgu of $As_2\!:\!t'$ and $Bs_1\!:\!u$.

With the above change, edges can use partial results having a different stack, but we still need some way of avoiding the recomputation of such results. We can achieve this by modifying the membership test. Now, whenever an edge of the form:

$$edge(ts_1\!:\!t,\ ts_1\!:\!t,\ \hat{p}_0,\ [l_0, \hat{p}_1, \ldots, \hat{p}_n, l_n])$$

is removed from the agenda, it is combined with the edges in the chart only if there is no edge of the form:

$$edge(ts_2\!:\!t,\ ts_2\!:\!t,\ \hat{p}_0,\ [l_0, \hat{p}_1, \ldots, \hat{p}_n, l_n])$$

in the chart. In addition, we can ignore an edge labeled with $\hat{p}_0 \longrightarrow \epsilon$ removed from the agenda if there is a similar edge in the chart already, having a different stack. If an edge of the form:

$$edge(ts_1\!:\!t,\ ts_1\!:\!t',\ \hat{p}_0,\ [\,])$$

is removed from the agenda, it is combined with the edges in the chart only if there is no edge of the form:

$$edge(ts_2\!:\!t,\ ts_2\!:\!t',\ \hat{p}_0,\ [\,])$$

in the chart.

4.3.1. Implementation

The URL we gave above also contains the Prolog code of an inference system based on the above changes. This inference system computes each permutation of each sublist *exactly once* when applied to the *perm* program. By contrast, Prolog may compute some partial results for the *perm* program many times. When given the goal $\leftarrow perm([a, b, c, d], Zs)$, for instance, Prolog computes *six* times the (only) permutation of each singleton list: $[a]$, $[b]$, $[c]$, and $[d]$.

Our inference system also avoids recomputation in the following program for solving the Towers of Hanoi problem:

$$h(1, A, B, C, [\mathit{from}, A, \mathit{to}, B]) \leftarrow$$
$$h(N, A, B, C, \mathit{Moves}) \leftarrow N > 1,\ N' \mathit{\ is\ } N-1,$$
$$h(N', A, C, B, L),$$
$$h(N', C, B, A, M), \mathit{append}(L, [\mathit{from}, A, \mathit{to}, B|M], \mathit{Moves})$$

For instance, moving four disks from peg a to peg b using auxiliary peg c, requires twice the result of moving two disks from peg a to peg b using auxiliary peg c. Our code computes this result only once. In fact, the number of edges produced by this program is linear in the number of disks.

The same phenomenon occurs in a doubly recursive, naive definition of Fibonacci numbers:

$$\mathit{fib}(0, 1) \leftarrow$$
$$\mathit{fib}(1, 1) \leftarrow$$
$$\mathit{fib}(N, F) \leftarrow N > 1,\ N_1 \mathit{\ is\ } N-1,\ \mathit{fib}(N_1, F_1),$$
$$N_2 \mathit{\ is\ } N-2,\ \mathit{fib}(N_2, F_2),\ F \mathit{\ is\ } F_1 + F_2$$

in which our method uses memory space linear in the range of the Fibonacci number computed.

The research of [26] was done exclusively with M chain programs in mind, as at that time we had not yet developed I chain programs. An inference system for M chain programs does not require to compute variants of unit program clauses or full unification. However, it is easy to see that the Prolog code in [26] is also valid for I chain programs. The reason is that such a code, as well as the chart parser of [12] on which it is based, employ Prolog's `findall`. This metapredicate computes variants of program clauses and uses full unification.

The `findall` metapredicate is normally implemented with the extra-logical "predicates" `assert` and `retract`. In the next section we will see that chain programs are also useful for implementing `findall` with a logical basis. In fact, our chart-based inference system can be regarded as a metainterpreter.

5. Deterministic Metainterpreters

A proof procedure consists of a set of inference rules and a search strategy. The inference rules determine a search space and the search strategy determines in turn the discipline for traversing such a space. In Sect. 4. we saw how chain programs may help in the design of inference systems inspired by parsers. We will now illustrate the development of search strategies also with chain programs. Since our object of interest in this section is the description of search strategies, we will employ ordinary SLD resolution and consider traversals of the usual SLD search space, namely the SLD tree.

5.1. Two First Deterministic Metainterpreters

It is common to write logic programs at the metalevel defining the provability relation. However, such metainterpreters are usually nondeterministic, and hence the search space is implicit. Consider for example the following *demop* predicate [18, 19] for propositional object programs:

$$\begin{aligned}
&\mathit{demop}(T, P) \leftarrow \mathit{axiom}(T, P \leftarrow Q),\ \mathit{demop}(T, Q)\\
&\mathit{demop}(T, P \wedge Q) \leftarrow \mathit{demop}(T, P),\ \mathit{demop}(T, Q)\\
&\mathit{demop}(T, \mathit{true}) \leftarrow
\end{aligned}$$

Here, $\mathit{demop}(T, P)$ is intended to hold if conclusion P can be demonstrated form theory T. This definition is nondeterministic because it is not determined, in the first clause of the definition, what axiom in the theory T, having conclusion P, might be needed to demonstrate P [19, p. 229].

Since we cannot select the axiom to be applied in each step, it is impossible to establish a particular search strategy at the metalevel with nondeterministic metainterpreters such as *demop*. To be able to reason about search strategies, we need instead an explicit representation of the search space. Such an explicit representation is achieved with a deterministic metainterpreter, able to select the axiom to be applied at each step. Writing such deterministic metainterpreters, however, is a complex task. To appreciate the difficulty of such a task, we will refer to the work of Clark and Gregory [6].

Clark and Gregory [6] were perhaps among the first to publish a deterministic metainterpreter. Their motivation was that of providing a means for committed-choice processors, which are deterministic, to execute nondeterministic logic programs. A slightly modified version of their metainterpreter appears in Fig. 11.

In this and other metainterpreters, we interpret $\wedge$ both as conjunction and as a (right-associative) infix list constructor, terminated by *true*. Thus every conjunction has a final conjunct *true*. Without danger of ambiguity "$\leftarrow$" names "$\leftarrow$."

The intended meanings of some of the predicates in this metainterpreter are as follows. Assume that the set of answer substitutions to the goal having A as its only subgoal is $\{\theta_1, \ldots, \theta_n\}$. Then the predicate $\mathit{single\_call\_set}(A, A\theta s)$ is intended to hold when $A\theta s$ is a list of the form $[A\theta_1, \ldots, A\theta_n]$.

The predicate $\mathit{set}(A, \mathit{Bs}, A\theta s)$ is a generalization of *single_call_set*. In this case the goal *Bs*, which may have more than one subgoal, is of the form $B_1 \wedge \ldots \wedge B_m \wedge \mathit{true}$, and $A\theta s$ is of the form $[A\theta_1, \ldots, A\theta_n]$, where $\{\theta_1, \ldots, \theta_n\}$ is the set of answer substitutions for *Bs*.

The predicate $\mathit{all\_set}(\mathit{ABs}, A\theta s)$, in turn, can be viewed as a generalization of *set*, where *ABs* is a list of clauses $[A_1 \leftarrow \mathit{Bs}_1, \ldots, A_m \leftarrow \mathit{Bs}_m]$ and $A\theta s$ is of the form $[A_1\theta_{1,1}, \ldots, A_1\theta_{1,n_1}, \ldots, A_m\theta_{m,1}, \ldots, A_m\theta_{m,n_m}]$, where $\{\theta_{i,1}, \ldots, \theta_{i,n_i}\}$ is the set of answer substitutions for Bs_i. We refer the reader to [6] for a thorough discussion of this metainterpreter.

Clark and Gregory's metainterpreter has two features that in our opinion are undesirable. First, is it not clear how the metainterpreter was obtained. Moreover, it is not clear either how to modify it in case we wished to add features to it. In particular, modifying this metainterpreter requires being concerned about *the set of unifiers of the children of a node*

Example of object-program representation:

$$
\begin{aligned}
&\mathit{definition}(ap(\_,\_,\_), [ap([\,], L, L) \leftarrow \mathit{true},\\
&\qquad\qquad\qquad ap([A|L'], M, [A|N]) \leftarrow (ap(L', M, N) \wedge \mathit{true})\\
&\qquad\qquad\quad]\\
&\quad) \leftarrow
\end{aligned}
$$

Example of goal: $\leftarrow \mathit{single\_call\_set}(ap(X, Y, [a, b]), A\theta s)$

Metainterpreter:

$$
\begin{aligned}
&\mathit{single\_call\_set}(A, A\theta s) \leftarrow \mathit{definition}(A, ABs),\\
&\qquad\qquad \mathit{all\_matches}(A, ABs, AB\theta s'),\\
&\qquad\qquad \mathit{all\_set}(AB\theta s', A\theta s)\\
&\mathit{all\_set}([\,], [\,]) \leftarrow\\
&\mathit{all\_set}([A \leftarrow Bs|ABs], A\theta s) \leftarrow \mathit{set}(A, Bs, A\theta s_1),\\
&\qquad\qquad \mathit{all\_set}(ABs, A\theta s_2),\\
&\qquad\qquad \mathit{append}(A\theta s_1, A\theta s_2, A\theta s)\\
&\mathit{set}(A, \mathit{true}, [A]) \leftarrow\\
&\mathit{set}(A, B \wedge Bs, A\theta s) \leftarrow \mathit{single\_call\_set}(B, B\theta s),\\
&\qquad\qquad \mathit{term\_instances}(B, B\theta s, A \leftarrow Bs, AB\theta s),\\
&\qquad\qquad \mathit{all\_set}(AB\theta s, A\theta s)\\
&\mathit{all\_matches}(A, [\,], [\,]) \leftarrow\\
&\mathit{all\_matches}(A, [A\theta \leftarrow B\theta s|ABs], [A\theta \leftarrow B\theta s|AB\theta s']) \leftarrow \mathit{copy}(A, A\theta'),\\
&\qquad\qquad \mathit{unify}(A\theta, A\theta'),\ !,\\
&\qquad\qquad \mathit{all\_matches}(A, ABs, AB\theta s')\\
&\mathit{all\_matches}(A, [A' \leftarrow Bs|ABs], ABs') \leftarrow \mathit{all\_matches}(A, ABs, ABs')\\
&\mathit{term\_instances}(B, [\,], C, [\,]) \leftarrow\\
&\mathit{term\_instances}(B, [B\theta|B\theta s], C, [C\theta|C\theta s]) \leftarrow \mathit{copy}(f(B, C), f(B\theta', C\theta)),\\
&\qquad\qquad \mathit{unify}(B\theta, B\theta'),\\
&\qquad\qquad \mathit{term\_instances}(B, B\theta s, C, C\theta s)
\end{aligned}
$$

Figure 11. *A deterministic, exhaustive-traversal metainterpreter for arbitrary definite programs. For readability, we use a string $X\theta$ as the name of a variable taking as value an instance of the value of X. Similarly, $X\theta s$ is the name of a variable taking as value a list of instances of the value of X.*

in the derivation tree (which can be seen, for example, in the *term_instances* predicate). This is an additional difficulty, absent in usual nondeterministic metainterpreters.

Second, this metainterpreter does not follow Prolog's search strategy. Under a leftmost computation rule, this metainterpreter computes first all answers for the leftmost subgoal, and then uses each such answer to compute all answers for the next subgoal, and so on.

This regime results in a traversal having both breadth-first and depth-first characteristics. A metainterpreter following the ordinary top-down left-to-right discipline would be more useful than Clark and Gregory's, as such a discipline is often taken as the default search strategy. Thus, it is natural to attempt to write, in the style of Clark and Gregory's, a deterministic metainterpreter following Prolog's search strategy. Such an exercise would enable us, first, to have an idea of what conceptual difficulties are involved, and second, how intuitive the meanings of the different predicates in such a metainterpreter are. We have written one such metainterpreter, and can conclude not only that this task involves indeed considerable difficulties, but also that the meanings of the predicates are arguably less intuitive than those of Clark and Gregory's. The Appendix shows this metainterpreter, together with possible meanings for its predicates.

Note that this metainterpreter employs variables of the metalevel in the representation of the object program. Although the same practice is usually followed in the familiar Vanilla metainterpreter, strictly speaking this use of metavariables is incorrect. This nonground representation of the object program is motivated by efficiency reasons, but then a problem appears from a theoretical point of view. In the case of the Vanilla metainterpreter, several explanations have been given as to why in spite of the incorrectness such a metainterpreter works [14, 15, 20, 23]. Hence, it would be desirable to give as well an explanation of why a nonground, deterministic metainterpreter works.

In contrast to these drawbacks, we will now turn our attention to a feature that we do wish to preserve from Clark and Gregory's metainterpreter. At first sight it might appear that a metainterpreter computing *all answers* to a query is not adequate for studying deterministic metainterpreters in general. Nevertheless, note that all-answer metainterpreters capture in fact the essence of arbitrary deterministic metainterpreters. It could be argued that if we only wish one answer, there is no need to traverse the whole search space. Observe, however, that if we are aiming at any kind of completeness, we do need to be able to traverse the whole space, as we will have to do so in the worst of cases. An all-answer metainterpreter could then be modified to obtain the desired variation. For example, we could change such a metainterpreter so as to compute only one answer, and/or to count the number of inference steps. Therefore, in the rest of this section we will limit ourselves to metainterpreters computing all the answers to a query.

The shortcomings of Clark and Gregory's approach suggest utilizing more formal tools for arriving at an all-answer metainterpreter. More precisely, we will start from a familiar nondeterministic metainterpreter usually called *demo*, representing the object program with ground terms. Next, we will observe that chain programs enable us to simplify the *demo* metainterpreter. We give both a version for I and for M chain object programs. Finally, from the *demo* metainterpreter simplified for M chain programs, we obtain a deterministic version.

5.2. The *Demo* Metainterpreter

Consider the familiar *demo* metainterpreter [3]. This metainterpreter uses the predicate $demo(T, As)$, which expresses that conclusion As can be demonstrated from the theory named T.

$$
\begin{aligned}
&demo(T, true) \leftarrow \\
&demo(T, A \wedge As) \leftarrow axiom(T, B \leftarrow Bs), \\
&\qquad rename(B \leftarrow Bs, A \wedge As, B' \leftarrow Bs'), \\
&\qquad unify(A, B', \theta), \\
&\qquad append_{\wedge}(Bs', As, BsAs), \\
&\qquad apply(BsAs, \theta, BsAs\theta), \\
&\qquad demo(T, BsAs\theta)
\end{aligned}
$$

Here and throughout, we will employ sequences of Greek letters for names of variables ranging over substitutions. The predicate $axiom(T, B \leftarrow Bs)$ expresses that $B \leftarrow Bs$ is a clause represented explicitly as an axiom in T. The predicate $rename(B, A, B')$ states that B' is a variant of B having no variables in common with A. The predicate $unify(A, B, \theta)$ denotes the relationship which holds between atoms A, B, and their mgu θ. The predicate $apply(A, \theta, A\theta)$ holds when $A\theta$ results from applying the substitution θ to A. The predicate $append_{\wedge}(As, Bs, AsBs)$ is like the ordinary *append*, but for lists constructed using $\wedge$.

The *demo* predicate is the top level of a representation of definite-clause provability. For simplicity, however, Bowen and Kowalski [3] omitted the answer substitution. Since we are interested in writing metainterpreters computing all answers to a query, let us first undo such a simplification. Referring again to the representation of provability, we must, in addition, (1) compose the unifier of an SLD resolution step with the answer substitution of the subsequent SLD resolution steps, and (2) restrict such a composition to the variables of the query. We will, however, omit the theory argument for conciseness. The resulting metainterpreter would be:

$$
\begin{aligned}
&demo(true \leftarrow true) \leftarrow \\
&demo(A \wedge As \leftarrow \theta\sigma') \leftarrow axiom(B \leftarrow Bs), \\
&\qquad rename(B \leftarrow Bs, A \wedge As, B' \leftarrow Bs'), \\
&\qquad unify(A, B', \theta), \\
&\qquad append_{\wedge}(Bs', As, BsAs), \\
&\qquad apply(BsAs, \theta, BsAs\theta), \\
&\qquad demo(BsAs\theta \leftarrow \sigma), \\
&\qquad composition(\theta, \sigma, \theta\sigma), \\
&\qquad restricted(\theta\sigma, A \wedge As, \theta\sigma')
\end{aligned}
$$

We will represent a substitution by a conjunction of equations (terminated by *true*). As an example object program, we give the *append* predicate:

$$
\begin{aligned}
&axiom(app([\,], y, y) \leftarrow true) \leftarrow \\
&axiom(app([w|x], y, [w|z]) \leftarrow app(x, y, z) \wedge true) \leftarrow
\end{aligned}
$$

With respect to the metalevel, w, x, y, and z, are constants. Sometimes, terms of the object level are named at the metalevel by terms such as

$$struct(cons, [var(1), var(2)])$$

This metalevel term might name the object-level term $[W|X]$, where $cons$ names the list-constructor function symbol, $var(1)$ names the variable W, and $var(2)$ names the variable X. However, for simplicity, we will represent $[W|X]$, say, by $[w|x]$ (where w and x are metalevel constants).

A goal and an answer for such a goal are:

$$\leftarrow demo(app(x, y, [a, b]) \wedge true \leftarrow \theta)$$

$$\{\theta \,/\, y = [b] \wedge x = [a] \wedge true\}$$

5.3. The *demo* Metainterpreter Specialized to I Chain Programs

Let us now see how the *demo* metainterpreter gets simplified when the object program has chain form. We recall from Sect. 2. that both I chain and M chain programs have the property that we need only consider the output (i.e. the second argument place) to have an answer for a single-subgoal goal.

Note next that each goal has the form:

$$\leftarrow q_1(t, X_1),\ q_2(X_1, X_2),\ \ldots,\ q_n(X_{n-1}, X_n)$$

which we can represent by:

$$(t, [q_1, q_2, \ldots, q_n])$$

Hence, we can employ two argument places to denote a chain goal: X, which will represent t, and Qs, which will represent the list $[q_1, q_2, \ldots, q_n]$ of predicate symbols. In addition, we need to represent the output of the topmost subgoal: Z. Hence we have three argument places: $demo_{ch}(X, Qs, Z)$.

Let us now turn our attention to the representation of the object program. The I chain form of *append* is:

$$\widehat{ap}(Ws\!:\![\,]\!:\!Y\!:\!Y,\ Ws\!:\![\,]\!:\!Y\!:\!Y) \leftarrow$$
$$\widehat{ap}(U_0, U_3) \leftarrow l_0(U_0, U_1),\ \widehat{ap}(U_1, U_2),\ l_1(U_2, U_3)$$
$$l_0(Ws\!:\![W|X]\!:\!Y\!:\![W|Z],\ [W|Ws]\!:\!X\!:\!Y\!:\!Z) \leftarrow$$
$$l_1([W|Ws]\!:\!X\!:\!Y\!:\!Z,\ Ws\!:\![W|X]\!:\!Y\!:\![W|Z]) \leftarrow$$

The intended meaning of $\widehat{ap}(Ws\!:\!X\!:\!Y\!:\!Z,\ Ws'\!:\!X'\!:\!Y'\!:\!Z')$ is: Ws is Ws', X is X', Y is Y', Z is Z', and Z is X affixed in front of Y.

We will represent this program by:

$$unit(\widehat{ap},\ ws\!:\![\,]\!:\!y\!:\!y,\ ws\!:\![\,]\!:\!y\!:\!y) \leftarrow$$
$$nonunit(\widehat{ap},\ [l_0, \widehat{ap}, l_1]) \leftarrow$$
$$unit(l_0,\ ws\!:\![w|x]\!:\!y\!:\![w|z],\ [w|ws]\!:\!x\!:\!y\!:\!z) \leftarrow$$
$$unit(l_1,\ [w|ws]\!:\!x\!:\!y\!:\!z,\ ws\!:\![w|x]\!:\!y\!:\![w|z]) \leftarrow$$

Because unit and nonunit clauses in chain programs have different forms, the metainterpreter must treat them separately. In the nonunit case we can dispose of substitutions, and hence of renaming the program clause, the unification, and the application of the unifier:

$$\begin{aligned} \mathit{demo}_{ch}(X, [P|Ps], Z) \leftarrow\ & \mathit{nonunit}(Q \leftarrow Qs), \\ & \mathit{append}_{\wedge}(Qs, Ps, QsPs), \\ & \mathit{demo}_{ch}(X, QsPs, Z) \end{aligned}$$

In the unit case, by contrast, we can dispose of the concatenation of the goals. The composition and the restriction of substitutions can also be eliminated, as we are only interested in the output of subgoals.

$$\begin{aligned} \mathit{demo}_{ch}(X, [P|Ps], Z) \leftarrow\ & \mathit{unit}(P, X', Y'), \\ & \mathit{rename}((X', Y'), X, (X'', Y'')), \\ & \mathit{unify}(X, X'', \theta), \\ & \mathit{apply}(Y'', \theta, Y), \\ & \mathit{demo}_{ch}(Y, Ps, Z) \end{aligned}$$

5.4. The *demo* Metainterpreter Specialized to M Chain Programs

If the object program has M chain form, the metainterpreter can be further simplified for unit clauses, as the input X is ground. Hence, we need not rename the program clause:

$$\begin{aligned} \mathit{demo}'_{ch}(X, [P|Ps], Z) \leftarrow\ & \mathit{unit}(P, X', Y'), \\ & \mathit{unify}(X, X', \theta), \\ & \mathit{apply}(Y', \theta, Y), \\ & \mathit{demo}'_{ch}(Y, Ps, Z) \end{aligned}$$

5.5. A Deterministic Metainterpreter for M Chain Programs

Let us now convert the *demo* metainterpreter specialized to M chain programs to an all-answer deterministic version.

We posit the existence of the predicate $\mathit{defn}(B \leftarrow D)$ expressing that $B \leftarrow D$ is the complete definition of B. Such a definition is a disjunction of all the conditions of all the clauses having conclusion B. In addition to having its logical meaning as disjunction, $\vee$ can be interpreted as a right-associative list constructor, terminated by *false*. Thus every disjunction has a final disjunct *false*.

We deal now with the object-program representation. It will be convenient to assume that in the complete definition of predicates no unit clauses appear, and that unit clauses are represented separately. We can do so by introducing predicate symbols. For example, consider the following M chain program for splitting lists:

$$\begin{aligned} & \mathit{split}(Ws{:}Y,\ Ws{:}[\,]{:}Y) \leftarrow \\ & \mathit{split}(U_0, U_3) \leftarrow l_0(U_0, U_1),\ \mathit{split}(U_1, U_2),\ l_1(U_2, U_3) \\ & l_0(Ws{:}[W|Z],\ [W|Ws]{:}Z) \leftarrow \\ & l_1([W|Ws]{:}X{:}Y,\ Ws{:}[W|X]{:}Y) \leftarrow \end{aligned}$$

We will represent this program by:

$$\begin{aligned}
&\mathit{defn}'_{ch}(\mathit{split} \leftarrow [\mathit{split}_1] \vee [l_0, \mathit{split}, l_1] \vee \mathit{false}) \leftarrow \\
&\mathit{unit}'(\mathit{split}_1,\ ws\!:\!y,\ ws\!:\![\,]\!:\!y) \leftarrow \\
&\mathit{unit}'(l_0,\ ws\!:\![w|z],\ [w|ws]\!:\!z) \leftarrow \\
&\mathit{unit}'(l_1,\ [w|ws]\!:\!x\!:\!y,\ ws\!:\![w|x]\!:\!y) \leftarrow
\end{aligned}$$

With no loss of generality we will assume that each object predicate is defined by at most two clauses. Clearly, the demo'_{ch} metainterpreter is true of the deterministic version in the case of a single-clause definition, except that instead of the subgoal $\mathit{axiom}(B \leftarrow Bs)$, we would now have $\mathit{defn}(B \leftarrow Bs_1 \vee \mathit{false})$.

$$\begin{aligned}
\mathit{ddemo}'_{ch}(X, [P|Ps], Z) \leftarrow\ & \mathit{defn}'_{ch}(Q \leftarrow Qs \vee \mathit{false}), \\
& \mathit{append}_{\wedge}(Qs, Ps, QsPs), \\
& \mathit{ddemo}'_{ch}(X, QsPs, Z)
\end{aligned}$$

For two-clause definitions we need only replicate the same treatment for each clause:

$$\begin{aligned}
\mathit{ddemo}'_{ch}(X, [Q|Qs], Z_1 \vee Z_2) \leftarrow\ & \mathit{defn}'_{ch}(Q \leftarrow Ps_1 \vee Ps_2 \vee \mathit{false}), \\
& \mathit{append}(Ps_1, Qs, PsQs_1), \\
& \mathit{ddemo}'_{ch}(X, PsQs_1, Z_1), \\
& \mathit{append}(Ps_2, Qs, PsQs_2), \\
& \mathit{ddemo}'_{ch}(X, PsQs_2, Z_2)
\end{aligned}$$

On the other hand, unit clauses have only one answer, so that we can reuse the corresponding part of the nondeterministic version:

$$\begin{aligned}
\mathit{ddemo}'_{ch}(X, [P|Ps], Z) \leftarrow\ & \mathit{unit}(P, X', Y'), \\
& \mathit{unify}(X, X', \theta), \\
& \mathit{apply}(Y', \theta, Y), \\
& \mathit{ddemo}'_{ch}(Y, Ps, Z)
\end{aligned} \qquad (46)$$

Finally, because we wish all answers, we must cover failures:

$$\begin{aligned}
\mathit{ddemo}'_{ch}(X, [P|Ps], \mathit{false}) \leftarrow\ & \mathit{unit}(P, X', _), \\
& \mathit{not}\ \mathit{unify}(X, X', _)
\end{aligned} \qquad (47)$$

A drawback of this resulting metainterpreter is that the unification at the object level is interpreted at the metalevel [4]. This source of inefficiency can be eliminated by employing metalevel variables at the object level. The clauses (46) and (47) would then be respectively replaced by:

$$\begin{aligned}
\mathit{ddemo}'_{ch}(X, [P|Ps], Z) \leftarrow\ & \mathit{unit}(P, X, Y), \\
& \mathit{ddemo}'_{ch}(Y, Ps, Z) \\
\mathit{ddemo}'_{ch}(X, [P|Ps], \mathit{false}) \leftarrow\ & \mathit{unit}(P, _, _), \\
& \mathit{not}\ \mathit{unit}(P, X, _)
\end{aligned}$$

An example goal is:

$$\leftarrow ddemo'_{ch}([\,]:[a,b],\ [split],\ Zs)$$

Although we have arrived at a useful metainterpreter, in that it is conceptually simple and efficiently executable, we have not justified our introduction of the nonground representation. It would be desirable to prove the soundness of this introduction of metavariables in the object program in a formal way. However, we do not perform this task here, and leave it for future research.

6. Concluding Remarks

A proof procedure is a set of inference rules together with a search strategy on a space determined by all possible ways of applying the inference rules. Prolog employs a proof procedure having SLD resolution as its sole inference rule and a top-down, left-to-right regime as its search strategy. This proof procedure is convenient for many applications because of its simplicity. There are, however, important advantages in developing other, more sophisticated inference systems and search strategies.

6.1. Inference Systems

6.1.1. Inference Systems vs. Parsers

As an illustration of the need for a variety of inference systems for logic programs, we can consider the existing myriad parsers for context-free grammars [30]. The reason why this comparison is possible is that definite clauses are similar to context-free productions. There exist elaborate context-free parsers able to avoid some nonterminating loops, as well as the recalculation of some partial results. However, when logic-program inference systems and context-free parsers are put side by side, it immediately emerges that there are surprisingly few inference systems for logic programs compared with parsers for context-free grammars. A cause for this scarcity of inference systems could be an inherent difficulty in devising inference rules for definite programs. Writing logic-program inference systems with advantages similar to those of sophisticated parsers possibly requires more inventiveness than that demanded by the creation of such parsers.

6.1.2. Chain Programs

Chain programs simplify the design of definite-clause inference systems by relegating the role played by substitutions to unit clauses. In particular, parser-inspired inference systems for chain logic programs are readily obtained because of close connections between chain programs and context-free grammars. We showed how a sound inference system for chain clauses results from adding unification to the treatment of terminals in a context-free parser. Moreover, inference systems so obtained are also applicable to arbitrary definite programs when coupled with our transformation of definite programs into chain form. Completeness, however, is not normally achieved, and has apparently to be dealt with specifically for each particular resulting inference system. Also, as a consequence of our transformation into chain form, the inference system obtained may no longer detect nonterminating loops or previously computed partial results. We illustrated this effect in an inference system based on chart parsing. Here we have exhibited the retrieval of these advantages with slight modifications to the chart parser to which unification was added. In general, however, it is not clear how to recover these properties in case they are lost.

6.2. Search Strategies

6.2.1. Deterministic Metainterpreters

As an example of the utility of employing different search strategies within SLD resolution, we have chosen Kowalski's approach [19] for reconciling reactive and rational agents. Kowalski's reconciliation consists in using a metainterpreter able to count the number of steps in the search of a proof (as opposed to the number of steps of a proof). Such a metainterpreter is said to be deterministic, as it is able to determine the axiom applied at each step by employing an explicit search space. Although Kowalski's proposed metainterpreter traverses the search space following the same discipline as Prolog, this metainterpreter is also adequate for exhibiting techniques for describing different search strategies. The reason is that any such technique requires first an explicit representation of the search space.

Given the usefulness of deterministic metainterpreters, it is also noticeable that few such metainterpreters have been published. In [19] Kowalski only deals with the simplified, propositional case. In [6] Clark and Gregory do give a complete deterministic metainterpreter, for committed-choice processors. This metainterpreter, however, has several drawbacks. First, it does not follow Prolog's search strategy, as would be desirable, but rather a strategy having both breadth-first and depth-first components. In addition, it is plagued by substitutions applied to terms, which complicates its comprehension, compared with nondeterministic metainterpreters (such as the Vanilla metainterpreter), for example.

6.2.2. Our Method

Our approach has been first to write a deterministic metainterpreter having a clear separation between the metalevel and the object level by using terms having no variables of the metalevel (i.e. "ground" terms) for representing variables of the object level. Next, we observed a number of important simplifications resulting when the object program has chain form. From the nondeterministic metainterpreter for M chain programs we obtained a deterministic version. This metainterpreter is hopelessly inefficient [4] because of interpreting the unification of the object level. Next, we informally modified this ground-representation metainterpreter obtaining a nonground-representation version, thereby increasing its efficiency.

Our transformation of definite programs into chain form makes such simplifications valid also when object programs do not have chain form. The result is a deterministic metainterpreter using the underlying unification of the metalevel (hence efficiently executable). Furthermore, this metainterpreter is simple and therefore readily modifiable.

6.3. Transformations Into Chain Form

The design of both parser-based inference systems and conceptually simple deterministic metainterpreters are dependent on our being able to transform logic programs that do not have chain form into such a form. We gave two such transformations, one for arbitrary definite programs and another one for moded programs, using each argument place of a predicate either as input (instantiated) or as output (uninstantiated). The more general transformation, for arbitrary definite programs, might appear at first glance to supersede the more limited, moded-program version. However, the moded-program variant is useful, first, for explanation purposes, as it is simpler, and second, for efficiency reasons, as instead of full unification, one-way matching can be employed.

An important property of chain programs simplifying the design of inference systems based on parsers and the creation of deterministic metainterpreters is that we need only be concerned about the output (the second argument place) of a subgoal, and not about its input.

The moded-program transformation takes as input a moded logic program and produces a special kind of chain program, called M chain program, where

- unit clauses $p(t, t') \leftarrow$ satisfy $\mathrm{var}(t) \supseteq \mathrm{var}(t')$.

We saw how, if the topmost goal has a leftmost subgoal with a ground input, then we need only be concerned about computing the substitution received by the output of each subgoal.

The transformation taking an arbitrary definite logic program also produces a special kind of logic program, called I chain program, where

- each predicate $p(t_1, \ldots, t_n)$ of the original program is converted into a binary predicate $p'(t_1 : \ldots : t_n,\ t'_1 : \ldots : t'_n)$ denoting a subset of the identity relation.

This characteristic also results in our being interested only in the substitution received by the output of subgoals.

This property streamlines the construction both of proof trees and derivation trees. Normally, a proof tree is extended by applying a substitution to all terms occurring in such a tree. A proof tree for a chain program, by contrast, only requires the application of a substitution to a single term. Similarly, a derivation can be represented by recording only one term for each goal.

6.4. Future Work

6.4.1. Generative Nondeterminism

A number of open problems emerged all through this chapter. First, in spite of the close connections between chain programs and context-free grammars, there is a kind of nondeterminism in chain programs, absent in string parsing. This new kind of nondeterminism results from the fact that in general there is more than one way of extending a computation. In the parsing problem, an input string is given, and parse trees having such a string as frontier are constructed. In the inference problem, sequences of terms are extended, and proof trees having such sequences as frontier are built. The next term in each term sequence is determined by unit clauses. Any unit clause whose first argument unifies with the current term extends the term sequence. Thus, it is possible to have sequences of terms with a branching structure.

As a consequence, rather than associating chain-program inference with parsing, it would be more accurate to relate inference with *string generation*. The string-generation problem gets as input the first symbol of a set of strings of interest (together with a context-free grammar). Because this new kind of nondeterminism also occurs in the string-generation problem, we will refer to it as *generative nondeterminism*.

Generative nondeterminism is not normally dealt with by parsers. Our choice of chart parsers as the basis for parser-inspired inference systems was advantageous because these parsers employ memoing. Therefore, the generative nondeterminism present in chain programs is handled without having to add any special mechanism: Whenever a sequence of terms has more than one possibility for it to be extended, memoing records the pending possibilities in the agenda for future consideration.

In [28] we studied a parser-based inference system resulting from an LR parser, also using chain programs. Unlike chart parsers, LR parsers do not provide any method applicable to generative nondeterminism. However, because in [28] we implemented the inference system in Prolog, it was easy to handle generative nondeterminism with Prolog's backtracking device. We have thus found two mechanisms dealing with generative nondeterminism, but a more systematic approach to generative nondeterminism is clearly desirable.

6.4.2. Possible Loss of Parser Advantages

Another phenomenon deserving further study is the loss of some sought-after properties of a parser-based inference system when used in chain programs resulting from our transformations. We saw how the ability of chart parsers to avert some nonterminating loops and reuse some partial results disappears when a chart-based inference system is used in programs transformed into chain form. The culprit in this case is the stack added by the transformation. The inference system can then be modified in this particular case to disregard such a stack in certain situations when comparing two terms, and the lost benefits reappear.

The inference system of [28] based on LR parsing also loses some advantages present in the original LR parser. This time the cause is the set of predicates introduced by the transformation and defined by unit clauses (for which we chose the predicate symbols l_i). Sometimes these predicates can be deleted, and again the wished features reemerge. It would be interesting to address this problem from a general point of view.

6.4.3. Justification of Nonground Representation

Finally, our introduction of metavariables in the ground-representation deterministic metainterpreter is evidently unsatisfactory. Such introduction of metavariables is of prime relevance, as the metainterpreter becomes several orders of magnitude more efficient. Hence, we believe it is important to be able to justify this step in the derivation of our deterministic metainterpreter.

Acknowledgments

We gratefully acknowledge the facilities provided by IIMAS, UNAM. In addition, Ohmsha, Ltd. and Cambridge University Press kindly granted us permission to publish respectively revised versions of [26] and [27].

Appendix A

A Deterministic Metainterpreter in the Style of Clark and Gregory's, Following Prolog's Search Strategy

```
t( Athetas ) :-
        definition( ap(_,_,_), ABs ),
        top( ap(X,Y,[1,2,3]), ABs, Athetas ).

:- op( 700, xfx, <- ).

% top( A, ClList, AThetas ): holds iff every element of AThetas is
% an instance of A. In addition, such an instance of A is the root
% of the closed proof tree whose first clause is an instance of a
% clause from ClList.

top( A, [], [] ).
top( A, [false|Clauses], Zs ) :-
        top( A, Clauses, Zs ).
top( A, [H <- []|Clauses], [H|Zs] ) :-
        match( A, H <- [] ),
        top( A, Clauses, Zs ).
top( A, [H <- []|Clauses], Zs ) :-
        \+ match( A, H <- [] ),
        top( A, Clauses, Zs ).
top( A, [H <- [B|Bs]|Clauses], YsZs ) :-
        match( A, H <- [B|Bs] ),
        definition( B, BCs ),
        top2( A, H <- [B|Bs], BCs, Clauses, YsZs ).
top( A, [H <- [B|Bs]|Clauses], Zs ) :-
        \+ match( A, H <- [B|Bs] ),
        top( A, Clauses, Zs ).

% top2( A, Cl, ClList1, ClList2, AThetas ): holds iff every element
% of AThetas is an instance of A. In addition, such an instance of
% A is the root of a closed proof tree that either
% a) its first clause is an instance of Cl and its second clause
% (to the left) is an instance of an element of ClList1; or
% b) its first clause is an instance of an element of ClList2.

top2( A, Clause, [], Qs, Zs ) :-
        top( A, Qs, Zs ).
top2( A, Clause, [AB|ABs], Qs, YsZs ) :-
        resolve( Clause, [AB|ABs], QB, ABs1 ),
        top( A, [QB], Ys ),
        top2( A, Clause, ABs1, Qs, Zs ),
        append( Ys, Zs, YsZs ).
```

```
% resolve( Cl, ClList, Clres, ClListp ): holds iff Clres is the
% resolvent of Cl, wrt its leftmost body atom, and the first clause
% of ClList which is resolvable with Cl, if such a clause in ClList
% exists. If no such clause exists, then Clres is false. ClListp is
% the list of the clauses ClList without the clause used for
% resolution.

resolve( Clause, [], false, [] ).
resolve( A <- [B|Bs],
         [Btheta <- Cstheta|Clauses],
         Atheta <- CsBstheta,
         Clauses
        ) :-
        copy( A <- [B|Bs], Atheta <- [Bthetap|Bstheta] ),
        Btheta = Bthetap, !,
        append( Cstheta, Bstheta, CsBstheta ).
resolve( Clause, [_|Clauses], Clausep, Clausesp ) :-
        resolve( Clause, Clauses, Clausep, Clausesp ).

match( A, Atheta <- Bthetas ) :-
        copy( A, Athetap ),
        Atheta = Athetap.

append( [], Y, Y ).
append( [A|X], Y, [A|Z] ) :-
        append( X, Y, Z ).

cc(0).

copy( X, X1 ) :-
        abolish( cc/1 ),
        assert( cc(X) ),
        retract( cc(X1) ).

definition( ap(_,_,_), [ap([],L,L) <- [],
                         ap([A|Lp],M,[A|N]) <- [ap(Lp,M,N)]
                        ]
          ).

definition( del(_,_,_), [del(X,[X|Xs],Xs) <- [],
                          del(X1,[Y|Xs1],[Y|Ys]) <- [del(X1,Xs1,Ys)]
                         ]
          ).

definition( perm(_,_), [perm([],[]) <- [],
                         perm(Xs,[X|Zs]) <- [del(X,Xs,Ys),perm(Ys,Zs)]
                        ]
          ).
```

References

[1] Krzysztof R. Apt. *From logic programming to Prolog*. Prentice Hall, 1997.

[2] Edward Ashcroft, Zohar Manna, and Amir Pnueli. Decidable properties of monadic functional schemas. *Journal of the ACM*, **20**(3):489–499, 1973.

[3] Kenneth A. Bowen and Robert A. Kowalski. Amalgamating language and metalanguage in logic programming. In K. L. Clark and S-Å. Tärnlund, editors, *Logic Programming*, pages 153–172. Academic Press, 1982.

[4] Antony F. Bowers and Corin A. Gurr. Towards fast and declarative meta-programming. In Krzysztof Apt and Franco Turini, editors, *Meta-Logics and Logic Programming*, chapter 6, pages 137–166. MIT Press, 1995.

[5] Rodney A. Brooks. *Cambrian Intelligence*. MIT Press, 1999.

[6] Keith Clark and Steve Gregory. Notes on the implementation of Parlog. *The Journal of Logic Programming*, **1**:17–42, 1985.

[7] Keith L. Clark and M. H. van Emden. Consequence verification of flowcharts. *IEEE Transactions on Software Engineering*, **SE-7**(1):52–60, January 1981.

[8] A. Colmerauer. Metamorphosis grammars. In L. Bolc, editor, *Natural Language Communication with Computers*, pages 133–189. Springer-Verlag, 1978. Lecture Notes in Computer Science Vol. 63.

[9] Jay Earley. An efficient context-free parsing algorithm. *Communications of the ACM*, **13**(2):94–102, 1970.

[10] Joost Engelfriet. *Simple Program Schemes and Formal Languages*. Springer-Verlag, 1974. Lecture Notes in Computer Science Vol. 20.

[11] P. A. Gardner and J. C. Shepherdson. Unfold/fold transformations of logic programs. In Jean-Louis Lassez and Gordon Plotkin, editors, *Computational Logic. Essays in Honor of Alan Robinson*, pages 565–583. The MIT Press, 1992.

[12] Gerald Gazdar and Chris Mellish. *Natural Language Processing in Prolog. An Introduction to Computational Linguistics*. Addison-Wesley, 1989.

[13] Michael R. Genesereth and Nils J. Nilsson. *Logical Foundations of Artificial Intelligence*. Morgan Kaufmann, 1987.

[14] P. M. Hill and J. W. Lloyd. Analysis of meta-programs. In Harvey Abramson and M. H. Rogers, editors, *Meta-Programming in Logic Programming*, chapter 2, pages 23–51. MIT Press, 1989.

[15] Marianne Kalsbeek. Correctness of the Vanilla meta-interpreter and ambivalent syntax. In Krzysztof Apt and Franco Turini, editors, *Meta-Logics and Logic Programming*, chapter 1, pages 3–26. MIT Press, 1995.

[16] Donald M. Kaplan. Regular expressions and the equivalence of programs. *Journal of Computer and System Sciences*, **3**(4):361–386, 1969.

[17] Martin Kay. Algorithm schemata and data structures in syntactic processing. Technical Report CSL-80-12, Xerox Palo Alto Research Center, October 1980.

[18] Robert A. Kowalski. Problems and promises of computational logic. In J.W. Lloyd, editor, *Computational Logic. Symposium Proceedings*, pages 1–36. Springer-Verlag, 1990.

[19] Robert A. Kowalski. Using meta-logic to reconcile reactive with rational agents. In Krzysztof Apt and Franco Turini, editors, *Meta-Logics and Logic Programming*, chapter 9, pages 227–242. MIT Press, 1995.

[20] Giorgio Levi and Davide Ramundo. A formalization of metaprogramming for real. In David S. Warren, editor, *Proc. 10th International Conference on Logic Programming*, pages 354–373, 1993.

[21] J. W. Lloyd. *Foundations of Logic Programming*. Springer-Verlag, 2nd edition, 1987.

[22] David Maier and David S. Warren. *Computing with Logic. Logic Programming with Prolog*. Benjamin/Cummings, 1988.

[23] Bern Martens and Danny De Schreye. Two semantics for definite meta-programs, using the non-ground representation. In Krzysztof Apt and Franco Turini, editors, *Meta-Logics and Logic Programming*, chapter 3, pages 57–81. MIT Press, 1995.

[24] Fernando C.N. Pereira and David H.D. Warren. Parsing as deduction. In *21st Annual Meeting of the Association for Computational Linguistics*, pages 137–144, Cambridge, Massachusetts, 1983. Association for Computational Linguistics.

[25] Alberto Pettorossi and Maurizio Proietti. Transformation of logic programs: Foundations and techniques. *The Journal of Logic Programming*, **19**, 20:261–320, 1994.

[26] David A. Rosenblueth. Chart parsers as inference systems for fixed-mode logic programs. *New Generation Computing*, **14**(4):429–458, 1996.

[27] David A. Rosenblueth. Chain programs for writing deterministic metainterpreters. *Theory and Practice of Logic Programming*, **2**(2):203–232, 2002.

[28] David A. Rosenblueth and Julio C. Peralta. SLR inference: An inference system for fixed-mode logic programs, based on SLR parsing. *The Journal of Logic Programming*, **34**(3):227–260, 1998.

[29] J.D. Rutledge. On Ianov's program schemata. *Journal of the ACM*, **11**(1):1–9, 1964.

[30] Klaas Sikkel. *Parsing Schemata*. Springer-Verlag, 1997.

[31] Robert F. Stärk. A direct proof for the completeness of SLD-resolution. In E. Börger, H. Kleine Büning, and M. M. Richter, editors, *Computation Theory and Logic* **89**, pages 382–383. Springer-Verlag, 1990.

[32] H. Tamaki. Stream-based compilation of ground I/O Prolog into committed-choice languages. In *Proc. Fourth International Conference on Logic Programming*, pages 376–393, Melbourne, Australia, 1987.

[33] Hisao Tamaki and Taisuke Sato. Unfold/fold transformation of logic programs. In *Proc. Second International Logic Programming Conference*, pages 127–138, 1984.

[34] Kazunori Ueda. Making exhaustive search programs deterministic. *New Generation Computing*, **5**:29–44, 1987.

In: Computer Science Research Trends
Editor: Casey B. Yarnall, pp. 239-265
ISBN 978-1-60021-518-6

Chapter 8

REAL-WORLD EVOLUTIONARY DESIGNS: SECURE EVOLVABLE HARDWARE FOR PUBLIC-KEY CRYPTOSYSTEMS

Nadia Nedjah [*] ***and Luiza de Macedo Mourelle*** [†]
Department of System Engineering and Computation, Engineering Faculty,
State University of Rio de Janeiro,
Rua São francisco Xavier, 524, Sala 5022-D,
Maracanã, Rio de Janeiro, Brazil

Abstract

In this chapter, we propose a methodology based on genetic programming to automatically generate data-flow based specifications for hardware designs of combinational digital circuits. We aim at allowing automatic generation of balanced hardware specifications for a given input/output behaviour. It minimises space while maintaining reasonable response time. We show that the evolved designs are efficient and creative. We do so comparing the obtained circuits of some benchmarks against those that were produced by human designers as well as to other evolutionary ones.

To emphasize the applicability of the methodology to real-world problems, we use genetic programming as an alternative methodology to automatically generate secure and minimal hardware designs of public-key cryptosystems such as RSA encryption system. We evolve optimal hardware circuits for modular exponentiation, which a cornerstone operation in almost every cryptographic system. The evolved circuits minimize both space (i.e. required gate number) and time (i.e. encryption and decryption time). The evolved designs are shielded against side-channel leakage and hence secure. The structure of the cryptographic circuit is random and so the private key cannot be deduced using known attacks. We compare our results against existing well-known designs, which were produced by human designers based on the binary method.

* E-mail address: nadia@eng.uerj.br; www.eng.uerj.br
† E-mail address: ldmm@eng.uerj.br

1. Introduction

Designing a hardware that fulfils a given function consists of deriving from specific input/output behaviour, an architecture that is operational (i.e. produces all the expected outputs from the given inputs) within a specified set of constraints. Besides the input/output behaviour of the hardware, conventional designs are essentially based on knowledge and creativity. These are two human characteristics too hard to be automated.

The problem of interest consists of designing efficient and creative circuits that implement a given input/output behaviour without much designing effort. The obtained circuits are expected to be minimal both in terms of space and time requirements: The circuits must be compact i.e. use a reduced number of gates and efficient, i.e. produce the output in a short response time. The response time of a circuit depends on the number and the complexity of the gates forming the longest path in it. The complexity of a gate depends solely on the number of its inputs. Furthermore, the design should take advantage of the all the kind of gates available on reconfigurable chip of field programmable gate array (FPGAs).

The three most popular are minimisation techniques are: algebraic method, Karnaugh map [10] and Quine-McCluskey procedure [8]. The algebraic method consists of applying some known algebraic theorems and postulates. This method depends heavily on the designer ability, as it does not offer general rules to assist her/him in recognising the theorem to apply. The Karnaugh map [10] is a matrix-based representation of logical functions and allows minimisation of up to 5-input functions. McCluskey procedure [8] is a tabular method and allows one to minimise functions of any number of inputs. Both Karnaugh map and McCluskey procedure produce a minimal sum of products. A combinational circuit based on this minimal form offers the shortest response time, but not at all the smallest size. However, in some cases, the designer great concern is the minimisation of the number of gates of the circuit as well as the signal propagation delay. Moreover, the McCluskey procedure needs an execution time that grows exponentially with the number of input signals. Furthermore, Karnaugh map and McCluskey procedure produces design that only use AND, OR and NOT gates and ignores all the rest of gates. So the designer needs to perform further refinement on the circuit yield by these methods in order to introduce other kind of gates such as XOR gates [20].

Evolutionary hardware is a hardware that is yield using simulated evolution as an alternative to conventional-based electronic circuit design. Genetic evolution [7] is a process that evolves a set of individuals, which constitutes the population, producing a new population. Here, individuals are hardware designs. The more the design obeys the constraints, the more it is used in the reproduction process. The design constraints could be expressed in terms of hardware area and/or response time requirements. The freshly produced population is yield using some genetic operators such as crossover and mutation that attempt to simulate the natural breeding process in the hope of generating new design that are fitter i.e. respect more the design constraints. Genetic evolution is usually implemented using genetic algorithms.

In this work, we design innovative and efficient evolutionary digital circuits. Circuit evaluation is based on their possible implementation using CMOS technology [5], [18], [21]. The produced circuits are balanced i.e. use a reduced number of gate equivalent and propagate result signals in a reduced response time such that the factor area$\times$performance is minimised. We do so using genetic programming.

The remainder of this chapter is divided in five sections. In Section 2, we describe the principles of genetic programming. In Section 3, we describe the methodology we employ to evolve new compact and fast hardware for a given input/output behaviour. In Section 4, we compare the discovered hardware against existing most popular ones. Finally, we draw some conclusions.

2. Genetic Programming

Genetic programming [9] is an extension of genetic algorithms. The chromosomes are computer programs and the genes are instructions. In general, genetic programming offers a mechanism to get a computer to provide a solution of problem without being told exactly how to do it. In short, it allows one to automatically create a program. It does so based on a high level statement of the constraints the yielded program should obey to. The input/output behaviour of the expected program is generally considered as an omnipresent constraint. Furthermore, the generated program should use a minimal number of instructions and have an optimal execution time.

Starting form random set of computer programs, which is generally called initial population, genetic programming breeds a population of programs through a series of steps, called generations, using the Darwinian principle of natural selection, recombination also called crossover, and mutation. Individuals are selected based on how much they adhere to the specified constraints. Each program is assigned a value, generally called its fitness, which mirrors how good it is in solving the program. Genetic programming [9] proceeds by first, randomly creating an initial population of computer programs; then, iteratively performing a generation, which consists of going through two main steps, as far as the constraints are not met. The first step in a generation assigns for each computer program in the current population a fitness value that measures its adherence to the constraints while the second step creates a new population by applying the three genetic operators, which are reproduction, crossover and mutation to some selected individuals. Selection is done with on the basis of the individual fitness. The fitter the program is, the more probable it is selected to contribute to the formation of the new generation. Reproduction simply copies the selected individual from the current population to the new one. Crossover recombines two chosen computer programs to create two new programs using single-point crossover as shown in Figure 1(a) or two-points crossover as shown in Figure 1(b). Mutation yields a new individual by changing some randomly chosen instruction in the selected computer program. The number of genes to be mutated is called mutation degree and how many individuals should suffer mutation is called mutation rate.

3. Evolving Hardware for Combinational Digital Circuits

There three main aspects in implementation of genetic programming [9], [13]: *(i)* program encoding; *(ii)* crossover and mutation of programs; *(iii)* program fitness. In this section, we explain how we treat these three aspects in our implementation.

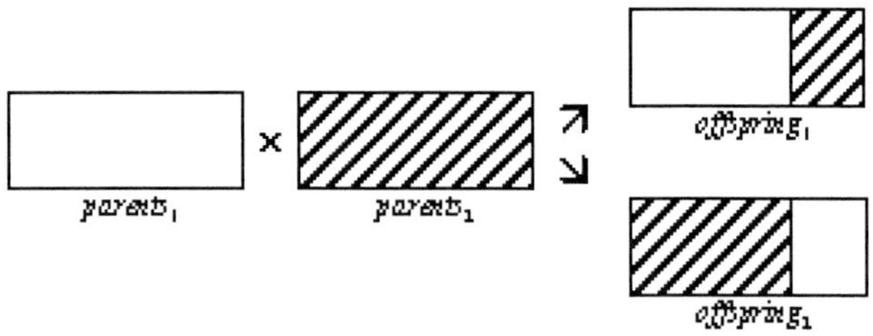

(a) single-point crossover

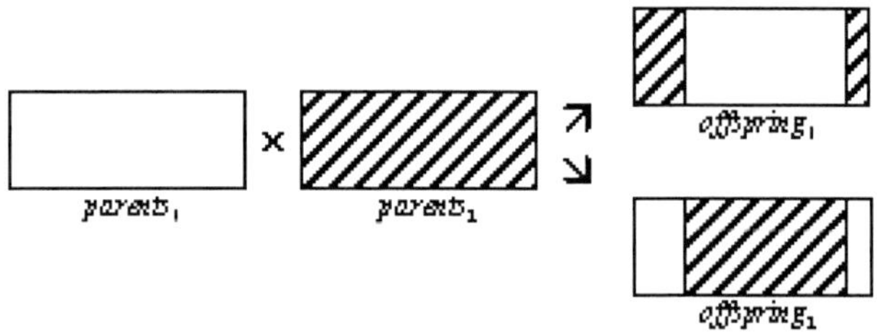

(b) double-point crossover

Figure 1. Types of crossover genetic operator.

3.1. Circuit Specification Encoding

Encoding of individuals is one of the implementation decisions one has to take in order to use evolutionary computation. It depends highly on the nature of the problem to be solved. There are several representations that have been used with success: *binary encoding* which is the most common mainly because it was used in the first works on genetic algorithms, represents an individual as a string of bits; *permutation encoding* mainly used in ordering problem, encodes an individual as a sequence of integer; *value encoding* represents an individual as a sequence of values that are some evaluation of some aspect of the problem; and *tree encoding* represents an individual as tree. Generally, the tree coincides with the concrete tree as opposed to abstract tree [1] of the computer program, considering the grammar of the programming language used.

Here a design is specified using register transfer level equations. Each instruction in the specification is an output signal assignment. A signal is assigned the result of an expression wherein the operators are those that represent basic gates in CMOS technology of VLSI circuit implementation and the operands are the input signals of the design. The allowed operators are shown in Table 1. Note that all gates introduce a minimal propagation delay as the number of input signal is minimal, which is 2.

A NOT gate inverts the input signal, an and-gate propagates a 1-signal when both input signals are 1 and 0-signal otherwise and an or-gate propagates a 0-signal when both input signals are 0 and 1-signal otherwise. An AND gate inverts the signal propagated by a NAND

Table 1. Node operators

Name	Symbol	Name	Symbol
NOT	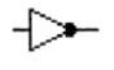	NAND	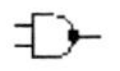
AND	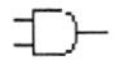	NOR	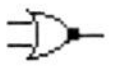
OR	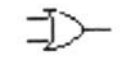	XNOR	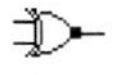
XOR		MUX	

gate while an OR gate inverts that propagated by a NOR gate. Note that, in CMOS technology, an and-gate is a NAND gate coupled with a NOT gate and an OR gate is a NOR gate followed by a NOT gate and not the inverse [5]. The XOR gate is a CMOS basic gate that has the behaviour of sum of products $x\bar{y} + \bar{x}y$ wherein x and y are the input signals. However, a XOR gate is not implemented using 2 AND gates, 2 NOT gates and an OR gate. A 2to1-multipliexer MUX is also a CMOS basic gate and implements the sum of products $x\bar{s} + ys$ wherein x and y are the first and the second input signals and s is the control signal. It is clear that a XOR and MUX gates are of the same complexity [5], [18].

For instance, a 2-bit multiplier has 4-bit result signal so an evolved register transfer level specification is as follows, wherein the input operands are $X = \langle x_1 x_0 \rangle$ and $Y = \langle y_1 y_0 \rangle$ and the output is the product $P = \langle p_3 p_2 p_1 p_0 \rangle$. The schematic of the digital circuit implementing the above specification is given in Figure 2.

$$\begin{array}{lcl} p_3 & \Longleftarrow & (x_0 \text{ AND } y_0) \text{ AND } (x_1 \text{ AND } y_1) \\ p_2 & \Longleftarrow & (x_0 \text{ NAND } y_0) \text{ AND } (x_1 \text{ AND } y_1) \\ p_1 & \Longleftarrow & (x_1 \text{ NAND } y_0) \text{ XOR } (x_0 \text{ NAND } y_1) \\ p_0 & \Longleftarrow & (y_0 \text{ AND } x_0) \text{ OR } y_0 \end{array} \tag{1}$$

We encode specifications using an array of concrete trees corresponding to its signal assignments. The ith tree represents the evaluation tree of the expression on the left-hand side of the ith signal assignment. Leaf nodes are labelled with a literal representing a single bit of an input signal while the others are labelled with an operand. The individual corresponding to above specification is shown in Figure 3.

3.2. Circuit Specification Reproduction

Crossover of circuit specification is implemented using a double-point crossover as described in Figure 1. One of the important and complicated operators for genetic programming is the mutation. It consists of changing a gene of a selected individual. The number of individuals that should suffer *mutation* is defined by the *mutation rate* while how many genes should be altered within a chosen individual is given by the *mutation degree*.

Here, a gene is the tree of the expression on the left hand side of a signal assignment. Altering an expression can be done in two different ways depending the node that was randomised and so must be mutated. A node represents either an operand or operator. In the former case, the operand, which is a literal representing a bit in the input signal, is

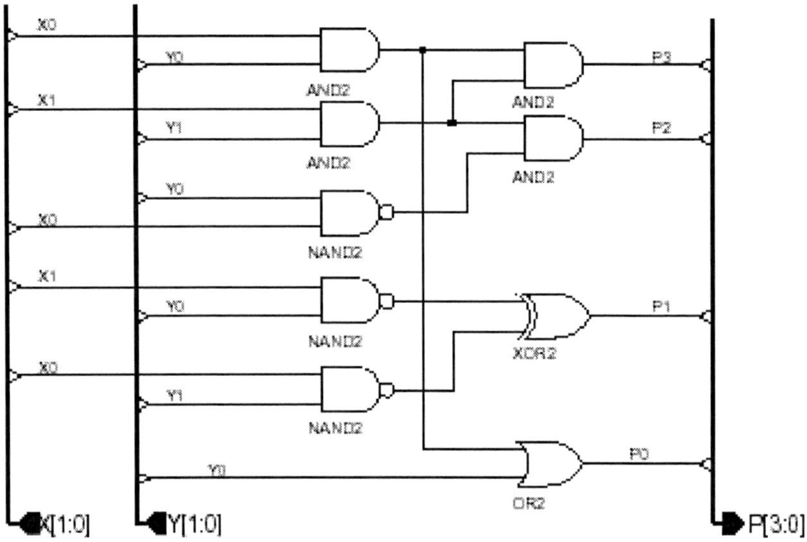

Figure 2. Evolved 2-bit multiplier.

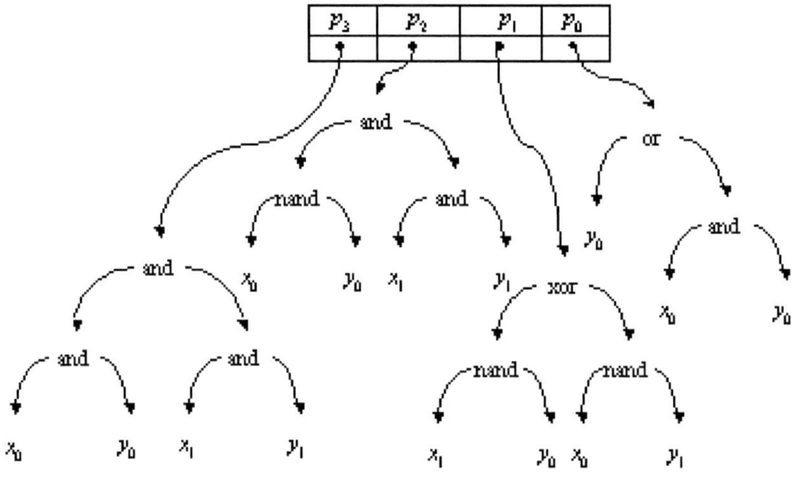

Figure 3. Chromosome for the evolved 2-bit multiplier.

substituted with either a literal or simple expression. The decision is random. In the case in which the operand has to be changed by another operand, the literal representing the bit of lesser significance in the binary notation of the input signal or that representing its most significant bit is used. This is performed as indicated by function mutate1 below, wherein $X = \langle x_{n-1}x_{n-2}\ldots x_1x_0\rangle$ is the signal obtained by the concatenation of all input signals:

$$mutate_1(x_i) = \begin{cases} x_{n-1} & i = 0 \\ x_{i-1} & \text{otherwise} \end{cases} \tag{2}$$

In the case of mutating an operand nodc to an operator node, we proceed as follows: First let x_i be the operand being mutated. We choose randomly an operator among those available. Let OP be this operator. Its first operand is x_i. So if the chosen operator is NOT then the operand node is mutated to NOT x_i. When the selected operator is binary, a new literal is generated using $mutate_1(x_i)$. Thus, in this case, x_i is mutated to either $x_i\text{OP}mutate_1(x_i)$, wherein OP is an available binary operator. If the chosen operator is MUX, then a third operand is generated using $mutate_1(mutate_1(x_i))$. Last but not least, when the selected operator is quaternary a fourth literal is generated in the same way, i.e. using $mutate_1(mutate_1(mutate_1(x_i)))$. This mutation procedure is implemented by function $mutate_2$ below wherein the notation $mutate_1^{[i]}$ represents the i times application of $mutate_1$ and #OP represents the arity of operator OP:

$$mutate_2(x_i) = \begin{cases} \text{NOT } x_i & \#\text{OP} = 0 \\ x_i \text{ OP } mutate_1^{[1]} & \#\text{OP} = 1 \\ x_i \text{ OP } mutate_1^{[1]} mutate_1^{[2]} & \#\text{OP} = 2 \\ x_i \text{ OP } mutate_1^{[1]} mutate_1^{[2]} mutate_1^{[3]} & \#\text{OP} = 3 \end{cases} \tag{3}$$

So far we explained how an operand node is mutated. Now, we describe the mutation process of an operator node. Let OP be the operator being changed. An operator node can be mutated to another operator node or to an operand node. In the latter case, a literal is randomised and used to substitute the operator node. In the former case, however, things become a little more complicated depending on the relation between the arity OP and that of the operator selected to substitute it, say OP/. So we mutate OP to OP/. When #OP = #OP/ we leave the operands unchanged. Note that this case happens only for binary operators. When #OP ¿ #OP/, we use only a random subset of OPs operands. Finally, i.e. when #OP ¡ #OP/, we generate a random set of literals using function $mutate_1$repetitively as in function $mutate_2$ above.

3.3. Circuit Specification Evaluation

Another important aspect of genetic programming is to provide a way to evaluate the adherence of evolved computer programs to the imposed constraints. In our case, these constraints are of three kinds. First of all, the evolved specification must obey the input/output behaviour, which is given in a tabular form of expected results given the inputs. This is the truth table of the expected circuit. Second, the circuit must have a reduced size. This constraint allows us to yield compact digital circuits. Thirdly, the circuit must also reduce the signal propagation delay. This allows us to reduce the response time and so discover

Table 2. Gate equivalent and propagation delays

Name	Gate equiv.	Delay (ns)
NOT	1	0.0625
AND	2	0.209
OR	2	0.216
XOR	3	0.212
NAND	1	0.13
NOR	1	0.156
XNOR	3	0.211
MUX	3	0.212

efficient circuits. In order to take into account both area and response time, we evaluate circuits using the $area \times performance$ factor. We evolve balanced digital circuits that implement a given behaviour that require a reduced hardware area and produce the result in a reduced time such that $area \times performance$ factor is minimal.

We estimate the necessary area for a given circuit using the concept of gate equivalent. This is the basic unit of measure for digital circuit complexity [5], [18]. It is based upon the number of logic gates that should be interconnected to perform the same input/output behaviour. This measure is more accurate that the simple number of gates [5].

When the input to an electronic gate changes, there is a finite time delay before the change in input is seen at the output terminal. This is called the propagation delay of the gate and it differs from one gate to another. Of primary concern is the path from input to output with the highest total propagation delay. We estimate the performance of a given circuit using the worst-case delay path. The number of gate equivalent and an average propagation delay for each kind of gate are given in Table 2. The data were taken form [5].

Let C be a digital circuit that uses a subset (or the complete set) of the gates given in Table 2. Let $Gates(C)$ be a function that returns the set of all gates of circuit C and $Levels(C)$ be a function that returns the set of all the gates of C grouped by level. For instance, applied to the circuit of Figure 2, it returns the set of sets $\{\{$AND, AND, NAND, NAND, NAND$\}$, $\{$AND, AND, XOR, OR$\}\}$. Notice that the number of levels of a circuit coincides with the cardinality of the set expected from function $Levels$. On the other hand, let $Value(T)$ be the Boolean value that the considered circuit C propagates for the input Boolean vector T assuming that the size of T coincides with the number of input signals required for circuit C. The fitness function, which allows us to determine how much an evolved circuit adheres to the specified constraints, is given as follows, wherein I represents the input values of the input signals while O represents the expected output values of the output signals of circuit C, n denotes the number of output signals that circuit C has and function $Delay$ returns the propagation delay of a given gate as shown in Table 2. For each difference between the evolved circuit output values and the expected output signals, penalty ψ is accumulated. Note that for a correct circuit the first term in the definition of function $Fitness$ is zero and so the value returned by this function is the factor $area \times performance$ of the evaluated circuit.

Table 3. Truth table of the example of circuit fitness evaluation

x_1	x_0	y_1	y_0	Z_2	Z_1	Z_0
0	0	0	0	0/0	0/0	0/1
0	0	0	1	0/0	0/0	0/1
0	0	1	0	0/0	0/0	0/1
0	0	1	1	0/0	0/0	0/1
0	1	0	0	0/0	0/0	0/1
0	1	0	1	0/0	0/0	0/1
0	1	1	0	0/0	0/0	1/0
0	1	1	1	0/0	0/0	1/0
1	0	0	0	0/0	0/0	0/1
1	0	0	1	0/0	0/0	1/0
1	0	1	0	0/0	1/1	1/1
1	0	1	1	0/0	1/1	1/0
1	1	0	0	0/0	0/0	0/1
1	1	0	1	0/0	0/0	1/0
1	1	1	0	0/0	1/1	1/0
1	1	1	1	1/1	0/0	0/0

$$
\begin{aligned}
Fitness(C) = & \sum_{j=0}^{n} \left(\sum_{i \mid Value(x_i) \neq y_{i,j}} \psi \right) \\
& + \sum_{g \in Gates(C)} GateEquiv(g) \times \sum_{l \in Levels(C)} \max_{g \in l} Delay(g)
\end{aligned} \tag{4}
$$

For instance, consider the evolved circuit of Figure 4. It should propagate the output signals of Table 3 that appear first (i.e. before symbol /) but it actually propagates the output signals that appear last (i.e. those after symbol /). Observe that signals Z_1 and Z_2 are correct for every possible input combination of the input signals. However, signal Z_0 is correct only for the combinations 1010 and 1111 of the input signals and so for the remaining 14 combinations, Z_0 has a wrong value and so the circuit should be penalised 14 times. Applying function $Gates$ to this circuit should return 5 AND gates and 3 NAND gates while function $Levels$ should return $\{\{$ AND, AND, NAND, NAND, NAND $\}, \{$ AND, AND, AND$\}\}$. If ψ is set to 10 then, function $Fitness$ should return $140+(5\times 2+3\times 1)+(0.209+0.209)$. This fitness sums up to 153.418.

In order to speed up the computation of the evolved circuit fitness, we take advantage of the parallelism of the central processing unit. This technique was first used by Poli in [16]. Instead of obtaining the output signal values one by one, one can compute them i.e. for all possible input signal combinations, in parallel. For instance, to compute the values of output signal $Z_2 \Longleftarrow (x_0 \text{ AND } y_0) \text{ AND } (x_1 \text{ AND } y_1)$ considering the circuit of Figure 4 and the values of Table 3, we proceed as follows:

1. Convert 0000111100001111, which is the content of column x_0 to integer value 3849 and 0101010101010101, which is the content of column y_0 to integer value 21849;

2. Compute the bitwise operation 3849 & 21849 = 2569;

3. Convert 0000000011111111, which is the content of column x_1 to integer value 255 and 0011001100110011, which is the content of column y_1 to integer value 51;

4. Compute the bitwise operation 256 & 21849 = 51;

5. Compute the bitwise operation 169 & 2569 = 1;

6. Convert 1 to its 16-bit binary representation 000000000000001, which is exactly the content of column Z_2.

The use of this technique to compute the first term of fitness of an evolved circuit speeds up the process to an order of magnitude of 10. Note that for circuits of more than 6 input signals, the bitwise operations need to be split out in several 16, 32 or 64-bit operations depending on the size of the memory word.

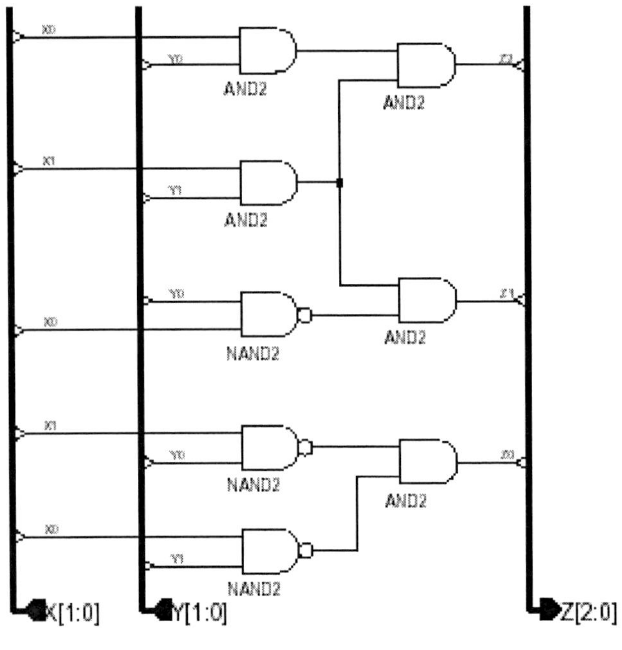

Figure 4. Evolved circuits for the input/output behavior of Table 3.

Table 4. Truth table of the first benchmark

x_2	x_1	x_0	Y
0	0	0	0
0	0	1	0
0	1	0	0
0	1	1	1
1	0	0	0
1	0	1	1
1	1	0	1
1	1	1	0

4. Evolutionary vs. Conventional Designs

In this section, we compare the evolutionary circuits yield by our genetic programming based evolution to those designed by a human as well as to those evolved by Coello's genetic algorithm [4].

The truth table of the first benchmark is given in Table 4. It has three-bits input signal $X = \langle x_2 x_1 x_0 \rangle$ and propagates a single-bit output signal Y.

For this circuit specified in Table 4, a human designer came with a digital circuit that uses 2 AND gates, 1 OR gate and 2 XOR gates. The output signal is computed as in signal assignment of Equation 5. The Coello's genetic algorithm evolved the circuit specified in signal assignment of Equation 6. It uses 1 XOR gate less than the human designed circuit.

$$Y \Longleftarrow x_0 \text{ AND } (x_2 \text{ XOR } x_1) \text{ OR } x_1 \text{ AND } (x_2 \text{ XOR } x_0) \tag{5}$$

$$Y \Longleftarrow x_0 \text{ AND } (x_2 \text{ OR } x_1) \text{ XOR } (x_2 \text{ AND } x_1) \tag{6}$$

Our genetic programming-based evolutionary computation yields two different circuits for the first benchmark. Both of them use 1 AND gate, 1 XOR gate and 1 MUX gate. The specifications of theses two circuits are given in signal assignment of Equation 7 and Equation 8 respectively:

$$Y \Longleftarrow \text{MUX } ((x_0 \text{ AND } x_1), (x_0 \text{ XOR } x_1), x_2) \tag{7}$$

$$Y \Longleftarrow \text{MUX } ((x_0 \text{ AND } x_2), (x_0 \text{ XOR } x_2), x_1) \tag{8}$$

The schematics of these two circuits are given in Figure 5. The circuit, we evolved needs less hardware area, propagates the output signal faster and so the factor area $\times$performance is minimised. The numerical figures are given in Table 6 at the end of this section.

Both the second and third benchmarks need a 4-bit input signal $X = \langle x_3 x_2 x_1 x_0 \rangle$ and yield a single-bit output signal Y. The fourth and fifth benchmarks also requires a 4-bit input signal X but the respective circuits propagate a 4-bit and 3-bit output signal respectively. The truth tables of the four benchmarks are summarised in Table 5 below. Note

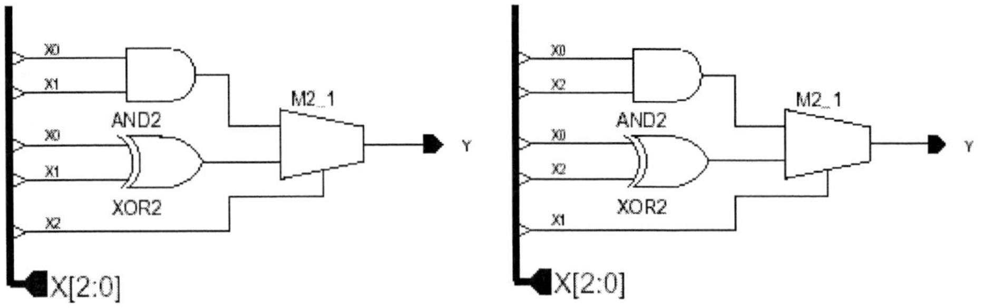

(a) First circuit (b) Second circuit

Figure 5. Schematics of the evolved circuits for the first benchmark.

Table 5. Truth tables of second, third, fourth and fifth benchmarks respectively

Input				2nd	3rd	4th Benchmark				5th Benchmark		
x_3	x_2	x_1	x_0	Y	Y	p_3	p_2	p_1	p_0	y_2	y_1	y_0
0	0	0	0	1	1	0	0	0	0	1	0	0
0	0	0	1	1	0	0	0	0	0	0	1	0
0	0	1	0	0	1	0	0	0	0	0	1	0
0	0	1	1	1	0	0	0	0	0	0	1	0
0	1	0	0	0	1	0	0	0	0	0	0	1
0	1	0	1	0	0	0	0	0	1	1	0	0
0	1	1	0	1	1	0	0	1	0	0	1	0
0	1	1	1	1	1	0	0	1	1	0	1	0
1	0	0	0	1	1	0	0	0	0	0	0	1
1	0	0	1	0	1	0	1	0	0	0	0	1
1	1	1	0	1	1	0	1	1	0	1	0	0
1	0	1	1	0	0	0	1	1	0	0	1	0
1	0	0	0	0	0	0	0	0	0	0	0	1
1	1	0	1	1	1	0	0	1	1	0	0	1
1	1	1	0	0	1	0	1	1	0	0	0	1
1	1	1	1	0	1	1	0	0	1	1	0	0

that the fourth benchmark is a simple 2-bit multiplier of $X = \langle x_3 x_2 \rangle$ times $Y = \langle x_1 x_0 \rangle$. (The notation of the input signals is purely for space sake!)

For the second example, a human designer came with a circuit that requires 4 AND gates, 1 OR gate, 2 XOR gates and 4 NOT gates. The specification of the signal assignments as follows:

$$Y \Longleftarrow ((\overline{x}_3 \text{ AND } x_1) \text{ XOR } (\overline{x}_0 \text{ AND } \overline{x}_2)) \text{ OR } ((\overline{x}_2 \text{ AND } x_0) \text{ AND } (x_3 \text{ XOR } \overline{x}_2)) \quad (9)$$

For the second benchmark, the Coello's genetic algorithm evolved the circuit specified in signal assignment of Equation 10. It uses 1 AND gate, 3 OR gates, 3 XOR gates and 1 NOT gate.

$$Y \Longleftarrow ((x_3 \text{ XOR } ((x_2 \text{ XOR } x_0) \text{ OR } (x_1 \text{ AND } x_0)) \text{ XOR } (\text{ NOT } ((x_3 \text{ OR } (x_1 \text{ OR } x_0))) \quad (10)$$

The schematics of the circuit we evolved are given in Figure 6. It needs less hardware area, but propagates the output signal a little bit slower than Coello's evolved circuit. However, the factor $area \times performance$ is the smallest. Again, the numerical figures are given in Table 6.

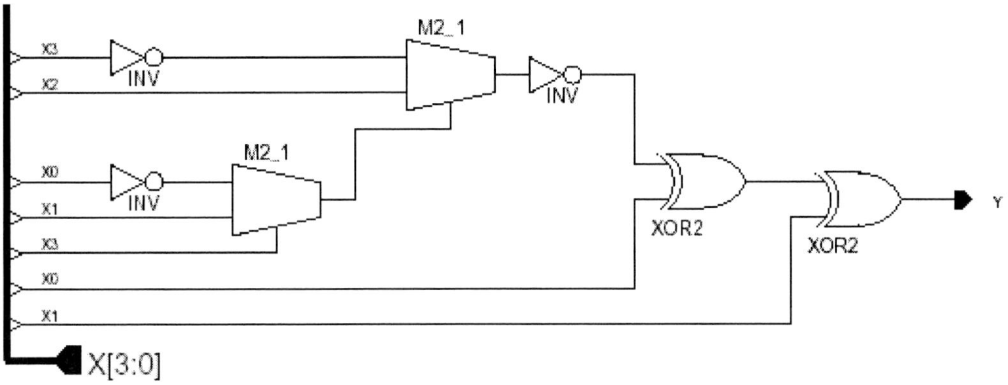

Figure 6. Evolved circuit for the second benchmark.

For the third benchmark, a human designer obtained a circuit that requires a total of 20 gates equivalent: 5 AND gates, 3 OR gates and 4 NOT gates. The specification of the signal assignment (11) is as follows:

$$Y \Longleftarrow ((\overline{x}_3 \text{ AND } \overline{x}_0) \text{ OR } (\overline{x}_3 \text{ AND } \overline{x}_2)) \text{ OR } ((x_2 \text{ AND } x_1) \text{ OR } (x_3 \text{ AND } \overline{x}_1 \text{ AND } x_0)) \quad (11)$$

For the third benchmark, the Coello's genetic algorithm evolved the circuit specified in signal assignment of Equation 12. It requires 2 AND gates, 2 OR gates, 2 XOR gates and 1 NOT gate.

$$Y \Longleftarrow \text{ NOT } (((x_2 \text{ AND } x_1) \text{ XOR } (x_2 \text{ OR } x_0)) \text{ AND } (x_1 \text{ OR } (x_3 \text{ XOR } x_0))) \quad (12)$$

The schematics of the circuit we evolved are given in Figure 7. The circuit, we evolved needs less hardware area, propagates the output signal faster than both circuits i.e. Coello's and the one designed by the human, and so the factor $area \times performance$ is minimised. Once more, the numerical figures about gate equivalent, delay and $area \times performance$ factor are shown in Table 6.

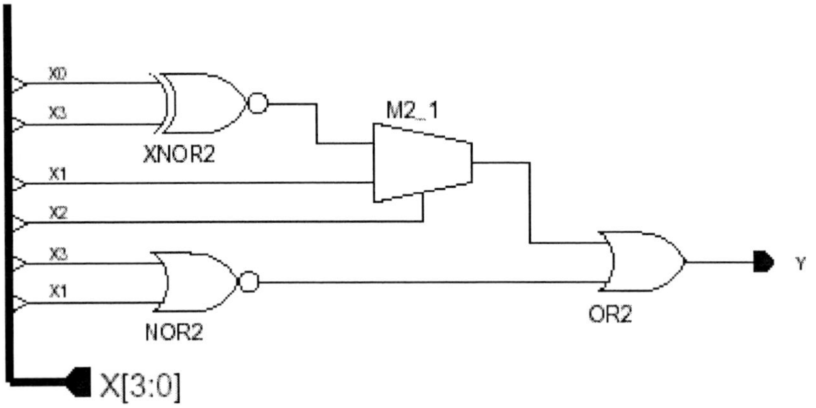

Figure 7. Evolved circuits for the third benchmark.

Another circuit was obtained for that benchmark. Its schematics are given in Figure 8 below. The circuit of is less efficient than that shown in Figure 7. However, it is more compact that the circuits obtained by the human designer and that evolved by Coello's genetic algorithm as it requires only 11 gates equivalent compared to 20 for the circuit designed by the human and 15 for Coello's evolved circuit. Moreover, the circuit of Figure 8 has a smaller propagation delay of 0.853ns compared to the 0.912ns required by the human designed circuit. The circuit presents a $area \times performance$ factor of 9.383.

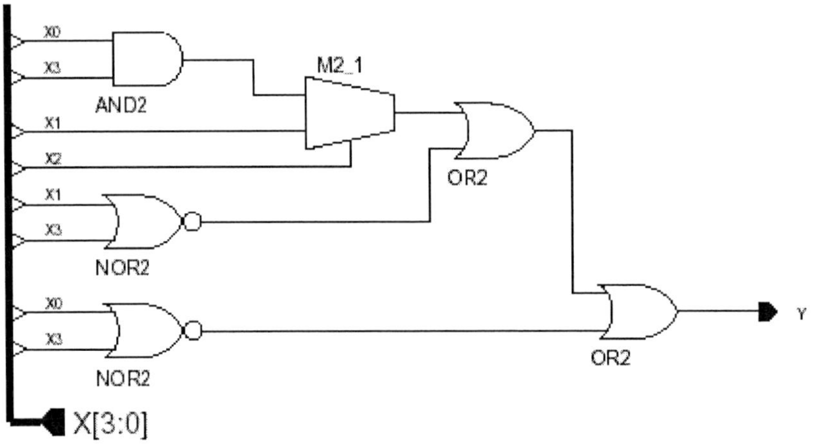

Figure 8. Less efficient evolved circuits for the third benchmark.

For the fourth benchmark, a human designer obtained a circuit that requires a total of 24 gates equivalent: 8 AND gates, 2 OR gates, 1 XOR gate and 1 NOT gate. The specification of the signal assignments is as follows (Equation 13), wherein $y_1 = x_3$ and $y_0 = x_2$ when Table 5 is used.

$$
\begin{aligned}
p_0 &\Leftarrow (x_0 \text{ AND } y_0) \\
p_1 &\Leftarrow (x_1 \text{ OR } x_0) \text{ AND } (y_1 \text{ OR } y_0) \text{ AND } ((x_1 \text{ AND } x_0) \text{ XOR } (y_1 \text{ AND } y_0)) \\
p_2 &\Leftarrow (x_1 \text{ AND } y_1) \text{ AND NOT } ((x_0 \text{ AND } y_0)) \\
p_3 &\Leftarrow (x_1 \text{ AND } y_1) \text{ AND } (x_0 \text{ AND } y_0)
\end{aligned}
\tag{13}
$$

For the fourth benchmark, the Coello's genetic algorithm evolved the circuit specified in the output signal assignments of Equation 14. It requires an area of 16 gates equivalent. That is 5 AND gates and 2 XOR gates.

$$
\begin{aligned}
p_0 &\Leftarrow (x_0 \text{ AND } y_0) \\
p_1 &\Leftarrow (x_0 \text{ AND } y_1) \text{ XOR } (x_1 \text{ AND } y_0) \\
p_2 &\Leftarrow (x_1 \text{ AND } y_1) \text{ XOR } ((x_0 \text{ AND } y_0) \text{ AND } (x_1 \text{ AND } y_1)) \\
p_3 &\Leftarrow (x_1 \text{ AND } y_1) \text{ AND } (x_0 \text{ AND } y_0)
\end{aligned}
\tag{14}
$$

The schematics of the circuit we evolved are given in Figure 9. The circuit we evolved needs the same hardware area as Coello's evolved circuit but it propagates the output signal faster than both circuits i.e. Coello's and the one designed by the human, and so the factor $area \times performance$ is minimised. The comparison of the numerical figures such as gate equivalent numbers, propagation delays and $area \times performance$ factors is detailed in Table 6.

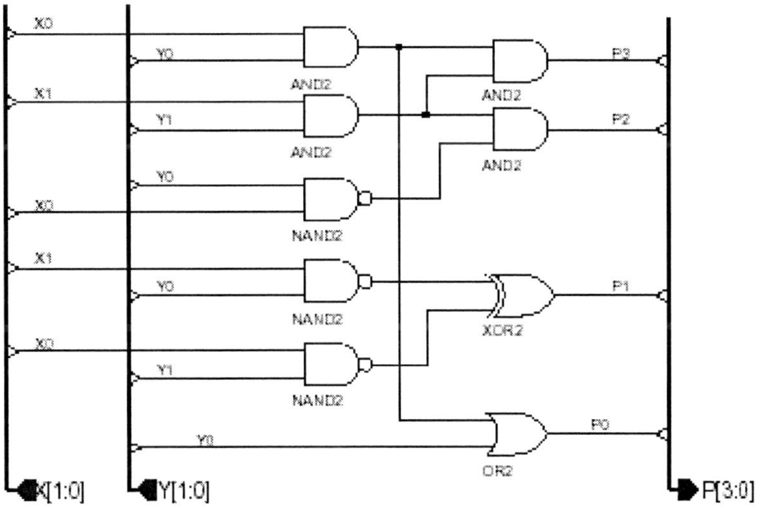

Figure 9. Evolved circuits for the fourth benchmark.

Finally for the fifth benchmark, a human designer engineered a circuit that requires a total of 34 gates equivalent, i.e. 7 AND gates, 4 OR gates, 2 XOR gate and 6 NOT gates. The specification of the signal assignments of Equation 15, wherein $y_1 = x_3$ and $y_0 = x_2$ when Table 5 is used.

$$\begin{aligned} y_0 &\Longleftarrow \text{NOT } (x_3 \text{ XOR } x_1) \text{ AND } \text{ NOT } (x_2 \text{ XOR } x_0) \\ y_1 &\Longleftarrow (\overline{x}_2 \text{ AND } x_0) \text{ AND } (\overline{x}_3 \text{ OR } x_1) \text{ OR } (x_3 \text{ AND } x_1) \\ y_2 &\Longleftarrow (\overline{x}_0 \text{ AND } x_2) \text{ AND } (\overline{x}_1 \text{ OR } x_3) \text{ OR } (\overline{x}_1 \text{ AND } x_3) \end{aligned} \quad (15)$$

For the same example, the Coelho's genetic algorithm evolved the circuit specified in the output signal assignments of Equation 16. It requires an area of 22 gates equivalent, which consist of 2 AND gates, 3 OR gate, 3 XOR gates and 3 NOT gates.

$$\begin{aligned} y_0 &\Longleftarrow \text{NOT } ((x_3 \text{ XOR } x_1) \text{ AND } (x_2 \text{ XOR } x_0)) \\ y_1 &\Longleftarrow (temp \text{ AND} \\ &\quad \text{NOT } (((x_3 \text{ XOR } x_1) \text{ AND } x_3 \text{ XOR } (x_0 \text{ OR } (x_3 \text{ XOR } x_1))) \text{ OR } temp)) \\ y_2 &\Longleftarrow \text{NOT } (((x_3 \text{ XOR } x_1) \text{ AND } x_3 \text{ XOR } ((x_0 \text{ OR } (x_3 \text{ XOR } x_1)) \\ &\quad \text{OR NOT } temp) \\ temp &\Longleftarrow (x_2 \text{ XOR } x_0) \text{ OR } (x_3 \text{ XOR } x_1) \end{aligned} \quad (16)$$

The schematics of the circuit that our genetic algorithm evolved are given in Figure 10. This circuit requires one gate equivalent more than Coello's evolved circuit but our circuit propagates the output signal much faster. Compared with the human designed circuit, our circuit has the same response time but needs a much smaller area. Furthermore, the factor $area \times performance$ for our circuit is minimal compared with the other two. The numerical figures such as gate equivalent numbers, propagation delays and $area \times performance$ factors are given in Table 6.

The convergence graphs of our evolutionary process for the benchmarks are shown in Figure 11. The best circuits for the 1st, 2nd, 3rd, 4th and 5th examples were obtained in 100, 280, 320, 370 and 540 generations.

In order to evolve the circuits for the proposed behaviours (see Table 5) and for all of the examples we used a population of 100 individuals. The double-point crossover was used with mutation rate of 0.5 and a mutation degree of 1.

Table 6 shows a comparison between the fittest circuits engineered by a human designer, Coello's genetic algorithm and our genetic algorithm, which is based on genetic programming. For each benchmark, the required hardware area, the necessary propagation delay and the product $area \times performance$ are detailed. The graphical representation of these figures is shown in the chart of Figure 12.

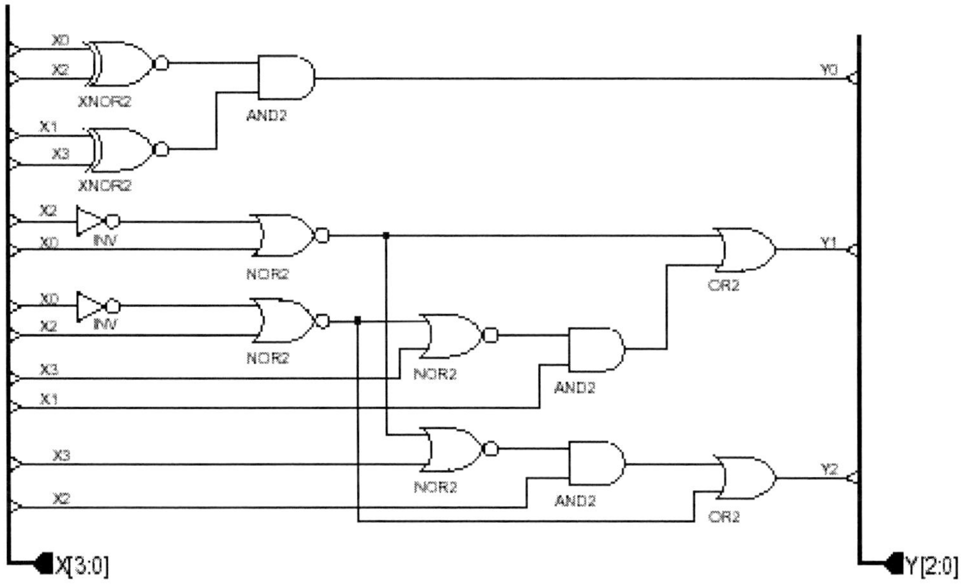

Figure 10. Evolved circuits for the fifth benchmark.

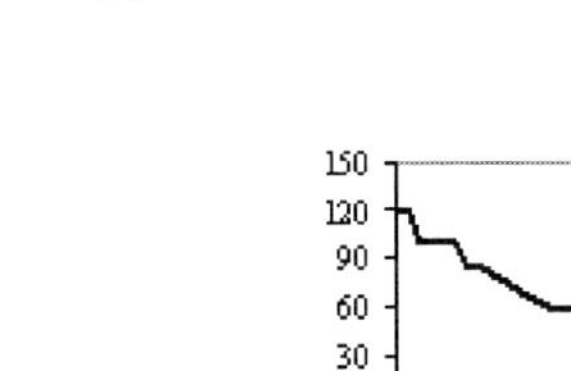

(a) First benchmark

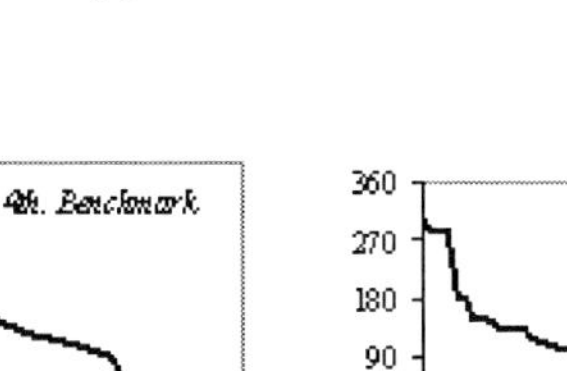

(b) Second benchmark

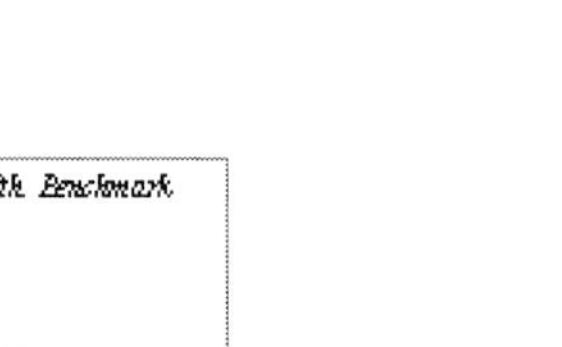

(c) Third benchmark

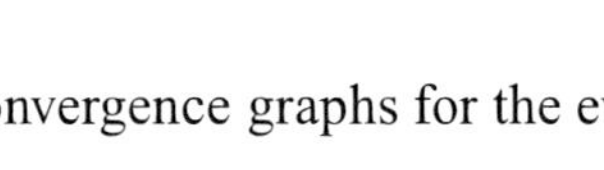

(d) Fourth benchmark

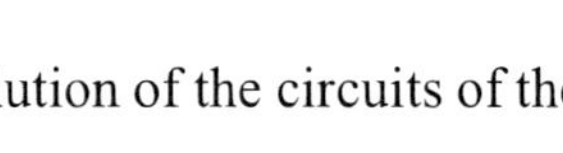

(e) Fifth benchmark

Figure 11. Convergence graphs for the evolution of the circuits of the benchmarks.

Table 6. Numerical comparison of the three methods

	area			delay			factor		
	Our	Coello	Human	Our	Coello	Human	Our	Coello	Human
1st	8	9	12	0.424	0.637	0.637	3.392	5.733	7.644
2nd	15	16	20	0.973	0.918	0.702	14.595	14.696	14.050
3rd	9	15	20	0.639	0.699	0.912	5.751	10.492	18.250
4th	16	16	24	0.425	0.842	0.853	6.800	13.472	20.472
5th	22	21	34	0.799	1.065	0.703	17.589	22.365	23.919

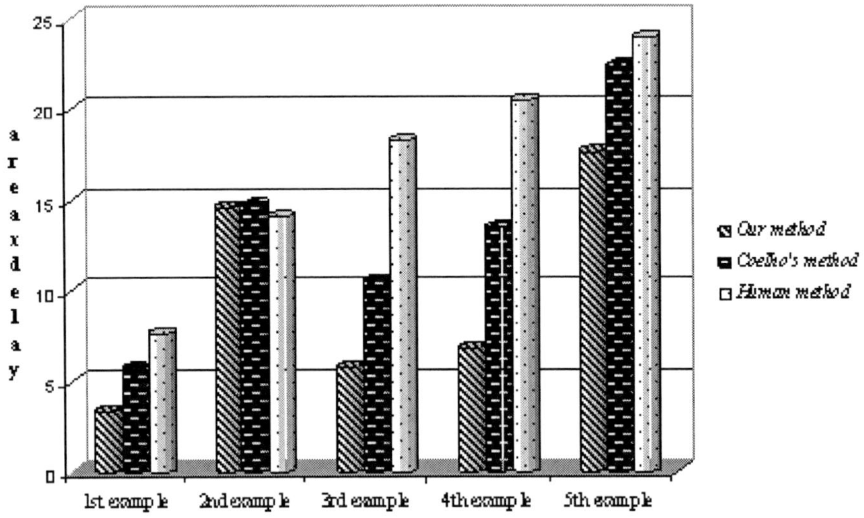

Figure 12. Graphical comparison of the $area \times delay$ factor for the three methods.

5. RSA-Based Cryptosystems

Cryptography is the science of keeping secrets secret. Its main task is to provide confidentiality by encryption methods. The original message, which can be some text, numerical data or any other kind of information, is usually called plaintext and the encrypted plaintext is called ciphertext. Information transmission between two parties through public channels occurs after plaintext T is encrypted into ciphertext C so that an eventual adversary third party in possession of c cannot derive any information about T. Cryptosystems must provide an encryption and a decryption algorithm. Existing cryptosystems can be classified into symmetric and asymmetric systems. Both encryption and decryption processes in symmetric cryptosystems depend on the same secret key while in asymmetric ones there exist a public key on which depends the encryption algorithm and another private key used by the decryption process.

A Rivest-Shamir-Adleman or simply RSA-based cryptosystem [17] is asymmetric. It consists of triple $\langle M, e, d\rangle$, which consists of the *modulus*, *public* and *private key* respectively. The modulus and the public key of the system are made public while the private key is kept secret. To build an RSA-based cryptosystem, one needs to:

1. Create two primes p and q;
2. Compute $M = p \times q$;
3. Calculate the value of *Euler totient* function defined for M as $N = \Phi(M) = (p-1)(q-1)$;
4. Choose e, such that the greatest common divisor of N and e is 1—$gcd(e, N) = 1$, with $e \neq 1$ and $e \neq N$;
5. Compute d such that $e \times d \equiv 1 \bmod N$. (This can be done using the extended Euclidean algorithm [11].)

Note the public and private keys of a given cryptosystem are non-negative integer smaller than its modulus, i.e. for the system defined by $\langle M, e, d\rangle$, we have $0 \leq e, d \leq M-1$. With modulus of reasonable length, i.e. about 1024 bits, solving the factoring problem i.e. discovering p and q, which will lead to discovering the private key is impossible considering the computation power and the factoring algorithms one disposes of nowadays.

Both the encryption and decryption algorithms in RSA-based cryptosystems are implemented using the same algorithm: modular exponentiation. That is, the *ciphertext* C is obtained from *plaintext* T by $C = T^e \bmod M$ and T is obtained from C by $T = C^d \bmod M$. This characteristic is very attractive and so it increased the popularity of RSA-based cryptosystems. Note that the plaintext and its corresponding ciphertext in a given RSA-based cryptosystem are non-negative integers smaller than the modulus.

The practicality of cryptosystem depends heavily on how fast the encryption and essentially decryption process can be done. Therefore, the practicality of RSA-based cryptosystems depends essentially on how fast modular exponentiation of large integers can be performed.

Clearly, modular exponentiation is the cornerstone operation in RSA-based cryptosystem. It consists of several successive modular multiplications. Modular multiplication is time consuming for large operands. Engineering fast public-key cryptography hardware needs either optimising the time consumed by a single modular multiplication or reducing the total number of modular multiplication performed or both of them [14], [3], [2], [19]. The so far engineered hardware designs using modular exponentiation as encryption process suffer from a very serious drawback that is called *side-channel leakage*. As the designs for modular exponentiation are regular and repetitive one can trace the data transfers between operations, which usually reveal the beginning of every long integer operation very clearly [12]. This allows one with an extra little effort to discover the private key of the cryptosystem. Here, we use evolutionary computation to discover new efficient, creative and above all secure hardware for RSA-based cryptosystems.

6. Evolutionary vs. Conventional Cryptographic Hardware

Several efficient designs for RSA-based cryptosystems were developed [14], [3], [2]. In the following, we compare two conventional designs: one sequential and the other parallel to the evolutionary design obtained.

First of all, we describe an sequential design based on the binary exponentiation method [6] we presented in earlier research work [14], [15]. Subsequently, we present the parallel design based on the same method.

The sequential straightforward binary exponentiation algorithm is given hereafter (Algorithm .1, wherein m is the number of digits in exponent e. Observe that the multiplication of line 5 of the algorithm depends on the result of the squaring of line 4.

The hardware architecture of Figure 13 includes two Montgomery modular systolic multipliers, i.e. MULTIPLIER$_1$ and MULTIPLIER$_2$.

Algorithm .1 Sequential binary modular exponentiation

Input. Plaintext/ciphertext T, private/public key e and modulus M
Output. Ciphertext/palintext R

1. int $R := 1$;
2. if $e_{k-1} = 1$ then $R := T$;
3. for $i := m - 2$ downto 0
4. $\quad R := R \times R \bmod M$;
5. $\quad$ if $e_i = 1$ then $R = R \times T \bmod M$;
6. return R; end.

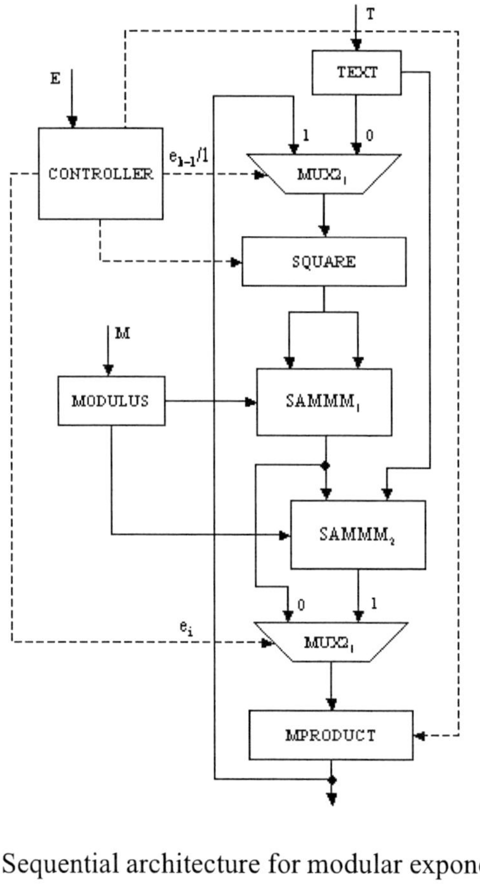

Figure 13. Sequential architecture for modular exponentiation.

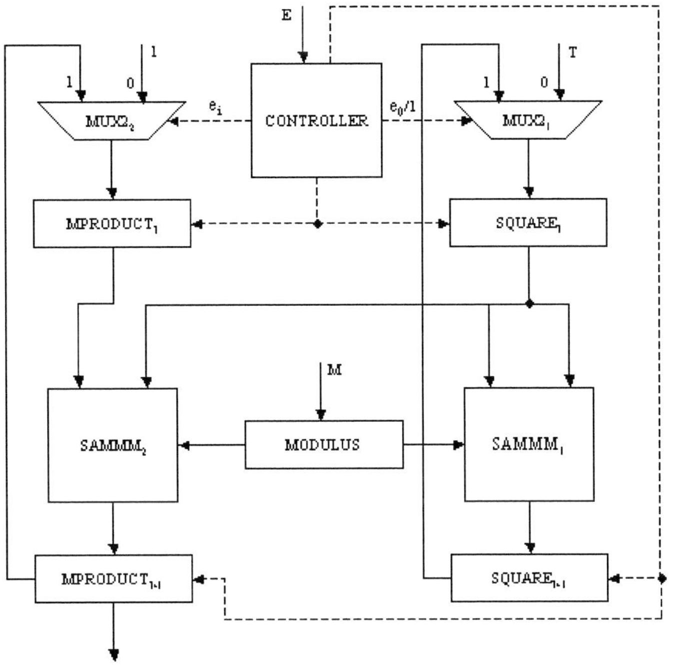

Figure 14. Parallel architecture for modular exponentiation

The parallel algorithm of binary exponentiation is given in Algorithm .2 and the parallel architecture in Figure 14.

Algorithm .2 Parallel binary modular exponentiation

Input. Plaintext/ciphertext T, private/public key e and modulus M
Output. Ciphertext/palintext R
1. int $R^{(0)} := 1$, $P^{(0)} := T$;
2. for $i := 0$ to $m - 1$
3. $P^{(i+1)} = P^{(i)} \times P^{(i)} \bmod M$;
4. if $e_i = 1$ then $R^{(i+1)} := R^{(i)} \times P^{(i)} \bmod M$
5. else $R^{(i+1)} := R^{(i)}$
6. return R;

end.

To illustrate the obtained results, we evolved a specification for two different modulus and keys, which are $M = 11$, $e = 5$ and $M = 13$, $e = 11$. The specification of the evolved RSA-based cryptographic hardware for the first case is given below, wherein the signals t_0 to t_3 are the bits constituting the plaintext from the less to most significant bit. For the sake of clarity, we use the expression prefix notation.

$$\begin{array}{lll} c_3 & \Longleftarrow & \text{AND}\ (\ \text{OR}\ (t_3,\ \text{NOR}\ (\ \text{NOR}\ (\bar{t}_0, t_2), \bar{t}_1)),\ \text{NAND}\ (\ \text{NOR}\ (\bar{t}_0, t_2), \bar{t}_2)) \\ c_2 & \Longleftarrow & \text{NOR}\ (\bar{t}_0, t_0) \\ c_1 & \Longleftarrow & \text{AND}\ (\ \text{NAND}\ (\ \text{NOR}\ (\bar{t}_0, t_2), \bar{t}_2),\ \text{OR}\ (t_3,\ \text{NOR}\ (\ \text{NOR}\ (\bar{t}_0, t_2), \bar{t}_1))) \\ c_0 & \Longleftarrow & \text{MUX}\ (\bar{t}_1,\ \text{NOR}\ (\bar{t}_0, t_2), \bar{t}_2) \end{array} \tag{17}$$

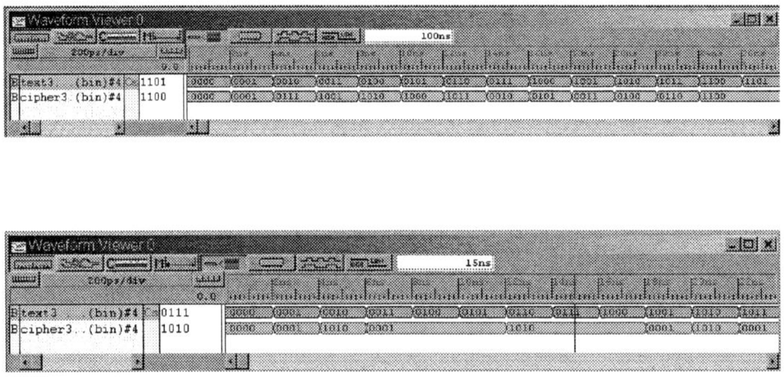

Figure 15. Simulation result of the evolved circuit behaviour.

The specification of the evolved RSA-based cryptographic hardware for the second case, i.e. $M = 13$, $e = 11$ is given below, wherein NUX stands for NOT MUX.

$$\begin{aligned}
c_3 &\Longleftarrow \text{NUX}\ (\ \text{AND}\ (\ \text{NAND}\ (t_2, \bar{t}_0),\ \text{NAND}\ (\bar{t}_1, t_2)), \\
&\quad \text{NOR}\ (\ \text{NOR}\ (\ \text{NOR}\ (\bar{t}_0, \bar{t}_2), \bar{t}_0),\ \text{AND}\ (\ \text{NAND}\ (t_2, \bar{t}_0), \bar{t}_1)), \\
&\quad \text{NOR}\ (\ \text{MUX}\ (\bar{t}_3, \bar{t}_1,\ \text{NOR}\ (\ \text{NOR}\ (\bar{t}_0, \bar{t}_2), \bar{t}_0)), t_3)) \\
c_2 &\Longleftarrow \text{NUX}\ (\ \text{NOR}\ (\ \text{MUX}(\bar{t}_3, 6,\ \text{NOR}\ (\ \text{NOR}\ (\bar{t}_0, \bar{t}_2), \bar{t}_0)), t_3), \\
&\quad \text{MUX}\ (\bar{t}_3, \bar{t}_1,\ \text{NOR}\ (\ \text{NOR}\ (\bar{t}_0, \bar{t}_2), \bar{t}_0)),\ \text{NAND}\ (\bar{t}_2, t_1)) \qquad (18) \\
c_1 &\Longleftarrow \text{MUX}\ (\ \text{NOR}\ (\ \text{NOR}\ (\bar{t}_0, \bar{t}_2), \bar{t}_0),\ \text{NOR}\ (\ \text{NOR}\ (\ \text{NOR}\ (\bar{t}_0, \bar{t}_2), \bar{t}_0), \\
&\quad \text{AND}\ (\ \text{NAND}\ (t_2, \bar{t}_0), \bar{t}_1)), \bar{t}_3) \\
c_0 &\Longleftarrow \text{AND}\ (\ \text{NAND}\ (\bar{t}_1, t_2),\ \text{MUX}\ (\ \text{NOR}\ (\ \text{NOR}\ (\bar{t}_3, \bar{t}_1), \\
&\quad \text{NOR}\ (\bar{t}_0, \bar{t}_2)), t_3,\ \text{NOR}\ (t_0, t_1)))
\end{aligned}$$

The schematics of the evolved circuit with the above given specification were generated automatically using the XILINX^{TM} Project Manager [22] and are shown in Figure 6.. The simulation waveform of the yielded circuit is depicted in Figure 15. The ciphertext for all possible values of the plaintext are considered.

We also generated automatically from the XILINX^{TM} Project Manager [22] the evolved circuit schematics using look-up tables. The basic unit is a four inputs and one output look-up table. The circuit requires 4 look-up tables as shown in Figure 17. We obtained and compared the size and response time for the evolved circuit with those corresponding to the sequential and parallel binary exponentiation implementations whose architectures are depicted in Figure 6 and Figure 14. Table 7 lists the collected data for $M = 13$ and $e = 11$.

The size of the circuits is expressed in terms of gate equivalent and the response time is nano-seconds. The data provide in this table show clearly that the evolved circuit is far better than the conventional designs: It requires much less hardware area and encrypts/decrypts much faster. Furthermore, it is shielded against side-channel leakage as it has no repetitive behaviour, as it is the case for conventional designs. However, the evolved circuit is not scalable. When a new cryptosystem with new modulus and/or key, a new design need be evolved from scratch.

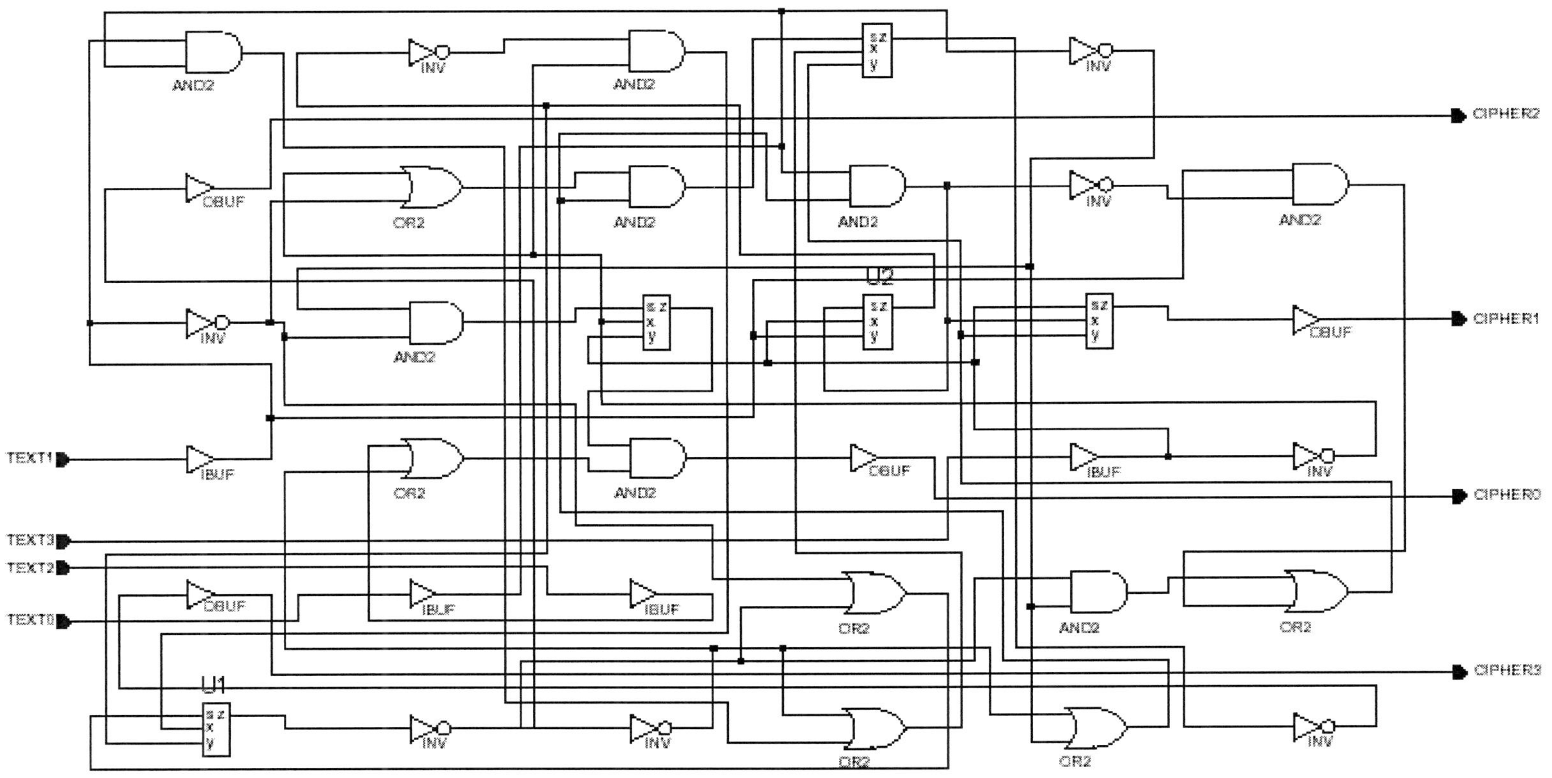

Figure 16. Schematics of the evolved RSA-based cryptographic hardware for M=13 and E=11.

Table 7. Conventional vs. evolutionary designs for the RSA-based cryptosystems

Design	Size	Time (ns)
Sequential Binary	524	7.321
Parallel Binary	992	4.992
Evolved circuit	24	1.313

7. Summary

In this chapter, we described an evolutionary technique to engineer compact, efficient and creative digital combinational circuit given the expected input/output behaviour. We explored the use of genetic programming and changing from the binary representation of circuits to a tree representation. We showed how to improve the evolution process by taking advantage of the central processing unit parallelism. An advantage of using genetic programming consists of the readability of the evolved circuit for synthesis using one of the available synthesis tools [15].

Our evolutionary process is multi-objective as it allows one to yield balanced i.e. compact and efficient digital circuits. The proposed fitness function evaluates a given circuit with respect to correctness, required hardware area and necessary propagation delay of output signals. It does so using the well-agreed-upon factor $area \times performance$ as a measure to appreciate the complexity of a digital circuit.

We evolved a better circuit for every example used by Coello et al. [12] compared to both human designs and evolved circuit that only consider the number of required gates to evaluate an evolved solution. On one hand, this proves that the fitness function we engineered is far more realistic than that of used by Coello et al. On the other hand, it also proves that evolutionary hardware can offer an alternative way to human design techniques to design efficient digital circuit. We showed how the evaluation of circuit fitness can be computed efficiently taking advantage of the inherent parallelism of the central processing units of the computers.

Using the evolutionary process described earlier, we automatically generate data-flow based specifications for hardware designs of public-key cryptosystems such as RSA-based encryption system. We focussed on evolving minimal hardware specifications, i.e. hardware that minimises both space (i.e. required gate number) and time (i.e. encryption and decryption time), for modular exponentiation. Modular exponentiation is the cornerstone operation of most public-key cryptosystems. The advantage of such evolved cryptosystems are shielded against side-channel leakage. However, the designs are not scalable, i.e. for new modulus or keys, one needs to evolve a new design. We compared our results against existing and well-known designs, which are based on the binary modular exponentiation method. The evolved is far more efficient in both required hardware area and encryption/decryption throughput.

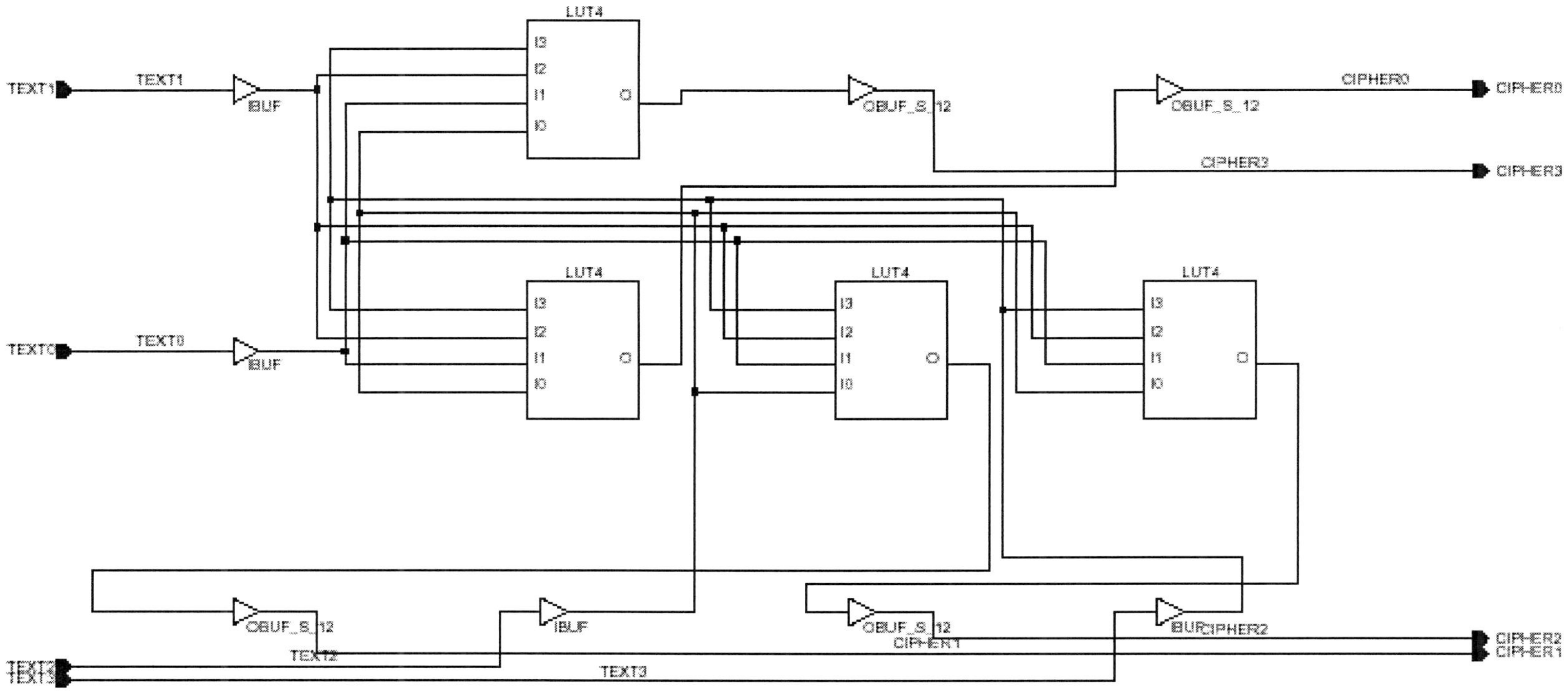

Figure 17. Circuit schematics using look-up tables generated by the Xilinx^{TM} project manager for the evolved circuit.

References

[1] Aho, A.V., Ravi, S. and Ullman, J.D., *Compilers: principles, techniques and tools*, Addison-Wesley, 1986.

[2] Blum, T. and Paar, C. Montgomery modular exponentiation on reconfigurable hardware, *Proceedings of the 14th. IEEE Symposium on Computer Arithmetic* , Australia, 1999.

[3] Brickell, E.F., A survey of hardware implementation of RSA, In G. Brassard, ed., Advances in Cryptology, *Proceedings of CRYPTO'98*, Lecture Notes in Computer Science 435:368-370, Springer-Verlag, 1989.13:39 3/6/2004

[4] Coello, C.A.C., Christiansen, A.D. and Aguirre, A.H., Towards Automated Evolutionary Design of Combinational Circuits, *Comput. Electr. Eng.*, **27**, pp. 1-28, 2001

[5] Ercegovac, M.D., Lang, T. and Moreno, J.H., *Introduction to digital systems*, John Wiley, 1999.

[6] Gordon, D.M., A survey of Fast exponentiation methods, *Journal of Algorithms* **27**, pp. 129-146, 1998.

[7] Haupt, R.L. and Haupt, S.E., *Practical genetic algorithms*, John Wiley and Sons, 1998.

[8] Karnaugh, M., A map method for synthesis of combinational logic circuits, Transactions of the AIEE, *Communications and Electronics*, **72**(I):593-599, November 1953.

[9] Koza, J.R., *Genetic Programming*. MIT Press, 1992.

[10] McCluskey, E.J., Minimisation of Boolean functions, *Bell Systems Technical Journal*, **35**(5):1417-1444, November 1956.

[11] Menezes, A.J., Van Oorschot, P.C., and Scott A. Vanstone. *Handbook of Applied Cryptography*. CRC Press, 1996.

[12] Dabbish, E.A. and Sloan, R.H., Power analysis attacks of modular exponentiation in smartcards, Proc. Cryptographic Hardware and Embedded Systems, *Lecture Notes in Computer Science*, vol. 1717, pp. 144-157, 1999.

[13] Miller, J.F. and Job, D., *Principles in the evolutionary design of digital circuits*

[14] Nedjah, N., Mourelle, L.M., Two hardware implementations for the Montgomery multiplication: sequential vs. parallel, *Proceedings of the 15th. Symposium on Integrated Circuits and Systems Design*, Porto Alegre, RS, Brazil, R. Reis and Calazans, N. (Eds.), IEEE Computer Society Press, pp. 3-8, 2002.

[15] Nedjah, N., Mourelle, L.M., Reconfigurable hardware implementation of Montgomery modular multiplication and parallel binary exponentiation, *Proceedings of the Euromicro Symposium on Digital System Design* , Dortmund, Germany, IEEE Computer Society Press, pp. 226-235, 2002.

[16] Poli, R., Efficient evolution of parallel binary multipliers and continuous symbolic regression expressions with sub-machine code GP, *Technical Report CSRP-9819*, University of Birmingham, School of Computer Science, December 1998.

[17] Rivest, R., Shamir, A. and Adleman, L., A method for obtaining digital signature and public-key cryptosystems, *Communications of the ACM*, **21**:120-126, 1978.

[18] Rhyne, V.T., *Fundamentals of digital systems design*, F.F. Kuo Ed. Prentice-Hall Electrical Engineering Series, 1973.

[19] Tiountchik, A., Systolic modular exponenti13:38 3/6/2004ation via Montgomery algorithm, *Electronic Letters*, **34**(9):874-875, 1998.

[20] Turton, B.C.H., Extending Quine-McCluskey for exclusive-or logic synthesis, *IEEE Transactions on Education*, **39**(1):81-85, February 1996.

[21] Thompson, A., Layzel, P. and Zebelum, R.S., Explorations in design space: unconventional design through artificial evolution, *IEEE Transactions on Evolutionary Computations*, **3**(3):81-85, February 1996.

[22] XILINX^{TM}, Inc., Foundation Series Software, `http://www.xilinx.com`, 2002.

In: Computer Science Research Trends
Editor: Casey B. Yarnall, pp. 267-278
ISBN 978-1-60021-518-6

Chapter 9

THE BIG BANG GRAPH—A COLORED-GRAPH REPRESENTATION OF SOFTWARE DESIGN

*Wei Li**
Computer Science Department, University of Alabama
in Huntsville, Huntsville, AL 35899

Abstract

A common approach of modeling software designs is to represent designs graphically. In the object-oriented design paradigm, the Unified Modeling Language (UML) is a widely used graphical design-modeling method. This paper discusses the big bang graph as an alternative or supplement to UML. We compare the big bang graph with the UML and present a translation framework between the two modeling methods. We show how to expand the big bang graph to model aspect-oriented and procedural designs. We discuss using the big bang graph as a design-analysis platform and the state space embedded in the graph. Finally, we discuss the potential applications of the big bang graph in formalizing software measures and calculating design.

1. Introduction

In designing a software system, we create models that serve several purposes. Design models help us archive designs; they help us communicate with customers and development partners; they provide a higher level of abstraction than source code for understanding designs; and they provide a platform for design analysis on various issues of interests, such as architecture, performance, and soundness of design. In this paper, we focus on the analysis-platform role of design models.

As an analysis platform, the Unified Modeling Language (UML) [12] provides multiple views on a design with easy visibility. For example, we can identify how many classes there are in a design and how these classes are generally coupled together (through the class relations depicted as directional edges) in the *class diagram*. If we want to know what users expect from a system, we can examine the *use case diagram*. We can find out what messages are sent and received in a system through the *sequence diagram*.

*E-mail address: wli@cs.uah.edu

In a design process, we often want to find information that is not directly visible in the UML diagrams. For example, the following two questions may interest us when we analyze a design:

- Q1: What is the set of objects that are declared as data attributes in a class?
- Q2: What is the set of objects that become visible in a class through parameter passing (via the methods)?

In UML, we have to analyze the text-based class specification to find the answer to Q1. We can also find the answer to Q1 in source code; however, source code often does not become available (probably piece by piece) until the end of the design process, thus making it difficulty to rely on source code to extract the information at early or middle stage of the design process. Finding the answer to Q2 takes more effort, although possible, from the UML modeling of a design. Once again, we have to analyze the text-based design specifications, subject to perhaps higher probability of making mistakes in the answer-finding process than before. Finding answers to additional questions in the UML models (diagrams) may get progressively more difficult. For example, the following question will take even more effort to answer:

- Q3: What is the intersection of the two type (class) sets for the two object sets?

We may want to know this intersection because we are curious about why objects of the same type (class) become visible in a class through two different means, and further, whether we can refactor the design to a better architecture (perhaps by reducing the size of the type-intersection set).

Finding the answers to these questions illustrates the difficulty of using UML as a design-analysis platform, especially when we want to explore the design features that are not visible in the UML diagrams. To address the concerns of design analysis, we want to find a design representation that can help answer these questions conveniently and efficiently. Li et al. introduced the *big bang graph* as an alternative or supplement to UML for modeling object-oriented designs [9]. For clarity, we briefly define the big bang graph in the following section before we move into the discussions on its use.

2. The Big Bang Graph

The big bang graph (BBG) is a colored, directed, and connected graph, which is modeled as BBG=(V, E), where V is a set of colored vertices and E is a set of colored and directed edges. The vertices of BBG represent design entities such as classes, objects, object references, and methods. The edges represent the primitive associations of the design entities. The objective of BBG is to model a software design that includes the most primitive (atomic) design features in a simple graph notation. We define a *primitive design feature* as a design notion that is irreducible (it cannot be further divided) in a particular paradigm. For example, the *object read* is a primitive design feature in the OO paradigm, whereas *object access* is not, because it can be further divided into two primitive features: *object read* and *object write*. It is worth noting that the inclusion of all primitive design features is the necessary but not sufficient condition for BBG, primarily because of the vertices. We can make all edges, but not all vertices, primitive for practical concerns. For example, the concept of a *class* is not primitive because it is composed of *attributes* and *operations*. Yet, we cannot represent attributes and operations without modeling classes in BBG. Therefore, it is sufficient to say that all edges in BBG represent primitive design features. BBG is a generic design representation and is capable of modeling aspect-oriented, object-oriented, and procedural designs. In this section, we only focus on the OO part of BBG for the convenience of comparing with UML; we will discuss how to use BBG to model aspect-oriented and procedural designs in the Flexibility of BBG section. Table 1 summarizes BBG vertices and their colors.

Table 1. BBG Vertices

Vertex	Color
Class	Red
Method	Black
Object	Cyan
Object Reference	Blue
System	Green

We assume that BBG models pure OO design where all variables are object references. The variables of the traditional primitive types—char, int, and float—that are popular in C++ and Java are abstracted as objects in BBG. The System vertex is the abstraction of all possible design entities that are outside the scope of a design. The design entities are linked through relations such as definition, reading from, writing to, and message passing. Each edge in BBG has a unique color which is based on the color of the source vertex and represents a semantics that goes from the source to destination vertex. Table 2 summaries the edges.

The From and To columns show the two vertices involved in a relation. The Rel. column defines a relation in the Z formal language [14]. The color of a relation is different from the color of its source vertex.

3. The State Space in BBG

BBG is a simple design representation with only two syntactical symbols (vertex and edge) and embeds a state space for the architectural aspect of design. The design state space can be modeled using Z. The foundation of the state space is composed of sets of vertices and relations.

For any specific design, we introduce four basic types for the vertices as follows: $[CLASSES, OBJECTS, OBJECTREFERENCES, METHODS]$, where

- *CLASSES* is the finite set of all classes in the design;
- *OBJECTS* is the finite set of all objects in the design;
- *OBJECTREFERENCES* is the finite set of all object references in the design;

Table 2. The Object-Oriented Design Relations

From	To	Edge Color	Rel.	Edge Semantics
Class	Class	red1	↔	Aggregation
Class	Class	red2	↔	Association
Class	Class	red3	↔	Containment
Class	Class	red4	↔	Dependency
Class	Class	red5	→	Inheritance
Class	Interface	red6	↔	Inheritance
Class	Method	red7	↔	Private instance method definition
Class	Method	red8	↔	Public instance method definition
Class	Method	red9	↔	Private class method definition
Class	Method	red10	↔	Public class method definition
Class	Method	red11	↔	Private instance final method definition
Class	Method	red12	↔	Public class final method definition
Class	Object Reference	red13	↔	Private instance attribute declaration
Class	Object Reference	red14	↔	Public instance attribute declaration
Class	Object Reference	red15	↔	Private class attribute declaration
Class	Object Reference	red16	↔	Public class attribute declaration
Method	Class	black1	↔	Being invoked through class
Method	Class	black2	↔	Returning type from method
Method	Method	black3	↔	Class method overriding
Method	Method	black4	↔	Instance method overriding
Method	Method	black5	↔	Method to method message
Method	Object Reference	black6	↔	Being invoked through object reference
Method	Object Reference	black7	↔	Object read
Method	Object Reference	black8	↔	Object write
Method	System	black9	↔	Method to system message
Object	Class	cyan1	→	Object type
Object	Method	cyan2	→	Object returned from method invocation
Object	System	cyan3	→	Object returned from System
Object Reference	Class	blue1	↔	Being read through class
Object Reference	Class	blue2	↔	Being written through class
Object Reference	Class	blue3	↔	Object reference type
Object Reference	Method	blue4	↔	Visibility through class attribute
Object Reference	Method	blue5	↔	Visibility through inherited attribute
Object Reference	Method	blue6	↔	Visibility through local variable
Object Reference	Method	blue7	↔	Visibility through parameter
Object Reference	Method	blue8	↔	Visibility through return
Object Reference	Object	blue9	↔	Referring to
Object Reference	Object Reference	blue10	↔	Assignment by equality
Object Reference	Object Reference	blue11	↔	Being read through object reference
Object Reference	Object Reference	blue12	↔	Being written through object reference
Object Reference	Object Reference	blue13	↔	Binding by reference
Object Reference	Object Reference	blue14	↔	Binding by value
System	Method	green1	↔	System to method message

- *METHODS* is the finite set of all methods in the design;

We then introduce a basic type for each colored edge (a relation) in Table 2; in this case, we have 43 edges, thus 43 finite sets as the basic types. For brevity, we omit the formal introduction of the relation basic types.

The relationship between the graph and the state space is as follows:

$$V == CLASSES \cup OBJECTS \cup OBJECTREFERENCES \cup METHODS\ [1].$$

We did not include the System vertex in V because it is out of the scope of any particular design. The set of edges—E—in BBG is the union of all the relations in Table 2. When BBG is expanded to model more design features, E will include more edges pertaining to the expanded design features. The evolution of an OO design is the refinement of V and E. When BBG is expanded to cover more design features, V will include the additional vertices pertaining to the expanded design features.

4. A Platform for Design Analysis

We can now search for answers to Q1-3 in the state space of BBG. Assume that the class of our interest is c. The answer (A1) to Q1 is the domain-restricted relation ClassInstanceAttribute, i.e., A1 $== \mathrm{dom}(\{c\} \lhd \mathit{ClassInstanceAttribute})$. ClassInstanceAttribute can be calculated as follows:

$$\text{ClassInstanceAttribute} == \text{PrivateInstanceAttribute} \cup \text{PublicInstanceAttribute}$$

PrivateInstanceAttributre and PublicInstanceAttribute are two basic types; PrivateInstanceAttribute is the set of red13 edges and PublicInstanceAttribute is the set of red14 edges.

Finding the answer to Q2 takes some effort. ran $(\{c\} \lhd \text{ClassAllMethod})$ is the set of locally defined methods in c. ClassAllMehtod is calculated as follows:

$$\text{ClassAllMethod} == \text{ClassPrivateInstanceMethod} \cup \text{ClassPublicInstanceMethod} \cup \text{ClassPrivateClassMethod} \cup \text{ClassPublicClassMethod}$$

ClassPrivateInstanceMethod (red7), ClassPublicInstanceMethod (red8), ClassPrivateClassMethod (red9), and ClassPublicClassMethod (red9) are four basic types. BindingByReference (blue13) and VisibilityThroughParameter (blue7) are also two basic types. BindingByReference $\fatsemi$ VisibilityThroughParameter is the set of object reference-to-method pairs (object references that become visible in methods through parameter binding). Restricting the range of the set to the set of methods in c gives us all object reference-to-method pairs in c; its domain is the answer (A2) to Q2, i.e.,

$$A2 == \mathrm{dom}((\mathit{BindingByReference} \fatsemi \mathit{VisibilityThroughParameter}) \rhd (\{c\} \lhd \mathit{ClassAllMethod}))$$

[1]This definition of V is for the completeness of the graph, not for formal analysis in Z because the union of basic types does not make sense in Z.

$T1 == \operatorname{ran}(A1 \lhd \mathit{ObjectReferenceType})$ is the set of classes that are used as types for the objects in A1. $T2 == \operatorname{ran}(A2 \lhd \mathit{ObjectReferenceType})$ is the set of classes that are used as types for the objects in A2. $T1 \cap T2$ is the answer to Q3. If the sets are constructed by an automated design tool in the modeling process, finding the answers to Q1-3 become much easier and more accurate than in UML.

5. The State Space

The Z schema language allows us to specify a state via a state schema and an operation via an operation schema. When an operation schema is executed, it changes the system state from a state (the pre-state) to another state (the post state). The state space embedded in BBG provides an opportunity for formal specification and checking of architectural design. The state space is made of sets of vertices and edges in BBG. These sets are part of the architectural design of an OO system. We can use a state schema to describe a system state and an operation schema to define a design step that changes the system state. This specification allows us to precisely define each individual design action as it relates to the system architecture depicted by the state space in BBG. For example, we can specify an operation schema for adding a method into the architecture of a design by specifying those sets in the state space that the added method will potentially affect. We then define the constraints of adding the method in the predicate part of the operating schema by linking the method to classes, other methods, objects, and potentially other aspects of the architectural design that are related to use case, use-case scenarios, and aspects (we will show how to model these additional features in the Flexibility of BBG section). The operation schema gives us the opportunity to check the sanity of our thoughts about adding the method. For instance, we can use the operator *pre* to calculate the precondition to see whether our method-adding operation is a full or partial function; we probably want to convert a partial function into a full function. We can also check the effect of two architectural design operations by using schema calculus and the predicates in the two operation schemas. This step-by-step check in architectural design is largely assumed to be sane and correct in the current design practice.

6. Comparing BBG with UML

As an alternative modeling method to UML, what are the benefits and drawbacks of BBG? First, BBG offers precision in design modeling. To create a design in BBG, designers must be more precise about their design decisions than they do in UML. There is an argument that precision can be a hindrance to design modeling at early stage of design because we are not very certain about which direction the design should go and want to keep the modeling deliberately vague. This argument is valid. However, a design model will progress and eventually be refined to a more precise state; this is the time when BBG can help the most. Although we can refine UML models to a more precise state, UML relies on text description to specify more detailed design decisions, whereas the precise modeling of design in BBG is shown on the graph, The benefit of visible design precision, however, does bring a drawback—the crowded graph that is difficult to view in its entirety. Because we depict the lowest level of design decisions in BBG, we will definitely get an unwieldy graph with many colored edges connecting vertices. For this drawback, we acknowledge that BBG is a more effective and efficient modeling platform for design analysis (especially formal analysis) than it is for visual examination of designs. We can overcome this drawback partially if we view a region of the design at a time. For example, we may want to examine the portion of BBG for a particular class, object, or method.

The second benefit of BBG is its state space for design. As we illustrated in the examples of the previous section, the state space provides ample opportunity for conducting various design analyses. This benefit becomes more apparent when an automated tool constructs and updates the state space during design process. The answers to the three questions have precise representations in the design state space; thus it is easy for an automated tool to find them.

The third benefit of BBG is its syntactical simplicity. Any BBG has only two syntactical symbols: vertex and colored (and directional) edge. This benefit can become a drawback depending on your view point. UML has many syntactical symbols in many different diagrams. Although this feature of UML is not necessarily undesirable (because UML purposely create many different views of a design for various view points), it does, however, make analyzing a design across different view points more difficult than in BBG.

7. The Conversions Between the Two Models

If both UML and BBG correctly model the same design, we should be able to create one graph from the information in the other for the design features that are present in both graphs.

7.1. The Class Diagram

The class diagram of UML depicts two aspects of a design: the set of classes and their relations. The set of classes in a design is a basic type in BBG, i.e., CLASSES. The class relations are scattered in five primitive relation sets in BBG: Containment, Aggregation, Association, Dependency, and Inheritance; each one of them is a set of single-color edges. The conversion between the two graphs is straight forward. In an UML class diagram, the text-based class specification (the invisible part) may accompany the visible graph. Because there is no standard on how much (or little) specification must be in a class diagram, it is difficult to propose a formal conversion for text-based specification. However, whatever the information that is in the class specification of an UML class diagram is visible in BBG, thus present in the state space.

7.2. The Object Diagram

The object diagram of UML depicts a set of objects and their associations. In BBG, the object associations are manifested through the associations of their perspective object references. Therefore, the homogeneous relations on OBJECTREFERENCES include the necessary and sufficient information to draw the object diagrams (subject to domain or range restrictions to the set of objects of interest).

7.3. The Sequence Diagram

The sequence diagram in UML depicts three aspects of a design: a set of messages, an use case (or use-case scenario) that triggers the messages, and a time order of the messages. The modeling of use case and use case-related design features are in Table 4, which will be introduced later in the Flexibility of BBG section. We can find the association between an use case and the set of methods that are involved in implementing the use case through a series of relation operations involving *use case module* and *use case slice*; this set of methods corresponds to the set of messages in the sequence diagram. Here, we note one missing piece of information in BBG—the time order of the methods. The state space of a design in BBG is not capable of expressing time order, although we know the set of methods involved in response to a use case. This time order is implied in the top-down time line of the sequence diagram.

8. The Flexibility of BBG

BBG is a flexible modeling technique, i.e., we can expand BBG to cover more design features by adding more vertices and relations. This flexibility can extend to other design paradigms. For instance, we can use BBG to model aspect-oriented designs [1, 2, 4, 13] by expanding Table 1 and Table 2. We use the notations introduced by Jacobson and Ng [6] as an example to show how to model aspect- and use case-related design features in BBG. Table 3 is the addition to Table 1 and Table 4 is the addition to Table 2.

Table 3. BBG Additional Vertices

Vertex	Color
Actor	Magenta
Advice	Brown
Aspect	Gold
Interface	Purple
Pointcut	Pink
Use Case	Yello
Use Case Module	Cocoa
Use Case Slice	Lilac

If we expand the OO design state space by creating additional sets pertaining to the added vertices and relations in Table 3 and Table 4, we have the design state space for aspect-oriented designs.

We can also use BBG to model procedural designs. In procedural design, we already have two levels of graph modeling—the *structure chart* for the call-return architecture and *flow chart* for function design. Modeling flow chart in BBG is simple. All we need to do is to color the flow chart. Assume that we use four colors for the vertices in the flow chart: one for the entry vertex, one for the exit vertex, one for the sequential vertex, and one for the decision vertex. We use one color for the edge to indicate the execution flow change from

Table 4. The Aspect-Oriented (and Use-Case) Design Relations

From	To	Edge Color	Rel.	Edge Semantics
Actor	Use Case	magenta1	$\leftrightarrow$	Actor use
Advice	Pointcut	brown1	$\rightarrow$	Advice to Pointcut
Aspect	Pointcut	gold1	$\leftrightarrow$	Aspect pointcut inclusion
Component	Class	pumpkin1	$\leftrightarrow$	Component-class inclusion
Component	Component	pumpkin2	$\leftrightarrow$	Component usage
Component	Interface	pumpkin3	$\leftrightarrow$	Provided interface
Component	Interface	pumpkin4	$\leftrightarrow$	Required interface
Pointcut	Class	pink1	$\rightarrowtail$	Pointcut to class
Pointcut	Method	pink2	$\rightarrowtail$	Pointcut to method
Pointcut	Object Reference	pink3	$\rightarrowtail$	Pointcut to object reference
Pointcut	Pointcut	pink4	$\leftrightarrow$	Pointcut equivalence
Use Case	Use Case	yellow1	$\leftrightarrow$	UC extension
Use Case	Use Case	yellow2	$\leftrightarrow$	UC inclusion
Use Case	Use Case	yellow3	$\leftrightarrow$	UC generalization
Use Case	Use Case Module	yellow4	⤖	Use-case realization
Use Case	Use Case Scenario	yellow5	$\leftrightarrow$	Use-case implementation
Use Case Module	Use Case Module	cocoa1	$\leftrightarrow$	UCM extension
Use Case Module	Use Case Module	cocoa2	$\leftrightarrow$	UCM generalization
Use Case Module	Use Case Module	cocoa3	$\leftrightarrow$	UCM inclusion
Use Case Module	Use Case Slice	cocoa4	⤖	UCM-UCS specification slice
Use Case Module	Use Case Slice	cocoa5	⤖	UCM-UCS analysis slice
Use Case Module	Use Case Slice	cocoa6	⤖	UCM-UCS design slice
Use Case Module	Use Case Slice	cocoa7	⤖	UCM-UCS implementation slice
Use Case Module	Use Case Slice	cocoa8	⤖	UCM-UCS test design slice
Use Case Module	Use Case Slice	cocoa9	⤖	UCM-UCS test implementation slice
Use Case Slice	Aspect	lilac1	$\leftrightarrow$	UCS-aspect inclusion
Use Case Slice	Component	lilac2	$\leftrightarrow$	UCS-component inclusion
Use Case Slice	Method	lilac3	$\leftrightarrow$	UCS-method inclusion
Use Case Slice	UML	lilac4	$\leftrightarrow$	UCS implementation
Use Case Slice	Use Case Slice	lilac5	$\leftrightarrow$	UCS-UCS extension
Use Case Slice	Use Case Slice	lilac6	$\leftrightarrow$	UCS-UCS inclusion
Use Case Slice	Use Case Slice	lilac7	$\leftrightarrow$	UCS-UCS generalization
Use Case Slice	Use Case Slice	lilac8	⇸	UCS trace

one vertex to another. We assume that each decision vertex has already been normalized to a single primitive predicate. The colored flow chart can be easily integrated into BBG by linking the entry point of the flow chart with the method vertex where the flow chart belongs with a new colored edge underlying the *method execution* semantics.

Modeling structured chart in BBG is similar to the modeling of flow chart—we need to color the vertices and the call-return edges. However, we cannot tie the colored structure chart into an object-oriented or aspect-oriented design model as we can with a colored flow chart, because the call-return architecture is not compatible with the two design models.

9. Applications of the Big Bang Graph

In addition to modeling and analyzing designs, BBG can also be used to formalize software measures and help use calculate designs.

The BBG modeling of designs provides a platform for formally defining software measures and linking the formal definition explicitly to design features in BBG. For instance, we can define a characteristic set for the CTM metric [8] as follows:

$$
\begin{array}{l}
[C] \\
ctmCS : \mathbb{P}\ MethodToMethodMessage \\
\hline
C \subseteq CLASSES \\
\#C = 1 \\
ctmCS = \forall m : \mathbb{P}\ METHODS \mid m = \mathrm{ran}(C \lhd ClassInstanceMethod \cup \\
\quad ClassClassMethod) \bullet ctmCS = m \lhd MethodToMethodMessages \rhd m
\end{array}
$$

The cardinality of ctmCS set is the value of the CTM metric. The characteristic set (ctmCS) of the CTM metric has all the message edges that originate from the class and go to the object references (or other classes in case of static method invocations) of other classes in the design. The class that the metric measures is passed as the parameter to the definition. The messages destined for System were excluded from the metric definition because System is out of the scope of the design. In the context of formally defined metrics, we can express design heuristics or rules formally for verification purpose. For instance, for the ctmCS set, we have the statement: $\forall c: CLASSES; m1, m2: METHODS \mid m1 \mapsto m2 \in ctmCS[\{c\}/C] \bullet ctmCS[\{c\}/C] \Rightarrow (\exists\ or: OBJECTSREFERENCES \bullet m2 \mapsto or \in MethodBeingInvokedThroughObject \land or \in \mathrm{dom}\ (Visibility \rhd \{m1\}) \lor (\exists\ c: CLASSES \bullet m2 \mapsto c \in MethodBeingInvokedThroughClass)$

> For any correct and non-empty design, the message-receiving method has to be invoked through a design unit: an object reference or a class. If the message-receiving method is invoked through an object reference, the object reference must be visible in the message-sending method (a class in the *CLASSES* set is visible to other classes by default). This statement is not a theorem in the BBG-Z system because it cannot be deduced from the definition predicate. However, it has an important empirical implication: methods can only send messages to those object references or classes that are visible to them.

The formally defined metrics in BBG has three benefits. First, the metrics are precisely defined in a formal language. Second, the definition of a metric is directly tied with certain design features that are directly visible in BBG. Last, as the CTM metric example illustrated, we can build empirical design experience (heuristics) into statements and check the correctness of design against these empirical experience via design and metrics analyses.

We can use BBG as a platform for calculating an optimal design structure. For instance, given an established BBG, adding a method to the design is equivalent to finding a position in BBG for the added method and link the method with the rest of the graph via various colored edges that are determined by a set of constraints. Among many possible means of putting a method into BBG, perhaps a better or optimal place for the added method can be calculated through graph theories or known mathematical techniques. The current design practice determines where to put a method based on the designer's intuition: a less scientific decision than the calculation via mathematics.

We can use BBG to study the ramifications of graph theories in software design. We can also use BBG to investigate many social phenomena such as the small-world phenomenon [11, 5, 7], the link prediction [10], and clustering [3]. The study of graph theories and the graph-related phenomena is possible on BBG, but not on UML diagrams.

10. Conclusion

We presented the big bang graph as a new graph-based design modeling technique. This new technique can be used as either an alternative or supplement to UML. We showed how to use the big bang graph to model object-oriented, aspect-oriented, and procedural designs. We also indicated several potential applications of the big bang graph. For designers who have used UML comfortably and efficiently, we do not recommend that the big bang graph replaces UML as the modeling method; rather the big bang graph can be used as a supplement to the UML design models for more precise and detailed design documentation, especially if designers want to perform some formal analysis on the design.

References

[1] Baniassad, E.; Clements, P.C.; Araujo, J.; Moreira, A.; Rashid, A.; and Tekinerdogan, B. Discovering Early Aspects *IEEE Software* 2006, (1), 61-69.

[2] Beuche, D. and Beust, C. AOP Has Yet to Prove Its Value *IEEE Software* 2006, 23(1), 73-74.

[3] Davis J.A. Clustering and structural balance in graphs *Human relations* 1967, 20, 180-187.

[4] Griswold, W.G.; Sullivan, K.; Song, Y.; Tewari, N.; Cai, Y.; and Rajan, H. Modular Software Design with Crosscutting Interfaces *IEEE Software* 2006, 23(1), 51-60.

[5] Guare, J. *Six Degree of Separation: A Play* Vintage Books 1990, New York, NY.

[6] Jacobson, I.; and Ng, P *Aspect-Oriented Software Development with Use Cases*; Addison Wesley: Upper Sanddle River, NJ, 2005.

[7] Kleinberg, J. The small-world phenomenon: an algorithmic perspective *The Proceedings of the 32nd ACM Symposium on Theory of Computing (STOC 2000)* 2000, 163-170.

[8] Li, W. Another metrics suite for object-oriented programming *J. Systems and Software* 1998, 44(2), 155-162.

[9] Li, W.; Zhang, H.; and Shatnawi, R. A Graph-Based Representation of Object-Oriented Design *Proceedings: International Conference on Software Engineering Research and Practice (SERP'06)* Las Vegas, Nevada, June, 2006.

[10] Liben-Nowell, D. and Kleinberg, J. The link predication problem for social networks *The Proceedings of the Twelfth Annual ACM International Conference on Information and Knowledge Management (CIKM'03)* 2003, 556-559.

[11] Milgram, S. The small world problem *Psychology Today* 1967, 60-67.

[12] Object Management Group (2005), Unified Modeling Language (UML), Version 2.0 http://www.omg.org.

[13] Diaz-Pace, J. A. and Compo, M. R. Analyzing the role of aspects in software design *Communications of the ACM* 2001, 44(10), 66-73.

[14] Spivey, M. *The Z Notation: A Reference Manual*; Prentice Hall International Computer Press: Upper Saddle River, NJ, 1992.

In: Computer Science Research Trends
Editor: Casey B. Yarnall, pp. 279-287

ISBN: 978-1-60021-518-6

Chapter 10

GRAPH BASED PRIVATE KEY CRYPTO-SYSTEM

Abderezak Touzene * ***and Vasyl Ustimenko*** [1#]
College of Science Sultan Qaboos University, Sultanate of Oman
[1] Institute of Mathematics, University of Maria Courie Sklodovska
Lublin 20-031, Poland

Abstract

Our symmetric key crypto-system is based on walks on a bipartite graph. The general idea is to treat vertices of a graph as messages and arcs of a certain length as an encryption tool. Starting from the plain text (vertex v_1 of graph), we consider a one-step walk as an arc that connect v_i to the next vertex v_{i+1} and which uses one character of the password. The adjacency matrix of this graph consists of a simple system of equations. A plain data is seen as an n-tuple in a Galois finite field GF(2^8). We show that using this special family of graphs, for any password of length m, $m<(n+5)/2$, any cipher data (vertex in the graph) will have a unique path (walk) in the graph. Furthermore, our crypto-system has a linear complexity and it resists to different type of adversary attacks.

Keywords: Cryptography, graphs, symmetric encryption, virtual organizations, e-commerce.

1. Introduction

Everyday, hundreds of thousands of people interact electronically, whether it is through e-mail, e-commerce (business conducted over the Internet), or cellular phones. The need for secure communications is more profound than ever. The emergence of e-organizations such as e-learning; e-business and e-government, shall rely on a secure way for online transactions. In order to secure data for storage or transmission, an encryption algorithm transform it into a cipher text (scrambled text) that would be difficult for any unauthorized person to discover its true meaning. Cryptographic techniques can be used to protect the privacy of data. It can provide "digital signature" to guarantee users authenticity.

---

* E mail address: touzene@squ.edu.om
# E mail address: vau@roller.ukma.kiev.ua

There are two classes of crypto-systems: private-key (symmetric key) and public key crypto-systems. Symmetric key encryption uses the same key for both encryption and decryption. The algorithm used to perform encryption may be well known. The most widely used algorithm is the Data Encryption Standard (DES), created during the 70's. DES is badly compromised today. Electronic Frontier Foundation put together a hardware box to crack DES within a day. Triple DES was the answer to many of the shortcomings of DES. It is a variant of DES existing software. It has also the advantage of proven reliability and a longer key length that eliminates many of the shortcut attacks. However, even this more powerful version of DES may not be strong enough to protect data for very much longer and needs replacement. To this end, the National Institute of Standards and Technology (NIST) developed the Advanced Encryption Standard (AES) as a replacement for DES.

In symmetric key crypto-systems both parties in communication (Encryption/Decryption) should have the same key. With a big organization you can physically distribute keys to users by some secure channel (courier, most likely). However, this is vulnerable if your courier is not secure. A bigger problem occurs when you want to communicate with someone you have never met before from another organization, symmetric key distribution problem.

The second class of crypto-systems is public key crypto-systems. It solves at least the problem of key distribution. In this case, there are two keys: one public, which means known to everybody. Any e-organization may have its specific public key published to all its customers. The public key, used only for encryption, when the private key is kept secret and it is used for decryption. The most famous public key crypto-system is RSA, which relies on the difficulty of fast factoring large prime numbers. In practice, public key crypto-systems are slow, compared to symmetric key crypto-systems, by an order of about 1,000. This leads to hybrid crypto-systems, where a public key system is used to distribute a "session key", and the symmetric key is used for the bulk of communications.

In this paper we propose a fast and reliable symmetric key encryption tool for any type of data, because it uses binary code. More precisely, the unit of information is the byte. Any type of data such as text file, word document, picture, sound or movie is in fact a succession of bytes. In [1] we presented an encryption tool based on walking on graph. This paper extends that work by proposing a new type of graph of high girth which is stronger in term of adversary attacks. The general idea is to treat vertices of a graph as messages and arcs of a certain length as an encryption tool (see [2], [3]). A plain text is seen as a succession of n bytes or more precisely, an n-tuple in a Galois finite field $GF(2^8)$ (see [4] [5]). Starting from the plain text (vertex v_1 of graph), we consider a one-step walk as an arc that connect v_1 to the next vertex v_2 using the first character of the password. A move from v_i to v_{i+1} involves an arc which consists of the ith character of the password. The adjacency matrix of this graph consists of a simple system of equations. This system of equations is expressed in term of operations (additions and multiplications) in the finite field $GF(2^8)$ [6].

The rest of this paper is organized as follows: Section 2 focuses on some theoretical background. Section 3, presents our encryption tool and its implementation. Section 4 presents some experimental measurements for our algorithm. Section 5, concludes the paper.

2. Theoretical Background

We consider the following general idea of walks on graphs as a nonlinear encoding tool. Let G be a simple bipartite graph and $V(G)$ its set of vertices. The vertices in $V(G)$ are n-tuple (x_0, x_2, ... , x_{n-1}), where x_i's are elements of $GF(2^8)$ (bytes which represent data to be encrypted) and n is the size in bytes of this data. We refer to v_1 the vertex, which represents the plain data before encryption. To encrypt the data we use a key or password of length m, $\rho = (p_1, p_2, \ldots, p_m)$, where p_i's are password characters such as p_i is different from p_{i+2}, $i=1, \ldots, m-2$. Each arc of the graph G represents one possible character. As an example the vertex v_1 (plain data) is adjacent to *256* vertices, each vertex v_2 corresponds to an encrypted message using the first element of the password p_1 (one-step walk). The second step walk consists on encrypting the message of the vertex V_2 using the second character of the password p_2 (arc labeled p_2) to reach a vertex v_3 and so on. The last step walk will be from vertex v_{m-1} to reach vertex v_m the final cipher, using the last character of the password p_m. See figure 1.

In our algorithm, we use a special cases of graphs, called parallelotopic graphs with no cycles, for which the probability *pkey* to guess the plain text can be easily computed. We assume without loss of generality that our graph is k-regular (k= 256). Parallelotopic graphs have the following graph coloring property: a special coloring of arcs induces the coloring of vertices, such that the neighborhood of each vertex is a set of vertices with different colors. Note that *parallelotopic* is also referred in the literature as *rainbow* [7]. In this situation, the string of colors (elements of the chosen alphabet) uniquely determines the walk (path). The decryption process corresponds to the reversed path. Let us consider this situation in more details. We consider the parallelotopic graphs for which arcs represents words in a certain alphabet M. We say that $G=(G, M, \pi)$ is a parallelotopic graph over a finite set M if we have a surjective function π:

$\{V(G)\} \rightarrow M$ such that for every pair (v, c), $v \in V(G)$, $c \in M$, there is a unique neighbor u of v satisfying $\pi(u)=c$. We refer to the function π as a labeling. It is clear that a parallelotopic graph $G = (G, M, \pi)$ is an $|M|$-regular graph. We can consider M as the set of colors, and π as a coloring of the vertices of G such that for any given vertex v, and any color c, there exists exactly one neighbor u of v of color c. Examples of parallelotopic graphs of high girth with the important extremal properties are given in [8]. Let G be a parallelotopic graph and let us consider an operator $N(t, v) = u$, where u is the neighbor with color t of a vertex v in the parallelotopic graph G. If $(t_1, t_2, \ldots, t_{n-1}, t_n)$, $t_i \in M$, is a tuple such that t_i is different from t_{i+2}, then the path $(v, v_1=N(t_1, v), v_2=N(t_2, v_1), \ldots, v_n=N(t_n + a, v_{n-1}))$, where a is the first byte of the plain text, is a path of the graph G. This path is the encoding sequence for any chosen vertex v. The decryption process uses the reverse path $(v_n, v_{n-1}=N^{-1}(t_n -1, v_n),), \ldots, v_1 =N^{-1}(t_2, v_3), v=N^{-1}(a, v_1)$. The decryption key is $(t_{n-1}, t_{n-2}, \ldots, t_2, a)$. Note that the value of a is available at the decryption process side as $a=f - t_n$, where f is the first byte of the final cipher text.

More topological properties of our bipartite graph G are discussed in [8] [9]. Different applications of this family of graphs can be found in [10]. In this paper, we will use these families of graphs to develop an efficient and secure encryption tool. In what follows we present in more details our encryption and decryption algorithm. We start by giving a definition of our graph vertices and then their adjacency. A simple system of equations describes the vertex adjacency. In our graph, we have two sets of vertices namely the set of points P and the set of lines L. The following will represent a vertex point *(p)* and a vertex line *[l]*:

$$(p)=(p_1, p_{1,1}, p_{1,2}, p_{2,1}, p_{2,2}, p'_{2,2}, p_{2,3}, p_{3,2}, p_{3,3}, p'_{3,3}, \ldots, p_{i,i}, p_{i,i+1}, p_{i+1,i}, p_{i+1,i+1}, p'_{i+1,i+1}, \ldots)$$

$$[l]=(l_1, l_{1,1}, l_{1,2}, l_{2,1}, l_{2,2}, l'_{2,2}, l_{2,3}, l_{3,2}, l_{3,3}, l'_{3,3}, \ldots, l_{i,i}, l_{i,i+1}, l_{i+1,i}, l_{i+1,i+1}, l'_{i+1,i+1}, \ldots).$$

The component of both *(p)* and *[l]* are elements of $GF(2^8)$. The set of vertices P and L are n-dimensional vector spaces over the finite field $GF(2^8)$. We define a walk by moving from a point vertex to a line vertex then from the line vertex a point vertex and so on (see figure 1).

We define the point and line adjacency relation by the following simple system of equations:

$$\begin{aligned}
l_{11} - p_{11} &= l_1 p_1 \\
l_{12} - p_{12} &= l_{11} p_1 \\
l_{21} - p_{21} &= l_1 p_{11} \\
l_{i,i} - p_{i,i} &= l_1 p_{i-1,i} \\
l'_{i,i} - p'_{i,i} &= p_1 l_{i,i-1} \\
l_{i,i+1} - p_{i,i+1} &= p_1 l_{i,i} \\
l_{i+1,i} - p_{i+1,i} &= l_1 p'_{i,i}
\end{aligned} \qquad (1)$$

(The last four equations are defined for $i \geq 2$). Note that l_1 or p_1 are the free parameter of the system of equation (1). In each walk number j, l_1 or p_1 will be set to α_j, the jth character of the password (see figure 1). α_j is also called the color of the incident vertex (cipher text).

We denote our bipartite graph $D(n, q)$, where $q=2^8$, corresponding to the elements of the Galois field $GF(2^8)$ and n is the size of the data to be encrypted (in bytes). It is easy to see that the graph $D(n, q)$ is regular of degree q and $|P|=|L|=q^n$.

Proposition1. The graph D(n, q) has:

- *No cycle of length 4, for $n=2$.*
- *No cycle of length 6, for $n=3$.*
- *No cycle of length $n+5$, for $n>3$.*

Proof. Uses induction on n, see [8].

The above proposition is very important, it states that if we use these graphs as an encryption tool for a data file of size n (bytes) with a password of length $m<(n+5)/2$, each password will have a unique walk path. Starting from the same plain data file different passwords will produce different cipher data files. In practice, the password length condition can be easily verified because in general the size of the data files n (kilo-bytes) is much larger than m the length of password (from *10* to *30* bytes). Since there is only a unique path password $(\alpha_1 \alpha_2 \alpha_3 \ldots \alpha_m)$ from the vertex v_1 plain data to the vertex v_m, which represent the encrypted data. For the decryption procedure, the same unique path traversed backward from

v_m to v_1 is used. In fact the decryption process uses the same algorithm as the encryption but using a reversed password $(\alpha_m \alpha_{m-1} \ldots \alpha_2 \alpha_1)$.

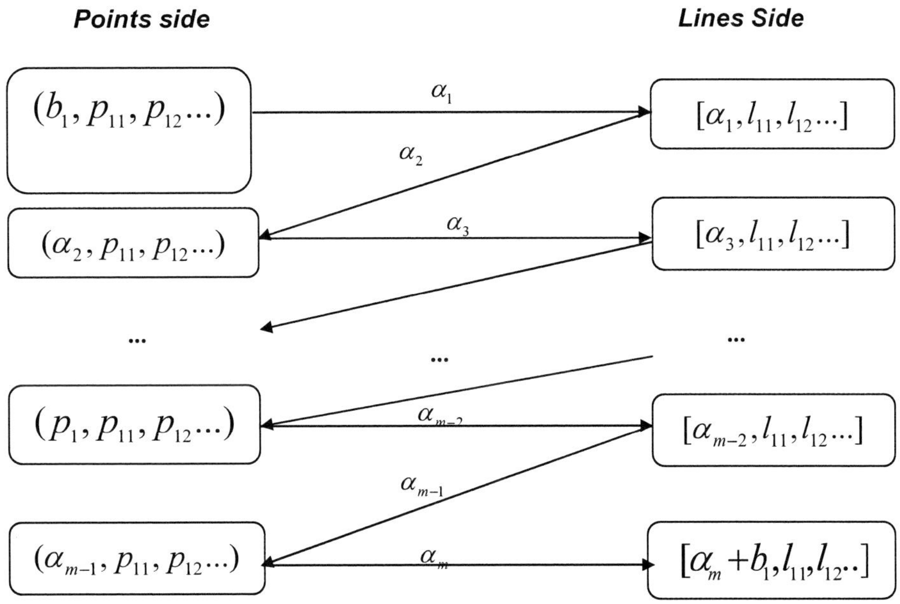

Figure 1. Walks using a password $\alpha_1\, \alpha_2\, \alpha_3 \ldots\, \alpha_m$

Example: We illustrate our encryption and decryption algorithm using a small size file $n=3$ bytes. Assume that the plain text vertex $v_1 = (p_1\, ,\, p_{1,1}\, ,\, p_{1,2}\,)$, where the $p_{i,j}$'s are byte values. We use a password of length two, *key*= $\alpha_1\, \alpha_2$. As discussed earlier, the encryption key is $(\alpha_1,\ \alpha_2 + p_1)$. Starting our encryption process from the plain text, point vertex v_1, a first walk step using the first character of the password α_1 reaches the line vertex $v_2 = [l_1\, ,\, l_{1,1}\, ,\, l_{1,2}]$ such as (see equations 1):

$$l_1 = \alpha_1\, ;\ l_{1,1} = l_1 p_1 + p_{1,1} = \alpha_1 p_1 + p_{1,1}\, ;\ l_{1,2} = l_{11} p_1 + p_{1,2} = (\alpha_1 p_1 + p_{1,1})\, p_1 + p_{1,2}\, .$$

From the vertex line v_2 using the second character of the password α_2, we move to the point vertex $v_3 = (pp_1,\ pp_{1,1},\ pp_{1,2})$ such as:

$pp_1 = \alpha_2 + p_1;\ pp_{1,1} = l_{1,1} - l_1\, pp_1 = (\alpha_1 p_1 + p_{1,1}) - \alpha_1\, (\alpha_2 + p_1)\ ;\ pp_{1,2} = l_{1,2} - l_{11}\, pp_1 = (\alpha_1 p_1 + p_{1,1})\, p_1 + p_{1,2} - (\alpha_1 p_1 + p_{1,1})(\alpha_2 + p_1)$. The final cipher text is: $v_3 = ((\alpha_2 + p_1),\ (\alpha_1 p_1 + p_{1,1}) - \alpha_1\, (\alpha_2 + p_1),\ (\alpha_1\, p_1 + p_{1,1})\, p_1 + p_{1,2} - (\alpha_1\, p_1 + p_{1,1})\ (\alpha_2 + p_1))$. $(\alpha_2 + p_1)$ is the color of the vertex v_3.

Now we consider the decryption process starting from the cipher text (vertex v_3) and using the decryption key $(\alpha_1,\ p_1)$. We apply equations (1) from point to line (v_3 is point vertex). From v_3 we reach the vertex $vv_2 = [ll_1,\ ll_{1,1},\ ll_{1,2}]$ such as:

$ll_1 = \boldsymbol{\alpha_1}\ ;\ ll_{1,1} = \alpha_1\, (\alpha_2 + p_1) + \alpha_1\, p_1 + p_{1,1} - \alpha_1\, (\alpha_2 + p_1) = \boldsymbol{\alpha_1\, p_1 + p_{1,1}}\ ;\ ll_{1,2} = (\alpha_1\, p_1 + p_{1,1})\, (\alpha_2 + p_1) + (\alpha_1 p_1 + p_{1,1})\, p_1 + p_{1,2} - (\alpha_1 p_1 + p_{1,1})\ (\alpha_2 + p_1) = \boldsymbol{(\alpha_1 p_1 + p_{1,1})\, p_1 + p_{1,2}}$.

The vertex vv_2 is in fact the vertex v_2. From the line vertex v_2 applying equations (1), we reach a point vertex $v=[m_1, m_{1,1}, m_{1,2}]$ such as:

$m_1 = \mathbf{p_1}$; $m_{1,1} = (\alpha_1 p_1 + p_{1,1}) - \alpha_1 p_1 = \mathbf{p_{1,1}}$; $m_{1,2} = ((\alpha_1 p_1 + p_{1,1}) p_1 + p_{1,2}) - (\alpha_1 p_1 + p_{1,1}) p_1 = \mathbf{p_{1,2}}$. The vertex v is exactly the vertex plain text v_1.

3. Algorithm Implementation and Complexity

We use walks on a regular bipartite graph as encryption and decryption tools. In our algorithm implementation for efficiency reasons in programming, we have changed the form of the system of equations (1) as follows: Point vertex (p)= $(p_0, p_1, ..., p_{n-1})$ and line vertex [l] = $[l_0, l_1, ..., l_{n-1}]$.

$$l_0 = \alpha_i$$
$$l_1 = l_0 p_0 + p_1$$
$$l_2 = l_1 p_0 + p_2$$
$$l_3 = l_0 p_{i-2} + p_3$$
$$l_i = l_0 p_{i-2} + p_i$$
$$l_{i+1} = p_0 l_{i-1} + p_{i+1}$$
$$l_{i+2} = p_0 l_i + p_{i+2}$$
$$l_{i+3} = l_0 p_{i+1} + p_{i+3}.$$

Note that all arithmetic operation (solving system of equations (1)) are in the finite field $GF(2^8)$. For implementation purposes a multiplication table of elements of $GF(2^8)$ is pre-computed and stored into memory. The cost of a multiplication is the cost of accessing in memory to the $GF(2^8)$ multiplication table [6].

We focus now on the cost of our encryption algorithm. We consider first, only walk step, say from a point vertex to a line vertex, and a data file of size n bytes. The cost of this walk step includes the cost of computing n line components using a formula of the form

$$l_i = l_0 p_{i-2} + p_i \ (\mathit{1\ addition\ and\ 1\ multiplication}).$$

Since the number of walks is equal to the length of the password m, the cost of the algorithm is then linear: mn (addition and multiplication). The experimental results in the next section confirm the linear complexity of our encryption algorithm.

A very important consequence of proposition 1 is the simple way to compute the probability to guess the plain data from the cipher data. In fact proposition 1 tells us that there is a unique walk (path) starting from the cipher data vertex back to the plain data vertex. The unique way to guess the plain data is to guess the reverse password. Let us compute the probability to guess the plain data from the cipher data, which is the same probability to guess the cipher data from the plain data. Starting from the plain data vertex, the probability to guess the next line vertex depends on the first password character. There are $q=2^8$ different possible line vertices. The probability to guess the first step walk is $1/q$. Now the probability to guess the next walk step using the second character is $1/(q-1)$, we remove the possibility to go back to the previous vertex. We do the same reasoning for the other successive step walks.

If the password to encrypt the data is of length *m,* the probability to guess the message is $pkey = 1/(q\ (q-1)^{m-1})$. See Figure 2. As an example, for passwords of length $m=10$, $pkey \approx 10^{-25}$. If $m=20$, $pkey \approx 10^{-49}$. This show how strong is our algorithm even with short passwords.

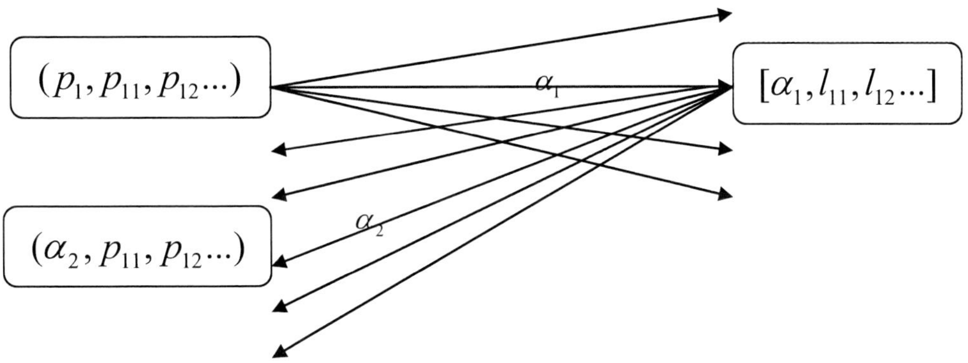

Figure 2. Guessing two steps walk.

To study the resistance from attacks of different types such as passive attacks where the intruder has both the plain and the cipher data, let us express our walks in the graph using algebraic polynomial factorization. The first point vertex corresponds to an *n*-dimensional vector of elements in the finite field $GF(2^8)$. The *n*-dimensional vector represents a polynomial $p(x)$ of degree $n-1$, where the polynomial coefficients are the vector components. Our encoding procedure corresponds to a multiplication of the polynomial $p(x)$ by another polynomial $q(x)$. The one-step walk reaches a vertex which corresponds to the polynomial $p(x)*q(x)$. Note that the coefficients themselves are polynomials in the finite field $GF(2^8)$. The last walk reaches the vertex (cipher data) is a polynomial $f(x)$ of degree $n-1$. Therefore, if an intruder intercepts the cipher data, it is almost impossible to compute the original polynomial (plain data). To do so, first the intruder should factorize the polynomial $f(x)$ into *m* product polynomials. This is already very difficult, especially with polynomial of high degree (*n* of order thousand and may be millions). In the second stage, the intruder should compute the product of the inverse of each polynomial factor, which is even harder. If we compare the resistance of our algorithm with the resistance of RSA, we can say that RSA rests on difficult factorization of large prime number. In our case, it is more difficult because it rests on factorization of polynomials of very high degree.

4. Experimental Measurements

To evaluate the performance of our algorithm, we measure the encryption time for our algorithm for different size of data files and using different password lengths. Figure 3 summarizes the results. It confirms the linear time complexity for our algorithm. It shows also that for password of length 5 and large files (9 Mega Bytes), our algorithm is capable to encrypt at speed 3.45 kilo-bytes per millisecond which is very fast. Our program is written in Java and it runs on Pentium 4. We expect better performance if we use compiled programming languages like C or C++.

Passwd.length *m*	**3000**	**6000**	**9000**
5	915	1760	2606
10	1830	3520	5211
15	2745	5280	7815
20	3666	7053	10440

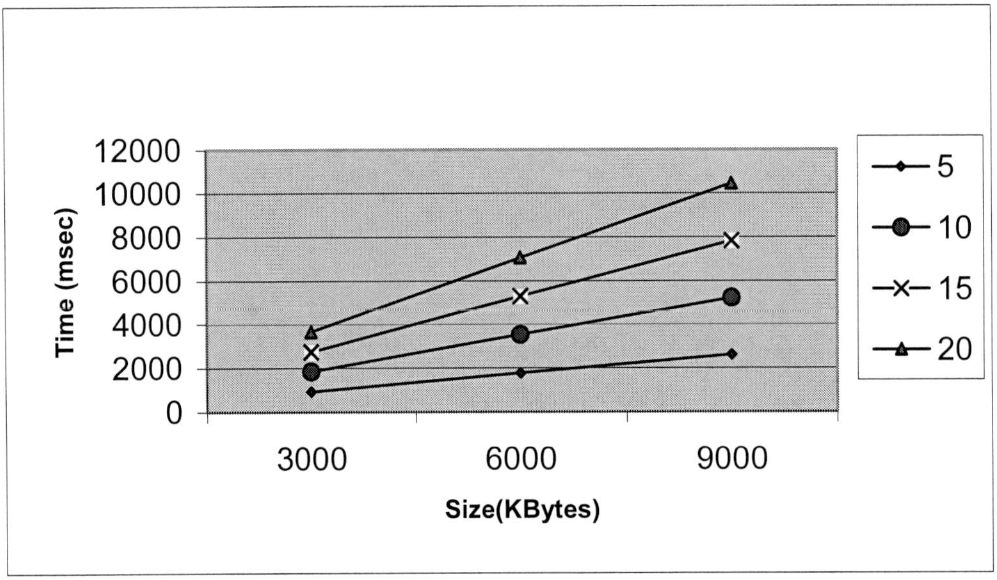

Figure 3. Run time for the encryption algorithm (ms).

5. Conclusion

We presented a new private key crypto-system based on walking on a special type of graphs. We have shown that these graphs do not have cycles and thus different passwords produce different cipher texts. We have also discussed attacks resistance for our algorithm. It is almost impossible to guess the plain data if the cipher data has been intercepted, unless you guess the password. We have shown that for these type of graphs, we can compute easily the probability to guess the message and it is very small (almost zero). Our algorithm uses binary code; it may encrypt/decrypt any data type. The complexity of our algorithm is linear which makes it very fast. We have developed prototype software written in Java. Our prototype software is a very attractive tool to secure virtual organization (e-learning, e-business, etc …). We are investigating the possibility to use the same graphs to develop a very strong public key crypto-system.

References

[1] Ustimenko, A. Touzene. *CRYPTALL-a System to Encrypt All types of Data.* Notices of Kiev Mohyla Academy, (June 2004), 57-63.

[2] V. Ustimenko, CRYPTIM: *Graphs as Tools for Symmetric Encryption.* In Lecture Notes in Computer Science, Springer, (2227), (2002), 278-287.

[3] V. Ustimenko. *Graphs with special arcs and Cryptography.* Acta Applicandae Mathematicae , (1974), 117-153.

[4] N. Koblitz. *A Course in Number Theory and Cryptography.* Second Edition, Springer, 1994.

[5] N. Koblitz. Algebraic *Aspects of Cryptograph,.* Springer, 1998.

[6] M. A. Hasan. Look-Up Table-Based Large Finite Field Multiplication in Memory Constrained Cryptosystems. *IEEE Trans. Comp.*, 49 **(7), (2000)** ,749-758.

[7] Woldar. *Rainbow graphs.* In: Codes and designs, K.T. Arasu and A. Seress Editors, deGruyter, Berlin 2002.

[8] F. Lazebnik, V. A. Ustimenko. *Explicit construction of graphs with an arbitrary large girth and of large size. Discrete Appl. Math.*, (**66**), (1995), 275-284.

[9] F. Lazebnik, V. A. Ustimenko and A. J. Woldar. *A New Series of Dense Graphs of High Girth.* Bull *(New Series) of AMS,* **32** (1), (1995), 73-79.

[10] V. Ustimenko, A. Woldar. *Extremal properties of regular and affine generalized polygons as tactical configurations, Europ. J. Com*, (**24**), (2003), 99-111.

INDEX

A

B

C

J

K

L

M

Q

R

S

T

U